Withdrawn from
Davidson College Library

Library of
Davidson College

International's Series in

ECONOMICS

Introduction to

Price Theory

Introduction to

Price Theory

second edition

MICHA GISSER

Associate Professor of Economics
The University of New Mexico
Albuquerque, New Mexico

INTERNATIONAL TEXTBOOK COMPANY

Scranton, Pennsylvania

338.5
G535i

Copyright ©, 1969 and 1966, by International Textbook Company

72-1629

All rights reserved. No part of the material protected by this copyright notice
may be reproduced or utilized in any form or by any means, electronic or me-
chanical, including photocopying, recording, or by any informational storage and
retrieval system, without written permission from the copyright owner. Printed
in the United States of America by The Haddon Craftsmen, Inc., Scranton,
Pennsylvania.

Library of Congress Catalog Card Number: 75-76407

Standard Book Number 7002 2226 X

To My Mother and Father

Preface to the Second Edition

The second edition of this price theory text has been revised and expanded based on classroom use, book reviews, and helpful suggestions from friends and colleagues. There are several features distinguishing this edition.

1) The chapter on capital was changed to include the theory of capital budgeting.
2) A chapter dealing with general equilibrium and welfare economics was added.
3) A non-mathematical chapter on linear programming has been included.
4) Separate chapters have been devoted to monopoly and to imperfect competition.
5) New problems have been added.

Classroom testing by Professor Nathaniel Wollman of The University of New Mexico has resulted in helpful additions, and in some cases deletions, to improve the presentation of the text material. Two separate book reviews by Professor Edwin Burmeister of The University of Pennsylvania have resulted in the incorporation of important new material. Gratitude is expressed to both of these scholars and much of the credit for the improvement of the text is a result of their efforts.

MICHA GISSER

Albuquerque, New Mexico
February, 1969

Preface to the First Edition

This textbook is the outgrowth of my experience in teaching an undergraduate course in price theory at Roosevelt University in Chicago. It is my conviction that undergraduate students can appreciate a course in price theory, provided that it is not mathematically involved. My experiences show that sometimes students who have little or no knowledge in mathematics may often become excellent practitioners when it comes to analyzing economic problems without having to resort to functions, derivatives, etc. Thus, every effort has been made to present the basic elements of price theory by using simple tools such as tables and diagrams. In fact, the student who utilizes this text need only be familiar with such simple skills as being able to draw a diagram, some knowledge of percentage changes, and similar vehicles.

An effort has been made to provide an intuitive discussion of each new concept prior to its theoretical development. This has been achieved by giving numerical and other examples before the theoretical analysis.

Some of the unusual features of this book are:

1. Each chapter contains examples relating to solving problems in price theory and applying them to reality.

2. Approximately eight problems are provided at the end of each chapter. Answers to numerical and "True, False, Uncertain" problems are given at the back of the book.

3. In addition to the pure theory of the price, some chapters are devoted to applications. Thus, price theory as applied to agriculture, indirect taxes, imperfect competition, the labor market, and the theory of capital can be found in chapters that are independent of each other.

4. Almost all the chapters are followed by an appendix. The appendix is designed for the student who is more analytically inclined.

5. A mathematical appendix is given at the end of the book. This appendix is designed for students who are interested in pursuing the mathematics of the presentation.

The chapters are preceded by an introduction which deals with the economic problems in every society. Chapters 1, 2, 3, and 4 deal with the consumer and derived problems which are related to the demand curve. Chapters 5, 6, 7, and 8 are concerned with the theory of the producer and the derived cost curves and the supply curve. In Chapter 9 the concepts of demand and supply are brought together, and the perfect market is analyzed. Chapter 10 deals with the problem of indirect taxes in the perfect market, and price theory as applied to agriculture is discussed in Chapter 11. The problem of monopoly and imperfect competition is analyzed in Chapter 12, with a special emphasis on imperfect competition. The market for factors of production is covered in Chapter 13. Price theory as applied to labor problems is dealt with in Chapter 14, and the market for capital in the short and the long run is analyzed in Chapter 15. The chapters are followed by answers to the problems and a mathematical appendix. Some of the problems at the ends of the chapters are taken from examinations that I have collected as a student at the University of Chicago. Since I do not claim originality, I have not listed the detailed obligations.

I want to thank Seymour Friedman and Donald Ohannes for their help in editing this text. I am also grateful to Eitan Berglas for his useful comments. I am especially indebted to my wife, Rivka, whose aid, patience, and encouragement made this book possible.

MICHA GISSER

Kfar Vitkin, Israel
February, 1966

Contents

excise taxes regressive? Are excise taxes good? Problems. Selected readings. *Appendix:* Welfare loss due to specific taxes. An alternate approach.

Introduction to
Price Theory

Introduction

Price theory is a science that concerns itself with three basic problems that confront every society. These are:

1. What goods can be produced and in what quantity?
2. How can the different goods be produced?
3. For whom are the different goods being produced and how can the goods be distributed?

Note that goods stand for both tangible commodities and services.

The first problem of what to produce and the second problem of how to produce exist in any society. Even Robinson Crusoe on his island was confronted with these two basic problems. Crusoe had limited resources, that is, his manpower, some tools, and primitive sources of energy. With these limited resources, he could have produced alternative combinations of goods. His basic economic problem was how much to produce of each. It is clear, however, that since Crusoe had limited resources, he could have produced more of one commodity only by sacrificing other goods. Prior to the arrival of Friday on the island, Crusoe was confronted with only two problems. The third problem of distribution did not exist because Crusoe provided both services of labor and capital. He was the sole owner of the capital on the island and the sole provider of labor services. The problem of distribution arose only after Friday joined Crusoe. Now, in addition to the problems of what and how, they confronted the third problem, namely, for whom?

Let us first focus on the problems of what and how much. Families receive their incomes in exchange for providing labor and capital services in the form of salaries, wages, rentals, interest, and profits. Part of the income which they earn is saved. The rest is spent on finished goods such as books, food, and furniture. To begin with, the decision concerning the problem of what fraction of income should be saved is determined in the market for capital. Having decided how much to save and how much to spend, the consumer can spend his budget on many goods and services that are available in the market. The first role of the theory of the price is to describe the behavior of the consumer in the market.

The consumer has a certain budget which he can spend on different

1

goods and services available in the market. Consumption is a process of voting with dollars in the market. The decision concerning the allocation of the budget is subject to the constraint of the budget. Also, since the consumer has a negligible share in the market, he has no influence over the prices of commodities in the market. For example, by his decision to double his consumption of oranges the individual consumer cannot affect the price of oranges in the market. Since market prices of different commodities change from one period of time to the next, the consumer is constantly engaged in reallocating his budget among the array of commodities that he consumes. In addition to changes in prices, from time to time the individual is faced with a change in income which also necessitates reallocation of the budget. Finally, reallocation of the budget may result from a change in the tastes of the consumer. For example, he may change his tastes in favor of margarine and against butter. If consumption were a process of picking commodities at random in the market place, then no theory would be necessary. The fact, however, is that consumers select commodities for consumption in a systematic manner. They consume more of a commodity whose price falls; they increase the consumption of one group of commodities and decrease the consumption of another group when income changes. To this one may add that consumers are affected by advertisements. In Chapters 1, 2, 3, and 4 a theoretical framework which summarizes the behavior of the consumer is provided. This convenient framework is known as the theory of the demand curve and demand shifts.

In order to complete the theory of the market for consumer's goods, producers have to be incorporated into the model of the market. If production were a process of picking resources at random and combining them for producing one commodity or another, the theory would be of little use. The fact is, however, that the process of selecting resources and combining them in production is systematic. Producers use more of a resource whose price falls, and they may use less of a resource whose price increases. They increase production when the price of a resource falls and decrease production when the price of a resource rises. When the price of the product rises, producers usually use more of most of the resources, and vice versa. Accordingly, it is necessary to provide a theory which rationalizes the behavior of producers. This is done in Chapters 5, 6, 7, and 8.

The problem of what to produce and how much is solved automatically in the market for finished goods and services. The market is governed by economic democracy; producers respond to the vote of consumers. For example, if there is a change in tastes in favor of butter and against margarine, then to the first approximation the price of butter will rise because more dollars will vote for a relatively limited amount of butter. At the same time the price of margarine will decline because consumers are shifting their dollars away from margarine to butter. But producers of butter will respond to this in a very systematic way: they will use more factors of production in order to increase the production of butter. On the other hand, producers of margarine will have an incentive to produce less, and so they will release resources which will be coaxed by the butter industry. A detailed discussion of the market place in which consumers vote with dollars for what producers offer is offered in Chapter 9. In Chapter 9 the thread of the consumer's analysis and the thread of the producer's analysis are brought together. In fact, there always are market forces which determine the price at which producers sell what consumers buy. This type of market democracy is desirable not only because of the mechanism which ensures a prompt response to the vote of consumers; it is also desirable because it does not require wasting human energy and tangible resources on planning the economy.

In other words, the market performs a good job of allocating resources and fixing prices at no cost to society. We shall show later that this is true provided that information about the market situation is available to both consumers and producers, and the market is not dominated either by a group of producers or a group of consumers. In contrast to this, in a planned economy the planner performs an insufficient job of allocating resources and fixing prices, and this at a very high cost to society. One of the most important roles of this text is to rationalize the market for consumer's goods in democratic societies.

Special problems arise in the market for goods and services (1) when the government places an excise tax on a certain commodity; (2) in the market for agricultural commodities; and (3) when the product is made by a sole producer or a small group of producers. Chapters 10, 11, 12, and 13 are devoted to these special problems.

We have already indicated that the market provides an automatic mechanism which allocates resources among the production of different commodities. The other role of the market is to set prices of factors of production. Thus, wages and salaries are determined in the labor market. Returns to capital in the form of interest or rents paid to landlords are determined in the market for capital. Accordingly, the distribution of income is also determined in the market place.

Chapters 14, 15, and 16 are devoted to the problem of distribution. The principle of distribution which was accepted by most Western societies is one in which factors of production, including workers, receive a fraction of the "cake" according to the value of their contribution to production. It is shown in these three chapters that in equilibrium the prices of factors of production, as determined by market forces, are tied to the value of the contribution of the factors to production. Moreover, when such a market equilibrium is upset, there are economic forces which propel the factor market into a new equilibrium in which the price of a factor is again equal to its value of productive contribution to society. Thus, the problem of distribution which deals in pricing of factors of production belongs to price theory.

The main task of price theory is not to tell which principle of distribution is morally desirable, but rather to analyze the market forces which determine through pricing of factors of production the process of distribution in Western countries.

In the free societies of the Western countries, individuals either own their capacity to work, or they own capital which renders productive services. They sell their labor and capital services to firms for a price which may be in the form of salaries, wages, interest, and profits. The market in which these prices are determined provides an automatic mechanism that allocates resources between different industries.

In a free society, if people desire more cars, the price of cars will rise at least in the short run. Entrepreneurs in the car industry will then have an incentive to expand. In order to expand, automobile manufacturers will have to hire more workers and other factors of production. This can be done by offering higher rewards to owners of capital and to workers. To the first approximation, higher wages and payments to owners of capital will coax more workers and capital into the automobile industry. The remainder of the analysis can be found in the text; but the point was made, namely, in a free-enterprise economy such as exists in Western countries, the process of allocating resources is achieved automatically by the labor market and other markets for factors of production. Thus, one role of the theory of pricing is to analyze the market mechanism that automatically allocates resources between alternative goods that are produced in the economy. The role of the factor market is not only to divide the total flow of production between different individuals but also to allocate the resources which are owned by individuals among the different industries. Coming to the moral issue of distribution, not much can be said for one system (or principle) or another. But when the practicality of the different systems is concerned, much can be said for the Western system which advocates the free-exchange market and private ownership of factors of production in most industries. In general, other systems, such as the Soviet Union, rely upon physical planning instead of the market, and state ownership of capital instead of private ownership: there is a state sovereignty in economic affairs. The planners set prices of both resources and consumer's goods, and they decide upon the allocation of resources among the different commodities in the economy. This system of a planned economy, in addition to giving rise to bottlenecks and surpluses in the economy, is dictatorial: it leaves the consumer very limited freedom, or no freedom at all, in the market for finished goods. The Western system, which relies on private ownership of capital and free exchange markets for setting prices and allocating resources, is both efficient and democratic. Price theory is the study of how free exchange markets set prices and allocate resources in the Western countries.

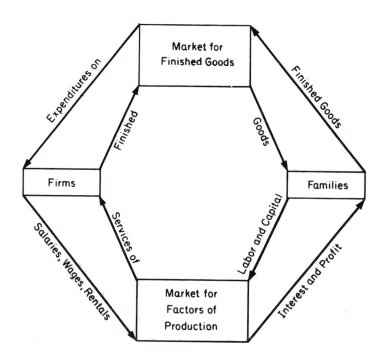

The role of the market in the economy is summarized in the accompanying figure: firms buy services of labor and capital in the market for factors of production. In return, families are paid in form of salaries, wages, rentals, interest, and profits. Families spend their incomes in the market for finished goods and services made by firms.

Thus, there are two flows in the economy, the monetary flow and the physical flow. In one direction there is the monetary flow of salaries, wages, interest, etc., which are payments of firms to families in return for services of labor and capital. The market for factors of production determines the rate of the monetary flow per unit of physical flow of labor and capital services. This monetary flow transforms into another monetary flow after it is received by families, namely, expenditures on finished goods, which are payments of families to firms in exchange for finished goods. The market for finished goods determines the rate of the monetary flow per unit of physical flow of finished goods.

If each industry had consisted of many small firms and if labor mobility and knowledge about market prices were perfect, then the role of price theory would boil down to a description and rationalization of the markets in our economy. Under such ideal circumstances the role of the government would be limited to imposing taxes on incomes in order to obtain the means necessary to run the army and the police, to maintain the schools which in most of the cases are in the hands of the public, and to alleviate poverty either through programs like nationalized social security or by directly subsidizing low-income classes. The real world is far from such an ideal picture. In the real world labor mobility may not be perfect. The reason is that moving from one geographical location to another involves a certain sacrifice. In the real world one industry may be monopolized by one firm or a few firms. If this is the case, the role of the theory, in addition to analyzing the behavior of the monopolist, is to advocate a policy to cope with possible exploitation of the consumer. In the case of the agricultural sector, labor mobility between rural farm and urban areas is far from perfect. As we shall see later, this gives rise to the farm problem which is characterized by a surplus of farm workers rather than farm output. Here, the role of the economist is to apply price theory in order to advocate the best policy which will raise farm income to a reasonable level and show the consequences of alternative policies. Other examples where price theory may cast some light on policy making are taxation and the labor market. In the case of indirect taxes, the role of price theory is to analyze the effect of imposing a specific tax on a certain product, like liquor. For example, an excise tax will affect the prices and quantities of the taxed commodity; it will cause a shift in resources involved in producing it, and also a welfare loss. In the case of labor, price theory sheds light on the process of wage determination in the labor market. Such an analysis enables one to see clearly the various circumstances under which the policies of the union help on one hand to promote the welfare of workers, and on the other achieve just the opposite result. All these problems are discussed in detail in Chapters 10, 11, 12, 13, 14, and 15. To illustrate the importance of price theory in the real world, consider the following statements:

1. By raising the price of liquor sufficiently, producers can shift the burden of the tax on to consumers.

2. Workers will always benefit from raising their wage rate as a result of the political pressure of the union.

3. Employers will always lose from a rise in the wage rate resulting from the pressure of the union.

4. Farmers will always benefit from a subsidy on fertilizers.

5. Farmers will benefit from favorable weather conditions.

6. A subsidy on farm output helps to solve the farm problem.

7. Farmers benefited from the invention of hybrid corn.

8. It does not pay a monopolist to charge a low price in one market while he charges a higher price in another market.

Common sense will probably tell you that the above statements are true. Note that in many cases economic policy which involves billions of dollars is based on such statements. By studying price theory you will find out that under *normal* conditions the above statements are false. Thus, it can be shown in many cases that if advocating one economic policy or another was based on price theory instead of common sense, billions of dollars could have been saved. Price theory, as other economic branches, became important in modern times mainly because it is capable of handling problems which common sense alone cannot cope with. Accordingly, you will find at the end of each chapter a few problems in which common sense and price theory disagree. You are urged to devote to these problems at least as much time as you do to reading the text.

Notice, finally, that some of the recommended articles in the list of selected readings at the end of the chapter assume a certain knowledge of calculus.

SELECTED READINGS

KNIGHT, FRANK H. *The Economic Organization*. Chicago, Ill.: The University of Chicago Press, 1933.

GALBRAITH, J. K. *The Affluent Society*. Boston, Mass.: Houghton Mifflin Company, 1958, Chapters 1 and 11.

chapter 1

The Theory of Demand

The role of the theory of demand is to describe and rationalize the behavior of the consumer. For our purpose, a consumer is the decision-maker in the household, or in any organization which is engaged in one type of consumption or another. From individual experience we know that there is some pattern in consumption. Accordingly, we know that consumers substitute cheaper commodities for expensive ones. We also realize that consumers do not concentrate on consuming one commodity or a group of commodities. Furthermore, we are aware of the fact that the decision-maker in the household is subject to the budget constraint when he has to make a decision. For instance, if one earns only $100 per week and A and B are the only two commodities in his budget, he can spend only $100 on A and B. In what follows we shall try to shed light on this process of decision-making subject to the constraint of the budget when the price of a certain commodity changes.

THE DEMAND CURVE

Consider an individual, or rather a consumer unit, whose income amounts to $100 per unit of time. Let the unit of time be one week and let our consumer unit be Joseph Smith. We are going to conduct several experiments upon Mr. Smith. Mr. Smith will be sent to an island where he can buy only four commodities. Let us denote them as W, X, Y, and Z. Now, each experiment is going to last one week, which, as you recall, is our unit of time.

At the outset of each week, Mr. Smith will receive only $100. An important condition of the experiment is that Mr. Smith must spend the entire $100 during the week in question. In other words, Mr. Smith is not allowed to save anything. This restriction is not important to our hypothesis because we could have made the assumption that Mr. Smith earns $120 per week and that he saves one-sixth of his income, which of course leaves him $100 to spend on commodities W, X, Y, and Z. In other words, the budget of Mr. Smith is limited. This is a realistic assumption since naturally the budget of each one of us is limited.

Another important condition under which the series of experiments are going to be conducted is that the prices of commodities X, Y, and Z are going to be held constant at $4, $3, and $1, respectively, throughout the period of experimentation. The price of commodity W will decline from one week to the next. Note, however, that Mr. Smith has no knowledge of the future changes in the price of W, nor can he make any predictions concerning the change. He finds out about the new price of W on Monday morning. Thus, as shown in Table 1-1, Mr. Smith is informed at the beginning of the first week that the price of W is set at $10. On Monday morning of the second week he is told that the price of W has dropped to $7, etc. Mr. Smith is going to adjust his allocation of income ($100) accordingly during the second week. He is going to increase his consumption of commodity W which has become cheaper. This is obvious because experience shows that we favor a commodity that becomes relatively inexpensive. Thus, if butter and margarine serve the same purpose in consumption, for example, as a spread on bread, then should margarine become relatively cheaper in price housewives will shift money from butter to margarine. We shall elaborate on this phenomena in Chapter 2.

Note that there is a functional relationship between the price of W and the quantity of W consumed per week. The lower the price of W, the larger the quantity of W consumed per week. In Table 1-1 we see that

TABLE 1-1

Period	Variable	Commodity				Nominal Income	Change in Apparent Real Income
		W	X	Y	Z		
1st week	Price—p	$10	$ 4	$ 3	$ 1		
	Quantity—q	4	5	4	28		
	$p \times q$	$40	$20	$12	$28	$100	
2nd week	Price—p	$ 7	$ 4	$ 3	$ 1		
	Quantity—q	6	4	3	33		
	$p \times q$	$42	$16	$ 9	$33	$100	$12
3rd week	Price—p	$ 5	$ 4	$ 3	$ 1		
	Quantity—q	9	3.5	2	35		
	$p \times q$	$45	$14	$ 6	$35	$100	$12
4th week	Price—p	$ 3	$ 4	$ 3	$ 1		
	Quantity—q	15	3	2	37		
	$p \times q$	$45	$12	$ 6	$37	$100	$18

when the price of W was \$10 apiece, the quantity consumed per week was four units. When the price dropped to \$7 apiece, Mr. Smith increased the quantity consumed from four to six units per week. During the third week, the price of W was set at \$5 per unit, and the quantity consumed increased to nine units of W per week; and finally, during the fourth week, the price of one unit of W dropped to \$3, and the quantity consumed reached a level of 15 units per week.

Note that (1) in this text consumption is identical with demand. In other words, "to consume" means "to demand." (2) We are always careful to specify the unit of time. This should be obvious because, after all, if one consumes 15 units of W per week, then one consumes 30 units per two weeks and about 780 units per annum.

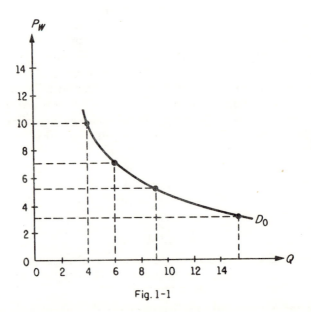

Fig. 1-1

The relationship between price and the quantity demanded is converted into a demand curve shown in Fig. 1-1. The technique of deriving the demand curve is simple. Let the vertical be the "price axis" and the horizontal be the "quantity axis." First, we plot points that represent pairs of prices and quantities, respectively, i.e., \$10 and 4 units, \$7 and 6 units, \$5 and 9 units and finally \$3 and 15 units—all taken from Table 1-1. Having plotted these points, we simply pass a curve through them. This curve, which is denoted by D_0, is the demand curve of Mr. Smith with respect to commodity W. Note that D_0 approximates the demand curve. The demand curve is practically unattainable simply because it is impossible to run an infinite number of experiments for infinite prices of commodity W. In what follows, however, we shall assume that D_0 is the demand curve.

VARIABLES THAT ARE KEPT CONSTANT ALONG THE DEMAND CURVE

Prices of All Other Commodities. Recall that prices of commodities X, Y, and Z are kept constant at \$4, \$3, and \$1, respectively, from one week to the next. The reason is that we are interested in the functional relationship between the price of W and the quantity of W demanded per unit of time. To illustrate this, assume that W is butter and X is margarine. If from one week to the next the price of margarine also changes, then the demand curve for butter becomes vague. Assume that the price of margarine rises along with the decline in the price of butter. Then one cannot tell whether Mr. Smith increased the quantity demanded for butter because of the decline in its price, the rise in the price of margarine (which is its closest substitute), or both

Thus, prices of all other commodities are kept constant along the demand curve. This rule must be followed especially with regard to commodities that are either close substitutes or close complements to the commodity under consideration. This problem of complementarity and substitutability will be covered in Chapter 3. Meanwhile it would suffice to note that when the price of a commodity falls, purchasing power and other prices remaining unchanged; the consumer will buy more of this commodity, more of its complementary commodity, and less of its substitute. Thus, Coca-Cola and Pepsi-Cola are substitutes for each other, and butter and bread are complements to each other.

Nominal Income. Recall that Mr. Smith's income was limited to \$100 per week. Whatever decision he makes, he must take into consideration the fact that his income is limited to \$100 per week. When the price of commodity W declines, Mr. Smith will reallocate his spending between W, X, Y, and Z—the only commodities in his budget. In general, Mr. Smith would attempt to shift money from substitutes to the commodity that becomes cheaper. Moreover, he would shift money to the complements of the commodity whose price falls. Thus, sugar and coffee are complementary to each other in consumption. If W is coffee, when the price of coffee declines Mr. Smith will reallocate more money to coffee and sugar, and relatively less to other beverages. This process of reallocating money between different commodities is always subject to the constraint of the budget. In Table 1-1 it is indicated that Mr. Smith is careful not to deviate from his budget of \$100. Although there are four commodities in his budget, when Mr. Smith reallocates his budget on Monday he only has to make three decisions. Assume that during the fourth week Mr. Smith has already made three decisions as follows: (1) to buy 15 units of W, (2) to buy 3 units of X, and (3) to buy 37 units of Z. Therefore, Mr. Smith must spend $45 + $12 + $37 = $94. There is nothing to decide in the case of commodity Y, because subtracting $94 from $100 leaves Mr. Smith $6. Since the price of Y is $3, Mr. Smith wants to buy 2 units of Y.

REAL INCOME ALONG THE DEMAND CURVE

One cannot hold both edges of a stick at the same time. Holding nominal income constant along the demand curve necessitates a sacrifice: *we cannot hold real income constant* along the demand curve. Of course, one can decide to hold real income constant along the demand curve, but then one loses the other edge of the stick. Everybody has his own tastes. We prefer to keep nominal income, rather than real income, unchanged. Real income may be defined as the purchasing power of nominal income over goods and services. To illustrate our point, consider the first week in Table 1-1. Nominal income amounts to $100. At the current prices of $10, $4, $3, and $1, 4 units of W, 5 units of X, 4 units of Y, and 28 units of Z are bought, respectively. If nominal income and prices are doubled, we can still purchase the orignal set of commodities. This is true because doubling nominal income and all prices leaves the purchasing power of nominal income over goods and services unchanged. When the price of one commodity declines, real income increases. After the price of one commodity falls, the consumer can buy the original combination of commodities and be left with a certain amount of money which economists call "the change in apparent real income." In other words, the consumer can buy the original set of goods and services and more; the purchasing power of his nominal income over commodities has increased. The change in apparent real income can be readily estimated. If one desires to estimate the change in the apparent real income of Mr. Smith resulting from a decline in the price of W, say from $10 apiece during the first week to $7 apiece during the second week, then one must go through the following arithmetics:

Had Mr. Smith bought the set of 4, 5, 4, and 28 units of W, X, Y, and Z, respectively, during the second week, he would be left with 12 unspent dollars as follows (see Table 1-1): he would spend the same amount on X, Y, and Z, but as far as W is concerned, he would spend only 7×4 units = $28 instead of 10×4 units = $40. This means that when the price of any commodity declines, real income increases provided that nominal income and all other prices are kept constant. Thus, when the price of W declines from $10 apiece to $7 apiece, apparent real income increases by $12, and so on.

Example: In Table 1-1, find the change in apparent real income when the price of W declines from $5 apiece to $3 apiece.

$$5 \times 9 \text{ units} = \$45$$
$$3 \times 9 \text{ units} = \$27$$
$$45 - \$27 = \$18$$

Some of the features of the demand curve can now be summarized:

The demand curve describes a functional relationship between a price of one commodity and the quantity demanded for that commodity per unit of time.

The demand curve is negatively sloped. Namely, when the price rises, the quantity demanded per unit of time declines, and vice versa, when the price declines, the quantity demanded per unit of time increases.

Nominal income and all other prices are kept constant along the demand curve. Real income changes along the demand curve. It increases going down the demand curve; it declines climbing up the demand curve.

THE AGGREGATE DEMAND CURVE

The aggregate demand schedule is obtained by horizontally totaling all the demand curves of all consumer units. To illustrate this, consider the totaling of the following two demand schedules of Mr. Smith and Mr. Johnson (Table 1-2):

The aggregate demand curve[1] can be drawn by plotting the following pairs: $10 and 7 units, $7 and 11 units, $5 and 15 units, $3 and 23 units.

TABLE 1-2

Price of Commodity W (1)	The Quantity Demanded Per Week		
	Mr. Smith (2)	Mr. Johnson (3)	Total (2) + (3) (4)
$10	4	3	7
7	6	5	11
5	9	6	15
3	15	8	23

This is left for the student as an exercise. In like manner, the aggregate demand curve for a certain commodity in the United States is obtained by *horizontally totaling* the demand curve of all the consumer units in the United States. Thus, the demand curve for potatoes in the United States can be derived in principle by horizontally totaling all the demand curves of families and other consumer units in the United States. A demand curve of this type summarizes the functional relationship between

[1] It is sometimes called the market demand curve.

the price of potatoes and the amount of potatoes bought in the United States. In other words, for every price per bushel there corresponds a quantity demanded per unit of time. The lower the price of potatoes, the larger the quantity demanded per unit of time.

A CHANGE IN TASTES

In addition to all other prices and nominal income, tastes are tacitly assumed to be the same along the demand curve. However, a change in tastes in favor of potatoes would mean increasing the demand leading to a rightward shift in the demand curve for potatoes. To illustrate this consider point S on the demand curve D_0 in Fig. 1-2.

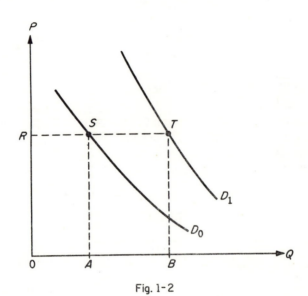

Fig. 1-2

At this point on the demand curve the price is $0R$ and the quantity demanded is $0A$. Now assuming tastes change in favor of potatoes and other things remaining unchanged, we would want to consume more potatoes at the same price. After the change in tastes occurs, we would like to consume $0B$ bushels of potatoes, which is by AB bushels larger than $0A$. Thus, T is a point on the new demand curve for potatoes. This is how the new demand curve denoted by D_1 is derived.

PRICE ELASTICITY

Absolute Change and Relative Change. Consider the following example: At the beginning of 1960, Robert weighed 95 pounds. At the end of 1960, Robert weighed 105 pounds. The absolute change in his weight during 1960 amounted to $105 - 95 = 10$ pounds. The absolute change is denoted by Δ (delta). Let original weight be denoted by W_0, the new weight by W_1 and the change in weight by ΔW, then: $\Delta W = W_1 - W_0 = 105 - 95 = 10$ pounds. The relative change in weight is the absolute change in weight divided by either the original weight, the new weight, or the average weight which we denote by $\overline{W}$. Note that $\overline{W} = (W_1 + W_0)/2$. Namely, the relative change is either $\Delta W/\overline{W}$, $\Delta W/W_0$, or $\Delta W/W_1$. Thus, in the above example,

$$\text{Relative change} = \frac{\Delta W}{\overline{W}} = \frac{W_1 - W_0}{\overline{W}} = \frac{10}{100} = 0.10$$

The relative change times 100 percent is the percentage change. For example, $0.10 \times 100\% = 10$ percent.

DEFINITION: Let the price elasticity of the demand curve be denoted by η (eta), the quantity demanded per unit of time by Q and price by P, then, the price elasticity is

$$\eta = \frac{\Delta Q/Q}{\Delta P/P} = \frac{\%\ \text{change in quantity}}{\%\ \text{change in price}}$$

which is the percentage change in the quantity demanded per 1 percent change in the price.

Example: In Fig. 1-3 estimate η in the neighborhood of point A on the demand curve D_0. Use $\overline{Q}$ (the average quantity) and $\overline{P}$ (the average price).

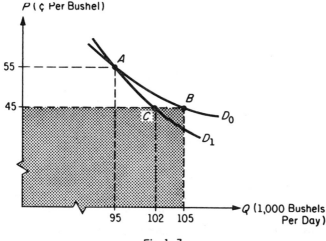

Fig. 1-3

Solution:

$$\overline{Q} = \frac{95 + 105}{2} = 100$$

$$\overline{P} = \frac{45 + 55}{2} = 50$$

$$\Delta Q = Q_1 - Q_0 = 105 - 95 = 10$$
$$\Delta P = P_1 - P_0 = 45 - 55 = -10$$

$$\eta = \frac{\Delta Q/\overline{Q}}{\Delta P/\overline{P}} = \frac{10/100}{-10/50} = \frac{10\%}{-20\%} = -\frac{1}{2}$$

If the changes in prices and quantities are small, Q_0, Q_1, P_0, and P_1, respectively, can be used to estimate η.

Example: If $\eta = -\frac{1}{4}$ and $Q_0 = 20$ units per unit of time, estimate ΔQ resulting from a 16 percent decline in the price of the commodity in question. Let X = percentage change in the quantity demanded, then

$$\frac{X}{-16\%} = -\frac{1}{4}$$

Multiplying both sides of the equation by -16% we obtain

$$X = \left(-\frac{1}{4}\right)(-16\%) = 4\%$$

Then, roughly speaking, ΔQ is 4 percent of 20 units, i.e., $\frac{8}{10}$ of one unit.

Example: Assuming $\eta = -2$, what is the change in price that will induce a 10 percent decline in the quantity demanded per unit of time? Let X = percentage change in the price. Then,

$$\frac{-10\%}{X} = -2$$

Multiplying both sides by X we obtain

$$-10\% = -2 \cdot X$$

Dividing both sides by -2 we obtain $X = 5$ percent, i.e., the price must rise 5 percent in order to induce a 10 percent decline in the quantity demanded.

Absolute Values. The reader can find the precise definition of an absolute value in almost any text in mathematics. By definition, the absolute value of a number is the negative number, ignoring its negative sign. Thus, the absolute value of -2, denoted by $|-2|$ is 2.

Elastic Demand Curve. When the demand curve has an elasticity whose absolute value is larger than unity, the demand curve is elastic.

Example: If $\eta = -3$, then $|\eta| = 3$ and the demand curve is elastic (because 3 is larger than 1).

A Demand Curve with Unitary Elasticity.   When $\eta = -1$, that is, $|\eta| = 1$, the demand curve has unitary elasticity.

Inelastic Demand Curve.   When the demand curve has an elasticity whose absolute value is smaller than unity, the demand curve is inelastic.

Example: If $\eta = -\frac{1}{4}$, $|\eta| = \frac{1}{4}$ which is smaller than unity.

Intuitively, if the demand curve is elastic, a 1 percent change in price will entail a change in quantity which is in absolute value larger than 1 percent. Thus, if $\eta = -3$, a -1 percent change in price will entail a 3 percent change in the quantity demanded. If the demand curve has a unitary elasticity, it simply means that a -1 percent change in price will entail a 1 percent change in quantity.

Finally, an inelastic demand curve means that in absolute value the percentage change in the quantity demanded is smaller than the percentage change in price. Thus, if $\eta = -\frac{1}{4}$, then a 1 percent change in price will bring about only a $-\frac{1}{4}$ percent change in the quantity demanded. Note finally that under normal conditions if the change in price is negative, the change in quantity is positive and vice versa.

SHORT-RUN AND LONG-RUN DEMAND CURVES

Consider the demand curve D_0 in Fig. 1-3. When the price drops down from 55 cents to 45 cents, quantity demanded per day increases from 95,000 bushels to 105,000 bushels. Here the time element is crucial. Thus, immediately after the price drops to 45 cents, the same amount of 95,000 bushels is demanded. This is true because no one has had time to learn about the change in price. It takes some time for the information to become known in the market. Even after the information is known, it takes time to adjust to the idea that a certain product is now cheaper. Assume that two weeks after the price per bushel dropped to 45 cents, quantity demanded per day was 102,000 bushels as indicated in Fig. 1-3. Also assume that after one month consumers do not adjust any more; they continue to buy 105,000 bushels per day. Then we can be sure that the long-run demand curve is some D_0 passing through A and B. There are many short-run demand curves that correspond to the period of time allowed for adjustment. One such demand curve corresponding to a two-week period of adjustment passes through A and C.

TOTAL REVENUE

Total revenue per unit of time is defined as the price times the quantity demanded per unit of time. The name total revenue is misleading because what is *total revenue* to the producers of cars is *total expenditures* to the buyers of cars.

In Fig. 1-3 total revenue at point B is the area marked by dots.

There the price is 45 cents per bushel, and at that price the quantity demanded is 105,000 bushels. Thus, total revenue is equal to $45 \times 105{,}000 =$ $4,725

Consider the following problem: Currently the price is $100 and the quantity is 100 units of output per unit of time. The price elasticity of demand is $- \frac{1}{2}$. This means that a 2 percent decline in price induces a 1 percent increase in quantity demanded. Originally, total revenue = 100×100 units = $10,000. After the price declines by 2 percent, i.e., by $2 (and the quantity increases by 1 unit) we obtain, total revenue = $98 \times 101 =$ $9,898. Namely, total revenue has decreased. Consider the same problem but assume that the price elasticity is $- 2$. Originally total revenue is $10,000, but after the price declines by 2 percent, the quantity demanded increases 4 percent, and total revenue amounts to 98×104 units = $10,192. The demand curve is inelastic in the first example and elastic in the second example. Let us now generalize it.

It is recalled that elasticity η is defined as

$$\frac{\Delta Q/Q}{\Delta P/P}$$

Let us consider the absolute value of elasticity as

$$|\eta| = \frac{|\Delta Q/Q|}{|\Delta P/P|}$$

It is clear that when the demand curve is inelastic, i.e., $|\eta|$ is smaller than unity, the denominator $|\Delta P/P|$ is larger than the numerator $|\Delta Q/Q|$. Now, when we go down the demand curve, the price declines and the quantity demanded increases. Total revenue is a product of the price and the quantity demanded. Thus, while the decline in price contributes to the shrinkage of total revenue, the increase in quantity demanded aids in increasing it.

Whether total revenue will increase or decrease will depend on which of the two, the decline in the price or the increase in the quantity demanded, will dominate. But we know that in case of an inelastic demand curve, the change in price is dominant because $|\Delta P/P|$ is larger than $|\Delta Q/Q|$. Accordingly, the effect of the decline in the price is to shrink total revenue and is stronger than the effect of a larger quantity demanded which is to increase total revenue. So, going down an inelastic demand curve results in a lower total revenue. Thus, in Fig. 1-4, D_0 is an inelastic demand curve. Going down from F to L would imply that total revenue is shrinking. Diagrammatically, the area indicated by $0KLM$ is *smaller* than the area indicated by $0EFG$. It is clear from Fig. 1-4 that going up the inelastic demand curve entails a rise in total revenue. In the case of an elastic demand curve $|\Delta P/P|$ is smaller than $|\Delta Q/Q|$. Accordingly, the effect of the decline in the price by itself is to shrink total revenue but is weaker than the effect of a larger quantity demanded. Therefore, total

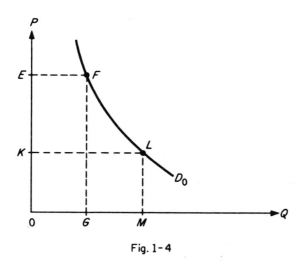

Fig. 1-4

revenue increases when we go down an elastic demand curve. The case of unitary elasticity is left for the student as an exercise. Let a rise be denoted by ↑, a decline by ↓ and no change by 0. For instance, a rise in

TABLE 1-3

Case	Demand Curve		
	Inelastic	Unitary Elasticity	Elastic
$Q\uparrow\ P\downarrow$	$TR\downarrow$	$TR\ \ 0$	$TR\uparrow$
$Q\downarrow\ P\uparrow$	$TR\uparrow$	$TR\ \ 0$	$TR\downarrow$

the price will be denoted by $P\uparrow$, etc. Table 1-3 summarizes the relationships between the price elasticity of the demand curve and total revenue.

AN IMPORTANT FORMULA

The relationships between total revenue and elasticity can be proved as follows: Let TR_0, Q_0 and P_0 denote original total revenue, original quantity demanded, and original price. Let TR_1, Q_1, and P_1 denote second total revenue, second quantity, and second price, respectively. Then

$$Q_1 = Q_0 + \Delta Q$$

and

$$P_1 = P_0 + \Delta P$$

Now,

$$TR_0 = Q_0 \cdot P_0$$

and

$$TR_1 = Q_1 \cdot P_1$$
$$= (Q_0 + \Delta Q) \cdot (P_0 + \Delta P)$$

then,

$$\Delta(TR) = TR_1 - TR_0 = (Q_0 + \Delta Q)(P_0 + \Delta P) - Q_0 \cdot P_0$$
$$= Q_0 \cdot P_0 + Q_0 \cdot \Delta P + \Delta Q \cdot P_0 + \Delta Q \cdot \Delta P - Q_0 \cdot P_0$$
$$= Q_0 \cdot \Delta P + \Delta Q \cdot P_0 + \Delta Q \cdot \Delta P$$

When the change in price is very small, the change in quantity demanded is also relatively small. Thus $\Delta Q \cdot \Delta P$ is negligible and it can be ignored. So,

$$\Delta(TR) = Q_0 \cdot \Delta P + \Delta Q \cdot P_0$$

Dividing through by ΔQ we obtain

$$MR = \frac{\Delta(TR)}{\Delta Q} = \frac{Q_0 \cdot \Delta P + \Delta Q \cdot P_0}{\Delta Q}$$
$$= Q_0 \frac{\Delta P}{\Delta Q} + P_0$$

Where MR stands for marginal revenue. By definition, marginal revenue is the extra revenue obtained from selling an extra unit. Factoring P_0 out and changing the order gives

$$MR = P_0 \left(1 + \frac{Q_0 \cdot \Delta P}{P_0 \cdot \Delta Q} \right)$$
$$= P_0 \left(1 + \frac{1}{\eta} \right)$$

Consider the following three cases:

1. *Elastic Demand Curve.* If $|\eta|$ is larger than unity, then $1/|\eta|$ is smaller than unity. Algebraically it is a negative number, thus $1 + 1/\eta$ is positive. Since P_0 is positive too, marginal revenue MR must be positive. Now, a positive marginal revenue means that total revenue increases when quantity demanded increases and it decreases when quantity demanded decreases.

2. *Unitary Elasticity.* If $|\eta| = 1$, then $1/|\eta| = 1$. Algebraically it is negative, thus $1 + 1/\eta = 1 - 1 = 0$. Namely, marginaly revenue is 0, which means that a change in quantity does not induce a change in total revenue.

3. *Inelastic Demand Curve.* If $|\eta|$ is smaller than unity, then $1/|\eta|$ is larger than unity. Algebraically it is a negative number. Thus $1 + 1/\eta$ is negative. Since P_0 is positive, marginal revenue must be negative too. Now, a negative marginal revenue means that total revenue decreases when quantity demanded increases, and total revenue increases when quantity demanded decreases.

PROBLEMS

1-1. Price elasticity of A is equal to $-\frac{1}{2}$. What will be the percentage increase in the consumption of A, following a decrease of 10 percent in the price of A?

1-2. If $\eta = -\frac{1}{2}$, what is the change in the price of A which will induce a 15 percent increase in the consumption of A?

1-3. Assuming $\eta = -\frac{1}{4}$ by how much will total revenue change as a result of a 4 percent increase in the quantity demanded?

1-4. The same as 3, except that $\eta = -1$.

1-5. The same as 3, except that $\eta = -4$.

1-6. Solve 3, 4, and 5 assuming a 4 percent *decrease* in the quantity demanded.

1-7. The price elasticity of agricultural commodities is very inelastic. It is known that bad weather conditions are followed by bad crops, while favorable conditions are followed by good crops. Which kind of weather, bad, normal, or good is the most favorable for farmers? (Assume that the cost of planting and harvesting is not affected by weather.)

1-8. The same as 7, except that $\eta = -1$.

1-9. Your income is $100. The prices of A, B, C, and D are $10, $4, $3, and $1. The quantities are 4, 5, 4, and 28, respectively. As a result of 20 percent decrease in the price of A, you increase your consumption of A by 50 percent, you consume 5.5 units of B, and you do not change your consumption of C. Will you change your consumption of D, and if so, by how much?

SELECTED READINGS

MARSHALL, A. *Principles of Economics*. London: The Macmillan Company, 1952, Book III, Chapter 4.

STIGLER, G. J. *The Theory of Price*. New York: The Macmillan Company, 1966, Chapter 3.

chapter 2

The Theory of Utility

PART I: THE NEOCLASSICAL THEORY OF UTILITY

In Chapter 1 we have defined the demand function as a function relating the quantity demanded to the price. The assumption that the demand curve has a negative slope was based on market observations: when the price of a commodity with which the consumer is faced falls, the quantity demanded for that commodity increases; and when the price rises, the quantity demanded decreases. At this point we could have proceeded to Chapters 3 and 4 where the demand shifts due to the changes in income and prices of other commodities are analyzed. To put it in other words, we could have derived the theory of the behavior of the individual consumer from market observations where the demand curve forms a convenient framework for organizing material.

Studying the theory of utility gives rise to two advantages. First, the student gains some insight into the theory of demand. Second, it is convenient to analyze practical issues, such as commodity rationing and index numbers, with the aid of indifference curves.

WHAT IS UTILITY

Not much can be added to the Benthamite[1] doctrine in which utility is power in objects which would normally create satisfaction; and the happiness of the individual is the sum total of his satisfactions. According to Bentham, the guiding principle of right action is "the greatest happiness principle," or what is known as maximization of utility. For Bentham, the question whether one ought to follow the principle of maximization of utility was irrelevant. It was equivalent to asking whether one ought to do what one does anyway.

Let us elaborate on the concept of utility. We know that there is some property common to all goods in the budget of the consumer. For

---

[1] Jeremy Bentham, a ninetenth century English philosopher.

example, goods are substituted for one another and thus they must have something in common. This common property is the creation of the mind of the consumer. It was called a *power* by Bentham, but one can give it any name, provided that one knows that the name is only a symbol. From experience we know that people substitute toward a commodity that becomes relatively cheaper. Also we know that generally consumers do not concentrate on one commodity or a group of a few goods. The role of the theory of utility is to shed light on the behavior of the individual consumer. Notice that we do not yet have a theory of utility. So far, utility is a name given to the common property of all the commodities in the budget of the consumer. In order to have a theory, one must formulate laws capable of rationalizing the behavior of the individual consumer. Before formulating the laws of utility governing the behavior of the consumer, we shall have to dispose of the problem of cardinal and ordinal utility.

CARDINAL AND ORDINAL UTILITY

In order to choose among the various commodities that are available in the market, we must rank them according to their importance to us. The act of choice is the act of ranking goods or desires according to their importance. Ranking can be performed in terms of cardinal numbers or ordinal numbers. Cardinal numbers are quantitatively related to one another. Thus, let us agree to measure utility by utils, where one util is an arbitrary amount of utility. Let us consider three combinations of goods denoted by A, B, and C. Let A be associated with 20 utils, B with 40 utils, and C with 120 utils. The three combinations are ranked cardinally: B yields twice the utility of A, and C yields three times the utility of B. This concept of cardinal utility was adopted by the classical economists. The more refined version of it, which was developed in the twentieth century, is known as the neoclassical theory of utility which is the subject of this part. In contrast to cardinal utility, the consumer can rank combinations A, B, and C according to ordinal numbers, that is, A is first, B is second, and C is third. In other words, B is preferred to A, and C is preferred to B. Unlike in the case of cardinal utility where it is evident that C is preferred to A (C has six times the utility of A), in the case of ordinal utility we add an axiom stating that if B is preferred to A, and C is preferred to B, then C is preferred to A. Although ordinal utility has more appeal because in reality consumers rank commodities ordinally, it is not necessarily a better theory. In fact, both approaches have their own advantages and shortcomings, and the reader will have to decide for himself whether he likes the cardinal utility approach which is the subject of this part or the ordinal utility approach which will be the subject of the next part.

MARGINAL UTILITY

Marginal utility is defined as the extra utility obtained from the consumption of one additional unit of a given commodity when taste and the consumption of all other goods are remaining unchanged. To illustrate this, assume that when one drinks 2 glasses of milk and a certain set of all other commodities per day, his total utility amounts to 37 utils a day. When one drinks 4 glasses of milk and the same set of all other commodities per day, his total utility increases to 45 utils a day, then the marginal utility of milk per day is calculated as follows:

$$\text{Marginal utility of milk} = \frac{\Delta U}{\Delta Q} = \frac{U_1 - U_0}{Q_1 - Q_0} = \frac{45 - 37}{4 - 2} = 4 \text{ utils}$$

where U stands for (total) utility and Q for quantity.

THE LAW OF DIMINISHING MARGINAL UTILITY

The law of diminishing marginal utility states that *ceteris paribus*, the marginal utility derived from consuming a certain commodity diminishes when the quantity of that commodity consumed per unit of time increases. Notice that *ceteris paribus* means that tastes and the consumption of all other goods are remaining unchanged. The law of diminishing marginal utility summarizes our experience that the more we consume of one commodity per unit of time the less important to us is one additional unit of it.

Having explained what marginal utility is, we can run the following experiment:

We shall measure the total utility of Mr. Smith for different quantities of coffee consumed per unit of time. The unit of time is one day. From one day to the next we shall change the amount of coffee available to him while keeping consumption of all other commodities constant. Having measured his total utility, we can derive his marginal utility by dividing the change in total utility by the change in the quantity consumed per unit of time.

We shall run two similar experiments. In one, the amount of sugar available per day will be kept constant at 4 teaspoons. During the second experiment, the amount of sugar will be held constant at a larger quantity per day, say 6 teaspoons. The results of the first experiment are shown in Table 2-1 and of the second experiment in Table 2-2.

For 6 cups of coffee the marginal utility was derived in the following manner:

$$MU = \frac{\Delta U}{\Delta Q} = \frac{42 - 30}{6 - 5} = \frac{12}{1} = 12 \text{ utils}$$

where MU is marginal utility. In what follows, MU_a will stand for the marginal utility of commodity A, MU_b for the marginal utility of commodity B, etc.

TABLE 2-1
(Four Teaspoons of Sugar per Day)

Cups of Coffee per Day	Total Utility	Marginal Utility
5	30	
6	42	12
7	52	10
8	59	7
9	64	5

TABLE 2-2
(Six Teaspoons of Sugar per Day)

Cups of Coffee per Day	Total Utility	Marginal Utility
5	38	
6	54	16
7	69	15
8	79	10
9	85	6

The two tables are plotted into marginal utility curves as shown in Fig. 2-1, which conveys the following idea. When the quantity of sugar has increased, the MU curve of coffee has shifted upwards. This assumption stems from our intuitive feeling that the MU of commodity A will increase if we consume a larger quantity of its complementary commodities. The case of substitutes will be postponed to a later time.

A LAW OF LOGIC

In what follows we shall assume that consumption is a smooth process, that is, the case where commodities are indivisible is absent. Moreover, utility is a smooth function of consumption.

It was assumed that each individual maximizes the amount of utility derived from consumption. If this assumption is accepted, then it can be shown that in equilibrium, utility is maximized when the marginal utility derived from spending the last dollar on commodity A is equal to the marginal utility derived from spending the last dollar on commodity B and so on. Formally, this law can be summarized as follows:

$$\frac{MU_a}{P_a} = \frac{MU_b}{P_b} = \cdots = \frac{MU_n}{P_n} = \text{common } MU \text{ per income dollar}$$

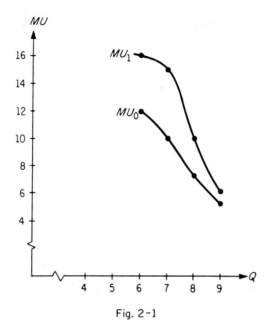

Fig. 2-1

Where P_a is the price of commodity A, MU_a is the marginal utility of A, etc.

Note that MU_a/P_a is equal to the marginal utility derived from spending the last dollar on commodity A. Suppose $MU_a = 30$ utils and $P_a = \$10$. Then, on the margin, the consumer has to pay an additional amount of \$10 for obtaining 30 utils. Thus, simple arithmetic will show that if 30 additional utils cost \$10, then with one additional dollar one can "buy" $30/10 = 3$ additional utils.

Assume that the only goods consumed are A and B. Suppose the law of logic is not followed, say MU_a/P_a is larger than MU_b/P_b. This can be written as

$$\frac{MU_a}{P_a} > \frac{MU_b}{P_b}$$

The marginal utility derived from the last dollar spent on A is by α utils larger than the marginal utility derived from the last dollar spent on B. Then, by transferring one dollar from spending on B to spending on A the consumer will gain α additional utils. This means that the consumer has not yet maximized his total utility. The consumer will continue to shift money from B to A. Now, for simplicity assume that there is no dependence between MU_a and the quantity of B consumed, and MU_b and the quantity of A consumed. Then it is obvious that the role of the law of diminishing marginal utility is crucial. When money is being transferred from B to A, MU_a declines, MU_b rises, just until a new point of equilibrium is achieved. In other words, the consumer gains less than α utils from transferring the second dollar from B to A, etc. Finally, due to the law of diminishing marginal utility, the utility gained from transferring money from B to A will equal zero.

This process is illustrated in Table 2-3. We assume that originally

TABLE 2-3

Price		MU		$\dfrac{MU}{P}$		α	Expenditures		
B	A	B	A	B	A	(6-5)	B	A	Total (8) + (9)
(1)	(2)	(3)	(4)	(5)	(6)	(7)	(8)	(9)	(10)
$5	$4	50	40	10	10	0	$22	$18	$40
5	2	50	40	10	20	10	22	9	31
5	2	55	38	11	19	8	20	11	31
5	2	60	34	12	17	5	17	14	31
5	2	75	30	15	15	0	14	17	31

the consumer has \$40 to spend per unit of time. The only commodities in his budget are A and B. We start from a point of equilibrium where the price of A is \$4 apiece. Then this equilibrium is upset by lowering the price of A to \$2 apiece. At that point, the change in apparent real income which amounts to \$9 is confiscated. The consumer starts to transfer money from B to A. By so doing he gives rise to increasing MU_b and decreasing MU_a until a new point of equilibrium is established. In the particular example shown in Table 2-3, a new point of equilibrium is achieved when MU of commodity B rises to a new level of 75 utils, while MU of commodity A falls to a new level of 30 utils. There are, however, many other solutions to this problem.

Assume that there is no dependence between MU_a and the quantity of B consumed and between MU_b and the quantity of A consumed. Also assume that the law of diminishing marginal utility is not in existence. This leads to a constant (or increasing) marginal utility. For simplicity we shall assume that MU is constant. Following the first line in Table 2-3, we have

$$\frac{MU_a}{P_a} = \frac{40 \text{ utils}}{\$4} = 10 \text{ utils per dollar}$$

$$\frac{MU_b}{P_b} = \frac{50 \text{ utils}}{\$5} = 10 \text{ utils per dollar}$$

Also, originally the consumer spends $22 on B and $18 on A. After the price of A falls from $4 to $2, the change in apparent real income (equals $9) is confiscated. This time

$$\frac{MU_a}{P_a} - \frac{MU_b}{P_b} = 20 - 10 = 10 \text{ utils}$$

which is constant. The consumer will gain 10 utils from transferring the first dollar, 10 utils from transferring the second dollar from B to A, up to the last dollar. Altogether he will gain $22 \times 10 = 220$ utils. Thus the above assumptions of the nonexistence of dependence and diminishing marginal utility lead to the logical conclusion that the consumer will concentrate on a single commodity (commodity A in our example) until the price of another commodity (commodity B) will fall sufficiently to persuade him to shift his entire budget to the other commodity. In reality, however, we hardly find consumers who spend their entire budget on one commodity. Rather, consumers shift only small fractions of their budgets resulting from a change in the price of one commodity. This justifies the assumption that diminishing marginal utility and/or dependence exist.

Let us elaborate on the case of dependence and diminishing marginal utility when two substitutes, A and B are considered.

Assume that the law of diminishing marginal utility does not exist, but instead there is positive dependence between MU_a and the quantity of B consumed, and MU_b and the quantity of A consumed. The equilibrium $MU_a/P_a = MU_b/P_b$ is upset when the price of A declines. It pays the consumer to transfer money from spending on B to spending on A. Although the law of diminishing marginal utility does not exist, when more of A is consumed, MU_b increases, and when less of B is consumed, MU_a diminishes. This is due to the assumption of positive dependence. Accordingly, the extra utility gained from transferring an additional dollar from B to A diminishes just until a new equilibrium is achieved.

If both the law of diminishing marginal utility and the positive dependence exist, the extra utility gained from transferring an additional dollar from B to A will diminish due to both laws. It follows that if there is negative dependence between MU_a and the quantity of B consumed, and MU_b and the quantity of A consumed, the law of diminishing marginal utility must dominate, otherwise the consumer will spend his entire budget either on A or on B.

In order for complementarity to exist, there must be more than two commodities in the budget of the consumer. This stems from the fact that complementarity as well as substitutability is defined *only for a fixed level of real income*. Consider again Table 2-3. After the price of A declines, $9 are confiscated and the consumer can, with the remaining

$31, buy the original combination of 4.4 units of B and 4.5 units of A. If the consumer decides to divert one dollar away from B, he would decrease the consumption of B by 0.2 units. If A and B were complements, then, following the definition of complementarity, the consumer should also reduce the consumption of A. But since there are only two commodities in his budget, with the dollar released from spending on B the consumer must buy an additional amount of 0.5 units of A. This contradicts the assumption of complementarity, and thus A and B *must* be substitutes for each other.

While in the case of substitutes we could rationalize the behavior of the consumer with, or without, dependence, in the case of complements we must assume dependence.

For example, assume that there are three commodities in the budget of the consumer, ground coffee, sugar, and orange juice. The following tabulation describes the original equilibrium:

	Ground Coffee	Sugar	Orange Juice
MU	30	15	21
P	10	5	7
MU/P	3	3	3

Ground coffee and sugar are complements to each other, while both ground coffee and sugar are substitutes for orange juice. Now, when the price of ground coffee drops down from $10 to $6, a certain amount of ground coffee is being substituted for orange juice. But, complementarity between ground coffee and sugar cannot be explained unless we assume either positive dependence between ground coffee and sugar or negative dependence between orange juice and sugar or both. To the first approximation, unless the MU of sugar will rise to a level higher than 25 utils, the quantity of sugar consumed will not increase.

If fixed proportions in consumption are assumed between complements, then the problem is simplified. Instead of considering ground coffee and sugar separately, one could consider a cup of coffee which includes a fixed amount of ground coffee and a fixed amount of sugar. Now, when the price of ground coffee falls, the price of one cup of coffee also decreases. Accordingly, the consumer will substitute cups of coffee for other commodities, thus increasing his demand for sugar. Finally, if you consider a consumer who drinks coffee and tea, then sugar is probably a complementary commodity to coffee and tea, and the rise in the demand for sugar which results from a larger consumption of coffee may be offset by a fall in the demand for sugar which results from a smaller consumption of tea (under the assumption that the price of ground coffee falls and other prices are unchanged).

INCOME EFFECT AND SUBSTITUTION EFFECT COMBINED

A Change in Real Income. When the price of commodity A declines (keeping nominal income and all other prices constant), the consumer becomes better off. This is true because if the consumer were forced to consume the original set of goods and pay the new price of A, he would be left with a windfall equal to the change in his apparent real income. Although we do not know by how much real income has changed, we know for sure that it has increased because the consumer is better off. At this point the reader should review Table 1-1 and make sure he understands what the change in apparent real income is, and why real income increases going down the demand curve and decreases going up the demand curve.

Superior and Inferior Commodities. Let the price of commodity A and all other commodities be held constant. If you consume more of A as you become better off (i.e., your real income increases), then A is said to be superior for you. However, if under the same circumstances you consume less of A, A is said to be inferior for you.

The Change in Apparent Real Income Approximates the Change in Real Income. Consider Table 2-3. It is recalled that if I currently consume 4.5 units of A and the price is $4 apiece, and if the price of A falls to $2, then, other things the same, the change in my apparent real income is going to be $-4.5 (2 - 4) = \$9$. Thus $9, which is the change in my apparent real income, is an *estimate* of the change in my real income. In fact, it is the best estimate available. Since we cannot measure the exact change in real income, we shall have to use this estimate instead. Moreover, it can be proved that the change in apparent real income is relatively closer to the change in real income, the smaller the change in price.

The Income Effect and Substitution Effect. Consider Fig. 2-2. Originally the price of A is $4 per unit, and the quantity demanded is 4.5 units. D_0 is the demand curve of a certain consumer. Now, when the price falls to $2 apiece, the consumer becomes better off. The change in his apparent real income is $-4.5 (2 - 4) = \$9$ per unit of time. If we want to separate between the income effect and the substitution effect, we should introduce them separately. So, let us eliminate the income effect by imposing a $9 tax (per unit of time) on the consumer. Then, he can still consume 4.5 units of A and the original set of all other commodities (4.4 units of commodity B) and be neither better off nor worse off. But from the theory of utility we know that since P_a has declined, marginal utility derived from the last dollar spent on A is now larger, compared

with other commodities. Then the consumer will start transferring money
from spending on other commodities which are substitutes for commodity
A to spending on A. This he will do until a new equilibrium is achieved.
Following Table 2-3, assume that a new equilibrium is attained when the
consumer increases the quantity of A from 4.5 units to 8.5 units. The
substitution effect is the cause of increasing consumption by 4 units indicated by the distance KL in Fig. 2-2. At this point we return the $9

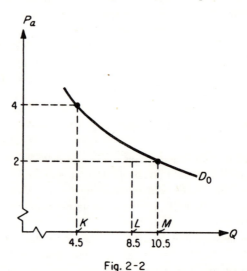

Fig. 2-2

to the consumer. Let us now assume that A and B, respectively, are
superior goods. The consumer is going to consider the windfall of $9 as a
change in his real income because the prices of A ($2) and all other com-
modities ($P_b = \$5$), respectively, are now constant. Assume that out of
the windfall $4 will be spent on A and $5 on B. Thus, the consumer will
increase the consumption of A from 4.5 units to 10.5 units, where the
income effect is the cause of increasing consumption by 2 units as indicated by LM in Fig. 2-2. Note that for the purpose of illustration we
have overemphasized the role of the income effect. Normally, the role
of the income effect is negligible compared with the role of the substitution effect. In summary we have

$$\text{Total effect} = \underbrace{\text{substitution effect}}_{} \text{ plus } \underbrace{\text{income effect}}_{}$$
$$\underbrace{}_{KM} \qquad \underbrace{}_{KL} \qquad \underbrace{}_{LM}$$

INTERPERSONAL COMPARISON OF UTILITY

The problem of interpersonal comparison of utility arises with respect to income taxes. In Western countries the principle of a progressive

income tax has long been adopted. A progressive income tax is one in which the higher your income, the higher the rate of the tax. (A regressive income tax is one in which the higher your income, the lower the rate of the tax; and a proportional income tax is one in which the rate is the same regardless of the size of your income.) The reason for imposing a progressive income tax is that governments believe in distributing the burden of the tax according to ability to pay, and ability to pay increases more than proportionately with income.

There are economists who try to justify the progressive income tax upon a law of diminishing marginal utility with respect to income. They claim that the marginal rate should be such that the sacrifice in utility, rather than the pecuniary sacrifice, should be equal on the margin: when the marginal sacrifices of utility of all individuals are equal, the aggregate sacrifice of utility of all individuals is a minimum. (Why?) This leads to a progressive rate of income tax under the assumption of a diminishing marginal utility with respect to income. For example, if you earn $2,000 and your marginal utility is two utils per penny of income and I earn $7,000 and my marginal utility is one util per penny of income, then, if the marginal rate of the tax is 10 percent for you, it should be 20 percent for me. This is true because by paying 10 cents per the last dollar you earn, you give up 10 cents times 2 utils which is 20 utils. When I pay 20 cents from the last dollar I earn, I give up 20 cents times 1 util which is also a sacrifice of 20 utils. Namely, such a progressive income tax results in an equal marginal sacrifice measured by utility. This makes sense if, and only if, your function of utility with respect to income is known and can be compared with my function of utility with respect to income. The truth of the matter is that interpersonal comparison of utility is impossible. Thus, in the example above, although my marginal utility with respect to income may be diminishing, its value when an income of $7,000 is earned may be 4 utils, which means that the marginal rate of the tax must be lower for me.

Moreover, the law of diminishing marginal utility as it is stated with respect to one commodity may not hold with respect to income as a whole. It is possible that my marginal utility of $7,000 is larger than my marginal utility of $2,000. It follows that the theory of utility does not provide a logical foundation for the progressive income tax.

THE CONSUMER'S SURPLUS

Let us start with the intuitive notion that in many cases the consumer pays for a commodity a price which is less than the benefit derived from this commodity. If you do not believe that this is true, simply ask yourself the following question: How much would you be willing to pay for that commodity rather than go without it altogether? A good example is water. You probably pay a negligible amount of money for water, but if the alternative was "all or nothing," you would agree to pay much more rather than to give up the consumption of water. Another example is air. It is not at all unrealistic to assume that you would be willing to pay an extremely high price for air rather than try to live without it.

Economic science cannot say much about this subject of consumer's benefit versus the cost. But, the little that it can say is sometimes of great importance when it comes to advocating policies concerning indirect taxes and other public activities.

The process of estimating the pecuniary value of the consumer's surplus is illustrated by Fig. 2-3. D_0 is the demand curve of one consumer. For simplicity it is assumed to be a 45 degree line. When the price is $7 per pound, the consumer buys one unit only. The utility which the consumer derives from this pound of meat is equal to the utility which he could obtain by spending it alternately on other goods. When the price falls to $6, the consumer could, if he wanted, continue to buy only one pound of meat and thus get for $6 what was worth $7 to him. This is a surplus of utility which is $7 minus $6 equals $1. When the price falls to $5, the surplus of utility per the first unit is worth $7 − $5 = $2, and per the second unit it is worth $6 − $5 = $1. Altogether it is $3. When the price falls to $2, the surplus of utility is roughly estimated at $5 + $4 + $3 + $2 + $1 = $15, which is indicated by the shaded area. This is a

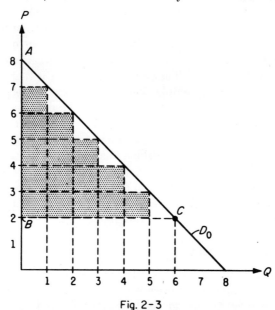

Fig. 2-3

downward biased estimate. In fact, if we considered very small units of meat, then the consumer surplus would become the area of the triangle indicated by ABC.

As far as economic policy is concerned, there may be a case where a public utility cannot break even. Then, if it can be shown that total cost (which is larger than total revenue) is smaller than total revenue plus the consumer's surplus, the government should subsidize the product which is made by the public utility.

PROBLEMS

2-1. $MU_a = 30$ utils and $P_a = \$10$. $MU_c = 9$ utils and $P_c = \$3$. This equilibrium is destroyed by a 40 percent decline in the price of A. Assume that A and C are substitutes. (a) How much utility will the consumer gain by transferring the first dollar from C to A? (b) Will the consumer gain the same amount of utility from transferring the second dollar from C to A?

2-2. The same as Prob. 2-1, except that the consumer is not subject to the law of diminishing marginal utility, nor is there any dependence between MU of one good and the consumption of other goods. What would the consumer do after realizing that P_a has declined 40 percent? Does it matter by how much P_a falls?

2-3. A and B are substitutes for Mr. Smith. Originally $MU_a = 30$ utils, $MU_b = 21$ utils, $P_a = \$10$, and $P_b = \$7$. What will Mr. Smith do if the price of A declines 40 percent? (Supplement your answer numerically.)

2-4. X and Y are the only two commodities in my budget. Currently $MU_x = 50$ utils, $MU_y = 35$ utils, $P_x = \$10$, and $P_y = \$7$. My tastes change in favor of X, e.g., to the first approximation, MU_x doubles. What should I do? Why?

2-5. In the accompanying figure D_0 is a legitimate demand curve. The commodity in question is a "prestige-good," say a mink coat. Could you rationalize the shape of D_0 below P_0? Apply the theory of utility.

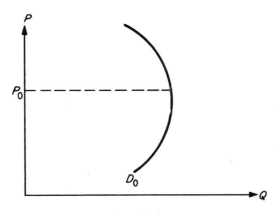

Prob. 2-5

PART II: INDIFFERENCE CURVE ANALYSIS

The classical economists based their theory of utility on the assumption that combinations of commodities can be ranked in terms of cardinal numbers. Late in the nineteenth century, the English economist F. Y. Edgeworth introduced the indifference curve analysis, which was the first challenge to cardinal utility.[2] But until the 1930's, indifference curve analysis was unpopular. In 1934 R. G. D. Allen and J. R. Hicks attacked cardinal utility with heavy artillery.[3] They developed the indifference curve technique which swept into the textbooks of economics. But after the attack was over, cardinal utility regained its popularity, and today cardinal utility and ordinal utility are equally popular. The popularity of cardinal utility was boosted again by the Neumann-Morgenstern method of measuring utility.[4] To illustrate this method consider the following experiment:

A person consumes 5 bottles of wine per unit of time. He is offered a 50-50 chance of winning or losing one bottle. He rejects the offer. Then he is offered a 51-49 chance. He rejects the offer. In such a manner the chance of winning is gradually increased until he is just barely induced to accept an offer of 70-30 odds. In other words, he is just indifferent between a 70 percent chance of gaining one bottle and a 30 percent chance of losing one bottle. Let the marginal utility of the fifth bottle be arbitrarily set at 10 utils. Since the expected gain in utility from gaining one bottle now equals the expected loss of utility from losing one bottle, we obtain the following actuarial equation:

$$0.7 \times \text{gain in utility} = 0.3 \times 10$$

then,

$$\text{Gain in utility} = \frac{0.3 \times 10}{0.7} = 4.3 \text{ utils}$$

That is, once we agree on an arbitrary scale, utility can be measured. In our example, if the marginal utility of the fifth bottle of wine is set at 10 utils, then the marginal utility of the sixth bottle is 4.3 utils. This experiment, however, exists only in theory. The theory is not very useful because such experiments can be conducted only in situations involving uncertainties. In reality, in most of the cases, consumers rank combinations of commodities by assigning them ordinal numbers, in situations which do not involve uncertainty. This is why ordinal utility is so attrac-

[2] F. Y. Edgeworth, *Mathematical Psychics,* C. K. Paul and Co., 1881.

[3] J. R. Hicks and R. G. D. Allen, "A Reconsideration of the Theory of Value," *Economica,* 1, 1934.

[4] J. von Neumann and O. Morgenstern, *Theory of Games and Economic Behavior* (3d ed.), Princeton University Press, 1954.

tive to many economists. Ordinal utility will be the subject of this part.

THE INDIFFERENCE CURVE

We start by considering a consumer who has only two commodities in his budget, A and B. It is convenient to think of A as any commodity and of B as a lump-sum of all other commodities. We assign the horizontal axis for A and the vertical axis for B. Thus each point in Fig. 2-4 represents a pair of two numbers, e.g., so many units of A per unit of time and so many units of B per unit of time. Consider any pair, say point K. Now, suppose we took away one unit of B (KQ) from the consumer and asked him the following question: "What is the additional amount of A which

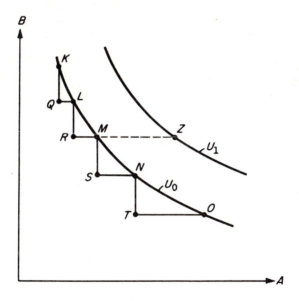

Fig. 2-4

will compensate you for the loss of one unit (KQ) of B?" The consumer would think for a while, and he would come out with the following answer: "The additional amount of A that will compensate me for the loss of one unit of B is QL." Thus, the consumer is indifferent between being on K or being on L. We repeat the same experiment by asking the consumer to forego the consumption of a second unit of B (LR), and he tells us that this time an additional amount of RM of A will compensate him. The loss of the third unit B (MS) is compensated by adding SN of A, and the loss of the fourth unit of B (NT) is compensated by adding TO. Thus the consumer is indifferent between the pairs of A and B represented by K, L, M, N, and O. To put it differently, the consumer derives the same amount of utility from combinations $K, L, M, N,$ and $O,$ respectively. By using smaller and smaller units of B we can obtain as many points as we wish on the indifference curve. Assume that this is the curve shown in Fig. 2-4. Note that the indifference curve is concave from above. The reason is that the scarcer the good, the larger the quantity of the other good which must be added in order to compensate for a sacrifice of one unit of the first good. This is equivalent to the law of diminishing marginal utility. Thus, $QL < RM < SN < TO.$ We can construct as many indifference curves as we want, in fact we could fill the space in Fig. 2-4 with many of them and call the space the *indifference map*. Note that being on one of the points of an indifference curve which lies to the right of another indifference curve means to achieve a higher level of utility.

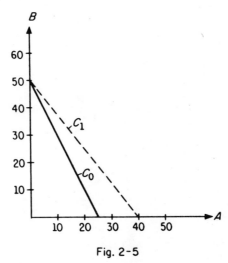

Fig. 2-5

Thus, compare any point on U_1 to being on U_0. For instance, consider point Z on U_1. At this point the consumer has available a certain combination M plus MZ of A. It is clear that the consumer is better off on Z which belongs to U_1. *Consumers simply prefer more to less.* Since this analysis can be applied to each point on the indifference curve U_1, we know that U_1 is preferred to U_0. Thus, the consumer is better off on U_1, but once there he does not gain or lose any utility by moving along the curve. It is left for the reader to show that the two indifference curves cannot intersect.

THE BUDGET LINE

Assume that the consumer has a budget of $100 per unit of time. Also assume that the price of A is $4 and the price of B is $2. Then, the consumer can spend his entire budget on A and buy 25 units of A per unit of time. Alternatively, he can also spend his entire budget on B and buy 50 units of B, or he can buy different combinations of A and B. All these combinations or pairs of A and B lie on a straight line, provided that the entire budget is spent. Start from 25 units of A. If the consumer foregoes consuming one unit of A, \$4 are released with which he can buy 2 additional units of B. This is true regardless of what the combinations of A and B are. Thus, the rate of substitution in consumption is fixed: it is always 1 unit of A for 2 units of B. The budget line relating to \$100 per unit of time and to $P_a = \$4$ and $P_b = \$2$ is C_0 in Fig. 2-5. It is left up to the reader to show that if the price of A falls to \$2.5, the new budget line is C_1.

IMPOSING THE BUDGET LINE ON THE INDIFFERENCE MAP

The budget line is imposed on the indifference map in Fig. 2-6. We assume that the consumer moves along the budget line until he hits the best

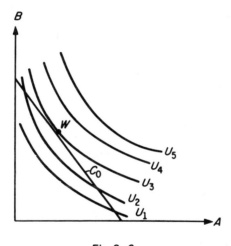

Fig. 2-6

point there. It should be noted that the points to the right are unattainable by the consumer due to the budget constraint. However, points to the left are attainable. Because we assume that the entire budget is spent on A and B, the consumer restricts his movements to the budget line. The best point on the budget line is that point at which utility is maximized, or on the highest indifference curve. This is point W. At W the budget line C_0 just touches the indifference curve U_3, or, in other words, C_0 is tangent to U_3 at W. When the consumer moves along the budget line the following must hold:

$$\Delta A \cdot P_a = - \Delta B \cdot P_b$$

Davidson College Library

For instance, if $\Delta A = 1$ unit, $P_a = \$4$. Then, since the price of B is \$2 apiece, with \$4 released from foregoing the consumption of 1 unit of A the consumer can buy 2 additional units of B. Thus, $\Delta B = 2$ units. Dividing the equality $\Delta A \cdot P_a = -\Delta B \cdot P_b$ by $\Delta B \cdot P_a$ we obtain $\Delta A/\Delta B = -P_b/P_a$. Next, let the change in quantity along the indifference curve be denoted by $\overline{\Delta}$. Then, due to the principle of compensation the following must hold along the indifference curve:

$$\overline{\Delta A} \cdot MU_a = -\overline{\Delta B} \cdot MU_b$$

Dividing this equality by $\overline{\Delta B} \cdot MU_a$ gives

$$RCS = \frac{\overline{\Delta A}}{\overline{\Delta B}} = -\frac{MU_b}{MU_a}$$

Since W is a point of tangency, at W the following must hold:

$$\frac{\overline{\Delta A}}{\overline{\Delta B}} = \frac{\Delta A}{\Delta B}$$

thus we obtain

$$\frac{MU_b}{MU_a} = \frac{P_b}{P_a}$$

Multiplying this equality by MU_a/P_b gives

$$\frac{MU_b}{P_b} = \frac{MU_a}{P_a}$$

which is the law of logic as previously stated.

THE DERIVATION OF THE DEMAND CURVE

Recall that when the price of B falls, we obtain a new budget line as indicated in Fig. 2-5. In general, the new quantity of A demanded will be determined by the point of tangency between the new budget line C_1 and another indifference curve as indicated by the indifference map.

Consider Fig. 2-7. Originally the budget line is C_0. Note that C_0 touches U_0 at E at which A_1 is the quantity of A demanded. After the price of A falls, the new budget line is C_1. Also, C_1 touches another indifference curve U_1 at H at which A_4 units of A is the quantity demanded. Thus, the total effect of reducing the price of A was to increase the quantity demanded from A_1 to A_4. By assigning different prices to A, we can derive different quantities of A from the indifference map. Plotting the pairs of prices and corresponding quantities will yield the demand curve. If we forced the consumer to stay on the same indifference curve U_0 after the

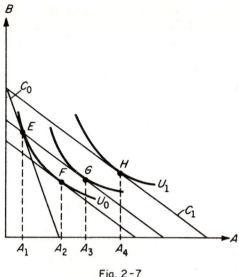

Fig. 2-7

price of A has changed, the consumer would move on the same U_0 curve to point F. This is true because at F a line which is parallel to C_1 touches U_0, namely, F is the point at which the law of logic holds for the new price of A. Note that A_2 is the quantity corresponding to F. By definition, the change in quantity demanded from A_1 to A_2 is the Hicksian substitution effect.[5] The proper way to achieve this effect on the quantity demanded is to force the consumer to stay with the same utility (i.e., on the same indifference curve) after the price of the commodity in question changes. The income effect is a residue, namely, it is the total effect minus the substitution effect, which is equal to $A_4 - A_2$. In summary we have

$$
\underbrace{\text{Total effect}}_{A_4 - A_1} \;=\; \underbrace{\overset{\text{Hicksian}}{\text{substitution effect}}}_{A_2 - A_1} \;+\; \underbrace{\text{income effect}}_{A_4 - A_2}
$$

This definition of the substitution effect is impractical because utility cannot be observed.

We can define the substitution effect as the change in the quantity demanded subject to the condition that the "windfall," that is, the change in apparent real income, is taken away from the consumer. Recall that after the change in apparent real income is confiscated the consumer is left with a budget sufficient to buy the original set of commodities. In Fig. 2-7 the original set is indicated by point E, i.e., the new budget line

[5] J. R. Hicks, an English economist, the author of *Value and Capital,* London: Oxford University Press, 1946, pp. 29-33.

corresponding to the original budget minus the "windfall" must pass through E. But it must be parallel to C_1 which reflects the new price of A. Thus, confiscating the change in apparent real income is equivalent to restricting the consumer to a budget line which is parallel to C_1 and which passes through point E. As indicated in Fig. 2-7, such a budget line touches an indifference curve at G. The quantity A_3 corresponds to G. Accordingly, we have another substitution effect which is the change from A_1 to A_3. This is the Slutsky substitution effect.[6] Here, the residue $A_4 - A_3$ is the income effect. In summary

$$\underbrace{\text{Total effect}}_{A_4 - A_1} = \underbrace{\text{Slutsky substitution effect}}_{A_3 - A_1} + \underbrace{\text{income effect}}_{A_4 - A_3}$$

Note finally that it can be proved that the difference between the two substitution effects, that is, $A_3 - A_2$, shrinks faster than $A_2 - A_1$, $A_3 - A_1$, $A_4 - A_3$, and $A_4 - A_2$, respectively, when the change in price is becoming smaller and smaller. In other words, the Slutsky effect is a good proxy for the Hicksian effect.

APPLICATIONS

Allotment. Assume that there are two commodities in the economy, X and Y. Consider two consumers with the same budget. (They have the same budget line C_0.) Originally one consumer prefers combination R,

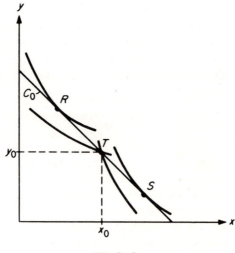

Fig. 2-8

[6] Eugen Slutsky, "On the Theory of the Budget of the Consumer." Reprinted in *Readings in Price Theory,* eds. K. Boulding and G. Stigler, Homewood, Ill.: Richard D. Irwin, Inc., 1952.

and the other prefers combination S. Now, the government decides to pay both consumers with goods. Each of them is allotted the combination of X_0 units of X and Y_0 units of Y. In other words, each of them consumes the combination indicated by point T (Fig. 2-8). But, by asking the consumer to move to T, the government in fact forces him to move to a lower indifference curve as indicated in Fig. 2-8. Namely, allotment involves a loss of utility to society.

Next, consider the case of allotment when income is not equal (Fig. 2-9). Originally the rich consumes the combination indicated by S, and

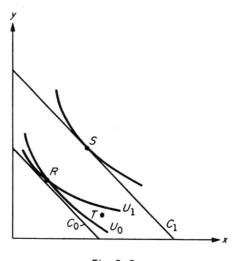

Fig. 2-9

the poor consumes the combination indicated by R. The government decides to give each of them the same allotment as indicated by T. Clearly, the rich consumer is now worse off because T belongs to an indifference curve which is lower than the one passing through S. As far as the poor consumer is concerned, we cannot say much. If U_0 is the indifference curve that passes through R, then he is better off; if U_1 is the one, then he is worse off. Note, however, that had the government simply decided to transfer money from the rich to the poor, i.e., had the government allowed the poor to move along a budget line that passes through T and is parallel to C_0, then there would be no doubt about the improvement in the welfare of the poor.

Commodity Rationing. This program is illustrated in Fig. 2-10. Assume that immediately after the war commodity X is scarce. The government decides to guarantee each citizen a certain amount X_0 units of X at the prevailing price of X in the market. There is a strict law forbidding

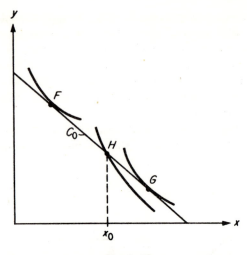

Fig. 2-10

the trade in commodity X. The consumer who used to consume the combination indicated by point F is not affected by the law. But a consumer who used to consume the combination indicated by G is affected: he must move to point H, which belongs to a lower indifference curve.

Next consider the case where citizens are allowed to trade in commodity X (Fig. 2-11). Let us make the realistic assumption that the market price of X denoted by P_m is higher than the rationing price denoted by P_r. First consider the consumer who used to be at point F. Now it pays

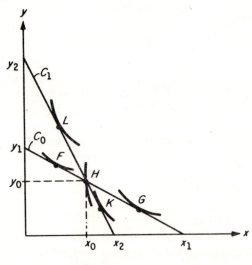

Fig. 2-11

him to buy the rationed X_0 units of X at P_r and sell them at P_m. This would increase his budget by $X_0(P_m - P_r)$. Originally, his budget amounted to C_0 and it cut the Y axis at $Y_1 = C_0/P_y$ and the X axis at $X_1 = C_0/P_r$. After trade is allowed, his new budget amounts to $C_1 = C_0 + X_0(P_m - P_r)$, and the new budget line cuts the Y axis at $Y_2 = [C_0 + X_0(P_m - P_r)]/P_y$ and the X axis at $X_2 = [C_0 + X_0(P_m - P_r)]/P_m$.

The new budget line C_1 intersects with the original budget line C_0 at point H. This is true because at point H the following equations are satisfied:

$$C_1 = X_0 \cdot P_m + Y_0 \cdot P_y$$
$$C_0 = X_0 \cdot P_r + Y_0 \cdot P_y$$
$$C_1 - C_0 = X_0 \cdot (P_m - P_r)$$

Clearly, the result of allowing trade is a gain in utility: the consumer who used to be at point F will move to a higher level of utility at point L. The consumer who wanted to be at G but was forced to move to H will either remain at H or, if there is a higher indifference curve touching C_1, move to point K.

PROBLEMS

2-6. By drawing the proper indifference map, show that if consumption is governed by increasing MU (and no dependence) the consumer will concentrate on consuming one good.

2-7. How will the consumer behave if consumption is governed by constant MU (and no dependence)? Apply indifference curve analysis.

2-8. Prove that two indifference curves cannot intersect.

2-9. Draw the indifference map for the case where one commodity is a source of utility and the other is a source of disutility.

2-10. A person earns \$600 a month. He is just barely induced to accept an 80-20 chance of winning or losing \$100. What is his marginal utility of the seventh \$100 if the marginal utility of the sixth \$100 is set at 10 utils?

2-11. Repeat Prob. 2-10, except that the odds are 20-80. Does his marginal utility of income diminish?

2-12. In Fig. 2-7, the Slutsky substitution effect is larger than the Hicksian substitution effect. What does this imply? Under what assumption will the opposite occur?

PART III: INDEX NUMBERS AND REVEALED PREFERENCE

QUANTITY INDICES

Assume that a consumer has only two commodities in his budget, denote them as X and Y. The consumer buys these two commodities in two distinct time periods, zero and one. In what follows we shall refer to *time period zero* as the *base time period*. Also, unless otherwise stated, we shall assume that the consumer's taste does not change from the base time period to time period one. Put in economic terms, the indifference map is the same in the two time periods. We shall refer to the various baskets of goods and services as combination A, combination B, etc.

Consider Fig. 2-12. In the base time period the consumer has an

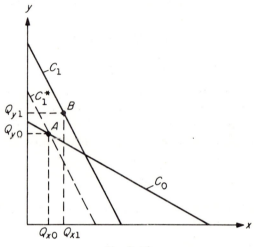

Fig. 2-12

income of C_0 dollars, the prices confronting him are P_{x0} and P_{y0}, and he prefers point A to all other points on the budget line C_0. At point A he consumes Q_{x0} units of X and Q_{y0} units of Y. That is, $C_0 = Q_{x0} \cdot P_{x0} + Q_{y0} \cdot P_{y0}$. This may be written as $C_0 = \Sigma Q_0 \cdot P_0$, and extended to any number of commodities. In time period one the income of the consumer is C_1 dollars, and at the prices P_{x1} of commodity X and P_{y1} of commodity Y he prefers point B to other points. At point B he buys Q_{x1} units of X and Q_{y1} units of Y. That is $C_1 = Q_{x1} \cdot P_{x1} + Q_{y1} \cdot P_{y1}$. This may be written as $C_1 = \Sigma Q_1 \cdot P_1$ and extended to any number of commodities.

Could the consumer buy in time period one combination A (of the base time period) at prices prevailing in time period one? Geometrically we answer this question by passing a budget line C_1^* parallel to C_1 through point A. This means that $C_1^* = Q_{x0} \cdot P_{x1} + Q_{y0} \cdot P_{y1}$. It may be written as $C_1^* = \Sigma Q_0 \cdot P_1$. As seen from Fig. 2-12, the consumer could have purchased combination A (Q_{x0}, Q_{y0}) at prices of time period one (P_{x1}, P_{y1}) because the budget line C_1^* is lower than the budget line C_1. Since the consumer has not done what he could do, we conclude that he prefers combination B to combination A. The fact that $C_1 > C_1^*$ may be written in the general form as

$$\Sigma Q_1 \cdot P_1 > \Sigma Q_0 \cdot P_1$$

Dividing both sides of the inequality by $\Sigma Q_0 \cdot P_1$ gives

$$Q_p = \frac{\Sigma Q_1 \cdot P_1}{\Sigma Q_0 \cdot P_1} > 1$$

This is known as the Paasche quantity index. Notice that Q stands for quantity and the subscript p for Paasche. In order to determine whether the consumer could buy combination B (of time period one) in the base time period, we reproduce parts of Fig. 2-12 in Fig. 2-13. In order to buy

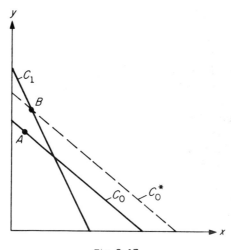

Fig. 2-13

combination B at prices prevailing in the base time period the consumer had to have a budget $C_0^* = Q_{x1} \cdot P_{x0} + Q_{y1} \cdot P_{y0}$. Its general form is $C_0^* = \Sigma Q_1 \cdot P_0$. But, as seen from Fig. 2-13, the budget the consumer actually had in the base time period, C_0, is smaller than C_0^*, and accordingly combination B is preferred to combination A. The inequality $C_0^* > C_0$ may be written as

$$\Sigma Q_1 \cdot P_0 > \Sigma Q_0 \cdot P_0$$

Dividing the above inequality by $\Sigma Q_0 \cdot P_0$ gives

$$Q_L = \frac{\Sigma Q_1 \cdot P_0}{\Sigma Q_0 \cdot P_0} > 1$$

This is known as the Laspeyre quantity index. Notice that here Q stands for quantity and the subscript L for Laspeyre.

We may summarize it as follows:

If the tastes of the consumer have not changed from one time period to another (the indifference map has not changed), then if Paasche and Laspeyre quantity indices are, respectively, greater than unity, then the consumer is better off in time period one as compared with the base time period.

Notice that when the Paasche quantity index is used, quantities of both time periods are weighted by prices of time period one. When the Laspeyre quantity index is used quantities are weighted by prices of the base time period.

It is left as an exercise for the reader to show that if in Fig. 2-13 the places of points A and B and lines C_0 and C_1, respectively, are changed, then the consumer is better off in the base time period and Paasche and Laspeyre quantity indices are respectively smaller than unity.

Consider now Fig. 2-14. C_1^* is smaller than C_1. Accordingly the con-

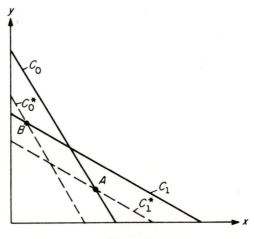

Fig. 2-14

sumer could in time period one buy combination A (of the base time period) at the prices of time period one. The inequality $C_1 > C_1^*$ may be written as

$$\Sigma Q_1 \cdot P_1 > \Sigma Q_0 \cdot P_1$$

Dividing through by $\Sigma Q_0 \cdot P_1$ gives

$$Q_p = \frac{\Sigma Q_1 \cdot P_1}{\Sigma Q_0 \cdot P_1} > 1$$

But C_0^* is smaller than C_0. Thus the consumer could in the base time period buy combination B (of time period one) at prices of the base time period. *This leads to ambiguity: we cannot determine whether A is better than B or B is better than A.* The inequality $C_0^* < C_0$ may be written as

$$\Sigma Q_1 \cdot P_0 < \Sigma Q_0 \cdot P_0$$

Dividing through by $\Sigma Q_0 \cdot P_0$ gives

$$Q_L = \frac{\Sigma Q_1 \cdot P_0}{\Sigma Q_0 \cdot P_0} < 1$$

Notice that the assumption of unchanging tastes is inconsistent with the way points A and B are plotted in Fig. 2-14. *Thus we are led to the conclusion that if Paasche quantity index is greater than unity while Laspeyre quantity index is smaller than unity, then the tastes of the consumer must have changed.*

In Fig. 2-15 we describe a situation in which in time period one the

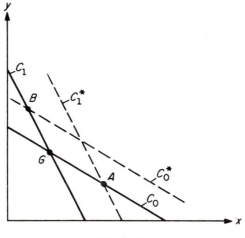

Fig. 2-15

consumer could not buy combination A (of the base time period) at prices of time period one. In the base time period the consumer could not buy combination B (of time period one) at the prices of the base time period. This is summarized as follows: The inequality $C_1 < C_1^*$ may be written as

$$\Sigma Q_1 \cdot P_1 < \Sigma Q_0 \cdot P_1$$

Dividing through by $\Sigma Q_0 \cdot P_1$ gives

$$Q_p = \frac{\Sigma Q_1 \cdot P_1}{\Sigma Q_0 \cdot P_1} < 1$$

The inequality $C_0^* > C_0$ may be written as

$$\Sigma Q_1 \cdot P_0 > \Sigma Q_0 \cdot P_0$$

Dividing through by $\Sigma Q_0 \cdot P_0$ gives

$$Q_L = \frac{\Sigma Q_1 \cdot P_0}{\Sigma Q_0 \cdot P_0} > 1$$

We may summarize it as follows:

If the Paasche quantity index is smaller than unity and Laspeyre quantity index is greater than unity, the assumption that the tastes of the consumer do not change from one time period to the next does not aid in determining whether the consumer is better off in time period one. We leave it for the reader to show that the indifference curve touching C_1 at point B may be either higher or lower than the indifference curve touching C_0 at point A. In other words, it is impossible to determine whether combination B represents a higher or a lower level of utility compared with combination A.

If either point A or point B is at the intersection of the budget lines (for example G in Fig. 2-15), then either Paasche or Laspeyre is equal to unity. These cases are left for the reader as exercises.

PRICE INDICES

We assume that the consumer buys two commodities X and Y in two time periods. The time periods are the base time period and time period one. In Fig. 2-16, C_0 is the budget of the consumer in the base

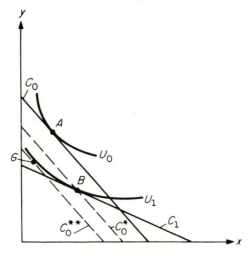

Fig. 2-16

time period, and given the prices in the base time period the consumer prefers combination A to all other possibilities on C_0. In time period one the budget of the consumer amounts to C_1 dollars, and given the prices in time period one the consumer prefers combination B to all other points on C_1.

The cost of combination B at time period one is C_1. The cost of the same combination B at prices of the base time period is C_0^*. C_0^* is a budget line parallel to C_0 and passing through point B. The Paasche price index measures the cost of combination B (of time period one) at prices of time period one relative to the cost of the same combination B at the base time period prices. This is written as

$$P_p = \frac{C_1}{C_0^*} = \frac{\Sigma P_1 \cdot Q_1}{\Sigma P_0 \cdot Q_1}$$

where P stands for price and the subscript p stands for Paasche. Notice that C_0^{**} is a budget line parallel to C_0 and touching the indifference curve U_1 at point G. U_1 passes through B. C_0^{**} tells what is the budget required for "buying" the same level of utility U_1 at prices of the base time period. Recall that the "cost" of U_1 at time period one is C_1. Thus, the *ideal* Paasche price index is

$$\text{Ideal } P_p = \frac{C_1}{C_0^{**}} > \frac{C_1}{C_0^*} = P_p$$

That is, the Paasche price index is smaller than the *ideal* Paasche price index. Since the shape of indifference curve is not known, the Ideal Paasche price index cannot be estimated. But the above inequality does indicate that the Paasche price index is downward biased. For example, if the Paasche price index is 1.20, then the correct statement is "*the price level has increased by at least 20 per cent.*"

Fig. 2-16 is partially reproduced in Fig. 2-17. Instead of focusing on combination B of time period one we now focus on point A of the base time period. The cost of combination A (of the base time period) at prices of the base time period is C_0. The cost of combination A at prices of time period one is C_1^*. Geometrically C_1^* is a budget line parallel to C_1 and passing through A. The Laspeyre price index measures the cost of combination A (of the base time period) at the prices of time period one relative to the cost of the same combination A at the base time period. This is written as

$$P_L = \frac{C_1^*}{C_0} = \frac{\Sigma P_1 \cdot Q_0}{\Sigma P_0 \cdot Q_0}$$

Here P stands for price and L for Laspeyre. Notice that C_1^{**} is a budget

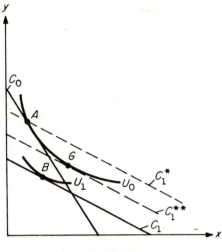

Fig. 2-17

line parallel to C_1 and touching the indifference curve U_0 at point G. U_0 passes through A. C_1^{**} tells what is the budget required for "buying" the same level of utility U_0 at prices of time period one. Recall that the "cost" of U_0 at the base time period is C_0. Thus the *ideal* Laspeyre price index is

$$\text{Ideal } P_L = \frac{C_1^{**}}{C_0} < \frac{C_1^{*}}{C_0} = P_L$$

That is, the Laspeyre price index is greater than the *ideal* Laspeyre price index. This indicates that the Laspeyre price index is upward biased. For example, if the Laspeyre price index is 1.25, then the correct statement is "the price level has increased by *at most* 25 per cent."

We leave it for the reader to explain why, under normal conditions, the Laspeyre price index is greater than the Paasche price index.

Let Y_1 denote the nominal income of the consumer in time period one, and Y_0 denote the nominal income of the consumer in the base time period, i.e.,

$$Y_1 = \Sigma Q_1 \cdot P_1 \qquad \text{and} \qquad Y_0 = \Sigma Q_0 \cdot P_0$$

The change in nominal income, (nominal income in time period one relative to nominal income in the base time period) is

$$\frac{Y_1}{Y_0} = \frac{\Sigma Q_1 \cdot P_1}{\Sigma Q_0 \cdot P_0}$$

The change in real income may be calculated by dividing the change in nominal income by the change in prices. If the Laspeyre price index is used we obtain

$$\text{change in real income} = \frac{\dfrac{Y_1}{Y_0}}{P_L} = \frac{\dfrac{\Sigma Q_1 \cdot P_1}{\Sigma Q_0 \cdot P_0}}{\dfrac{\Sigma P_1 \cdot Q_0}{\Sigma P_0 \cdot Q_0}} = \frac{\Sigma Q_1 \cdot P_1}{\Sigma Q_0 \cdot P_1} = Q_p$$

In other words, deflating the change in nominal income by a Laspeyre price index gives a Paasche quantity index. *Since P_L has an upward bias, then Q_p has a downward bias.* Alternatively, deflating the change in nominal income by a Paasche price index gives a Lespeyre quantity index as follows

$$\text{change in real income} = \frac{\dfrac{Y_1}{Y_0}}{P_p} = \frac{\dfrac{\Sigma Q_1 \cdot P_1}{\Sigma Q_0 \cdot P_0}}{\dfrac{\Sigma P_1 \cdot Q_1}{\Sigma P_0 \cdot Q_1}} = \frac{\Sigma Q_1 \cdot P_0}{\Sigma Q_0 \cdot P_0} = Q_L$$

Since P_p is downward biased, Q_L must be upward biased. Or in other words since the Paasche price index is smaller than the ideal Paasche price index, had we divided the change in nominal income by the ideal Paasche price index instead of the Paasche price index we would have received a smaller (ideal) Laspeyre quantity index.

PROBLEMS

2-13. Show that if in Fig. 2-13 the places of points A and B and lines C_0 and C_1, respectively, are interchanged, then the consumer is better off in the base time period and Paasche and Laspeyre quantity indices are, respectively, smaller than unity.

2-14. Show that in Fig. 2-14 the indifference curve touching C_1 at point B must cut the indifference curve touching C_0 at point A.

2-15. Show that if in Figs. 2-13, 2-14, and 2-15 either point A or point B coincides with the intersection of C_0 and C_1, then either Laspeyre or Paasche quantity index take on unity. Analyze the welfare change of the consumer in each of these cases.

2-16. Show that in Fig. 2-15 the indifference curve touching C_1 at point B may be either higher or lower than the indifference curve touching C_0 at point A.

2-17. Explain why under normal conditions the Laspeyre price index is expected to be greater than the Paasche price index.

SELECTED READINGS

HICKS, J. R. *Value and Capital*. London: Oxford University Press, 1946, Chapters 1, 2, and 3.

STIGLER, G. J. *The Theory of Price*. New York: The Macmillan Company, 1966, Chapter 4.

chapter 3

Demand Shifts Due to Changes in Income

The demand for a certain good is determined by the following factors: (1) the price of the good under consideration, (2) the income of the consumer, (3) prices of other commodities, (4) the taste of the consumer. It is convenient to separate between these factors in the analysis of the consumer's behavior. Thus, in Chapter 1 we defined the demand curve such that tastes, income, and all other prices are unchanged. The only factor that changes along the demand curve is the price of the commodity under consideration. It is convenient to define the demand curve in such a manner. For example, if the commodity under consideration is margarine, and the price of margarine declines, more margarine is demanded. But, if we allow the price of butter and income, respectively, to increase, then we cannot tell whether the demand for margarine has increased due to the decline of its own price, the rise in the price of butter, or the increase in income.

In Chapter 1 we focused mainly on a change in the quantity demanded due to a change in the price of the commodity. A change in demand when the price of the commodity is held constant was analyzed only with respect to a change in tastes. But the demand may also increase or decrease resulting from a change in income and a change in the prices of other commodities. In this chapter we shall discuss the change in demand due to a change in income, leaving the problem of a change in demand due to changes in prices of other commodities to the following chapter. At this point the attention of the reader is called to the difference between a change in the quantity demanded and a change in demand. A change in the quantity demanded refers to moving along the demand curve. A change in demand means moving from one demand curve to another, in other words, shifting the demand curve. Before going any further the reader should make sure that he understands what the difference is between an inferior and a superior commodity (Chapter 2).

A CHANGE IN NOMINAL INCOME

Consider one point on the demand curve. At this point the price is given. By definition all other prices are also given. Thus, analyzing the effect of the change in nominal income when one point on the demand curve is considered is equivalent to analyzing a change in nominal income when the prices of all commodities in the budget of the consumer are fixed. Assuming that prices are fixed, a positive change in nominal income means a positive change in real income, etc. This is true because if your nominal income increases while prices do not change, then you can buy more of each commodity that is in your budget.

How will the consumer allocate the additional income between various commodities? First of all he will shift from inferior to superior commodities. He may shift from an old car to a brand new car, from a cheap car to a luxurious one, etc. Secondly, the consumer will maximize his total utility. This is equivalent to saying that he will see to it that the marginal utility derived from spending the last dollar on each commodity, respectively, is the same. To illustrate this, consider an individual who has only two commodities in his budget. For simplicity assume that these two commodities denoted by A and B are superior, and also that there is no dependence between MU_a and the quantity of B consumed and MU_b and the quantity of A consumed. Let us assume that the price of A is \$4 and the price of B is \$2. A dollar's worth of A, then is $1/4$ of one unit of A, and a dollar's worth of B is $1/2$ of one unit of B. Originally, the nominal income of the consumer amounts to \$80. As it is indicated in Fig. 3-1, he allocates \$20 for spending on A and \$60 for spending on B because, as seen from the diagram, by so dividing his income he equates

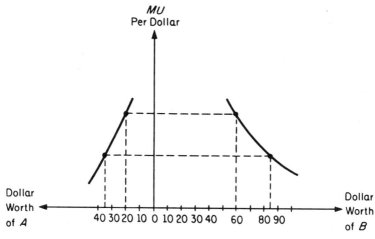

Fig. 3-1

the marginal utility derived from the last dollar spent on A with the marginal utility derived from the last dollar spent on B. After his income increases by $40, he allocates 16 additional dollars to A and 24 additional dollars to B. Again, it is shown in Fig. 3-1 that the consumer equates the marginal utilities derived from the last dollar's worth of A and the last dollar's worth of B. Note that out of his additional income the consumer allocates more money to B. The reason is that the marginal utility curve relating to dollars of B is flatter compared with the marginal utility curve relating to dollars of A. Or, to put it differently, the marginal utility curve relating to dollars of A is falling off very rapidly.

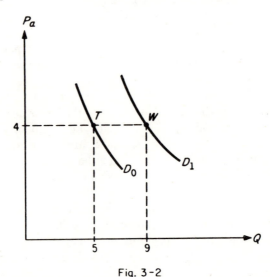

Fig. 3-2

Originally, the quantity demanded for A per unit of time was $20/$4 = 5 units. After the positive change in income occurs, the quantity demanded of A is $36/$4 = 9 units. Namely, the demand has changed by $9 - 5 = 4$ units. This idea of a change in demand (and *not* in quantity demanded) is illustrated in Fig. 3-2.

At T, which belongs to D_0, the quantity demanded was originally equal to 5 units of A. But after income has increased from $80 to $120, demand has increased by 4 units, and the new demand is indicated by W. In fact, W is a point on a new demand curve D_1 which corresponds to a higher level of income.

INCOME ELASTICITY

Let income be denoted by I, and demand by Q, then income elasticity which is denoted by n_I is

$$\eta_I = \frac{\Delta Q/Q}{\Delta I/I} = \frac{\% \text{ change in demand}}{\% \text{ change in income}}$$

It is recalled again that when income changes the prices of all commodities are kept constant

In Fig. 3-2 income elasticity can be estimated as

$$\eta_I = \frac{\Delta Q/Q}{\Delta I/I} = \frac{4/7}{40/100} = 1.42$$

which is the estimate of income elasticity at point T. To each point on D_0 there corresponds a different income elasticity. Moreover, to different changes in income there may correspond different values of income elasticity. This, however, is not a serious problem, because in most of the cases the economist is interested in the sign of income elasticity. To put it differently, if the commodity is superior, then income elasticity is positive. This is true because *ceteris paribus* a positive change in income entails a positive change in the consumption of the superior commodity. If the commodity is inferior, then income elasticity is negative. This is true because a positive change in income entails a negative change in the consumption of an inferior commodity. To say that the economist is interested in the sign of income elasticity is equivalent to saying that the economist is interested in the direction of the shift. If income elasticity is positive, then a rising income will give rise to increasing demand leading to a rightward shift in the demand curve. If income elasticity is negative, then a rising income will give rise to a decrease in demand leading to a leftward shift in the demand curve.

The order of magnitude of income elasticity is secondary in importance to its sign. In fact, you will hear economists say the following: "The income elasticity of agricultural commodities is usually smaller than unity. It is in the order of magnitude of $\frac{1}{2}$ or $\frac{1}{4}$." Also, economists define a luxury as a commodity whose income elasticity is larger than unity.

Example: Assuming that $\eta_I = -\frac{1}{2}$, estimate the change in demand for commodity A resulting from a 12 percent increase in nominal income. Originally, $Q_0 = 10$ units. Let the change in demand be denoted by X. Then

$$\eta_I = \frac{\% \text{ change in } Q}{\% \text{ change in } I} \qquad \text{or} \qquad -\frac{1}{2} = \frac{X}{12\%}$$

Solving for X gives $X = -6$ percent. Namely, the demand curve will shift leftward. Six percent of 10 units is 0.6 units, and, roughly speaking, ΔQ is estimated at -0.6 units.

Example: Assume that $\eta_I = 1.5$. What is the change in income which is necessary for inducing a 15 percent increase in the demand for the commodity in question? Let the percentage change in income be denoted by X. Then, we have

$$\eta_I = \frac{\% \text{ change in } Q}{\% \text{ change in } I} \quad \text{or} \quad 1.5 = \frac{15\%}{X}$$

Solving for X gives

$$X = 10\%$$

MARGINAL PROPENSITY TO CONSUME

Marginal propensity to consume with respect to a certain commodity is defined as the rate of change of total spending on that commodity per unit of change of income. For instance, in Fig. 3-1 it is shown that a change in total income from \$80 to \$120 gave rise to changing spending on commodity A from \$20 to \$36. Thus, we can estimate marginal propensity to consume as follows:

Let marginal propensity to consume with respect to commodity A be denoted by M_a, then

$$M_a = \frac{\Delta \text{ spending on } A}{\Delta I} = \frac{36 - 20}{120 - 80} = \frac{16}{40} = 0.4$$

This result may be interpreted as follows: 40 cents out of each additional dollar are spent on commodity A.

Average propensity to consume (denoted by K_a) with respect to A is defined as total spending on commodity A divided by total income. Consider Fig. 3-1. Before the change in income occurred, average propensity to consume with respect to commodity A is \$20/\$80 = 0.25.

It can be proved that income elasticity with respect to a certain commodity is equal to the marginal propensity to consume that commodity divided by the average propensity to consume that commodity. This is left as an exercise for the reader.

GROWTH AND INCOME ELASTICITIES

It is recalled that the aggregate demand curve is the horizontal sum of all individual demand curves. When income of individuals rises, some will demand more of a certain commodity and others will demand less of it. In other words, a commodity which is superior for your neighbor may be inferior for you. This, however, is not a real problem, because we are interested in the net shift of the aggregate demand curve. Thus, if there is a net increase in demand leading to a rightward shift of the aggregate demand curve resulting from a positive change in average income per capita, the commodity in question is superior. If the net shift of the demand curve is to the left, then the commodity is inferior. Note that the probable variable to use here is average income per capita which is national income divided by population. It is wrong to use national income as such because the population may grow faster than national income, i.e., while national income is increasing, average income per capita may be falling off. Let us restrict ourselves to the normal case where national income grows faster than the population. Then industries which are engaged in producing superior commodities are confronted with an increasing aggregate demand leading to a rightward shift in the demand curve over a period of time. Industries which are engaged in producing inferior commodities are confronted with an aggregate demand curve that either shifts leftwards over a period of time or an aggregate demand curve that shifts slowly to the right.

Econometric estimates of income elasticity enable economists to estimate future demands. Suppose average population this year was 1,000,000 people, and each person consumed 10 units of commodity X. If income elasticity is estimated at 2, population will grow at a rate of 3 percent per annum and disposable income per capita will increase 5 percent per annum. Then, we can estimate the change in aggregate demand as follows:

Demand this year = $10 \times 1,000,000 = 10,000,000$ units of X

$$2 = \frac{\text{percentage change in demand}}{5\%}$$

Percentage change in demand = $5\% \times 2 = 10\%$
110% of 10 units of X = 11 units of X
3% of 1,000,000 people = 30,000 people

The demand (per annum) in one year from now is estimated at $11 \times 1,030,000 = 11,330,000$. The absolute change in demand amounts to 1,330,000 units which is a change of 13.3 percent. Notice that a rough estimate of the percentage change in the aggregate demand can be obtained by adding the percentage shift of the demand of each individual (10 percent) to the percentage shift in population (3 percent). Thus, if the commodity is inferior, whether it will increase, leading to a rightward shift, or decrease, leading to a leftward shift, will depend on whether the percentage growth of population will be larger than the percentage shift of the demand curve of the average consumer, or vice versa.

THE INDIFFERENCE CURVE APPROACH

Consider a consumer who has only two commodities in his budget. Denote them as A and B. Changing income when the relative prices of A and B are unchanged means shifting the budget line upwards such that the new budget line is always parallel to the original one. In Fig. 3-3 when the budget line shifts from C_1 to C_2, C_3, etc., the points of tangency of the budget lines with the indifference curves, respectively, change from K to L, from L to M, and so on. Connecting points K, L, M, and so on yields the consumption curve denoted by CC. Note that CC represents a case where A and B are superior commodities; CC_A represents a case where A is an inferior commodity; and CC_B represents a case where B is inferior.

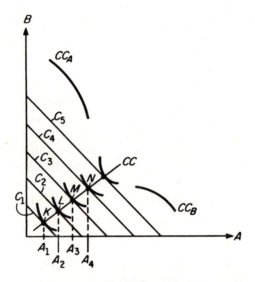

Fig. 3-3

A curve which relates the consumption of A to income can be derived from Fig. 3-3. Such a curve, known as the Engel curve, is derived in Fig. 3-4, where income is measured on the horizontal axis and the consumption of A on the vertical axis. Thus, I_1 is the income corresponding to the budget line C_1, and so on. The income elasticity in the range MN (Fig. 3-4) is

$$\eta_{IA} = \frac{\Delta A / \bar{A}}{\Delta I / \bar{I}} = \frac{(A_4 - A_3) / \bar{A}}{(I_4 - I_3) / \bar{I}}$$

where

$$\bar{A} = \frac{A_4 + A_3}{2} \quad \text{and} \quad \bar{I} = \frac{I_4 + I_3}{2}$$

If A were an inferior good, the Engel curve would have a negative slope.

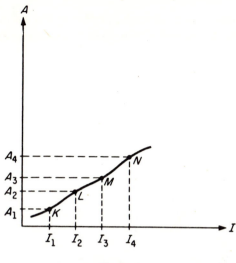

Fig. 3-4

AN IMPORTANT FORMULA

Let saving be defined as a commodity. Then the additional income is spent entirely on commodities. This can be summarized as

$$P_a \cdot \Delta A + P_b \cdot \Delta B + \cdots + P_n \cdot \Delta N = \Delta I$$

Dividing through by ΔI we obtain

$$\frac{P_a \cdot \Delta A}{\Delta I} + \frac{P_b \cdot \Delta B}{\Delta I} + \cdots + \frac{P_n \cdot \Delta N}{\Delta I} = 1$$

Consider the expression

$$\frac{P_a \cdot \Delta A}{\Delta I}$$

Multiplying the numerator and denominator of this expression, respectively, by $I \cdot A$ gives

$$\frac{P_a \cdot A}{I} \cdot \frac{\Delta A \cdot I}{\Delta I \cdot A} = K_a \cdot \eta_{Ia}$$

where K_a is the fraction of total income which is spent on commodity A. Thus we obtain

$$K_a \cdot \eta_{Ia} + K_b \cdot \eta_{Ib} + \cdots + K_n \cdot \eta_{In} = 1$$

Another important formula, which decomposes price-elasticity into the substitution-component and income-component, is derived in the Appendix.

PROBLEMS

3-1. Mr. Johnson's income has increased from $24 to $26 per day. As a result, he decreased his consumption of oleomargarine by 2 percent. Estimate his income elasticity with respect to oleomargarine. Use the mean income in your computation.

3-2. If your income elasticity with respect to potatoes is − ½, by how much will you increase or decrease your demand for potatoes as a result of a 4 percent increase in your income?

3-3. My income elasticity with respect to bologna is estimated at − ⅓. What is the change in my income that will induce me to decrease my consumption of bologna by 10 percent?

3-4. Raisers of cattle consume more meat when the price of meat rises. This implies that meat is (a) an inferior good or (b) a superior good. Circle the correct answer. (HINT: When you treat the raiser of cattle, separate between his role as a consumer and his role as a producer of meat.)

3-5. Suppose you heard of a raiser of cattle who consumes less meat when the price of meat rises. Could you rationalize it? Must you assume that meat is an inferior good?

3-6. Assume that (a) the aggregate demand for food is proportional to the population and (b) income elasticity with respect to food is − ¼. The population grows at a rate of 2 percent per annum and income per capita at a rate of 1 percent per annum. By how much does the aggregate demand curve for food shift over a period of one year?

3-7. Prove that the income elasticity of demand for one commodity is the marginal propensity to consume that commodity divided by the average propensity to consume that commodity.

3-8. If Mr. Smith has only two commodities in his budget, the two commodities cannot be inferior. Explain by applying the appropriate formula.

3-9. You receive your income in kind: three units of commodity X and four units of commodity Y. The prices of commodities X and Y are known, and X and Y are the only commodities in your budget. Draw the budget line. How will the budget line change when (a) the prices of X and Y, respectively increase 10 percent; (b) the price of X declines 10 percent, and (c) the price of Y declines 10 percent?

3-10. Mr. Smith has only three commodities in his budget, they are bread, wine, and milk. Mr. Smith currently allocates 20 percent of his budget to bread, 50 percent to wine and 30 percent to milk. What is the income elasticity of milk if the income elasticity of bread is 3 and of wine is − 1?

SELECTED READINGS

FRIEDMAN, M. "The Marshallian Demand Curve," *Journal of Political Economy,* Vol. LVII, December, 1949.

APPENDIX

VARIATIONS ON PRICE ELASTICITY

Having developed the concept of income elasticity, we can show how it may be helpful to break the price elasticity into two components, i.e., the substitution component and the income component. Parts of Fig. 2-7 are reproduced in Fig. 3-5. It is recalled that originally the budget

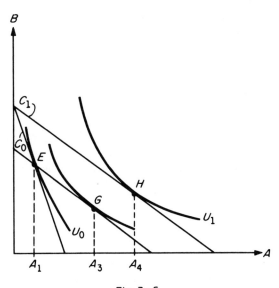

Fig. 3-5

line C_0 touches an indifference curve at point E. After the price of A falls, the new budget line is C_1, and it touches an indifference curve at H. The quantity demanded increases from A_1 to A_4. The change in the quantity demanded is $\Delta A = A_4 - A_1$. The change in price is ΔP_a It is recalled that $\Delta A = A_4 - A_1 = (A_3 - A_1) + (A_4 - A_3)$, where $A_3 - A_1$ is the Slutsky substitution effect and $A_4 - A_3$ is the income effect. Let us adopt the following notations:

$$\text{Total effect} \quad\quad = A_4 - A_1 = \Delta A$$
$$\text{Substitution effect} = A_3 - A_1 = \overline{\Delta}A$$
$$\text{Income effect} \quad\quad = A_4 - A_3 = \Delta^*A$$
$$\Delta A = \Delta\overline{A} + \Delta^*A$$

It is recalled that the change in apparent real income is equal to the original quantity of A demanded times the change in the price of A, which is denoted by $-A \cdot \Delta P_a$. Now, if the marginal propensity to consume with respect to A is M_a, then out of the change in apparent real income $- M_a \cdot A \cdot \Delta P_a$ dollars will be spent on commodity A. To illustrate it, assume that originally I consume 100 units of A, and the original price of A is \$10. Next, the price of A falls to \$9. Then, the change in apparent real income is $- A \cdot \Delta P_a = - 100 \cdot (9 - 10) = \$100$. Assume that $M_a = 0.36$, then, out of this change of \$100, \$36 will be spent on commodity A. If you are interested in estimating the additional amount of A that will be consumed due to the change in apparent real income, simply divide \$36 by the price of A. In this case \$36/\$9 = 4 units.

In summary, the change in the quantity demanded resulting from the change in apparent real income is

$$\Delta^* A = \frac{- M_a \cdot A \cdot \Delta P_a}{P_a}$$

Thus we obtain

$$\Delta A = \overline{\Delta} A - \frac{M_a \cdot A \cdot \Delta P_a}{P_a}$$

The negative sign of the second expression in the right-hand side of the equality takes care of the fact that a negative ΔP_a gives rise to a positive change in real income. In our example, $\Delta P_a = 9 - 10 = \$ - 1$. But the change in real income is positive. Thus, the change in apparent real income was $-100(9 - 10) = -100(- 1) = \$100$. Multiplying the equality above by $P_a/(A \cdot \Delta P_a)$ we obtain

$$\frac{P_a \cdot \Delta A}{A \cdot \Delta P_a} = \frac{P_a \cdot \overline{\Delta} A}{A \cdot \Delta P_a} - M_a$$

Now the left-hand side of the new equality is simply η. The first expression on the right-hand side is the price elasticity relating to the substitution effect only. Let us denote it by $\overline{\eta}$. This gives

$$\eta = \overline{\eta} - M_a$$

It is recalled that M_a is the additional spending on commodity A divided by the additional income, or

$$M_a = \frac{P_a \cdot \Delta^* A}{\Delta I}$$

Multiplying the numerator and denominator, respectively, by $I \cdot A$ we obtain

$$M_a = \frac{P_a \cdot A \cdot \Delta^* A \cdot I}{I \cdot \Delta I \cdot A} = K_a \cdot \eta_I$$

where K_a is the average propensity to consume of A, or simply the fraction of total income spent on commodity A. It is recalled that η_I is income elasticity with respect to commodity A. Substituting $K_a \cdot \eta_I$ for M_a we obtain

$$\eta = \bar{\eta} - K_a \cdot \eta_I$$

ABNORMAL DEMAND CURVES

If A is a superior commodity, then η_I is positive, and the expression $-K_a \cdot \eta_I$ is negative. $\bar{\eta}$ is always negative; thus, η which is obtained by adding two negative expressions must be negative too. In other words, the demand curve for a superior commodity must have a negative price elasticity. Accordingly, it is always negatively sloped—or, in other words, it is normal. This generalization excludes the case of a "prestige-commodity." Note that this is a case where it may be assumed that $\bar{\eta}$ with respect to mink coats may take on positive values when the price of a mink coat becomes very low. One cannot deny the possibility of a positive $\bar{\eta}$. Thus, you will find producers of cheap compact cars putting the following piece of advertisement in magazines: "Even though our price per car is very low, our price per kilogram of a car is the highest!" But let us restrict ourselves to commodities with negative $\bar{\eta}$. If commodity A is inferior, then η_I is negative, and the expression $- K_a \eta_I$ is positive. Now if $| - K_a \cdot \eta_I| < |\bar{\eta}|$, then η is still negative and the demand curve is negatively sloped. However, if $| - K_a \cdot \eta_I| > |\bar{\eta}|$, then the demand curve is positively sloped because η is positive. To put it differently, a rise in the price of an inferior good might entail increasing the quantity demanded for that good. To be sure, it will give rise to a larger quantity demanded if the income effect dominates the substitution effect. The income effect has a chance of dominating the substitution effect if K_a, or $|\eta_I|$, or both are relatively very large. Thus, one can conceive of a case where in an underdeveloped country a lower price of rice induces a smaller quantity demanded for rice. There it is realistic to assume that (a) rice is inferior and (b) a significant fraction of the national income is spent on rice. Namely, if rice is denoted by A, it is possible that $| - K_a \cdot \eta_I| > |\bar{\eta}|$.

EXERCISES

3-1. Using the formula of elasticity, show that the necessary condition for a positively sloped demand curve is an inferior commodity.

3-2. If $\bar{\eta} = -\frac{1}{4}$ and $\eta_{Ia} = -3$, K_a must be larger than _____ (fill in the blank) in order for η to be positive.

3-3. When the price of a prestige commodity falls, its MU also falls. Show that such relationship between the price and MU of a prestige commodity is the necessary condition! What is the sufficient condition? (When you answer this problem, assume that the income effect is negligible and can be ignored.)

chapter **4**

Demand Shifts Due to Changes in Prices of Other Commodities

In this chapter we shall complete the analysis of the consumer's behavior. In Chapter 1 we focused on the change in the quantity demanded for one commodity resulting from a change in the price of that commodity. For example, in Table 1-1 the price of commodity W changed from $10 in the first week to $7 in the second week and as a result, the quantity demanded for W increased from 4 units in the first week to 6 units in the second week. In Chapter 1 we paid little attention to the demand for other commodities. For example, the decline in the price of W entailed a reduction in the demand for commodity X which declined from 5 units in the first week to 4 units in the second week. This decline in the demand for commodity X is a leftward shift in the demand curve for X because at the price of $4 the demand curve for commodity X has shifted from 5 units to 4 units due to a decline in the price of commodity W. This chapter will be concerned with this problem of a change in the demand for one commodity due to a change in the price of another commodity. At the end of this chapter we shall have completed the model of a demand curve which summarizes conveniently the consumer's behavior in the market. In fact, the consumer may change his consumption of a certain commodity due to changes in the price of that commodity and in tastes (discussed in Chapter 1), a change in income that was discussed in the previous chapter, and a change in prices of other commodities to be discussed in this chapter.

SUBSTITUTES AND COMPLEMENTS

From experience we know that the following is a list of pairs of substitutes: Coca-Cola and Pepsi-Cola, margarine and butter, chicken and turkey, and coffee and tea. One can easily provide a list of pairs of complements, as follows: coffee and cream, tea and sugar, bread and butter, housing and furniture, and paper and ink. One can arrange such pairs of items simply because the following difference between the two groups is observable: Normally, when the price of a commodity falls, you tend to buy more of this commodity and less of its substitute. Thus, when the price of Coca-Cola falls consumers will buy more of it and relatively less of other Colas. The reason for this is the following: Assume that A and B are substitutes. Originally, the following equality holds

$$\frac{MU_a}{P_a} = \frac{MU_b}{P_b}$$

If the price of A falls, MU_a/P_a rises, i.e., the marginal utility derived from spending the last dollar on A is larger than the marginal utility derived from spending the last dollar on B. Accordingly, it pays the consumer to transfer money from spending on B to spending on A. Or, in reality, the consumer will shift money from a Cola to an orange drink because after the price of an orange drink falls to the first approximation, additional utility can be gained from shifting money from the Cola to the orange drink. This problem was discussed in Chapter 2. The reader is advised to review the relevant parts in Chapter 2.

Now consider a pair of complements, such as coffee and cream. It is known that in the United States, cream is added to coffee but seldom to tea. After the price of coffee falls, consumers will buy more coffee and less tea, or, in other words, they will transfer money from tea to coffee. Cream is complementary to coffee. From experience we know that consuming more coffee entails a larger consumption of cream. Or, if one were to use economic terminology, he would say that consuming more coffee and/or less tea gives rise to a higher marginal utility of cream. Since the price of cream is unchanged, at least to the first approximation, the marginal utility derived from spending the last dollar on cream increases, and as a result the consumer has an incentive to spend more money on cream. Consider the demand curve for cream D_0 in Fig. 4-1.

Let us focus our attention on one point which belongs to D_0, say G. At point G the price is P_0 and quantity of cream is Q_0. After the price of coffee falls, the demand for cream will increase for two reasons: (1) consumers will substitute coffee for tea and (2) consumers will be better off; their real income will increase. To illustrate this, assume that originally 100 units of coffee per unit of time are consumed, and the price of one unit is $10. After the price falls to $9, the consumer can buy the original set of all other commodities and 100 units of coffee. But instead of paying $1,000 for coffee, he now pays $900 for the same quantity

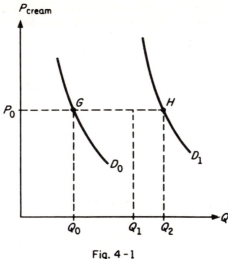

Fig. 4-1

which indicates that the change in his apparent real income is $1,000 − $900 = $100. In order to separate between the income effect and the substitution effect, we impose a $100 tax per unit of time on the consumer. Thus, we eliminate the effect of the change in income resulting from the decline in the price of coffee. Because of the pure substitution effect, the consumer starts to transfer money from tea and other beverages to coffee. But, as indicated before, when more coffee is consumed, the marginal utility of cream rises and more cream is demanded. Let us assume that the demand for cream increases from Q_0 to Q_1. At Q_1 there is no further motive to substitute cream and coffee for other beverages. Thus the segment $Q_1 − Q_0$ is the substitution effect. Next, we return the $100 to the consumer. It is clear that this $100 is comparable with increasing the income of the consumer by $100. It is also clear that the consumer will increase his consumption of superior commodities. Assuming that cream is superior, then a fraction of the additional $100 and what is released from decreasing the consumption of inferior commodities will be spent on buying more cream, say $Q_2 − Q_1$ units as indicated in Fig. 4-1. This can be summarized as follows: as a result of falling prices of coffee, more cream is demanded. In fact, at P_0 the total effect is to increase the demand for cream by $Q_2 − Q_0$. The total effect is divided between the income effect and the substitution effect as follows:

$$\underbrace{\text{Total effect}}_{Q_2 - Q_0} = \underbrace{\text{substitution effect}}_{Q_1 - Q_0} + \underbrace{\text{income effect}}_{Q_2 - Q_1}$$

Note that Q_2 in Fig. 4-1 corresponds to point H. Point H belongs to a new demand curve D_1. In order to derive D_1, one has to apply the same analysis to each point on D_0. In summary, a lower price of coffee induces a rightward shift in the demand curve for cream. In fact, the demand curve has shifted from D_0 to D_1. Having illustrated how the direction of the demand shift is determined, we can summarize the possible cases of demand shifts due to changes in prices of other commodities. Note that in order to determine the direction of the change, you must know whether the commodity in question is a complement or a substitute with respect to the commodity whose price changes and also whether the commodity is superior or inferior.

An example in which there are two substitutes can be derived from Table 2-3. There, B and A are two substitutes. After the price of A falls

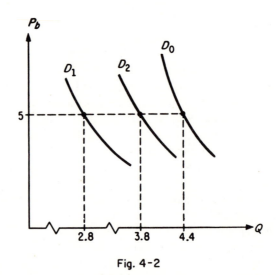

Fig. 4-2

from \$4 to \$2, a sum of \$9, which is the change in apparent real income, is confiscated. As a result of the substitution effect, \$8 are transferred from spending on B to spending on A. Since the price of B is \$5, this means that the consumption of B declines by 1.6 units. Thus, the substitution effect in that example is to shift the demand curve for commodity B by 1.6 units to the left (at $P_b = \$5$). It was assumed that the change in apparent real income is divided into \$4 for spending on A and \$5 for spending on B. Accordingly, the income effect is to shift the demand curve for commodity B by one unit to the right. This is summarized in Fig. 4-2 as follows: the substitution effect shifted the demand curve from D_0 to D_1, and the income effect from D_1 back to D_2.

CROSS ELASTICITY

Cross elasticity is defined as the relative change in the demand for one commodity divided by the relative change in the price of another commodity, or rather, the percentage change in the demand for one commodity per 1 percent change in the price of another commodity. The formula of cross elasticity is

$$\eta_{AP_b} = \frac{\Delta A/A}{\Delta P_b/P_b} = \frac{\% \text{ change in } A}{\% \text{ change in } P_b}$$

Example: A 10 percent decline in the price of commodity B induces an increase of 5 units in the demand for A. Originally the demand for A was 97.5 units. Estimate the value of η_{AP_b}. Use the mean quantity in your computations.

$\bar{A} = (97.5 + 102.5)/2 = 100$. The percentage change in the demand for A is equal to $(5/100)\ 100\%$, that is, 5 percent. Then, $\eta_{AP_b} = 5\%/-10\% = -\frac{1}{2}$.

Example: Assume that $\eta_{AP_b} = 1.5$. Estimate the percentage change in the demand for A resulting from a 3 percent decline in the price of B. Denote the percentage change in demand for A by X; then, $X/-3\% = 1.5$.

Solving for X we obtain $X = -4.5$ percent; namely, the demand will fall by 4.5 percent.

Example: Assume that $\eta_{AP_b} = -2$. What is the necessary change in the price of B which will induce a 4 percent increase in the demand for A? Denote the percentage change in the price of B by X; then, $4\%/X = -2$.

Solving for X we obtain $X = -2$ percent.

Note that as in the case of income elasticity, to each point on the demand curve there corresponds a different value of cross elasticity with respect to the price of a certain substitute or complement. Again, this does not always create a problem because we are often interested in the sign of the cross elasticity rather than in its precise magnitude.

DEMAND SHIFTS

In what follows we are going to analyze the shift in the demand curve for commodity A resulting from a change in the price of commodity B. In order to exhaust all possible cases, different relationships will be assumed between A and B, and A will play the role of superior and inferior commodity, respectively. In order to save space, the marginal utility derived from the last dollar spent on A will be denoted by $\$MU_a$. It is important to emphasize here that the change in the price of B is external. The tastes of the consumer are assumed unchanged. Suddenly, the price of B changes; and being confronted with a new price of B, the consumer changes his demand for A, leading to a shift in the demand curve for A.

Finally, note that the aggregate demand curve will shift in the same direction if it can be assumed that the consumer under consideration is a typical one.

CASE I

Here, P_b falls; A and B are substitutes; A is superior.

Substitution Effect: $\$MU_b$ is larger than $\$MU_a$. Thus, the consumer transfers money from A to B, and the demand curve for A shifts leftward.

Income Effect: Apparent real income increases. The consumer buys more of superior commodities, since A is superior, the consumer buys more of A, and the demand for A shifts rightward.

Total Effect: This is uncertain because the two effects are in opposite directions. (However, under normal conditions one can assume that the substitution effect will dominate the income effect, and the net effect would be to shift the demand curve for A to the left.)

The Sign of the Cross Elasticity: Ambiguous (positive under normal conditions).

CASE II

The same as in Case I, except that P_b rises. It is left for the reader to show that here the substitution effect is to shift the demand curve for A to the right, and income effect is a shift to the left. The total effect is uncertain, but as in Case I, one can assume that the substitution effect dominates the income effect. The sign of the cross elasticity is ambiguous (positive under normal conditions).

CASE III

Here P_b falls; A and B are substitutes; A is inferior.

Substitution Effect: The same as in Case I.

Income Effect: Apparent real income increases. The consumer buys less of inferior commodities. Accordingly, the demand curve for A shifts leftward.

Total Effect: Both the substitution effect and the income effect are to shift the demand curve for A to the left. Thus, the total effect is to shift the demand curve for A leftward.

The Sign of the Cross Elasticity: Positive (because ΔP_b and ΔA, respectively, are negative).

CASE IV

The same as in Case III, except that P_b rises.

It is left for the reader to show that here both income effect and the substitution effect are to shift the demand curve for A to the right, and the sign of the cross elasticity is positive.

CASE V

Again P_b falls; A and B are complements; A is superior.

Substitution Effect: $\$MU_b$ is larger than $\$MU$ of substitutes for B. The consumer transfers money from substitutes to B. But when more of B is consumed, $\$MU_a$ increases, and more money is spent on A. Thus, the substitution effect is to shift the demand curve for A to the right.

Income Effect: The Same as in Case I; that is, a rightward shift.

Total Effect: Both the substitution effect and the income effect are to shift the demand curve for A to the right. Thus, the total effect is to shift the demand curve for A to the right.

The Sign of the Cross Elasticity: Negative (because ΔP_b is negative and ΔA is positive).

CASE VI

The same as Case V, except that P_b rises.

It is left for the reader to show that both the substitution effect and the income effect are to shift the demand curve for A to the left. The sign of the cross elasticity is negative (because ΔP_b is positive and ΔA is negative).

CASE VII

Again P_b falls; A and B are complements; A is inferior.

Substitution Effect: The same as in Case V; a rightward shift.

Income Effect: The same as in Case III, a leftward shift.

Total Effect: Uncertain, because the two effects are in opposite directions. (Again, under normal conditions the substitution effect will dominate, and the demand curve for A will shift rightward.)

The Sign of the Cross Elasticity: Ambiguous (negative under normal conditions).

CASE VIII

The same as in Case VII, except that P_b rises.

It is left for the reader to show that the substitution effect is to shift the demand curve to the left while the income effect is to shift it to the right. Thus, the total effect is uncertain and the sign of the cross elasticity is ambiguous (negative under normal conditions).

THE INDIFFERENCE CURVE APPROACH

Consider a consumer who has only two commodities in his budget; denote them as A and B. The demand curve of commodity A shifts as a result of a change in the price of commodity B. Assume that the price of B falls, A and B are substitutes for each other, and A is an inferior commodity (Case III).

Originally, C_0, the budget line touches the highest indifference curve U_0 at point R. At point R, A_0 units of A are consumed. After the price of B falls, the new budget line is C_1, which touches another indifference

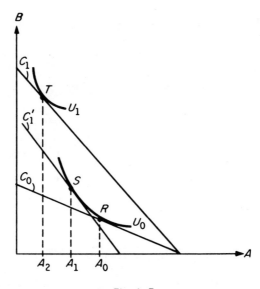

Fig. 4-3

curve U_1 at point T. At point T, A_2 units of A are consumed. The Hicksian substitution effect is obtained by drawing a new budget line C'_1 which touches the indifference curve U_0 at point S. Thus, the (negative) distance $A_1 - A_0$ is the substitution effect, and $A_2 - A_1$ is the income effect.

Recall from Chapter 2 that if there are only two commodities in the budget of the consumer, then the two commodities must be substitutes for each other. Accordingly, a two-dimensional diagram like Fig. 4-3 cannot describe the case of two commodities that are complements to each other.

The Appendix to this chapter is devoted to developing a formula which decomposes the cross-price-elasticity into the substitution-component and the income-component. Table 4-1 provide a convenient summary of the subject.

THE CASE OF TWO SUBSTITUTES

It can be proved that if X and Y are two commodities then the following equality holds:

$$\frac{\bar{\Delta}X}{\Delta P_y} = \frac{\bar{\Delta}Y}{\Delta P_x}$$

where $\bar{\Delta}X$ is the change in X due only to the substitution effect. Thus, the above equality is useful only when the changes in the prices of Y and X are small. Multiplying both sides by $P_y \cdot P_x$ gives

$$P_y \cdot P_x \frac{\bar{\Delta}X}{\Delta P_y} = P_y \cdot P_x \cdot \frac{\bar{\Delta}Y}{\Delta P_x}$$

Multiplying the left-hand side by $X \cdot P_y / X \cdot P_y$ and the right-hand side by $Y \cdot P_x / Y \cdot P_x$ we obtain

$$X \cdot P_x \frac{P_y \cdot \bar{\Delta}X}{X \cdot \Delta P_y} = Y \cdot P_y \frac{P_x \cdot \bar{\Delta}Y}{Y \cdot \Delta P_x}$$

which is

$$X \cdot P_x \bar{\eta}_{xP_y} = Y \cdot P_y \cdot \bar{\eta}_{yP_x}$$

where $\bar{\eta}_{xP_y}$ and $\bar{\eta}_{yP_x}$ *are substitution* cross elasticities. This formula is very useful in cases where K_x and K_y, respectively, are negligible. (Why?)

Consider two monopolists who produce two substitutes. Even though a monopolist was not yet defined, for our purpose a monopolist is the sole producer of one commodity. Assume that the fraction of national income spent on X and Y, respectively, is very small. Now, let us make the assumption that the monopolist who produces commodity Y has a good reason to believe that, $\bar{\eta}_{yP_x} = 1$. In other words, he believes that a 5 percent decline in the price of X will entail a 5 percent decline in the demand for his product Y, etc. Now the producer of Y is interested in estimating the loss that he can inflict on the producer of X by cutting down the price of Y. Assume that $Y \cdot P_y$ is \$20 million while $X \cdot P_x$ is \$10 million, then

$$\bar{\eta}_{xP_y} = \frac{Y \cdot P_y}{X \cdot P_x} \cdot \bar{\eta}_{yP_x} = \frac{20}{10} \cdot 1 = 2$$

Namely, by cutting down the price of Y by 5 percent, the monopolist who produces Y will inflict a 10 percent loss in demand on the producer of X.

PROBLEMS

Indicate whether each of the following statements is true (T), false (F) or uncertain (U). Briefly justify your answer. Assume that nominal income and other prices are kept constant.

4-1. If the price of A rises, the demand curve for B always shifts rightward so long as A and B are substitutes.

4-2. If X and Y are substitutes, a decline in the price of X can lead to a rightward shift in the demand for Y only if Y is an inferior good.

4-3. If the price of steel rises, the demand curve for tires will shift leftward. Assume that tires are superior, and steel and tires are complements.

4-4. A decline in the price of bread will lead to a leftward shift in the demand for potatoes. Assume that bread and potatoes are substitutes, and potatoes are superior.

4-5. If the substitution effect dominates the income effect, then the demand curve for lemons will shift over to the left as a result of a decline in the price of oranges. Assume that lemons and oranges are substitutes, and lemons are superior.

4-6. The demand curve for cream will shift rightward as a result of a rise in the price of coffee. (Assume that you are now in England!)

4-7. A decline in the price of cars will entail a shift to the right in the demand curve for gasoline.

APPENDIX

VARIATIONS ON CROSS ELASTICITY

Consider the following proposition: as a result of a change in the price of commodity B, the demand for commodity A also changes. Denote the change in the price of B by ΔP_b and the change in the demand for A by ΔA which is the total effect. Let the substitution effect be denoted by $\bar{\Delta} A$ and the income effect by $\overset{*}{\Delta} A$. Then the following equality holds:

$$\Delta A = \bar{\Delta} A + \overset{*}{\Delta} A$$

But $\overset{*}{\Delta} A$ is equal to the marginal propensity to consume with respect to A times the change in apparent real income divided by the price of A. (Why?) It was shown that the change in apparent real income is $- B_0 \cdot \Delta P_b$. Thus we get

$$\overset{*}{\Delta} A = - \frac{M_a \cdot B \cdot \Delta P_b}{P_a}$$

Substituting, we obtain

$$\Delta A = \bar{\Delta} A - \frac{M_a \cdot B \cdot \Delta P_b}{P_a}$$

Dividing through by ΔP_b we obtain

$$\frac{\Delta A}{\Delta P_b} = \frac{\bar{\Delta} A}{\Delta P_b} - \frac{M_a \cdot B}{P_a}$$

(Since ΔB is very small, B is either B_0 or B_1.) Multiplying through by P_b/A we obtain

$$\frac{P_b \cdot \Delta A}{A \cdot \Delta P_b} = \frac{P_b \cdot \bar{\Delta} A}{A \cdot \Delta P_b} - \frac{M_a \cdot B \cdot P_b}{P_a \cdot A}$$

or it can be written as

$$\eta_{AP_b} = \bar{\eta}_{AP_b} - \frac{M_a \cdot B \cdot P_b}{P_a \cdot A}$$

Consider the expression

$$\frac{M_a \cdot B \cdot P_b}{P_a \cdot A}$$

Recall that

$$M_a = \frac{P_a \cdot \overset{*}{\Delta} A}{\Delta I}$$

Then we have

$$\frac{M_a \cdot B \cdot P_b}{P_a \cdot A} = \frac{\overset{*}{\Delta} A \cdot B \cdot P_b}{\Delta I \cdot A} = \frac{I \cdot \overset{*}{\Delta} A \cdot B \cdot P_b}{I \cdot \Delta I \cdot A} = \frac{B \cdot P_b \cdot I \cdot \overset{*}{\Delta} A}{I \cdot A \cdot \Delta I} = K_b \cdot \eta_{I_a}$$

Substituting in it we obtain

$$\eta_{AP_b} = \bar{\eta}_{AP_b} - K_b \cdot \eta_{I_a}$$

where $\bar{\eta}_{AP_b}$ is the substitution cross elasticity, K_b is the fraction of income spent on commodity B, and η_{I_a} is income elasticity with respect to commodity A. The sign of cross elasticity is either positive, negative, or ambiguous. This is illustrated in Table 4-1.

TABLE 4-1

	A is inferior, $\eta_{Ia} < 0$	A is superior, $\eta_{Ia} > 0$
A and B are complements, $\bar{\eta}_{AP_b} < 0$	If $\lvert - K_b\eta_{I_a} \rvert > \lvert \bar{\eta}_{AP_b} \rvert$ then $\eta_{AP_b} > 0$ If $\lvert - K_b\eta_{I_a} \rvert < \lvert \bar{\eta}_{AP_b} \rvert$, then $\eta_{AP_b} < 0$	$\eta_{AP_b} < 0$ because $\bar{\eta}_{AP_b} < 0$ and $- K_b\eta_{I_a} < 0$
A and B are substitutes, $\bar{\eta}_{AP_b} > 0$	$\eta_{AP_b} > 0$ because $\bar{\eta}_{AP_b} > 0$ and $- K_b\eta_{I_a} > 0$	If $\lvert - K_b\eta_{I_a} \rvert > \lvert \bar{\eta}_{AP_b} \rvert$, then $\eta_{AP_b} < 0$ If $\lvert - K_b\eta_{I_a} \rvert < \lvert \bar{\eta}_{AP_b} \rvert$, then $\eta_{AP_b} > 0$

EXERCISES

4-1. Solve Probs. 4-1 to 4-7 by using the formula

$$\eta_{AP_b} = \bar{\eta}_{AP_b} - K_b \cdot \eta_{I_a}$$

THE STATUS OF THE THEORY OF DEMAND

The student who is interested in pursuing the mathematics of the presentation of demand theory is referred to the Mathematical Appendix. In fact, short of minor mathematical refinements, very little was added to the modern theory of demand which is due to Marshall, Slutsky, and Hicks. It is probably safe to predict that per se very little will be added in the future to the theory of demand.

Another field which is yet to be explored is the statistical determination of demand functions. While it is not our intention to survey the studies that were conducted in this area, we would like to refer the reader to a few important studies.

In most cases, the economist is interested in the theoretical demand curve rather than the empirical demand curve. For example, in a free enterprise economy in which mobility of factors of production is fairly certain, it may be interesting to note that in the past the demand for shoes has increased faster than the supply of shoes, and thus the prices of shoes have increased. But since no "economic policy to cope with the shoe problem in the United States" is in existence, there is no reason why the economist would want to estimate the value of price elasticity of the demand for shoes. There are, however, cases where the statistical demand curve for a certain commodity, or a group of commodities, may be helpful in advocating policy. For example, in Chapter 11 we shall show that the farm problem arises due to both low income elasticity and price elasticity of the demand for agricultural output and also due to insufficient mobility of the farm labor. Here, the empirical estimate of the elasticities of the demand for agricultural products may be useful in gaining insights into the farm problem.

The first study concerning the statistical determination of the demand curve was conducted by Henry Schultz. His book, *The Theory and Measurement of Demand*,[1] contains, for the first time in the history of economic theory, an econometric estimate of the demand function for various agricultural commodities. Since Schultz's pioneer research, many economists have been engaged in estimating demand curves both for consumer's goods and producer's goods. For the student who is interested in

[1] Henry Schultz, *The Theory and Measurement of Demand*, Chicago, Ill.: University of Chicago Press, 1938.

further pursuing this area, we recommend, in addition to Schultz's book, E. J. Working's article "What Do Statistical 'Demand Curves' Show?"[2] Also, the student who is familiar with calculus and matrix algebra might enjoy J. Johnston, *Econometric Methods*.[3]

[2] E. J. Working, What Do Statistical 'Demand Curves' Show? *Readings in Price Theory,* eds. K. Boulding and G. Stigler, Homewood, Ill.: Richard D. Irwin, Inc., 1952.

[3] J. Johnston, *Econometric Methods,* New York: McGraw-Hill Book Company, 1963.

The Theory of Production

PART I: THE PRODUCTION FUNCTION

Having covered the theory of demand in some detail, we can turn our attention from the consumer to the producer. Chapters 5, 6, 7, and 8 are devoted to the theory of the producer. Chapter 5 starts with the theory of the production function which deals with the economic aspects of production. Chapter 6 will be concerned with the firm in competition; in Chapter 7 we shall focus on some interesting features of cost curves; and, finally, in Chapter 8 we shall develop the theory of supply. The order of the following four chapters is not accidental. Rather, Chapter 8 is based on Chapters 7 and 6, and Chapters 7 and 6 draw heavily on Chapter 5.

When we use the term *process of production* we usually have in mind an entrepreneur who is currently busy in combining factors of production in the process of producing a certain product. For example, following an acceptance of an unusually large order for his plant, the entrepreneur has to figure out how many additional man-hours, tons of coal, and raw materials are necessary in order to meet the extra order. He may save on coal by employing more workers or he may save on the wage bill by using more coal and less labor. When the entrepreneur determines the set of resources that it takes to produce a certain amount of output, he probably has a certain rule in mind. This may be a rule of thumb, but it is this rule of thumb that is based on past experience and technological knowledge which is provided by the engineer.

In economics this rule which relates output to input is called the *production function.*

To be more specific about the name, the production function is *the technical relationship telling the maximum amount of output that can be produced by each combination of specified factors of production.* Note that the production function relates maximum outputs to sets of resources.

It does not relate sets of resources to levels of outputs. The reason for this is the following:

To each set of resources there corresponds many attainable levels of output, but there is only one maximum level. We are interested in this maximum level rather than in other attainable levels. On the other hand, to each level of output there corresponds many sets of resources. For instance, it may take 10 minutes of labor and 10 minutes by a milking machine to produce one gallon of milk, or alternatively, it may take 30 minutes of labor without the use of a milking machine to produce the same gallon of milk. There are probably intermediate combinations such as 20 minutes of labor and 12 minutes by a milking machine if one uses a certain model of a milking machine. Intuitively, one understands that the first combination would be common in areas where capital is rather inexpensive, while the second combination would be accepted in areas where labor tends to be cheap.

REALITY VERSUS THE PRODUCTION FUNCTION

In reality, only a finite number of separate processes of production is known to the firm. This number may be very large if enough time is allowed for adjustment, or it may be limited to a few processes if a short period of time is considered. For example, one process of production may be the following: It takes 2 man-hours, 3 machine-hours, and 5 pounds of steel to produce one unit of output. Usually the assumption is made that this process can be used at different levels, e.g., it takes 4 man-hours, 6 machine-hours, and 10 pounds of steel to produce two units of output and so on. In this case, another process of production could be labor-saving, e.g., it takes 1 man-hour, 4.5 machine-hours, and 5 pounds of steel to produce one unit of output and so on. If 100 distinct processes of production are known to the firm, then the technology of this firm is represented by a table of 100 by 3. In reality, if one is interested in maximizing the profit of a specific firm, one has to consider this table. However, it would be a sheer accident to find a mathematical function that summarizes such a table in a single relation.

On the other hand, if one is interested in the general nature of production of a typical firm rather than in the technology of one specific firm, it is very convenient to pretend that the technology of the firm can be summarized by one production function. This production function has no specific algebraic, trigonometric, or exponential form. For example, if A and B are the only two factors participating in production, then the general form of the production function is

$$Q = f(A, B)$$

where A and B can take on any pair of real values, and to any one pair of A and B there corresponds one value of Q which stands for output.

In what follows we shall see that several restrictions are imposed on the production function.

In order to liven up the presentation and avoid the use of mathematics, instead of using the production function in its general form, we shall use a specific production function $Q = \sqrt{A \cdot B}$, where A will stand for man-hours and B will stand for machine-hours. There is the danger that the student might get the wrong impression that such specific production functions can be known to firms, but since the marginal gain of convenience dominates the extra loss of generality, we shall go along with it.

THE TIME ELEMENT

Many readers may react to this idea of production function as follows: "Well, this is another toy invented by economists to confuse laymen! After all, proportions of the resources used are fixed by technology." It is true that in the short run proportions are fixed. But, if enough time is allowed for adjustment, then proportions are not fixed. Consider the entrepreneur who produces pipes in this country. He gets an offer to invest in a pipe-producing plant in India. The first thing that he is going to do is to call his chief engineer and ask him to work on a conceivable plant where more labor and less machinery is used. The incentive to change the proportion in favor of labor stems from the fact that labor is relatively cheaper in India. Accordingly, the concept of a production function involves an element of time. This element of time is the period necessary for transferring from one process of production to another. To put it in other words, the degree of substitutability between factors of production is very high provided that a transitional period of adjustment is allowed.

AN EXAMPLE OF A PRODUCTION FUNCTION

Consider an imaginary plant which produces logs in the forest. For simplicity, assume that the trees are free: whoever needs timber simply comes and cuts as many trees as he wants. Again, for simplicity, assume that the production function of a certain plant producing timber is

$$Q = \sqrt{A \cdot B}$$

where Q is the number of logs, A is man-hours, and B is machine-hours, all per unit of time. This production function allows for any proportion between capital and labor. Thus, 1 man-hour and 100 machine-hours will produce 10 logs, but 1 machine-hour and 100 man-hours are also capable of producing 10 logs, and of course, there are many other combinations such as 4 man-hours and 25 machine-hours, etc.

MARGINAL PHYSICAL PRODUCT (MPP)

The marginal physical product of a factor of production is the change in total production per unit of change in the factor when all other factors are kept constant. To put it differently, it is the extra output added by employing one extra unit of a certain factor while other factors are being held constant. Here again, we refer to output and factors used per unit of time. Note also that here *factors* are short notations for man-hours, machine-hours, or land-hours; namely, flows of services. The marginal physical product of factor A is denoted by MPP_a and so on. Formally, MPP_a is

$$MPP_a = \frac{\Delta Q}{\Delta A}$$

where ΔQ is the change in output and ΔA is the change in the flow of factor A, and it is assumed tacitly that all other factors are kept constant.

Consider our log-producing plant. Presently it employs 3 man-hours and 3 machine-hours with which it produces $\sqrt{3 \cdot 3} = 3$ logs. Let us approximate MPP_a by increasing the employment of labor by 2 man-hours, and keeping machine services fixed at 3 hours. Then we have

$$Q_0 = \sqrt{3 \cdot 3} = \sqrt{9} = 3$$
$$Q_1 = \sqrt{5 \cdot 3} = \sqrt{15} = 3.9$$
$$\Delta Q = Q_1 - Q_0 = 3.9 - 3 = 0.9$$
$$\Delta A = A_1 - A_0 = 5 - 3 = 2$$
$$MPP_a = \Delta Q / \Delta A = 0.9/2 = 0.45$$

It should be noted here that the smaller ΔA is, the finer the approximation of MPP_a.

RETURNS TO SCALE

When a certain plant increases the employment of all factors per unit of time, one can say that the plant is increasing its scale of operations. The change in scale is defined quantitatively only for cases where the amount of each factor used is changed at the same rate. Thus, to say that the amount of each factor used has doubled is equivalent to saying that the scale has doubled.

Consider three plants. Let us assume that in each of the three plants the amount of each factor used is raised K percent. This entails less than K percent increase in the level of production in the first plant, exactly K percent increase in output in the second plant, and more than K percent increase in output in the third plant—all per unit of time. Then, the first plant is said to be governed by decreasing returns to scale, the second plant by constant returns to scale, and the third plant by increasing returns to scale.

By the way, our long-producing plant is governed by constant returns to scale. Originally $Q_0 = \sqrt{A_0 \cdot B_0}$ if both factors are multiplied by C we obtain

$$Q_1 = \sqrt{C \cdot A_0 \cdot C \cdot B_0} = \sqrt{C^2 \cdot A_0 \cdot B_0} = \sqrt{C^2} \cdot \sqrt{A_0 \cdot B_0}$$
$$= C \cdot \sqrt{A_0 \cdot B_0} = C \cdot Q_0$$

Namely, by multiplying each factor by the coefficient C we also multiply production by the same coefficient. Logically we reject the assumption of increasing or decreasing returns to scale. We accept the assumption of constant returns to scale. The reason is as follows: Consider a plant that employs factors $A, B, C, \ldots, N$. If $A_0, B_0, C_0, \ldots, N_0$ are used per unit of time, an output of Q_0 is produced. Using $2A_0, 2B_0, 2C_0, \ldots, 2N_0$ per unit of time is equivalent to using $A_0, B_0, C_0, \ldots, N_0$ in the first plant and the same amount of $A_0, B_0, C_0, \ldots, N_0$ in an identical plant during the same period of time. This process must yield $2Q_0$ units of output. When one writes about decreasing returns to scale, one probably has in mind a case of diminishing marginal physical product. And when one refers to increasing returns to scale, one probably has in mind a case of indivisibility, in which MPP_a is rising and is positive, and MPP_b is negative. Our $Q = \sqrt{A \cdot B}$ cannot yield such relationships.

THE LAW OF DIMINISHING MARGINAL PHYSICAL PRODUCT

The law of diminishing marginal physical product tells us that if the use of one factor of production is increased while all other factors are kept constant, total productivity beyond a point will increase at a decreasing rate; or in other words, marginal physical product is diminishing. Formally, this law is identical with the law of diminishing marginal utility. You will find it interesting to write down the law of diminishing marginal utility, then substitute *factor of production* for *good*, *product* (or productivity) for *utility*, and *production* for *consumption*. The result will be the law of diminishing marginal product. Thus, the consumer can be conceived of as a plant which produces utility. In the process of producing utility, this peculiar plant uses different *factors of production*, i.e., different goods.

To illustrate the law of diminishing marginal productivity, let us return to our primitive production function. Let us keep the amount of machine-hours constant at 2 and increase the amount of man-hours from 2 to 6. Let A denote labor. We derive MPP_a in Table 5-1.

TABLE 5-1

Machine Hours B	Man Hours A	Total Output $Q = \sqrt{B \cdot A}$	ΔQ	$MPP_a = \dfrac{\Delta Q}{\Delta A}$
(1)	(2)	(3)	(4)	(5)
2	2	$\sqrt{2 \cdot 2} = 2$		
2	3	$\sqrt{2 \cdot 3} = 2.45$	0.45	$0.45 / 1 = 0.45$
2	4	$\sqrt{2 \cdot 4} = 2.83$	0.38	$0.38 / 1 = 0.38$
2	5	$\sqrt{2 \cdot 5} = 3.16$	0.33	$0.33 / 1 = 0.33$
2	6	$\sqrt{2 \cdot 6} = 3.46$	0.30	$0.30 / 1 = 0.30$

Next, suppose we keep machine-hours constant at 3. Then we shall have the schedule of MPP_a which is derived in Table 5-2.

TABLE 5-2

Machine Hours B	Man Hours A	Total Output $Q = \sqrt{B \cdot A}$	ΔQ	$MPP_a = \dfrac{\Delta Q}{\Delta A}$
(1)	(2)	(3)	(4)	(5)
3	2	$\sqrt{3 \cdot 2} = 2.45$		
3	3	$\sqrt{3 \cdot 3} = 3.00$	0.55	$0.55 / 1 = 0.55$
3	4	$\sqrt{3 \cdot 4} = 3.46$	0.46	$0.46 / 1 = 0.46$
3	5	$\sqrt{3 \cdot 5} = 3.87$	0.41	$0.41 / 1 = 0.41$
3	6	$\sqrt{3 \cdot 6} = 4.24$	0.37	$0.37 / 1 = 0.37$

Finally, the two schedules are transformed into two curves in Fig. 5-1. The reader can see that the choice of $\sqrt{A \cdot B}$ for illustration was a successful one because it obeys the law of diminishing marginal product. Moreover, it is governed by a second important law which tells us that there is positive dependence between MPP_a and B and MPP_b and A. To put it differently, when more of other factors are employed, MPP_a is larger, or, the MPP_a curve shifts rightward when more of other factors are used and leftward when less of all other factors are used.

A LAW OF LOGIC

In the next chapter we shall define and explain the concepts of *competition* and *a competitive firm*. For our purpose, it would suffice to

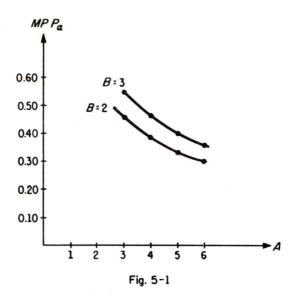

Fig. 5-1

emphasize the fact that a competitive firm has a negligible share in the market. The firm cannot affect the price of either the resources it uses or the price of the product it sells in the market. Thus, regardless of the firm's scale of operations, it is confronted with fixed prices of factors which are secured in the labor and capital market. It also faces a certain price of the product which it sells in the market. This price cannot be affected by the decisions taken by the entrepreneur.

The law of logic tells us that in order to minimize the cost of production, regardless of how many units the firm produces, the marginal product obtained from spending the last dollar on factor A must equal the marginal product obtained from spending the last dollar on factor B, and so on up to the last factor used. Note that this law does not provide a rule by which the firm can decide how much to produce. Given the level of output, this law tells the entrepreneur how to allocate the various inputs in order to minimize the cost. Another approach would be to maximize output given a certain outlay. The result is the same. For n inputs the law of logic can be written

$$\frac{MPP_a}{P_a} = \frac{MPP_b}{P_b} = \cdots = \frac{MPP_n}{P_n}$$

where P_a, P_b, . . . , and P_n are not influenced by the decisions of the firm. Again, this law is formally identical with the law of logic relating to the utility theory. Consider a plant in which only two factors A and B are employed. Let $MPP_a = 30$ units, and $MPP_b = 21$ units, $P_a = \$3$, and $P_b = \$3$. Then, we have

$$\frac{MPP_a}{P_a} = \frac{30}{\$3} = 10 \text{ units of output per dollar}$$

$$\frac{MPP_b}{P_b} = \frac{21}{\$3} = 7 \text{ units of output per dollar}$$

It is clear that by transferring the first dollar from B to A the entrepreneur can gain 3 units of output and spend the same amount of money. This is true because by spending one dollar less on B he loses 7 units, but by spending one additional dollar on A he gains 10 units, and the net gain is $10 - 7 = 3$ units. Shifting the second dollar will yield a gain which is smaller than 3 units because of the law of diminishing marginal physical product and dependence. When money is being transferred from B to A, MPP_a shrinks because of two reasons: (1) applying a larger quantity of A means going down the MPP_a curve—which is the law of diminishing marginal product and (2) a smaller quantity of B means that the MPP_a curve shifts downward.

While MPP_a is shrinking, MPP_b increases because of two reasons: (1) using less B means going up the MPP_b curve, and (2) since a larger quantity of A is employed, the MPP_b curve shifts upward. This process is summarized in Figs. 5-2 and 5-3.

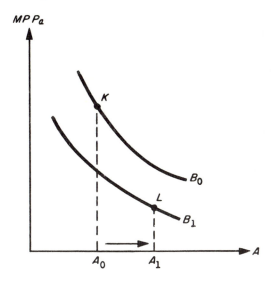

Fig. 5-2

When A increases from A_0 to A_1, MPP_a falls from A_0K to A_1L as indicated in Fig. 5-2. Note that MPP_a falls off because of the downward shift in the MPP_a curve and because MPP_a is negatively sloped.

In other words, both the dependence and the law of diminishing marginal product are responsible for achieving the new point of equilibrium.

If we assume that all factors are governed by constant or increasing marginal products, and no dependence, then all entrepreneurs would be concentrating only on one factor of production. Accordingly, if in the above example you assume no dependence and, say constant MPP_a and

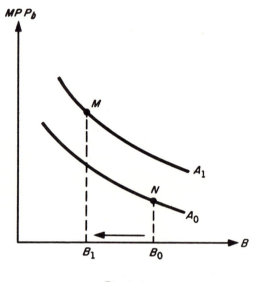

Fig. 5-3

MPP_b, respectively, it pays the entrepreneur to transfer the entire fraction of his budget which is currently spent on B to factor A, because under such assumptions he can gain 3 units of output per each dollar shifted, to the last dollar!

THE RELATIONSHIP BETWEEN DIFFERENT FACTORS OF PRODUCTION

Some confusion arises when it comes to the problem of complementarity and substitutability in production. For example, a student may easily succumb to the following line of argument: Labor without raw material cannot yield product. Or, equipment and machinery without labor can yield no output. Thus, even though two factors of production are to some extent substitutes for each other, they also co-operate in the process of production and thus they are complementary to each other at the same time. And so the vague conclusion to which a student may some time be exposed is that the prevailing situation in production is one in which a group of complementary factors is required between which, however, a degree of substitutability exists.

Let us try to clarify this problem by using our simple production function. First of all, substitution between two factors is defined only for a fixed level of output. For instance, when 4 man-hours and 25 machine-hours are used, output amounts to $\sqrt{4 \cdot 25} = 10$ units. Now we can ask the following question.

Keeping output *fixed at 10 units,* how many units of labor will substitute for 5 units of machine-hours that are diverted from production? As indicated by the production function, the answer is one man-hour because $\sqrt{5 \cdot 20} = 10$ units. You see immediately that there is no vagueness involved here. Labor and machinery co-operate in producing logs in the forest, but they are a substitute for each other.

Note that if only two factors of production are engaged in producing a certain product, they cannot be complements to each other. This stems from the fact that complementarity as well as substitutability is defined *only for fixed output.* If in our example, labor and machinery were complements, then using more labor would be followed by using more machinery which would entail larger production. This, however, is inconsistent with the assumption of fixed output. In order to illustrate complementarity in production, consider a wheat grower who combines labor with tractor services in growing wheat. The wheat farmer could have produced the same amount of wheat by using less labor hours and more tractor hours. But, using more tractor hours would mean burning more gasoline. That is, gasoline and tractor services are complements to each other. In many cases factors of production which are complements to each other are used in fixed proportions, and so, such factors can be treated as one. Moreover, sometimes we are interested in a broad analysis in which only two or three factors play a role in production. An example is labor, land, and capital properly defined. When factors are classified in such broad categories, the possibility of complementarity can be ignored for all practical purposes.

Note, finally, that the assumption of positive dependence is consistent with either a case of complements (if proportions are not fixed) or the case of substitutes. This is true because dependence is defined in an experiment in which only one factor changes. But if more of factor A is used in production, other factors get to cooperate with more units of A. Accordingly, other factors become more efficient and their respective marginal physical product increases.

PART II: THE ISOQUANT APPROACH

THE ISOQUANT AND THE ELASTICITY OF SUBSTITUTION

Consider a process of production where only two factors are combined in producing a certain commodity. It is clear that if we allow sufficient time for adjustment, we can produce the same amount of output with different combinations of the factors A and B. Thus, consider the production function $Q = \sqrt{A \cdot B}$. Currently, $A = 4$ man-hours and $B = 25$ machine-hours. The output is $\sqrt{4 \cdot 25} = 10$ units. Supposing the entrepreneur must cut down in machine-hours; he can use only 20 machine-hours. What is the additional amount of labor that he must employ in order to remain at the same level of production? To put it differently, what is the additional amount of man-hours that must be employed in order to compensate for the loss of 5 machine-hours? The answer is given by the production function; namely, the entrepreneur must increase the employment of labor by one unit. Thus $\sqrt{(4+1) \quad (25-5)} = \sqrt{5 \cdot 20} = 10$. Next, if only 15 machine-hours are to be used, then $6\frac{2}{3}$ hours of labor must be used; namely, in order to maintain the same level of production of 10 units, the loss of 5 machine-hours must be compensated with an extra amount of $1\frac{2}{3}$ hours of labor: The scarcer one factor is (in this case B), the more difficult it becomes to replace it by another factor (A). Thus, when 25 machine-hours are used. a diversion of 5 machine-hours from production can be substituted for by one additional man-hour. But when 20 machine-hours are used, a diversion of 5 machine-hours is replaced by $1\frac{2}{3}$ man-hours. This is true because of the law of diminishing marginal product and/or dependence. In order to stay at the same level of production, the following must hold:

$$- \Delta A \cdot MPP_a = \Delta B \cdot MPP_b$$

For example, if $\Delta A = -2$ man-hours and $MPP_a = 4.5$ units, and if $MPP_b = 3$ units, then ΔB must be 3 machine-hours if we want to stay at the same level of production. By reducing A by 2 man-hours, we induce a loss of $2 \times 4.5 = 9$ units of output. But by adding 3 machine-hours, we increase production by $3 \times 3 = 9$ units. Namely, production foregone due

TABLE 5-3

A	B	$Q = \sqrt{A \cdot B}$
1	100	10
2	50	10
3	$33\frac{1}{3}$	10
4	25	10
5	20	10
6	$16\frac{2}{3}$	10
7	$14\frac{2}{7}$	10
8	$12\frac{1}{2}$	10
9	$11\frac{1}{9}$	10
10	10	10

to the reduction in A is exactly compensated by production gained due to employing more B. Geometrically, we are simply tracing a *production indifference curve* which is denoted by *isoquant*. Accordingly, by definition an isoquant is a curve that includes all the pairs of A and B yielding the same output. Thus, combinations of A and B which belong to the same isoquant are shown in Table 5-3. This isoquant corresponds to a level of production of 10 units, and the production $Q = \sqrt{A \cdot B}$.

It is left up to the reader to draw the isoquant relating to Table 5-3. In case you are not sure how to go about it, review Part II of Chapter 2.

Now consider any isoquant, say the one indicated by S_0 in Fig. 5-4.

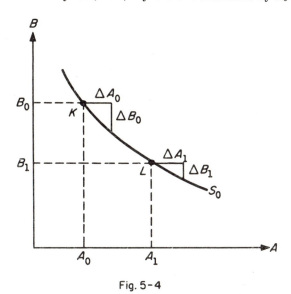

Fig. 5-4

When you move from point K to point L, $\Delta B/\Delta A$ changes. As shown in Fig. 5-4, it shrinks. But so does the ratio B/A. Let us denote $\Delta B/\Delta A$ by r and B/A by R; then the elasticity of substitution σ is

$$\sigma = \frac{\Delta R/R}{\Delta r/r}$$

where all Δs are very small (namely, when ΔA, ΔB, respectively, are small and K is close to L).

It can be proved that σ measures substitutability. If σ is a fixed parameter, then comparing the substitutability of one production function with another boils down to comparing the value of σ of the two production functions.

The elasticity of substitution will prove useful in Chapters 14 and 15.

THE LEAST COST COMBINATION OF FACTORS OF PRODUCTION

The theory of production is formally identical with the theory of consumption. Indifference curves are convex to the origin due to the law of diminishing marginal utility. Isoquants are convex to the origin due to the law of diminishing marginal physical product. Also, in the case of consumption to each budget there corresponds a certain budget line. In the case of production, to each outlay there corresponds a certain outlay line. In Fig. 5-5 we illustrate a case where the firm uses only two factors, A and B. The slope of the outlay lines, which are parallel to each other, is the ratio of the price of A to the price of B. The least cost combination corresponding to outlay L_1 is represented by point E_1

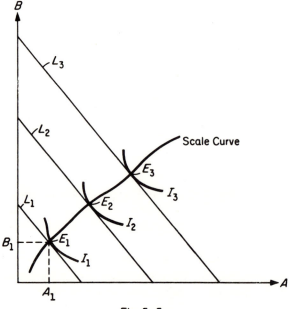

Fig. 5-5

(where E_1 represents a pair of A_1 units of A and B_1 units of B). At point E_1 the outlay line touches the highest isoquant denoted by I_1. Another way of saying the same thing is that at E_1 we minimize the outlay given a level of output as indicated by I_1. For larger outlays, we obtain other points of least cost combination of factors of production. In Fig. 5-5, when outlay increases to L_2 the least cost combination of factors A and B is E_2, and so on. If we continue to vary the outlay, a series of least cost combination points E_1, E_2, E_3, . . . will be yielded. A line passing through the locus of each of these points is defined as the scale curve.

Since going along an isoquant curve must satisfy $- \Delta A \cdot MPP_a = \Delta B \cdot MPP_b$, then the following equality must hold:

$$RTS = - \frac{\Delta B}{\Delta A} = \frac{MPP_a}{MPP_b}$$

where RTS is the marginal *rate of technological substitution*. The marginal rate of technological substitution tells us what the extra amount of input B is that must be added per one unit of input A diverted from the process of production, in order to maintain a certain fixed level of output. Going along an outlay line must satisfy $- \Delta A \cdot P_a = \Delta B \cdot P_b$. Accordingly, the marginal rate of substitution along the outlay line is

$$- \frac{\Delta B}{\Delta A} = \frac{P_a}{P_b}$$

At points like E_1, E_2 and E_3, where the outlay lines are tangent to the isoquant curves, the RTS are equal to the Rates of Substitution along the outlay lines, thus, at these points

$$\frac{P_a}{P_b} = \frac{MPP_a}{MPP_b}$$

Rearranging the above equality we get

$$\frac{MPP_a}{P_a} = \frac{MPP_b}{P_b}$$

which is the law of logic.

We leave it for the reader to show that if the process of production is governed by constant returns to scale and all factors of production are variable then (1) the scale curve is a straight line starting at the origin, and (2) output changes in proportion to the change in inputs.

In reality, only a finite number of processes is known to the producer. In Fig. 5-6 we illustrate a case where only two processes are known to the producer. Here only two scale lines are considered by the producer. If the outlay lines are parallel to a line passing through K and between G and I_1, then the producer will expand along the Scale Line 2. If the outlay lines are parallel to GH, the producer will be indifferent between Scale Line 1 and Scale Line 2. In other cases the producer will expand along Scale Line 1. When we are dealing with a specific firm, we are interested in this finite number of processes of production which is illustrated by Scale Line 1 and Scale Line 2 in Fig. 5-6. On the other hand, when we are considering the typical firm rather than a specific firm, we can assume that the number of processes of production is very large, and thus for all practical purposes the isoquants can be assumed to be smooth curves that are convex to the origin.

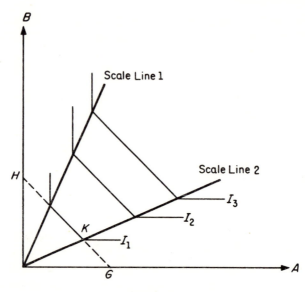

Fig. 5-6

EULER'S THEOREM

Euler's theorem states that if the production function is governed by constant returns to scale, then the sum of the products of quantities of factors used times their respective marginal physical products equals total output. For example, if only three factors are employed, say A units of labor, B units of machinery, and C units of raw material, we obtain

$$A \cdot MPP_a + B \cdot MPP_b + C \cdot MPP_c = Q$$

where Q stands for output. You will find it instructive to illustrate Euler's theorem by going to the case where $A = 8$ man-hours and $B = 2$ machine-hours in $Q = \sqrt{A \cdot B}$. For proof, see the Mathematical Appendix.

PROBLEMS

5-1. The production function of a plant is $Q = \sqrt{A \cdot B}$, where Q is output, A is man-hours, and B is machine-hours. Assume that $A = 5$ and $B = 20$. The cost of one man-hour is \$2 while the cost of one machine-hour is \$1. (a) Estimate MPP_a ($\Delta A = 1$). (b) Estimate MPP_b ($\Delta B = 1$). (c) What is MPP_a per dollar spent on A? (d) What is MPP_b per dollar spent on B? (e) You are the manager of the plant. You receive a loan with which you can increase the scale of the plant. On which of the two factors A or B will you start to spend money? Justify your answer numerically. (f) At what point will you become indifferent between investing in A and investing in B? (g) You double the amount of A and B, respectively. By how much will production increase?

5-2. Assume that the production function is $Q = (A + B)/2$. Currently, $A = 10$ man-hours and $B = 20$ machine-hours. Estimate MPP_b. (Assume that $\Delta B = 1$).

5-3. Repeat Prob. 5-2, except that $A = 20$ man-hours and $B = 20$ machine-hours.

SELECTED READINGS

MARSHALL, A. *Principles of Economics* (8th ed.). New York: The Macmillan Company, 1952, Book IV.

FRIEDMAN, M. *Price Theory, A Provisional Text*. Chicago, Ill.: Aldine Publishing Company, 1962, Chapter 6.

APPENDIX

THE COBB-DOUGLAS PRODUCTION FUNCTIONS

Among other things, the purpose of price theory is to help us explain the likely results of different economic policies. In order to do this we often have to assume that a certain industry is governed by a certain process of production and the laws relating to this process of production. We have agreed to accept *constant returns to scale, the law of diminishing marginal physical product and positive dependence* as the three laws by which all processes of production abide. (Note that the law of logic relates to the entrepreneur. This is the rule that tells him what is the least cost combination of factors of production). It would be very convenient if we could find a mathematical production function which would obey these three laws and be handy at the same time. The Cobb-Douglas production function serves these purposes. It is written

$$Q = KA^{\alpha}B^{\beta}C^{\gamma}$$

where Q is output; K is a coefficient; A, B, and C are quantities of factors of production; and α, β, and γ are coefficients. Note that the Cobb-Douglas function may include as many factors as one wishes. Our $Q = \sqrt{A \cdot B}$ is a Cobb-Douglas production function, where $K = 1$, $\alpha = \frac{1}{2}$, and $\beta = \frac{1}{2}$. (Why?) The first quality of the Cobb-Douglas production function is the fact that α, β, γ, etc. are elasticities of production. Namely

$$\alpha = \frac{\Delta Q/Q}{\Delta A/A}$$

The proof is mathematically involved and is left for the Mathematical Appendix. Thus, if $\alpha = \frac{1}{2}$, a 10 percent increase in A will entail a 5 percent increase in Q. If β is $\frac{1}{4}$, then a 10 percent increase in B will entail a 2.5 percent increase in Q, and so on.

CONSTANT RETURNS TO SCALE

The Cobb-Douglas production function can be made to obey the law of constant returns to scale. Assume that originally $Q_0 = KA_0^a B_0^\beta C_0^\gamma$. Next, multiply each factor by m. This gives

$$Q_1 = K(mA_0)^a \cdot (mB_0)^\beta \cdot (mC_0)^\gamma = m^{a+\beta+\gamma} \cdot KA_0^a \cdot B_0^\beta \cdot C_0^\gamma = m^{a+\beta+\gamma} \cdot Q_0$$

If we impose the equality $a + \beta + \gamma = 1$, we get

$$Q_1 = m^{a+\beta+\gamma} \cdot Q_0 = m^1 \cdot Q_0 = mQ_0$$

That is, multiplying all factors by the coefficient m results in multiplying Q_0 by the same coefficient.

THE LAW OF DIMINISHING MARGINAL PRODUCT

Recall that there must be at least two factors of production, otherwise one cannot increase the amount of one factor used *while keeping constant the amount of all other factors*. Since there are more than two factors and since we assumed that $a + \beta + \gamma = 1$, then a, β, and γ, respectively, have to be smaller than unity if each of them is positive. Accordingly, it is possible to prove the following:

1. $MPP_a = a \cdot \dfrac{Q}{A}$, $MPP_b = \beta \cdot \dfrac{Q}{B}$, $MPP_c = \gamma \cdot \dfrac{Q}{C}$

2. $MPP_a = a \cdot \dfrac{Q}{A}$ diminishes when A increase, and so on. The expression $a \cdot \dfrac{Q}{A}$ is very convenient to handle when the problem of distribution is analyzed.

DEPENDENCE

Suppose we keep A fixed at a certain level. Then, if we increase the amount used of any other factor, Q increases. Since a is a constant coefficient and A is by assumption unchanged, $a \cdot \dfrac{Q}{A}$ must increase when Q increases.

It is left up to the reader to show that if B is increased by 10 percent, then MPP_a increases by $\beta \times 10$ percent.

OTHER ADVANTAGES OF THE COBB-DOUGLAS FUNCTION

A *neutral shift* in the production function can be achieved by changing K. Thus, consider the following example. Originally $Q_0 = K_0 A_0^a B_0^\beta C_0^\gamma$. If you want to shift the production function by 5 percent, simply assign a new coefficient K_1. Where $K_1 = 1.05 \cdot K_0$,

$$Q_1 = K_1 A_0^a \cdot B_0^\beta \cdot C_0^\gamma = 1.05 \cdot K_0 A_0^a \cdot B_0^\beta \cdot C_0^\gamma = 1.05 \cdot Q_0$$

In other words, if the same original set of the factors of production is employed, a higher level of production is achieved. This is due to technological innovations. In the above example, the new level of production is 5 percent higher than the original level. Note, however, that the shift in the production function need not be neutral. The shift may be either labor-saving or capital-saving. Thus, consider the Cobb-Douglas function and assume that A stands for labor, B for land and C for capital. Originally, $K = K_0$, $a_0 = 0.4$, $\beta_0 = 0.3$, and $\gamma_0 = 0.3$. A labor-saving shift may be $K_1 = 1.10 \cdot K_0$, $a_1 = 0.2$, $\beta_1 = 0.5$, and $\gamma_1 = 0.3$.

THE DISADVANTAGE OF THE COBB-DOUGLAS PRODUCTION FUNCTION

It can be proved that the elasticity substitution σ is always unity for a Cobb-Douglas production function. Accordingly, one cannot benefit from the *services* rendered by this convenient function when the problem under consideration involves the elasticity of substitution. Later on we shall examine the effect of the decline in the price of factor B on the demand for factor A. The total effect on the demand curve for A has two sources: the substitution effect and the expansion effect. Clearly, it is not useful to impose a unitary elasticity of substitution between two factors of production. But this is exactly what one does if he accepts the Cobb-Douglas function for such a purpose.

AGGREGATE PRODUCTION FUNCTIONS

Economists try to explain growth as a function of the changes in labor, capital and technology. In order to estimate growth and attribute it to the different factors of production, economists make the assumption that production in the economy can be approximated by a single production function. For example, an economist may assume that the aggregate production function has the form

$$Q = e^{K \cdot t} \cdot C^a \cdot L^{1-a}$$

where Q is the gross national product, C and L, respectively, denote capital and labor, and the coefficient $e^{K \cdot t}$ takes care of the contribution of the change in technology which is a function of time. The statistical determination of such aggregate production functions is helpful in gaining insights into the problem of growth. For example, an economist may be interested in advocating policies concerning stimulating growth. For this, one might be interested in the immediate effect of accelerating the investment in tangible capital on the growth of gross national product. If capital formation is a vehicle for carrying technical change into effect, then the indirect effect of investment on growth through technology might be more important than the direct effect of investment on growth.

SELECTED READINGS

ARROW, K. J. "The Economic Implications of Learning by Doing," *Review of Economic Studies, The,* Vol. XXIX, June, 1962.

BERGLAS, E. "Investment and Technological Changes," *Journal of Political Economy,* April, 1965.

JOHNSTON, J., *op. cit.*

SOLOW, R. M. "Technical Change and the Aggregate Production Function," *Review of Economics and Statistics,* Vol. XXXIX, August, 1957.

————. "Technical Progress, Capital Formation and Economic Growth," *American Economic Review,* Vol. LII, May, 1962.

chapter 6

The Competitive Firm

When a large number of small firms are engaged in the production of a certain product, then the firms are said to be competitive, provided that the following is true:

1. Each individual firm has no influence over the price of the product it sells in the market.

2. The firm does not exert any influence over the prices of factors of production.

The statement that each individual firm *has no influence* over the price of the product it sells in the market could have been changed to the following: The firm has a *negligible influence* over the price of the product it sells in the market, and for all practical purposes we may assume that it has no influence over this price. To illustrate this point, consider an industry consisting of 1,000 firms. Thus, on the average, the individual firm shares 1/1,000 of the total production. Assume that the demand curve facing this industry has an elasticity of $-\frac{1}{2}$. By its decision to double production the firm will increase the total output of the industry by 1/1,000. If X stands for the unknown percentage change in price, we have

$$-\frac{1}{2} = \frac{\frac{1}{10}\%}{X\%}$$

And thus, X equals -0.2 percent. For example, if originally the market price was $10, after one individual firm has doubled its production, the new market price is set at $9.98. The inability of the firm to exert any significant influence over the market price means that the firm is faced with a horizontal demand curve for its product. This demand curve, which is shown in Fig. 6-1, may be called the price line.

Agriculture is a typical competitive industry. In the United States there are millions of wheat growers. One wheat grower cannot affect the price of wheat by increasing his production tenfold or by discontinuing production altogether. Laymen tend to associate competition with rivalry.

The opponents of the free enterprise system usually describe competitive firms as rival producers who are at each other's throats. The truth is, however, that competition and rivalry are two distinct phenomena. In a competitive industry, the individual producer has an infinitesimal share in total output. Thus, by his decision to produce more or less he cannot affect the welfare of other producers. Only in an industry which is dominated by a small number of producers can the decision of one producer affect the welfare of another.

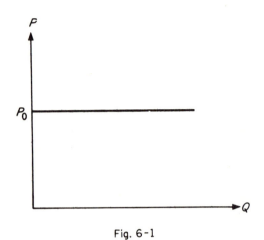

Fig. 6-1

The share of the competitive firm in the markets for factors of production is also negligible. Thus, one individual firm cannot raise the price of electricity by using more of it. Accordingly, in a competitive industry one individual firm cannot inflict losses upon another firm through raising the cost of resources in the market.

Competition fosters freedom. The individual producer cannot force the consumer to buy a low quality product because of the existence of other producers from whom the consumer can buy. The individual consumer cannot compel the producer to sell at a certain price because of the existence of other consumers to whom the producer can sell. The employer cannot mistreat the employee because of the presence of other producers for whom the employee can work, and so on along the line.

The opponents of the free enterprise economy sometimes argue that capitalistic economics are governed by monopolies and imperfect markets. This of course depends on where one draws the line between perfect and imperfect markets. For example, in the United States, about 50 percent of the gross national product is produced in markets which are competitive, or nearly so. Farm output, retail services rendered by cleaners, restaurants and small shops, some kinds of wholesale services and the like are produced in competitive industries. The other half of the gross national product is sold in imperfect markets. Conspicuous commodities such as cars, refrigerators, and soft drinks are sold in imperfect markets. In Chapter 13, we shall show that in spite of the imperfection of the markets for these commodities, the element of competition is still dominant there.

MARGINAL REVENUE

Marginal revenue is defined as the change in total revenue per unit of change in total production or simply the extra revenue resulting from the production of one·additional unit. The assumption is made here that each additional unit produced is eventually sold in the market. If total revenue is denoted by TR, then the formula of marginal revenue is

$$MR = \frac{\Delta(TR)}{\Delta Q}$$

where MR stands for marginal revenue. Note that since the competitive firm faces a given price of the product, for it $\Delta(TR)$ is equal to $\Delta Q \cdot P$. To illustrate this, if an extra three units are produced, that is, $\Delta Q = 3$ and the price is \$2, then the additional total revenue is $3 \times \$2 = \$6$. Accordingly, if we substitute $\Delta Q \cdot P$ for $\Delta(TR)$, we obtain

$$MR = \frac{\Delta Q \cdot P}{\Delta Q} = P$$

That is, for a competitive firm, price is identical with marginal revenue, and the horizontal demand curve in Fig. 6-1 is also the marginal revenue curve with which the firm is confronted. Finally, if you prefer common sense to arithmetics, simply note that the price must be identical with marginal revenue because each additional unit produced (and sold in the market) adds to total revenue an additional amount of money which is equal to the price. For a competitive firm, marginal revenue also equals average revenue, denoted by AR, where AR is total revenue divided by total output. Since total revenue equals $Q \cdot P$ we obtain

$$AR = \frac{TR}{Q} = \frac{Q \cdot P}{Q} = P$$

Accordingly, $AR = MR = P$.

The assumption that a competitive firm cannot influence the prices of the factors of production it uses is generally realistic. In few unimportant cases the firm may use a factor which is specific to a few firms. There, the firm may have to raise the price of the factor in order to be able to use more of it or pay a lower price when the firm decreases its use of the factor.

PRICES OF FACTORS OF PRODUCTION

Alternative Cost.   Let a firm use factors $A, B, \ldots, N$, *where A, B,
$\ldots, N$* also denote the quantities of services rendered by the factors per
unit of time. Let $P_a, P_b, \ldots, P_n$ be the prices of the factors. These prices are
established for the firm in the market. Note that one of the factors is
the entrepreneur; let it be factor N. The price of the entrepreneur, or
rather the cost of his services per unit of time, is his alternative cost.
The notion of alternative cost is somewhat vague. In order to get an
insight into the whole problem, assume that you are an entrepreneur
and you would like to find out what your alternative cost is. One morning
you dictate a letter to your secretary. In this letter you inform those
who may be concerned about your glorious achievements in the past. If
possible, you get a few friends to write letters of recommendation for you.
Then you mimeograph about thirty copies and send it to firms and
organizations which may have an opening. In a few weeks you may
collect fifteen answers. If you have had experience in the market you
would not run to the desk calculator to figure out what the average offer
is; nor would you grab the highest bid. The highest offer probably involves inconvenient hours, or altogether an inconvenient contract. The
lowest offer may give free on-the-job training. Moreover, it may offer
free training which can be applied elsewhere without committing you
to work in that specific place. To make a long story short, although you
cannot determine your alternative cost precisely, you can get some idea
about its order of magnitude. Let us assume that your alternative cost is
around \$10,000 per year. Thus, \$10,000 will stand for the cost of entrepreneurial services rendered per annum.

So far as labor is concerned, simply multiply the number of hours
worked by the hourly wage rate. If A stands for labor, then $A \cdot P_a$ is
total expenditure on labor. Note that $A \cdot P_a$ should cover fringe benefits
which is paid by the employer.

Raw Materials.   For simplicity assume that there is only one type of
raw material; denote it by B. Here we are interested only in the amount
of raw material used up in the process of production during a specific
period of time. This equals raw material bought during the specific period
of time minus the closing inventory plus the beginning inventory of raw
material.

The same procedure applies for sources of energy such as coal, oil,
etc. It is worth mentioning that these items of labor, raw material, and
sources of energy are called *current expenditures*.

The problem of estimating the cost of capital items is more involved.
One cannot multiply the price of the machine by the number of machines
and claim that this accounts for total expenditures on machinery per
unit of time. If the lifetime of a typical machine is twenty years, then

its price should be spread over a period of twenty years. In other words, the cost of the services of a machine per unit of time is the depreciation attributed to that period of time rather than the entire price of the machine. But depreciation does not constitute the entire cost of a service rendered by a machine per unit of time. The rate of interest charged on the value of the machine must be added to depreciation. This is true because if the entrepreneur has to rent the services of a machine, he would have to pay the rental price per unit of time. If we assume that a perfect market exists, then the rental price per annum is the rate of interest charged on the value of the machine plus the annual rate of depreciation.

In Chapter 16, the subject of capital budgeting and related topics are covered in detail.

Definitions of Cost Functions. Having explained in detail what the prices of factors of production are, we can define the total cost. Recall that $A, B, \ldots, N$ are flows of factors of production (services rendered per unit of time) and $P_a, P_b, \ldots, P_n$ are prices of the services of factors properly defined, then we have

$$TC = A \cdot P_a + B \cdot P_b + \cdots + N \cdot P_n$$

where TC stands for *total cost.*

Average cost is simply defined as total cost divided by output. Let output be denoted by Q, then

$$AC = \frac{TC}{Q}$$

where AC stands for average cost.

Finally, marginal cost is defined as the change in total cost per unit of change in output, or

$$MC = \frac{\Delta(TC)}{\Delta Q}$$

where MC stands for marginal cost. The reader should be aware of the possible separation between average fixed cost denoted by AFC and average variable cost denoted by AVC. Total fixed costs are costs incurred by factors that are fixed to the firm, such as depreciation on the building, some overhead items, and so on; and one may also add, fixed taxes. Total variable costs are costs incurred by variable factors such as raw materials, power, labor, etc. Depreciation may be classified either way, depending on the circumstances. Accordingly, average variable cost is total variable cost divided by output, and average fixed cost is total fixed cost divided by output. A variable factor is one that varies with output. On the other hand, a factor that is fixed regardless of the level of production is called a fixed factor.

COST CURVES

Let us consider the case where all factors can be varied, and the production function is governed by constant returns to scale. Consider our simple production function $Q = \sqrt{A \cdot B}$. Assume that the prices of the factors of production are $P_a = \$0.25$ and $P_b = \$1$. Let us help the entrepreneur to find a combination of A and B so that the following equality is satisfied

$$\frac{MPP_a}{\$0.25} = \frac{MPP_b}{\$1}$$

Assume that through a process of trial and error we finally find such a combination, namely, $A_0 = 8$ man-hours and $B_0 = 2$ machine-hours. Let us estimate MPP_a and MPP_b. It is recalled that the smaller ΔA and ΔB are, respectively, the finer is our estimate of MPP_a and MPP_b. Thus, we shall assume that $\Delta A = 0.10$ man-hours and $\Delta B = 0.10$ machine-hours.

The Estimate of MPP_a: Here, B is unchanged at $B_0 = 2$ machine-hours and $A_0 = 8$ man-hours, $A_1 = 8.1$ man-hours. Thus,

$$Q_0 = \sqrt{A_0 \cdot B_0} = \sqrt{8 \cdot 2} = \sqrt{16} = 4$$
$$Q_1 = \sqrt{A_1 \cdot B_0} = \sqrt{8.1 \cdot 2} = \sqrt{16.2} = 4.025$$

Accordingly,

$$MPP_a = \frac{\Delta Q}{\Delta A} = \frac{Q_1 - Q_0}{A_1 - A_0} = \frac{4.025 - 4}{8.1 - 8} = \frac{0.025}{0.1} = 0.25$$

The Estimate of MPP_b: Here, A is unchanged at $A_0 = 8$ man-hours, $B_0 = 2$ machine-hours, and $B_1 = 2.1$ machine-hours. Thus,

$$Q_1 = \sqrt{A_0 \cdot B_1} = \sqrt{8 \cdot 2.1} = \sqrt{16.8} = 4.1$$
$$MPP_b = \frac{\Delta Q}{\Delta B} = \frac{Q_1 - Q_0}{B_1 - B_0} = \frac{4.1 - 4}{2.1 - 2} = \frac{0.1}{0.1} = 1$$

and we have

$$\frac{MPP_a}{P_a} = \frac{0.25 \text{ units}}{\$0.25} = \frac{MPP_b}{P_b} = \frac{1 \text{ unit}}{\$1}$$

What is the marginal cost? In our example, the entrepreneur can produce one additional unit by doing one of the following three things:

1. Employ four additional man-hours keeping the use of machinery constant. Since $MPP_a = 0.25$ units, four additional units of A will increase production by $4 \times 0.25 = 1$ unit of output. The cost $4 \cdot P_a = 4 \times \$0.25 = \$1$. Namely, the extra cost involved in producing one additional unit is $1.

2. Employ one additional machine-hour keeping labor constant. Since $MPP_b = 1$, one additional machine-hour will give rise to one additional unit of output. But since $P_b = \$1$, namely, one additional machine-hour costs $1, the extra cost involved in producing one additional unit is $1.

Note that in cases 1 and 2, the extra cost, which is another notation for the marginal cost, was obtained by dividing the price of the factor by its MPP. Thus we had

$$\frac{P_a}{MPP_a} = \frac{P_b}{MPP_b} = MC$$

$$\frac{MPP_a}{P_a} = \frac{MPP_b}{P_b} = \frac{1}{MC}$$

3. Increasing output by 1 unit (from 4 units to 5 units) amounts to a 25 percent change. Since the function $Q = \sqrt{A \cdot B}$ is governed by constant returns to scale, this change may be obtained by increasing A and B, respectively, by 25 percent. Accordingly,

$$A_1 = 1.25 \cdot A_0 = 1.25 \cdot 8 = 10 \qquad B_1 = 1.25 \cdot B_0 = 1.25 \cdot 2 = 2.5$$

Thus,

$$Q_1 = \sqrt{A_1 \cdot B_1} = \sqrt{10 \cdot 2.5} = \sqrt{25} = 5$$

Note that,

$$\Delta A = A_1 - A_0 = 10 - 8 = 2 \qquad \text{and} \qquad \Delta B = B_1 - B_0 = 2.5 - 2 = 0.5$$

The extra cost involved is equal to

$$\Delta A \cdot P_a + \Delta B \cdot P_b = 2 \cdot 0.25 + 0.5 \cdot 1 = \$1$$

Namely, when cost is minimized, the marginal cost is the same regardless of whether the extra unit is achieved by a small increase in the use of input A alone, by a small increase in the use of input B alone, or by slightly increasing the use of both factors.

It can be proved that if the production function is governed by constant returns to scale, both MPP_a and MPP_b are functions of A/B. Thus, if we multiply A and B by K, then MPP_a and MPP_b are functions of $(K \cdot A)/(K \cdot B)$. But $(K \cdot A)/(K \cdot B) = A/B;$ thus, if the factors A and B are increased at the same rate, MPP_a and MPP_b retain the same values. This rule also holds true when more than two factors are employed. You will find it instructive to show that when, say, $2 \times 8 = 16$ man-hours and $2 \times 2 = 4$ machine-hours are used, MPP_a is the same 0.25 units and MPP_b is the same one unit of output. Since $MC = P_a/MPP_a = P_b/MPP_b$ and since P_a, MPP_a, P_b, and MPP_b, respectively, are given at $0.25, 0.25 units, $1, and 1 unit, in our case MC is always equal to $1 regardless of the level of production. This long run marginal cost curve which is denoted by MCL is derived in Fig. 6-2.

The reader may find it somewhat difficult to convince himself that MPP_a and MPP_b do not change when all factors are changed proportionately. An intuitive explanation goes as follows: To double all factors of production is identical with having two identical plants where each plant employs exactly the same set of factors of production. (The two plants have identical entrepreneurs.) Then, if each plant produces Q_0

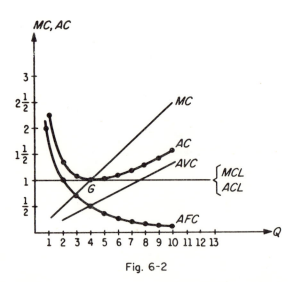

Fig. 6-2

units, the marginal cost is the same in both plants. But the marginal cost in one of them is also the marginal cost at a level of $2Q_0$ when both plants are counted as one firm. Accordingly the marginal cost corresponding to a level of $3Q_0$ is identical with the marginal cost of one plant where three identical plants are producing Q_0 units each by using an identical set of factors.

The Average Cost. In the above example, total cost is estimated as

$$TC = A \cdot P_a + B \cdot P_b = 8 \cdot \$0.25 + 2 \cdot \$1 = \$4$$

Total output is $Q = 4$ units; thus, average cost is estimated as

$$AC = \frac{TC}{Q} = \frac{\$4}{4} = \$1$$

It is clear, however, that average cost is always the same because if all factors are increased proportionately, total cost increases in the same proportion and so does output due to the assumption of constant returns to scale. Thus, the long run average cost curve ACL coincides with the long run marginal cost curve MCL, which is a horizontal curve. To illustrate this, multiply both factors by 2.

Thus,

$$A = 8 \cdot 2 = 16 \qquad B = 2 \cdot 2 = 4$$

and

$$Q = \sqrt{16 \cdot 4} = \sqrt{64} = 8 \qquad TC = 16 \cdot \$.25 + 4 \cdot \$1 = \$8$$

Then,

$$AC = \frac{TC}{Q} = \frac{\$8}{8} = \$1$$

What are MPP_a and MPP_b at this level of production? As before, let

$$\Delta A = 0.10$$

Then,

$$Q_0 = \sqrt{16 \cdot 4} = \sqrt{64} = 8$$
$$Q_1 = \sqrt{16.1 \cdot 4} = \sqrt{64.4} = 8.025$$

and

$$MPP_a = \frac{\Delta Q}{\Delta A} = \frac{Q_1 - Q_0}{A_1 - A_0} = \frac{8.025 - 8}{16.1 - 16} = \frac{0.025}{0.1} = 0.25$$

Next, let

$$\Delta B = 0.1$$

Then,

$$Q_1 = \sqrt{16 \cdot 4.1} = 8.1$$

and

$$MPP_b = \frac{\Delta Q}{\Delta B} = \frac{Q_1 - Q_0}{B_1 - B_0} = \frac{8.1 - 8}{4.1 - 4} = \frac{0.1}{0.1} = 1$$

THE CASE OF A FIXED FACTOR

The horizontal MC curve which coincides with the AC curve is obtained under the assumption that all factors are variable. Once we find a point of equilibrium where the following holds

$$\frac{MPP_a}{P_a} = \frac{MPP_b}{P_b} = \cdots = \frac{MPP_n}{P_n} = \frac{1}{MC}$$

we know that the marginal cost curve is a horizontal line obtained by changing all factors of production proportionately. This horizontal line represents a marginal cost which is equal to P_a/MPP_a (or the price of any

other factor divided by its MPP). In reality, however, factors cannot
be changed in the same proportion. One can imagine a firm which is
stuck with a certain building and machines in the short run. This firm
may increase output by employing more labor and other current items
while employing the same building and machines. If the prices of all
factors including machines are unchanged, the firm has an incentive to
increase the services rendered by the building and machines proportionately, thus maintaining equilibrium between the different factors, or differently, moving along the horizontal MC curve. But installing new machines
is a time-consuming process, and until new machines can be installed the
firm must deviate from its long-run MC curve. Consider the long run
in the sense that enough time is available to change all tangible factors
of production in the same proportion. There might be one factor of production which is fixed to the firm. This is the entrepreneurial capacity.
Accordingly, in most of the cases, even in the long run, the MC curve
is not horizontal. Consider the simple cases of two factors, A which is
labor, and B which is capital services, or, say, machine-hours. If B cannot
be varied, then production can be increased by increasing the labor input
only. However, the law of diminishing marginal product tells us that
this implies a declining marginal physical product of A. But, for the
competitive firm, P_a is given; thus, MC which in this case is equal to
P_a/MPP_a, must rise.

To illustrate this, recall that when $B = 2$ machine-hours and
$A = 8$ man-hours, $MPP_a = 0.25$ units. Since the price of one man-hour
is \$0.25, $MC = \$0.25/0.25 = \$1$. Let us assume that B cannot be varied,
it is fixed at 2 machine-hours. Let us increase the amount of labor used
from 8 man-hours to say, 18 man-hours. Let $\Delta A = 0.1$ man-hours, then,

$$Q_0 = \sqrt{2 \cdot 18} = 6 \text{ units}$$
$$Q_1 = \sqrt{2 \cdot 18.1} = 6.016$$

and

$$MPP_a = \frac{\Delta Q}{\Delta A} = \frac{Q_1 - Q_0}{A_1 - A_0} = \frac{6.016 - 6}{18.1 - 18} = \frac{0.016}{0.1} = 0.16$$

Thus,

$$MC = \frac{\$0.25}{0.16} = \$1.56$$

That is, marginal cost rose from \$1 to \$1.56. Note that only factor A is
involved in the estimation of MC; the reason being that since A is the
only variable factor, an extra unit of output involves using more A, but
the same amount of B.

Let us now derive the MC and AC curves under the assumption that
B is fixed at 2 machine-hours. This is carried out in Table 6-1.

Note that the estimates of MC in column 6 differ from the estimates of MC in column 7; in column 6, the change in output is always one unit. In column 7, we used very small changes in A in order to achieve negligible changes in output. The cost curves are derived in Fig. 6-2.

TABLE 6-1

B Machine Hours	A Man Hours	$Q=\sqrt{A \cdot B}$ Units of Output	$TC=B \cdot P_b+A \cdot P_a$ $=FC+VC$ (in dollars)	$AC=TC/Q$ $=(4)/(3)$ $=AFC+AVC$ (in dollars)	MC (in dollars)	
					$\Delta(TC)/\Delta Q$	P_a/MPP_a
(1)	(2)	(3)	(4)	(5)	(6)	(7)
2	0	$\sqrt{2 \cdot 0}\ =0$	$2+\ 0\ =2.00$			
2	½	$\sqrt{2 \cdot ½}\ =1$	$2+\ 0.12=\ 2.12$	$2.00+0.12=2.12$	0.12	0.25
2	2	$\sqrt{2 \cdot 2}\ =2$	$2+\ 0.50=\ 2.50$	$1.00+0.25=1.25$	0.38	0.50
2	4½	$\sqrt{2 \cdot 4½}=3$	$2+\ 1.12=\ 3.12$	$0.66+0.38=1.04$	0.62	0.75
2	8	$\sqrt{2 \cdot 8}\ =4$	$2+\ 2\ \ =4$	$0.50+0.50=1.00$	0.88	1.00
2	12½	$\sqrt{2 \cdot 12½}=5$	$2+\ 3.12=\ 5.12$	$0.40+0.62=1.02$	1.12	1.25
2	18	$\sqrt{2 \cdot 18}\ =6$	$2+\ 4.50=\ 6.50$	$0.33+0.75=1.08$	1.38	1.50
2	24½	$\sqrt{2 \cdot 24½}=7$	$2+\ 6.12=\ 8.12$	$0.28+0.88=1.16$	1.62	1.75
2	32	$\sqrt{2 \cdot 32}\ =8$	$2+\ 8\ \ =10$	$0.25+1.00=1.25$	1.88	2.00
2	40½	$\sqrt{2 \cdot 40½}=9$	$2+10.12=12.12$	$0.22+1.12=1.34$	2.12	2.25
2	50	$\sqrt{2 \cdot 50}\ =10$	$2+12.50=14.50$	$0.20+1.25=1.45$	2.38	2.50

MC intersects with AC at the lowest point on AC. In other words, when AC is declining, MC is smaller than AC; and when AC is rising, MC is larger than AC. This is not only true in the specific case indicated in Fig. 6-2 but it is a general theorem that can be proved.

Let total cost be denoted C; then, if AC is declining, we have

$$\frac{C + \Delta C}{Q + \Delta Q} < \frac{C}{Q}$$

which gives

$$Q(C + \Delta C) < C(Q + \Delta Q)$$

that is,

$$Q \cdot C + Q \cdot \Delta C < C \cdot Q + C \cdot \Delta Q$$

Subtracting $Q \cdot C$ in both sides of the inequality gives

$$Q \cdot \Delta C < C \cdot \Delta Q$$

Dividing through by $Q \cdot \Delta Q$ gives

$$\frac{\Delta C}{\Delta Q} < \frac{C}{Q}$$

TO PRODUCE OR NOT?

Let us assume that the plant is stuck with two units of B; thus, the horizontal MC line is not relevant any more. Instead we have the rising MC curve and the U-shaped AC curve. Once the price falls below the minimum point G on the AC curve, the firm should get out of business. When the price is below the average cost, the entrepreneur incurs losses. The loss will amount to $Q(AC - P)$. Thus, if 3 units are produced and the price is \$0.75, then the loss per unit of time is $3(1.04 - 0.75) = 3 \times 0.29 = \$0.87$. Note, however, that it may pay the firm to continue to produce in the short run rather than to scrap the plant. To illustrate this, consider Table 6-1. If the fixed cost of \$2 (column 4) did not exist, the firm should produce 3 units of output at which $P = MC = \$0.75$ (column 7). At that point total revenue amounts to $3 \times \$0.75 = \$2.25$. As indicated in column 4, when 3 units are produced total variable cost equals \$1.12. Accordingly, net profit equals $\$2.25 - \$1.12 = \$1.13$. Let us now introduce the fixed cost of \$2 per unit of time. If this fixed cost cannot be avoided by going out of business, the firm should continue its production in the short run, because a loss of \$0.87 (\$2 − \$1.13) is preferred to a larger loss of \$2. In reality, such a situation arises when the firm uses a rented machine for which it must pay a contractual price of \$2 per unit of time. This cost is legally unavoidable. If the fixed cost is avoidable by discontinuing production, the firm should get out of business. In summary, if at the point where $p = MC$ the price is higher than the average variable cost and the fixed cost is unavoidable, the firm should continue to produce in the short run.

HOW MUCH TO PRODUCE?

If the price is above the lowest point of the AC curve, the firm should stay in business. It should produce exactly the amount indicated by the point of intersection between the price line and the MC curve, namely, where $P = MC$. You will recall that for a competitive firm $P = MR$. Consider either Table 6-1 or Fig. 6-2. Let us assume that the price per unit of output is \$2. If only six units are produced, the corresponding MC is \$1.38. By adding one unit of output, the entrepreneur will gain the price of \$2 which is the marginal revenue. He will pay an additional cost as indicated by the MC curve. In this case it is \$1.62. Thus his additional net gain is $\$2 - \$1.62 = \$0.38$ per unit of time. Accordingly, through a process of trial and error the entrepreneur will expand until he produces 8 units at which $MC = \$1.88$ and $P = \$2$, that is, MC is slightly below P. The reader should be able to show that if the entrepreneur happened to produce, say, 9 units, he would soon find out that he is losing \$0.12 per unit of time. In summary, even if the entrepreneur has not taken a course in economics, and even if he does not know anything about his MC curve, he will produce at the point where the price is equal to the marginal cost. He will reach this point by a process of trial and error. If MC is below the price, he will gain from increasing the scale of production. If MC is above the price, he will benefit from shrinking production.

RENT

Variable factors of production are paid their alternative cost. The entrepreneur cannot pay the owners of variable inputs less than their alternative cost, because owners can shift such mobile inputs to alternative uses. The entrepreneur does not have to pay more than the alternative cost because of the availability at a lower cost of these inputs elsewhere in the economy.

But returns to fixed factors of production may exceed their alternative costs. The difference between the alternative costs of fixed factors and their actual returns are called rents. We shall show later that rents are not the same as net earnings (profit) as defined by accountants. In what follows, we shall assume that rent accrues to the entrepreneur. In reality rents also accrue to landlords and others who happen to own fixed resources.

Consider Fig. 6-3. The price is P_0, at which Q_0 is produced, as indicated by the MC curve. The price is above the average cost and the

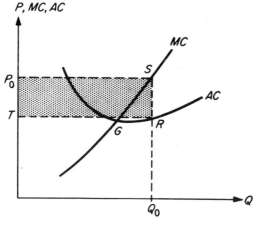

Fig. 6-3

difference between the price and the AC is RS. It is recalled that AC includes a component of the alternative cost of the entrepreneur. Accordingly, any price above AC gives rise to a net profit over and above what the entrepreneur can earn elsewhere. Thus $Q_0 \times RS$, which is equal to output times $(P - AC)$, is "extra profits" coming to the entrepreneur. Geometrically this *extra profit* is the shaded area indicated by the rectangle $TRSP_0$. This *extra profit* is sometimes called rent. Why does rent arise? First, rent may exist in the short run because of an innovation. In the following chapter we shall show that a firm that introduces an innovation into the process of production benefits from higher rent due to the decline in MC and AC (Fig. 6-3). But eventually other firms in the industry learn how to apply the new innovation. They increase their production (why?), and this leads to a lower market price. Thus, in the long run the rise of rent to the firm that first puts in the innovation may disappear. Other reasons why rent may arise in the long run are:

Undertaking Risk. Let us assume that your alternative cost is $10,000. That is, you can become an employee who earns $10,000 a year. Now you can enter the shoemaking industry and start to produce. There is uncertainty involved concerning your future income. Let us assume that your expectations are based on what other entrepreneurs in the shoemaking industry earn. As far as you are concerned, there is a 50 percent chance of earning $12,000 and a 50 percent chance of making only $8,000. Mathematically, you expect to earn $\frac{1}{2} \times \$12,000 + \frac{1}{2} \times \$8,000 = \$10,000$. If you are not a gambler by nature, taking such a risk is a nuisance, and unless somebody is ready to compensate you for the service of risk-bearing you will not enter the shoemaking industry.

Let us now make a different assumption. Your expectations (based on the situation in the industry) are the following: You have a 60 percent chance of earning $14,000 and a 40 percent chance of earning $8,000. The expected income is $0.6 \times \$14,000 + 0.4 \times \$8,000 = \$11,600$. Now the problem is simple. If you prefer your alternative income which is the certain $10,000 to the expected income of $11,600, you will not become an entrepreneur in the shoemaking industry. If you place the $11,600 which involves uncertainty above the certain income of $10,000, you will enter the industry and start making shoes. Note that you place the uncertain $11,600 above the certain $10,000 because the difference of $1,600 (which also is uncertain) is sufficient to compensate you for the service of the risk one must bear. Thus, the phenomenon of rent can be rationalized by assuming that entrepreneurs dislike riskiness. Unless they are paid an average rent which compensates them for undertaking the disliked risk, they cannot be persuaded to become businessmen. In our example, the entrepreneur had to be paid an expected positive premium of $1,600 in order to enter the industry. Accordingly, the assumption that businessmen dislike risk explains long-run rents in competitive industries.

Of course, one can take the view that the part of the rent which compensates the entrepreneur for undertaking the disliked risk is in fact an important component of the alternative cost of the entrepreneur. Accordingly compensation for risk-bearing is not rent.

Limited Supply of Specific Resources. Consider an industry which pays its entrepreneurs high rents. Let us assume that no risk is involved in entering the industry. If you have the required talents you can start to produce tomorrow. A situation may arise where potential entrepreneurs are scarce, thus no potential entrepreneur exists who will exploit the opportunity to enter the industry and earn a certain rent in addition to what he can earn by becoming an employee. Of course, if there are many potential entrepreneurs who are ready to enter the industry the moment a positive rent is paid, the rent will become a short-lived phenomenon. The rent will be eliminated by an influx of potential entrepreneurs who are eager to increase their certain income. The entry of additional producers to the industry will increase production, and so the price will continue to fall along the demand curve just to a point where no significant rents exist. However, if entrepreneurial services are in short supply, the rent may become a long-run phenomenon. In fact, the length of the run depends on the period of scarcity. Note that this is a case of natural scarcity: nature has not provided enough persons with the talents and character required to become businessmen.

Sometimes one firm rather than the whole industry may benefit from such scarcity. For example, a farmer may own extremely fertile land, and so his average cost curve may be extremely low. Or, one producer may be located very close to the market place. If transportation costs are important in the product which he makes, this would give rise to a relatively low average cost curve. All these are examples of natural scarcities which should be distinguished from contrived restrictions.

Contrived Scarcities. In New York, the municipal authority has restricted the number of taxicabs that are allowed to operate in the city. Thus, in spite of a rising demand for taxicab services, the supply is relatively fixed. This gives rise to relatively high incomes for cab drivers in New York. These incomes are relatively high because of the artificial scarcity in the supply of cab services: those who operate taxicabs in New York can get away with either a relatively higher price per mile of service, or they can offer more miles per day, or both.

Now consider one producer who is the sole owner of a patent. The patent gives rise to a lower average cost curve (and, of course, a lower marginal cost curve) and thus to a larger rent. As long as there is scarcity in the sense that other firms in the same industry cannot use the same patent, the owner of the patent will earn a special rent. It should be stressed here that this is a special case of contrived scarcity. While in other cases society should protect itself from contrived scarcity which boils down to exploiting the consumer, the case of a sole owner of a patent is different. Here, if you eliminate the rent which is reaped by the firm that owns the patent, you might kill the incentive to discover new methods of production. In other words, it may lead to a technological stagnation which no one advocates.

THE SUPPLY CURVE OF THE FIRM

The MC curve above point G (Fig. 6-3) is the supply curve of the firm. It tells us what are the quantities that will be supplied by the firm at different prices. One example is the Quantity Q_0 (Fig. 6-3) which is supplied at P_0 as indicated by point S on the MC curve. The shape of MC in Fig. 6-3 will depend on the time allowed for adjustment. We shall show in the following chapter that the longer the period of time allowed for adjustment, the flatter the MC curve. In the longest run, all factors of production might be variable and accordingly the supply curve of the firm is an horizontal line. If such an horizontal supply curve exists, then there is no limit to the size of the firm. This may lead either to a domination of the market by one firm, or to market instability where firms divide the market among themselves arbitrarily. In reality we observe either market domination by a sole producer (or a few producers), or a stable market which is shared by many small firms. By a stable market we mean that changes in prices do not lead to wide changes of production.

If the firm owns more than one plant, then each individual plant has its own MC curve. The firm will maximize its total rent by maximizing the rent in each individual plant. The supply curve of such a firm is obtained by horizontally totaling the MC curves of the individual plants.

ACCOUNTING VERSUS ECONOMIC COSTS

The economic rent which was defined in this chapter differs from net earnings which is computed by accountants. This difference arises primarily because the economist is interested in one thing and the accountant in another. You will recall that if there is a positive rent, the firm should stay in business. If the rent is negative, then in the long run the entrepreneur should dissolve the firm and find other employment. Thus, the rent which is based on economic costs tells the entrepreneur whether he is doing at least as well as he could alternatively do by investing his capital elsewhere and hiring himself out as an employee. On the other hand, the main purpose of the accountant is to furnish data concerning the state of business. Thus, among other things, the role of the accountant is to tell the owner of the firm what is left for him as taxable income after all expenses are paid. With proper adjustment, the data provided by the accountant may be used in economic analysis.

To illustrate this, consider a carpenter who is the proprietor of a small shop which produces furniture. Investment in assets amounts to $100,000. Let us assume that the alternative salary of the carpenter is $8,000. That is, the entrepreneur can be employed elsewhere for $8,000 a year. Let us assume that he owes $40,000 to the bank, and the interest charge is 5 percent. During the year net sales were $45,000, the cost of materials was $7,000, payments to labor amounted to $14,000, and depreciation and maintenance to $13,000. The income statement of the accountant is

Net Sales		$45,000
Less: Materials	$ 7,000	
Labor Cost	14,000	
Depreciation and Maintenance . .	13,000	
Interest Charges (5% on $40,000). .	2,000	
Total Costs		36,000
Net Earnings		$ 9,000

Let us now estimate the economic rent of the firm:

Net Sales (total revenue)		$45,000
Less: Materials	$ 7,000	
Labor Cost: (1) Hired	14,000	
(2) Entrepreneur . . .	8,000	
Depreciation and Maintenance . .	13,000	
Interest (5% on capital)	5,000	
Total (economic) Costs		47,000
Rent		−$ 2,000

In the above example even though net profit as estimated by the accountant amounts to $9,000, the economist shows that our carpenter would have done better had he invested his capital ($60,000) elsewhere and hired himself out. In fact, as indicated by the rent which is estimated by the economist, the carpenter would have been better off by $2,000 had he seriously considered other alternatives.

This is why total costs as defined by economists include the alternative cost of the entrepreneur. They do not include interest charges on loans, but rather they include interest charged on the entire capital.

The transformation from the accounting profit to the economic rent is simpler in the case of the corporation. Note that the alternative cost of the entrepreneur is already included in the item *Labor Cost*.

To illustrate this, assume that our shop, which is engaged in producing furniture, is a corporation. It was financed by issuing $40,000 bonds which pay 5 percent interest and 6,000 common shares of $10 each. It employs our carpenter as a manager and pays him $8,000 a year. The income statement of the corporation is

Net Sales		$45,000
Less: Materials	$ 7,000	
Labor Cost	22,000	
Depreciation and Maintenance. . .	13,000	
Interest (on bonds)	2,000	
Total Cost		44,000
Net Earnings		$ 1,000

If the corporation decides to pay the profit of $1,000 to stockholders, then the dividend paid will amount to about 17 cents per share, which is a rate of return of 1.7 percent. It is evident that stockholders are doing very badly. Had they invested their savings in alternative corporations they could have earned more.

If the prevailing rate of interest is 5 percent, then, on the average, they are losing $5\% - 1.7\% = 3.3\%$ per year. This is indicated by the fact that the rent is a negative $2,000! In the long run this will show up in the market price of the shares.

The income statement as viewed by the economist is illustrated in

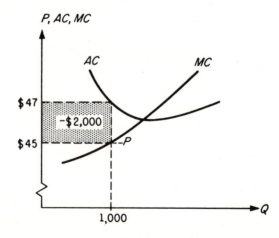

Fig. 6-4

Fig. 6-4. The firm sells 1,000 units of output per year. Currently the price is $45 apiece and average cost amounts to $47 as shown in the figure.

SOME IMPORTANT REMARKS ON COST CURVES

In Fig. 6-2 the MC (marginal cost), AC (average cost), AVC (average variable cost), and AFC (average fixed cost) are shown. The horizontal line represents both the MCL (long run marginal cost) and ACL (long run average cost) under the assumption that all factors of production are variable.

The AC and AFC curves have the shape of conventional cost curves. The AFC curve is a rectangular hyperbola. It approaches infinity when output is very small, and it approaches zero when output is very large. To use a mathematical terminology, it is asymptotic to the axes. If output is denoted by Q and fixed cost by FC, then we have $FC = Q \times AFC$. Since FC is constant, when Q is very small, AFC must be very large and vice versa. For example, if $FC = \$2,000$, then $AFC = \$1,000$ for $Q = 2$ units, $AFC = \$20$ for $Q = 100$ units and $AFC = \$1$ for $Q = 2,000$ units. For each unit of output, the AC curve is obtained by adding AFC to AVC. This is the reason why the AC curve is U-shaped. When output is very small, AVC is negligible; but AFC is very large, and accordingly AC is very large. When output increases, AFC declines rapidly which also causes the AC to decline. When production takes on large scales, AFC is negligible, but AVC becomes larger and larger and accordingly AC increases. Notice that the MC and AVC curves in Fig. 6-2 are constantly ascending. The "conventional" MC and AVC curves descend at first, reach their respective minimums, and then ascend. The reason for this is that our particular production function $Q = \sqrt{A \cdot B}$ cannot yield declining MC and AVC curves. If we assumed constant returns to scale without restricting ourselves to this type of production function, then we could have a stage in which the marginal physical product of the variable factor A increases. At this stage the marginal cost diminishes. (Why?) We can also find a stage at which the average physical product of the variable factor diminishes. At this stage the AVC rises. (Why?).

We can summarize the relationship between the MPP_a, MC, and TC as follows:

Stage I: MPP_a rises. MC $(= P_a/MPP_a)$ declines, and accordingly TC increases at a decreasing rate.

Stage II: MPP_a stays at the same level. MC is constant, and accordingly TC increases at a fixed rate.

Stage III: MPP_a diminishes. MC rises, and accordingly TC increases at an increasing rate.

Notice finally that the smooth marginal cost curve only approximates the real MC which, is step-shaped. For example, consider Table 6-1. If the units of output are indivisible then column 7 is irrelevant for optimum production decisions. Column 6 becomes the relevant MC function. The step-shaped MC curve is shown in Fig. 6-5.

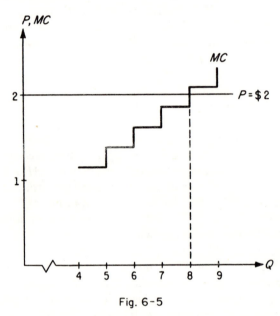

Fig. 6-5

On the quantity axis, the segment that lies between 4 and 5 represents the fifth unit, and so on. The MC of the fifth unit is \$1.12; then it rises vertically to \$1.38 which is the MC of the sixth unit, etc. At a market price of \$2, 8 units of output are produced. At a price of \$2.12, the firm is indifferent between producing 8 units or 9 units. At a price higher than \$2.12 but less than \$2.38 the firm should produce 9 units and so on.

In Fig. 6-6 we show the total cost curve (denoted by TC) and total revenue curve (denoted by TR). The TR curve is linear because a competitive firm cannot affect the price of the product it sells in the market. We leave it for the reader to show why the TR curve starts from the origin. The TC curve hits the TR curve at points E and G. Below E it does not pay the firm to produce in the long run. Point E is known as the break-even point. Beyond point G, TC is again higher than TR. Accordingly, Q_1Q_3 is the profitable range of the firm. Rent is maximized at Q_2. Recall from geometry that MC is the slope of TC and MR is the slope of TR. At point H the line g is tangent to TC and is also parallel to TR. Accordingly, at output Q_2 corresponding to H, MC equals MR and

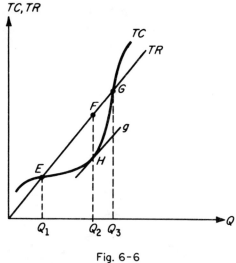

Fig. 6-6

rent denoted by HF is maximized. We leave it as an exercise for the reader to derive the AC and MC curves and price line from Fig. 6-6. (What occurs at Q_1, Q_2, and Q_3?)

A NOTE ON CONVENTIONAL COST CURVES

The $\sqrt{A \cdot B}$ type production function has a serious limitation: It only generates increasing MC curves. If production is governed by the $\sqrt{A \cdot B}$ function, then keeping the amount of factor B constant and vary-

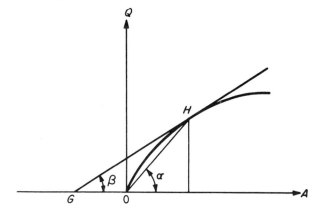

Fig. 6-7

ing factor A will yield a total output curve increasing at a decreasing rate as illustrated in Fig. 6-7.

Let average product of A be denoted by AP_a and, as before, marginal physical product of A be denoted by MPP_a; then, it is recalled from geometry that tan α equals AP_a and tan β equals MPP_a. If, as in Fig. 6-7, output increases at a decreasing rate, then tan α is always larger than tan β, and accordingly AP_a is always larger than MPP_a. (The line GH is tangent to the output curve at H, and the line $0H$ connects the point H with the origin.)

In Fig. 6-8 we show a more general case. Again, factor B is constant, and factor A is varied from zero to A_4. The output curve in Fig. 6-8a increases at an increasing rate from 0 to R, and it increases at a

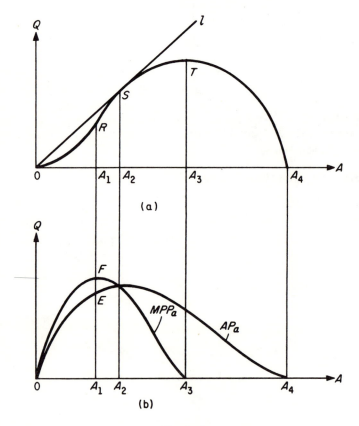

Fig. 6-8

decreasing rate from R to T. From T on, it decreases. Accordingly (in Fig. 6-8), MPP_a increases from 0 to A_1 .(corresponding to R) and it decreases from A_1 to A_3 (corresponding to T). From A_3 on, it takes on negative values. At any point between 0 and S on the output curve (Fig.

6-8a), the tangent cuts the A axis to the right of the origin. Accordingly, between 0 and A_2 (corresponding to S), MPP_a is larger than AP_a. Recall that if the marginal is larger than the average, the average increases. This is the reason why AP_a increases between 0 and A_2. The line denoted by l is tangent to the output curve at S, and it also connects S with the origin. Thus, at A_2, MPP_a equals AP_a. Beyond A_2 we are in a familiar world where both MPP_a and AP_a diminish.

If A is the only variable factor of production, then $MC = P_a/MPP_a$. Since P_a is given to the firm, MC will diminish in the range of output corresponding to $0A_1$. At the level of output yielded by $0A_1$, MC will attain its minimum point. This is true because MPP_a increases in the range $0A_1$, and beyond A_1, MPP_a diminishes. At any level of output corresponding to an input of A larger than $0A_1$, MC will be increasing. By the same reasoning, AVC will diminish up to the level of output corresponding to $0A_2$, and thereafter it will increase.

The elasticity of production with respect to factor A is the relative change in output divided by the relative change in the amount of factor A used. If we denote this elasticity by E, we obtain

$$E = \frac{\Delta Q/Q}{\Delta A/A} = \frac{\Delta Q}{\Delta A} \cdot \frac{A}{Q} = \frac{\Delta Q/\Delta A}{Q/A} = \frac{MPP_a}{AP_a}$$

Since in the range $0A_2$, MPP_a is larger than AP_a, E must be larger than 1. Assuming constant returns to scale this implies that MPP_b in the range $0A_2$ is negative. In order to prove this point, let us reproduce part of Fig. 6-8 in Fig. 6-9.

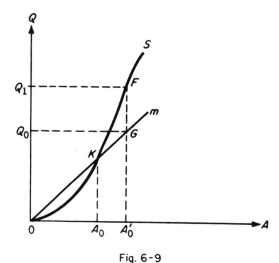

Fig. 6-9

Consider point K on the output curve (Fig. 6-9). If we increase factor A from A_0 to A'_0, and if at the same time we increase factor B by the same proportion of $(A'_0 - A_0)/A_0$, then output will also increase proportionately. Geometrically, the firm will expand along the line denoted by m passing through the origin and point K. The expansion will be from K to G. To point G corresponds an output of Q_0 units. If we divert the increment of factor B (ΔB) away from production, output will increase more than proportionately to $(A'_0 - A_0)/A_0$. In fact the firm will expand from K to F along the output curve, gaining an output of $Q_1 - Q_0$. Thus, the diversion of ΔB away from production gave rise to a gain of $Q_1 - Q_0$. Since $MPP_b = (Q_1 - Q_0)/\Delta B$, MPP_b must be negative because $Q_1 - Q_0$ is positive and ΔB is negative. If factor B were divisible, the firm could increase it (up to the amount in which it is fixed) proportionately to the increase in factor A, and MPP_b would not be negative. Thus we conclude that the negativity of MPP_b stems from the indivisibility of factor B which is fixed in the process of production.

We have stated without a proof that if the production function is governed by constant returns to scale, then AP_a and MPP_a are determined by the ratio of A/B. In Fig. 6-8, we derived the AP_a and MPP_a curves under the assumption that $B = B_0$. Thus, in Fig. 6-8, to A_1, B_0 correspond $AP_a = A_1E$ and $MPP_a = A_1F$. But the same AP_a ($= A_1E$) and MPP_a ($= A_1F$) will correspond to $2A_1, 2B_0$, or $3A_1, 3B_0$, or generally to KA_1, KB_0, where K is any positive number. In other words, in the case of constant returns to scale, the A axis in Fig. 6-8 can be replaced by an A/B axis. Notice however, that if A/B is used, the shape of the total output curve in Fig. 6-8a cannot be known.

In summary there are three stages of production. The first stage extends from the origin to all ratios equal to A_2/B_0. In this stage MPP_b is negative. The second stage extends from ratios equal to A_2/B_0 to ratios equal to A_3/B_0. In this stage both MPP_a and MPP_b are positive. The third stage extends from ratios equal to A_3/B_0 and on. In the third stage, MPP_a is negative. Thus the firm will avoid operating in the first and third stages. The first and the third stages are symmetrical. In the first stage MPP_b is negative because the ratio of B/A is very high: Too much of factor B is used per one unit of factor A. In the third stage MPP_a is negative because the ratio A/B is very high: Too much of factor A is used per one unit of B.

We leave it for the reader to draw the AP_b and MPP_b in Fig. 6-8b, where the ratio A/B increases from left to right and the ratio B/A increases from right to left.

MC AND UNAVOIDABLE FIXED COSTS

We have stated that in case the price is lower than the AC curve, the firm may not choose to discontinue production in the short run. This is illustrated in Fig. 6-10.

If the production function is $Q = \sqrt{A \cdot B}$, (or any other Cobb-Doug-

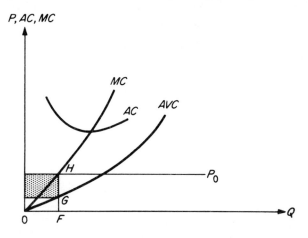

Fig. 6-10

las function) then both the MC and AVC curves are ascending. Both curves start at the origin, and the AVC curve is always lower than the MC curve. The price P_0 is lower than the AC (Fig. 6-10) and it intersects with the MC curve at point H. If the fixed cost is unavoidable, it will pay the firm to continue production in the short run at the $0F$ level: At zero production total loss would amount to the fixed cost. At a level of $0F$

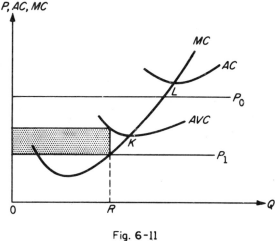

Fig. 6-11

units total loss would only amount to the fixed cost minus the shaded rectangle, where the shaded rectangle equals $0F$ times GH. If the fixed cost is avoidable by discontinuing production, then the firm would discontinue production in the short run.

If constant returns to scale is the only restriction imposed on the process of production then Fig. 6-11 rather than Fig. 6-10 illustrates the cost curves of the firm. If the price line is lower than L and higher than K, like P_0 in Fig. 6-11, then the analysis is similar to that of Fig. 6-10. However, if the price line is lower than point K, like P_1 in Fig. 6-11, then the firm would discontinue production in the short run: regardless of whether the fixed cost is avoidable or not, at the $0R$ level of production there is always an extra loss indicated by the shaded rectangle.

PROBLEMS

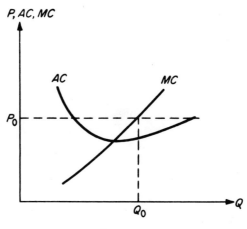

Prob. 6-1

6-1. You are the business manager of a firm which produces a certain commodity A. Your cost curves are described in the diagram. Currently the price is P_0, and you produce Q_0 of commodity A per unit of time. (a) Your friend suggests that you should lower the price in order to attract more customers. Do you agree? Why? (b) A relative of yours suggested that you should raise the price in order to increase profits. Do you agree? Why? (c) The government imposes on your firm a fixed tax of $500 per annum. Will you produce less after the law is enforced? (d) Labor is an important variable factor in your plant. After the wage rate rose 20 percent, your boss suggested that you increase production above Q_0 so as to catch up with what is lost on labor. Do you agree? Why?

Answer the following questions (6-2 to 6-7) as being True, False, or Uncertain.

6-2. Since by definition, there is only one price under competition, quantity discounts indicate the absence of competition.

6-3. A firm in a competitive industry does not have to know its marginal cost schedule in order to maximize profits.

6-4. An entrepreneur who operates two plants in a competitive industry should operate at a higher marginal cost in the larger plant.

6-5. The size of a competitive firm is indeterminate if all factors are variable.

6-6. Table 6-1 summarizes the cost curves of the firm. The price confronting the firm is $.80. The firm should not produce in the short run even if the fixed cost is unavoidable. Justify your answer numerically. Assume that the firm produces whole units.

6-7. The same as Prob. 6-6, except that the fixed cost is avoidable. The firm should not produce in the short run. Justify your answer numerically.

6-8. Show that when AC is rising,

$$\frac{\Delta C}{\Delta Q} > \frac{C}{Q}$$

SELECTED READINGS

KNIGHT, F. H. *Risk Uncertainty and Profit.* Boston: Houghton Mifflin Company, 1921.

SCITOVSKY, T. "A Note on Profit Maximization and Its Implications." Reprinted in *Readings in Price Theory*, eds. K. Boulding and G. Stigler. Homewood, Ill.: Richard D. Irwin, Inc., 1952.

STIGLER, G. J. *The Theory of Price.* New York: The Macmillan Company, 1966, Chapter 3.

APPENDIX

THE COBB-DOUGLAS CASE

Let $Q = K \cdot A^{\alpha} \cdot B^{\beta} \cdot C^{\gamma}$ be the production function. Recall that in equilibrium the entrepreneur will try to achieve the following equality:

$$\frac{MPP_a}{P_a} = \frac{MPP_b}{P_b} = \frac{MPP_c}{P_c} \quad \text{or} \quad \frac{\alpha Q/A}{P_a} = \frac{\beta Q/B}{P_b} = \frac{\gamma Q/C}{P_c}$$

or, if you consider two factors,

$$\frac{\alpha Q/A}{P_a} = \frac{\beta Q/B}{P_b}$$

then

$$\frac{P_b}{P_a} = \frac{\beta Q/B}{\alpha Q/A} \quad \text{or} \quad \frac{P_b}{P_a} = \frac{\beta \cdot A}{\alpha \cdot B}$$

METHODS OF DEPRECIATION

There are three methods of depreciation which are widely accepted.

We shall illustrate them by the following example: Consider a machine which is purchased at a price of $1,000. This machine, whose lifetime is 10 years, may be depreciated according to one of the following three methods which are customary in accounting.

1. *The Straight Line Method.* Here, the assumption is made that 1/10 of the original value of the machine is depreciated each year. Thus, 10 percent of the original value of the machine is the rate of depreciation. In general the rate is $(1/n)$ 100% for a lifetime of n years. In our example it is $100 per annum.

2. *The Declining Balance Method.* According to this method, instead of writing off an equal part each year one has to write off 10 percent of what is left over. Thus, during the first year, 10 percent of $1,000 is depreciated. This leaves $900. During the second year, 10 percent of $900 is written off which leaves $810, etc. Finally, whatever is left over for the tenth year is written off at the end of that year.

3. *The Sum of the Digits Method.* It can be proved that

$$1 + 2 + 3 + \cdots + (n - 1) + n = \frac{n(n + 1)}{2}$$

Thus,

$$1 + 2 + 3 + \cdots + 9 + 10 = \frac{10 \cdot 11}{2} = 55$$

Accordingly, during the first year 10/55 is written off, the rate for the second year is 9/55, and so on. The rate for the last year is 1/55. This method allows a generous depreciation during the "childhood" of the machine.

chapter 7

Some Problems Relating
to the MC Curve

In Chapter 6 we have shown that the marginal cost curve above the break-even point is also the supply curve of the firm. The student can at this point see for himself that the supply curve of the industry is the aggregate marginal cost curves of all the firms in the industry. The following chapter will be devoted to the process of aggregating the marginal cost curves of all the firms. However, before going into the process of adding all the marginal cost curves together, we ought to discuss some problems relating to shifting the marginal cost curve due to changes in prices of variable factors of production and changes in technology. This is carried out in this chapter. Other problems such as short- and long-run MC curves will also be disposed of in this chapter.

A CHANGE IN THE PRICE OF A FACTOR

When the price of a factor of production rises, the marginal cost also increases; or in other words, *ceteris paribus*, a rise in the price of a resource entails an upward shift in the MC curve, while a decline in the price of a factor gives rise to a downward shift in the MC curve.

Consider the case where only one factor is variable. Let us denote this factor by A. It is recalled that under such circumstances $MC = P_a/MPP_a$. When P_a rises, P_a/MPP_a rises too. When P_a falls, P_a/MPP_a falls too. In fact, it is obvious that when P_a increases, say 50 percent, P_a/MPP_a also increases 50 percent and accordingly MC increases 50 percent. Thus, consider our production function $Q = \sqrt{A \cdot B}$, where $A = 10$ man-hours and $B = 10$ machine-hours. Assume that the price of one man-hour is \$1. It is left up to the reader to show that $MPP_a = 0.50$ units. Then $MC = P_a/MPP_a = \$1/0.50 = \$2$. Namely, to a level of production of 10 units there corresponds a marginal cost of \$2. Since B is a factor which is fixed at 10 machine-hours regardless of what the price of A or B is, the only conceivable combination which will yield 10 units of output is 10 man-hours and the fixed amount of 10 machine-hours. Thus, if P_a rises to \$1.50, MC increases 50 percent, or

$$MC = \frac{P_a}{MPP_a} = \frac{\$1.5}{0.5} = \$3$$

Next, consider the case where all factors are variable. After the price of factor A rises, it pays the entrepreneur to substitute other factors for factor A. This is true because after P_a rises, the marginal product obtained from spending the last dollar on A is smaller than the marginal product obtained from spending the last dollar on factor B, from spending the last dollar on factor C, and so on up to the last factor. In order to determine the new magnitude of MC, we must substitute other factors for factor A while keeping the level of production unchanged. If we do not keep output fixed while we substitute other factors for A, we cannot say very much about the change in MC, because different values of MC may correspond to different outputs. In other words, MC will correspond to the original Q_0 units produced. Immediately after P_a rises, we have

$$\frac{MPP_{a0}}{P_{a1}} < \frac{MPP_{b0}}{P_{b0}} = \frac{MPP_{c0}}{P_{c0}} = \cdots = \frac{MPP_{n0}}{P_{n0}}, \; P_{a1} > P_{a0}$$

There is an incentive to substitute factors $B, C, \ldots, N$ for factor A. Due to the law of diminishing marginal productivity and/or dependence, a new point of equilibrium is reached where

$$\frac{P_{a1}}{MPP_{a1}} = \frac{P_{b0}}{MPP_{b1}} = \frac{P_{c0}}{MPP_{c1}} = \cdots = \frac{P_{n0}}{MPP_{n1}}$$

and the same Q_0 is produced. Our task is to show that the new MC, which is equal to P_a/MPP_a, P_b/MPP_b, etc., is higher than the original MC. Consider any of the other factors, say factor B. After the price of A rises the entrepreneur starts to change the proportion against factor A. This is done by employing more of all other factors and less of A.

As indicated in Figs. 7-1 and 7-2, when B is substituted for A, MPP_b falls from MPP_{b0} to MPP_{b1}. This is true because the MPP_b curve shifts downward (from the curve corresponding to A_0 to the curve corresponding to A_1) and also because of the law of diminishing marginal physical product (the MPP_b curve is negatively sloped!). But the price of B is unchanged at P_{b0}. Accordingly, we have

$$\frac{P_{b0}}{MPP_{b0}} < \frac{P_{b0}}{MPP_{b1}}$$

since

$$MPP_{b1} < MPP_{b0}$$

But the original MC was equal to P_{b0}/MPP_{b0} and the new MC is equal to P_{b0}/MPP_{b1}, thus the new MC is higher. Of course, the new MC is also equal to the new P_a/MPP_a, because B is substituted for A just until a new point of equilibrium is achieved where the same amount of Q_0 is produced and

$$\frac{P_{a1}}{MPP_{a1}} = \frac{P_{b0}}{MPP_{b1}} = \text{new } MC$$

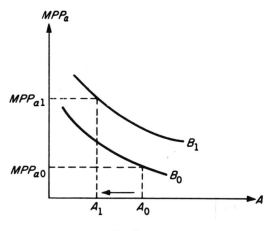

Fig. 7-1

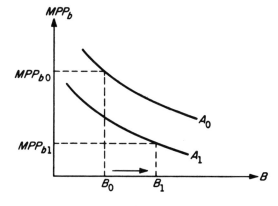

Fig. 7-2

Let us illustrate this by using our $Q = \sqrt{A \cdot B}$ production function. Assume that originally $P_a = \$1$, $P_b = \$1$, and $A = 10$ man-hours, $B = 10$ machine-hours. It is left up to the reader to show that $MPP_a = 0.50$ units and $MPP_b = 0.50$ units. Then the producer has no incentive to change the proportion between the factors because

$$\frac{P_a}{MPP_a} = \frac{P_b}{MPP_b} = MC = \$2$$

Let us assume that the price of A rises to $\$4$, We present the producer with the following problem: If you must produce 10 units as before, what is the *minimum* marginal cost corresponding to it? The minimum marginal cost will be attained by substituting enough B for A so as to come to a new equilibrium where $P_a/MPP_a = P_b/MPP_b$. The producer will substitute B for A just until $A = 5$ man-hours and $B = 20$ machine-hours. Output is the same because $\sqrt{5 \cdot 20} = 10$ units. It is left up to the student to show that now $MPP_a = 1$ unit and $MPP_b = 0.25$ units, thus

$$\frac{P_a}{MPP_a} = \frac{P_b}{MPP_b} = MC = \$4$$

$$\frac{\$4}{1} = \frac{\$1}{0.25}$$

Note, however, that MC does not increase in the same proportion as the increase in the price of the factor. This is true because in a case where the factors are variable, the entrepreneur can reduce the effect of the higher price of one factor by changing the proportion in favor of the relatively inexpensive factors.

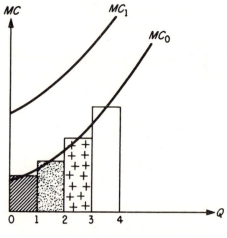

Fig. 7-3

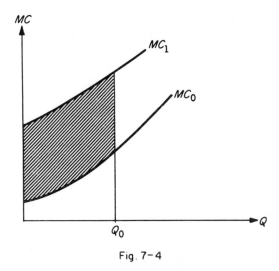

Fig. 7-4

Figure 7-3 summarizes this analysis: after the price of one of the factors rises, the MC curve shifts upwards from MC_0 to MC_1.

What about the AC curve? Where does it shift? Intuitively one feels that the AC curve should shift upward. This is true, and it can be proved as follows: The area below the MC curve is equal to total variable cost. Consider Fig. 7-3. When there is no production only total fixed cost exists. When one unit is produced, the additional variable cost involved is one unit times the corresponding MC, or the shaded rectangle. When the second unit is added, the additional variable cost is one unit times the corresponding MC, which is indicated by the dotted rectangle. When the third unit is added, the extra variable cost is the rectangle marked by pluses, and so on up to the last unit. But these rectangles approximate the area below the MC curve and thus the area below the MC curve is equal to total variable cost. Next, consider Fig. 7-4. After the MC curve shifted from MC_0 to MC_1, total variable cost incurred by producing Q_0 increased by an amount of money that is equal to the shaded area. This means that total cost and average cost have increased. In other words, the AC curve shifts upward along with the MC curve (this is not illustrated in Fig. 7-4).

On the other hand, a decline in the price of a factor of production entails a downward shift in the MC curve, and a downward shift in the AC curve.

TECHNOLOGICAL PROGRESS: A SPECIAL CASE

Technological progress is achieved through better organization and management, through changing the technical process of production, or by educating and training manpower. We shall now discuss a simple but useful case known as the neutral shift in the production function. The economist would summarize it as follows: A plant produces Q_0 units of output when employing a certain set of factors of production per unit of time. After the technological progress takes place, the same plant will produce more than Q_0 units by employing the same set of factors of production per unit of time. We can illustrate this with our simple production function as follows: Our production function is $Q = \sqrt{A \times B}$, where Q is output, A stands for labor, and B stands for services rendered by machines. This production function can be written

$$Q = K\sqrt{A \times B}$$

So far we assumed that $K = 1$; thus we could have ignored the coefficient K, because $1 \times \sqrt{A \times B} = \sqrt{A \times B}$. Let us assume that a technological innovation is introduced into the plant such that productivity increases 10 percent. Namely, employing the same set of factors of production will result in producing 10 percent more than prior to the change in technology. This means that after the change, K is equal to 1.1

Example: Prior to the change, employing 10 machine-hours and 10 man-hours would result in $Q = 1 \sqrt{10 \times 10} = 10$ units of output. After the change, the same set of 10 machine-hours and 10 man-hours yields $Q = 1.1 \sqrt{10 \times 10} = 11$ units of output.

Next, consider the marginal physical product of the factor of production A

$$MPP_a = \frac{\Delta Q}{\Delta A} = \frac{Q_1 - Q_0}{A_1 - A_0}$$

Let us denote output after the technological change by $\overline{Q}$. Also, let MPP_a and ΔQ after the change be denoted by $\overline{MPP_a}$ and $\Delta \overline{Q}$. Then

$$\overline{MPP_a} = \frac{\Delta \overline{Q}}{\Delta A} = \frac{\overline{Q_1} - \overline{Q_0}}{A_1 - A_0} = \frac{1.1\,Q_1 - 1.1\,Q_0}{A_1 - A_0}$$

$$= \frac{1.1\,(Q_1 - Q_0)}{A_1 - A_0} = \frac{1.1\,\Delta Q}{\Delta A} = 1.1\,MPP_a$$

Therefore, if the technological change is to increase productivity of the plant by 10 percent, then MPP_a will also increase 10 percent, or simply $\overline{MPP_a} = 1.1 \times MPP_a$. The same holds with respect to MPP_b, MPP_c, and other factors. Since MC equals the price of the factor divided by its MPP, the marginal cost will be lower as follows:

$$\frac{P_a}{1.1\,MPP_a} = \frac{P_b}{1.1\,MPP_b} = \cdots = \frac{P_n}{1.1\,MPP_n} = 0.9MC_0$$

As a result of a technological progress the marginal cost curve shifts downward. Percentagewise the downward shift in MC is not equal to the increase in productivity.

The problem of measuring technological progress is unsettled and very complicated. It is not in the scope of this chapter to enter into the technical details involved. However, a simple example may shed some light on the problem. Consider one particular industry, or the economy as a whole. Let us assume that over a period of time both employment of labor and capital services have doubled, but output, or Gross National Product $G.N.P.$ has tripled. Assuming constant returns to scale, doubling labor and capital would bring about doubled production. Accordingly, what is left as a residue can be explained by the technological progress. In the previous example, this can be rationalized as follows: Assume that originally $Q_0 = K\sqrt{A_0 \times B_0}$ where $K = 1$. Let us assume that during the period of time under consideration, productivity increased 50 percent. Thus, originally,

$$Q_0 = 1 \cdot \sqrt{A_0 \cdot B_0} = \sqrt{A_0 \cdot B_0}$$

and after a period of time,

$$Q_1 = 1.5\sqrt{2A_0 \cdot 2B_0} = 3\sqrt{A_0 \cdot B_0} = 3 \cdot Q_0$$

The student who is interested in the case where factors are not necessarily increased proportionately is referred to the Mathematical Appendix.

EXTERNAL DISECONOMIES

So far we have not defined the concept of supply which will be covered in the next chapter. For the time being, we shall be satisfied with the following definition of supply: The supply function tells what are the quantities supplied at different minimum prices. To put it differently, suppose you have in mind a certain quantity of a certain product per unit of time. Denote this quantity by Q_0. Then you ask the following question: What is the minimum price which will induce producers to supply Q_0 units of output per unit of time? If P_0 is the answer, then the pair Q_0 and P_0 is one point on the supply curve. Normally, in order to persuade producers to supply a quantity larger than Q_0, the price has to be larger than P_0; thus, *the supply curve is positively sloped*. One can conceive a supply curve of a factor of production as well as a supply curve of a commodity. Thus, one can conceive a positively sloped supply curve of labor. In order to increase the quantity supplied of labor, the minimum wage offered must increase.

An industry may be facing a positively sloped supply curve of labor. The common sense of this statement is the following: If the industry as a whole should expand it would like to employ more labor, but in order to attract more labor to the industry, wages will have to be raised. When one firm or a few firms decide to expand, they cannot exert influence on wages simply because the amount of labor employed by one firm or a few firms is negligible. But, when all firms decide to expand, they have to attract a significant additional amount of labor. They can do it only by raising wages. The reader should note that the industry may be facing positively sloped supply curves of factors of production other than labor. Labor was chosen only for the sake of demonstration. This is summarized in Fig. 7-5.

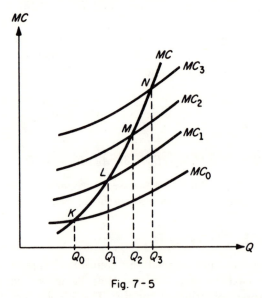

Fig. 7 - 5

Currently the firm produces Q_0. If the prices of factors of production are given to it, then MC_0 is the relevant curve. To put it differently, if the firm is the only one which is currently expanding, then it is expanding along the MC_0 curve. Let us assume that all firms decided to expand, and the firm under consideration also expanded. Assume that it has expanded from Q_0 to Q_1. Since the entire industry expanded, and assuming a positively sloped supply curve of labor, the firm faces a higher wage rate; and as shown earlier in this chapter, this implies an upward shift in the MC curve, say, from MC_0 to MC_1. Again, MC_1 is relevant if we assume that only one firm is expanding. But if all firms expand, then when our firm expands along with others, say from Q_1 to Q_2, the wage rate increases further, and the MC curve shifts upward from MC_1 to MC_2, and so on. Thus, when all firms expand, we may say that due to external diseconomies the relevant MC curve is the one passing through

KLMN. It should be noted that in this case this *MC* may be a short-run phenomenon. The reason is that there is a good chance that when one industry expands another industry contracts. Let the expanding industry be denoted by *X* and the contracting by *Y*. A change in tastes in favor of *X* and against *Y* may explain this phenomenon. To the first approximation the wage rate in *X* rises; thus, firms who are in industry *X* expand along an *MC*-type curve which passes through *KLMN* in Fig. 7-5 rather than along an MC_0-type curve. Meanwhile firms in the contracting industry *Y* lay off resources. These released resources will seek employment elsewhere. For example, workers will move to industry *X*, where wages are becoming more attractive. In other words, the supply of labor curve confronted by industry *X* will shift to the right. This is equivalent to saying that the minimum wage in industry *X* that is necessary to attract a certain amount of labor will be lower, or the *MC* curve passing through *KLMN* will, in the long run, be very close to MC_0. Here the *long run* means allowing a sufficient amount of time for resources released from industry *Y* to move to the expanding industry *X*.

SHORT- AND LONG-RUN MC CURVES

In Chapter 6 we have shown that if we assume constant returns to scale and two variable factors, the long-run *MC* curve is a flat line. If one factor plays the role of entrepreneurial capacity and assuming that the entrepreneurial capacity is fixed, then the long-run *MC* is an ascending curve. Let us assume that in addition to the entrepreneur, three other factors of production are employed. Denote them by *A*, *B*, and *C*. Then, along the long-run *MC* curve the following holds:

$$\frac{MPP_a}{P_a} = \frac{MPP_b}{P_b} = \frac{MPP_c}{P_c} = \frac{1}{MC}$$

This is the optimal situation, in the sense that *MC* is at its lowest level. Let us focus on Fig. 7-6. Consider point *S* on the long-run *MC* curve which corresponds to Q_0 units of output. If the firm expands, but it does not have sufficient amount of time to vary factor *A*, then factor *A* becomes temporarily fixed. Accordingly, the firm cannot attain the optimal arrangement where the marginal physical product obtained from the last dollar spent on *A* is equal to the marginal physical product obtained from the last dollar spent on *B* and on *C*, respectively. The only choice left for the firm is to maintain the equality

$$\frac{MPP_b}{P_b} = \frac{MPP_c}{P_c} = \frac{1}{MC_a}$$

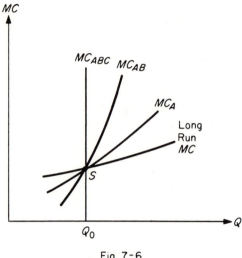

Fig. 7-6

But this is short of the optimum. To put it differently, the short-run MC_A which corresponds to a fixed factor A is higher than the long-run MC when quantity is larger than Q_0, etc. Thus, in this intermediate short run the firm would expand along MC_A.

If the period of adjustment is shorter so that both A and B are fixed, the proportions among the factors will be even "less optimal" than the proportion corresponding to moving along MC_A; namely, the firm would move along a higher MC curve which is denoted by MC_{AB}. Finally, if all factors are fixed, which happens in the shortest run, the firm cannot expand. This is indicated by the vertical MC_{ABC}.

THE PRODUCER'S SURPLUS

It is recalled that at the price P_0 the quantity supplied by the firm is Q_0 as indicated in Fig. 7-7. The area indicated by OQ_0GP_0 is total revenue, i.e., price times the quantity. The shaded area equals the total variable cost. Thus, the residue which is the dotted area equals the payments made to all fixed factors, one of which is the entrepreneur. If MC is the long-run curve in the sense that the entrepreneur is the only fixed factor, then the dotted area approximates the returns to the entrepreneur including both his alternative cost and the rent. This is sometimes called the *producer's surplus*.

.Consider a change in the producer's surplus due to a rise in the price from P_0 to P_1. This change equals the area indicated by EHP_1 minus EGP_0, which is P_0GHP_1. As stated before, the producer's surplus consists of a fixed cost which does not change plus rent. Let us denote the producer's surplus by PS. Then we have

$$EHP_1 = PS_1 = FC + \text{rent}_1$$
$$EGP_0 = PS_0 = FC + \text{rent}_0$$

$$P_0GHP_1 = PS_1 - PS_0 = FC - FC + \text{rent}_1 - \text{rent}_0$$
$$= \text{rent}_1 - \text{rent}_0$$

that is,

$$\Delta PS = \Delta \text{rent}$$

This proves that *change* in the producer's surplus equals the change in rent.

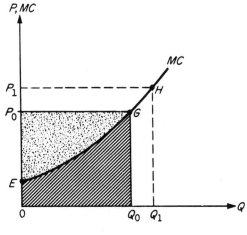

Fig. 7-7

JOINT PRODUCTS

Fixed Proportions. There are many cases where one industry is engaged in producing joint products in fixed proportions. For example, raisers of cattle produce many kinds of meat, and they produce them in fixed proportions. Let us simplify the whole complex by assuming that they produce good parts of meat which we denote by G and bad parts which we denote by B. Then it can be shown that the optimal point of production is just where $P_b + P_g = MC$, where MC relates to the unit which includes one part of B and one part of G. This is illustrated in Fig. 7-8. MC is the marginal cost with respect to the joint product. The marginal cost with respect to commodity G can be conceived as a residue; namely, it is MC of the joint product minus the price of B as determined

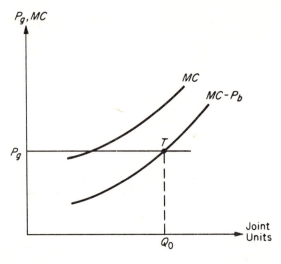

Fig. 7-8

in the market. Thus, MC of G, which is $MC - P_b$, intersects with the price at point T. There Q_0 joint units are produced. Also at T we have

$$P_g = MC - P_b$$

Adding P_b to both sides of the equality gives

$$P_b + P_g = MC$$

It is left up to the student to show the same thing by drawing the P_b price line and $MC - P_g$.

In summary, if more than two products are produced, say n products, then the firm will produce where the following holds:

$$MC = P_a + P_b + P_c + \cdots + P_n$$

Variable Proportions.   Consider the case where two or more products are made by the same plant, but the different products can be made in different proportions. Here, there are marginal costs and functions relating to each product separately. What are the combinations that will yield the maximum profit? If two commodities are produced by the firm, say X and Y, then the answer is

$$MC_x = P_x \qquad \text{and} \qquad MC_y = P_y$$

Note, however, that this theory is nonoperational. What we need in order to make the theory operational is the relationship between MC_x and Y and MC_y and X. We have already established that MC_x is positively sloped with respect to X. For the very same reasons, MC_x may rise when more of Y is produced and MC_y may rise when more of X is produced! Thus, let us assume that the equilibrium is disturbed by a decline in the price of Y. Then, less of Y is produced, but the MC_x shifts rightward, so that more of X will be produced. If the price of Y should rise, then the firm would increase the production of Y. But the MC_x would shift upward, thus less of X will be produced. It is left up to the reader to analyze the effect of a change in the price of X on both X and Y.

PROBLEMS

7-1. Labor is the only variable factor employed in your plant. Regardless of the level of production it always takes 2 man-hours to produce one additional unit of output. Currently the cost of labor is $1 per hour. (a) Draw the MC curve. (b) Draw the MC curve after the cost of labor rises to $1.25.

7-2. A competitive firm produces X and Y in fixed proportions: One unit of X with one unit of Y. The marginal cost of a joint unit of X and Y is given by the equation $MC = 1 + 2Z$, where Z is a joint unit. How many joint units should the firm produce if the market price of X is $2 and of Y $3?

7-3. The production of whatnots involves water pollution. In order to obtain the means necessary for clearing the water, the government imposed a tax of 5 cents per what-not produced. This tax is to be paid by firms producing what-nots. Draw the MC curve of a what-not-producing firm before and after the tax is imposed.

7-4. You produce a certain product A which is sold in a perfect market. Currently you produce 100 units per month. The price is $12 apiece. If you were to produce 106 units, extra costs would be as follows:

Labor	$15
Raw materials	35
Electricity	8
Other items	2

(a) Estimate MC when production is in the neighborhood of 100 units. (b) Should you expand or contract? (c) Suppose you have decided to expand to 106 units. By how much would the producer's surplus increase or decrease?

7-5. The marginal cost curve is currently $MC = 1 + 2Q$. A technological change gives rise to a 20 percent neutral shift in the production function. What is the new marginal cost curve?

7-6. Labor is a variable factor of production. A 20 percent rise in the price of labor will shift the marginal cost curve of the firm by *at most* 20 percent. Explain.

chapter 8

The Theory of Supply

In Chapter 6 we have shown that the marginal cost curve of an individual firm in competition is also its supply curve. In Chapter 7 we discussed some important problems relating to the marginal cost curve. In this chapter we shall derive the supply curve of the industry by aggregating the marginal cost curves of all the firms in the industry. Note that with this chapter, the theory of producers is completed, and we have all the tools necessary to analyze the competitive market.

THE RELATIONSHIP BETWEEN THE SUPPLY AND THE MC

The supply function of a certain commodity X is the total horizontal sum of all the MC functions of all the firms producing commodity X. Notice that all the firms producing commodity X constitute the industry of X. Or, to put it differently, the supply curve is obtained by horizontally adding all the MC curves (adjusted for external effects) of all the firms in one industry. A more general definition with which the student is familiar is the following: The supply function is a law telling us what the minimum price is which will induce producers in a particular industry to supply a certain quantity. Consider one individual firm. Recall that for the firm the MC curve tells us how much the firm will produce given a minimum price. Namely, the MC is the supply curve of the firm. Accordingly, the aggregate MC curve is the supply curve of the industry. Even though an industry is a concept which is understood intuitively, it is worth defining it as all the firms in the economy which are currently engaged in producing a certain commodity. The derivation of the supply curve from the marginal cost curves of four firms is illustrated in Table 8-1. Note that this is meant to be only a technical demonstration, because if there are only four firms, they probably cannot be competitive. Thus, the assumption is made that the firms behave as if they are competitive: they have no influence on the price of the commodity they make.

The supply curve can be drawn by plotting the points representing the following pairs: $0 and 0 units, $1 and 0 units, $2 and 0 units, $3 and 27 units, $4 and 68 units, etc. This is left up to the reader.

TABLE 8-1

Price	Supply of				
	Firm A	Firm B	Firm C	Firm D	Total (2)+(3)+(4)+(5)
(1)	(2)	(3)	(4)	(5)	(6)
0	0	0	0	0	0
1	0	0	0	0	0
2	0	0	0	0	0
3	27	0	0	0	27
4	40	28	0	0	68
5	60	49	41	0	150
6	61	62	47	0	170
7	69	68	53	35	225
8	73	47	60	40	250

There is not even one firm that can produce at a price below $3. The reason is that there are no firms with an average cost below $3. Firm A enters the industry when the minimum price is $3. In other words, the lowest point on its AC curve is in the neighborhood of $3. Firm B enters the industry when the price is $4 or more, and so on. The last firm to enter is D. The lowest point on its AC curve is around $7. Firm D whose *minimum AC* is the *highest* in the industry is sometimes called the *marginal firm*. Normally, the marginal firm is the least profitable in the sense that its rent is the smallest. It is recalled that the rent is estimated by $Q(P - AC)$, where AC includes a component of the alternative cost of the entrepreneurial services. Since the price is the same for all firms, and since the AC curve of the marginal firm occupies the highest position, $P - AC$ of the marginal firm is probably the lowest. However, the rent of the marginal firm will be the smallest only under the assumption that output of the marginal firm is either smaller than, or equal to the output of the other firms, respectively. But, it is possible that output of the marginal firm will be relatively large. This may make up for the small value of $P - AC$.

A RISE IN THE PRICE OF A FACTOR OF PRODUCTION

It was shown in Chapter 7 that a rise in the price of a variable factor of production gives rise to an upward shift in the MC curve, while a decline in the price of a variable factor of production results in a downward shift in the MC curve. Accordingly, for the industry as a whole, a rise in the price of a factor of production entails an upward shift in the supply curve, while a decline in the price of a factor of production entails a downward movement. (It is again recalled that a downward shift is identical with a rightward shift and an upward shift is identical with a leftward shift.)

The reader can verify that in the rare case where the supply curve is negatively sloped, a downward shift is identical with a leftward shift and vice versa. Notice that we refer to the MC curve passing through $K, L, M,$ and N in Fig. 7-5, which takes into consideration external diseconomies.

TECHNOLOGICAL PROGRESS

Sometimes the industry as a whole benefits from the same technological innovation. For example, the invention of hybrid corn increased the productivity of growing corn by about 15 percent. Sooner or later all farmers benefited technologically from this invention. The marginal cost curves of corn growers shifted downwards, and the supply curve shifted along with it. Normally, technological innovations are adopted by all the firms in the industry. Some firms adopt new methods of production immediately after they become available; other firms hesitate before they decide to use the new method.

There is a rise of profits for the firms that first put in the innovation. As shown in Chapter 7, the MC curve of the firm that uses the innovation shifts downward leading to an increase in its rent. This rise in rent induces other firms to adopt the same innovation, and eventually all the firms in the industry will be using it. All this is true provided that the innovation is available.

SHORT-RUN AND LONG-RUN SUPPLY CURVES

There are two reasons why there should be short-run and long-run supply curves. First, as indicated in Chapter 7, there are short-run and long-run MC curves corresponding to different firms. Thus, when the price is rising very rapidly, most of the firms can vary only one or two factors of production. These firms will expand along their short-run MC curves, and the short-run supply curve is simply the aggregate short-run MC curve. Secondly, a potential producer will not enter the industry immediately after the price is above the lowest point on his AC curve. The potential producer will start to produce only after he expects the new high price to be permanent. In order to become convinced that the new price is not a temporary one, the entrepreneur will wait a while before doing anything.

The same problem arises when the price falls. Facing a falling price, a firm will lay off only current resources such as labor and raw materials. It takes a short period of time to change the amount of current resources used in production. But changing the amount of services rendered by machines and buildings takes a longer period of time. It is very rare that a firm will sell a machine when the price of the product it makes is

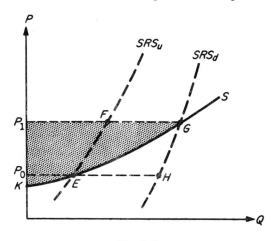

Fig. 8-1

falling. First of all, firms that produce the same product have an incentive to get rid of identical or comparable machinery. This fact reduces the chance of finding a customer for the machine. Furthermore, different firms employ engineers with different ideas. Thus, once installed in a particular plant, it becomes technically difficult to reinstall a machine elsewhere. So the only thing that is left for the entrepreneur to do is to either scrap a fraction of his machinery, or else use it until it is completely depreciated. Finally, when the price falls, marginal firms find themselves operating at a loss. Their AC curve is above the price line. These firms will quit producing sooner or later. As indicated in Chapter 6, even though these firms are not breaking even, they might continue to produce in the short run.

The mechanism that sets the price of a commodity in the market will be explained in the following chapter. So, in order to simplify we shall assume that the price is somehow determined in the market. Thus, in Fig. 8-1, for a long period of time the price was set at P_0. Suddenly, let us say by a miracle, the price of the commodity under consideration rose to P_1, and the price is going to stay at the level of P_1 for a long period of time. All that producers know is that they can sell as much as they want to at the

P_1 price. Originally, the industry was at point E as indicated by the long-run supply curve denoted by S. However, due to the reasons previously mentioned, the industry will expand along a short-run supply curve SRS_u. The temporary point of equilibrium is F. If the price is going to stay at P_1 for a long period of time, firms will be able to employ more factors that were considered fixed in the short run. Moreover, potential firms will enter the industry. If after a long enough period of adjustment not more than P_1G is forthcoming, then G is a point on the long-run supply curve. Assume that for a long period of time the price stayed at P_1, but then, for one reason or another it falls back to its original level of P_0. The industry will contract along the short-run supply curve denoted by SRS_d. Thus, in the short run, P_0H units of output will be supplied. But, allowing for a period of adjustment, firms that are still breaking even will have written off a sufficient fraction of their machinery and heavy equipment, and firms that are not breaking even will quit producing. This will bring the industry back to Point E on the long-run supply curve.

Let us now return to Fig. 8-1. When the price rises from P_0 to P_1, the industry expands along its supply curve. This expansion is achieved due to the fact that firms which are already in the industry produce more and new firms join the industry. Note that when the price of one commodity rises the price of another commodity probably falls, thus another industry probably cuts down in its production. This is achieved partly by firms that stay in the contracting industry producing less and partly through firms discontinuing production. This theory implies that in a dynamic economy that is governed by a free exchange competitive market many new firms will organize and many existing firms will go out of business each year. Statistics[1] indicate that this is the case. In 1950, 4,000,000 firms operated in the United States. In 1960 this figure reached·a level of over 4,500,000. During this period, about 350,000 new firms have organized annually, and some 300,000 firms have discontinued production each year.

THE PRODUCER'S SURPLUS

The producer's surplus is the shaded area indicated by $KEGFP_1$, in Fig. 8-1. It is left up to the reader to show that this area is the aggregate producer's surplus of all firms respectively.

THE SUPPLY OF FACTORS OF PRODUCTION

The same theory of supply applies both to the case of finished goods and to the case of factors of production which are sometimes called producer's goods.

[1] The figures given exclude farms and professional enterprises.

There is, however, an especially interesting case, which is the supply curve of labor. Consider first of all the supply curve of one worker. In Fig. 8-2, the horizontal axis represents hours supplied per week, and the vertical axis is the hourly wage rates. It is possible that when the wage rate is above a certain level W_2, the supply curve of labor relating to a particular worker will become negatively sloped. This can be explained as follows: the wage rate may also be looked at as the price of leisure. For

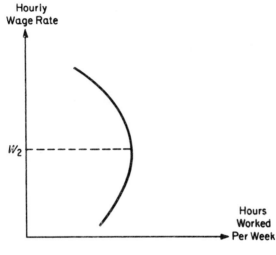

Fig. 8-2

example, if I decide to work an additional hour on Wednesday, it is equivalent to saying that I decide to sell one hour of leisure on Wednesday. On the other hand, if I decide to work seven hours instead of eight hours, it is equivalent to saying that I decide to buy one additional hour of leisure. In both cases the price per hour of leisure is equal to the hourly wage rate, because the sacrifice involved in obtaining one hour of leisure is roughly equal to the hourly wage rate foregone.[2]

Let us assume that leisure is a superior good. When the wage rate rises, the consumer has a higher income available. Accordingly, he tends to spend more on all superior commodities. Since leisure is superior, he tends to spend more on leisure, i.e., to work less hours. But, at the same time, a rising wage rate is identical with a rising price of leisure. When the price of leisure rises, the marginal utility derived from spendng the last dollar on leisure becomes smaller. Thus, the consumer has an incentive to substitute other commodities for leisure, or simply to work more hours.

---

[2] To be more precise, the price per hour of leisure equals the hourly wage rate minus a compensation for the unpleasantness involved in work.

In summary, the effect of the higher income is to buy more leisure, that is, to work less; but the substitution effect is to buy less leisure, i.e., to work more hours. In Fig. 8-2, when the wage rate is below W_2, the substitution effect dominates the effect of a larger income. When the wage rate is above W_2, the reverse holds. The so-called *backward-bending* supply curve of labor in Fig. 8-2 explains why there is a trend to work shorter weeks and shorter days in Western countries. The working day is now eight and sometimes seven hours instead of ten hours or more as it was a few decades ago. For many Americans the working week is five days. A working week of six days is not too far in the past. The shorter working period is due to the fact that in the United States and other advanced countries, the higher wage rate has reached a point above which the supply curve of labor is backward-bending.

THE INDIFFERENCE MAP APPROACH TO THE BACKWARD-BENDING SUPPLY CURVE OF LABOR

Consider the indifference map in Fig. 8-3. At point A, utility is maximized. This is true because we assume that the utility corresponding

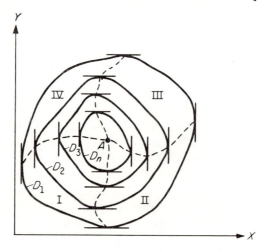

Fig. 8-3

to the indifference curve indicated by D_2 is larger than the utility corresponding to the indifference curve indicated by D_1, etc. It is left as an exercise for the student to show that in region I both X and Y are sources of utility. In region II, X is a source of disutility and Y is a source of utility. In region III, both X and Y are sources of disutility, and in region IV, X is a source of utility and Y is a source of disutility. (HINT: A commodity is a source of utility if, *ceteris paribus*, when you consume more of it your utility increases.)

Let us consider the process of laboring. Even though many workers will testify that for them the process of laboring involves pleasure, it is very likely that on the margin it is a source of disutility. Accordingly, if X is labor and Y is all other goods and services, region II in Fig. 8-3 is the relevant one.

What is the budget line representing different combinations of labor and all other commodities? The consumer faces fixed prices of all other commodities and the wage rate is given. If he does not work, the budget of the worker is zero. But when he starts to work, he moves on a straight budget line, because with an additional income paid for an additional hour of work he can get the same additional combination of goods and services with the provision that prices are given. It is left up to the reader to show that when the wage rate increases, the budget line rotates counter-clockwise about the origin. This is illustrated in Fig. 8-4, where the wage rate rises from W_1 to W_2, from W_2 to W_3, etc. When the wage rate rises from W_1 to W_2, the worker moved from point K to point L. At L he works more, but he can consume more of all other goods and services (excluding leisure). But, when the wage rate rises from W_2 to W_3 and from W_3 to W_4,

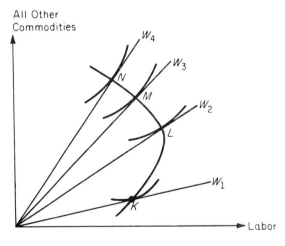

Fig. 8-4

the worker prefers to work less, as indicated by points M and N. In other words, from point L and on, when the wage rate is above W_2 the effect of a larger income dominates the substitution effect with respect to leisure.

Consider the following problem: You are an employer. You try to convince your workers to work more hours per day. You can try to do it either by raising the hourly wage rate, or, you can leave the hourly wage rate the same for the first eight hours, but increase the wage rate paid for the ninth hour, tenth hour, etc. You will find it instructive to use a diagram comparable to Fig. 8-4 in order to show that the second method is preferable to the first one.

SUPPLY ELASTICITY

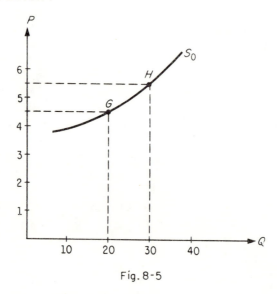

Fig. 8-5

The supply elasticity which is denoted by ϵ (epsilon) is defined as the relative change in the quantity supplied divided by the relative change in price. This is equivalent to the percentage change in the quantity supplied per 1 percent change in price. It can be written as

$$\epsilon = \frac{\Delta Q/Q}{\Delta P/P} = \frac{\%\ \text{change in quantity supplied}}{\%\ \text{change in the price}}$$

For example, S_0 in Fig. 8-5 is the supply curve of a certain commodity. When the price rises from \$4.5 to \$5.5, the quantity supplied increases from 20 billion bushels to 30 billion bushels. The supply elasticity in the neighborhood denoted by GH can be estimated as

$$\overline{P} = \frac{4.5 + 5.5}{2} = \$5$$

$$\Delta P = 5.5 - 4.5 = \$1$$

$$\overline{Q} = \frac{20 + 30}{2} = 25$$

$$\Delta Q = 30 - 20 = 10$$

then

$$\epsilon = \frac{10/25}{1/5} = \frac{40\%}{20\%} = 2$$

It is left up to the reader to explain why the supply elasticity is positive under normal conditions.

Example: The elasticity of the supply curve of labor faced by Industry Z is estimated as 4. By how much will the wage rate have to rise in order to increase labor employment by 16 percent. Denote the required change in the wage rate by X; then,

$$4 = \frac{16\%}{X}$$

Solving for X we obtain $X = 4\%$; namely, a 4 percent wage rise will entail a 16 percent increase in the amount of labor supplied.

Example: If the supply elasticity of a certain commodity is ⅓, by how much will the quantity supplied decrease resulting from a 9 percent decrease in the price? Let the change in the quantity supplied be denoted by X. then we have

$$\frac{1}{3} = \frac{X}{-9\%}$$

Solving for X gives

$$X = -3\%$$

Finally, note that the *quantity supplied* changes when we move along the same supply curve. The *supply* changes when we move from one supply curve to another. If supply elasticity is larger than one, then the supply curve is known to be elastic; and if the reverse holds, the supply curve is inelastic. In the case of an elastic supply curve, a small change in price will induce a relatively large change in the quantity supplied. For example, if supply elasticity is 2, then a 3 percent rise in price will induce a 6 percent increase in the quantity supplied. If the supply curve is inelastic, say supply elasticity is ½, then a 3 percent rise in price will only induce a 1.5 percent increase in the quantity supplied.

PROBLEMS

8-1. Supply elasticity is equal to 3. By how much will production increase as a result of a 10 percent rise in price?

8-2. It is believed that, other things unchanged, raising the salaries of teachers by 15 percent will entail a 30 percent increase in the number of people who apply for openings in schools. Estimate the supply elasticity of teachers!

8-3. Supply elasticity is $\frac{1}{2}$. $P_0 = 10\text{¢}$. What is the necessary (absolute) change in price which will induce a 10 percent increase in the quantity supplied?

8-4. Currently the supply of industry A amounts to 100 units. The prevailing price is $10, and elasticity is estimated at 2. Estimate the additional producer's surplus and additional total variable costs resulting from a $1 rise in the price. (Use P_0 and Q_0 to estimate ΔQ.)

Answer questions 8-5 to 8-8 as being True, False or Uncertain.

8-5. Raising the standards in economics departments will shift the supply curve of economists to the left.

8-6. Labor and electricity are the only variable factors of production in the whatnot industry. Currently the wage rate is $1 per hour. If the wage rate increases 25 cents, then the supply curve of whatnots will shift 25 percent upward. Assume that the whatnot industry cannot affect the wage rate in the labor market.

8-7. Labor is the only variable factor in the whatnot industry. Currently the wage rate is $1 per hour. If the wage rate increases 25 cents, then the supply curve of whatnots will shift 25 percent upward. Assume that the whatnot industry cannot affect the wage rate in the labor market.

8-8. Imposing an annual fixed tax of $5,000 per annum on each firm in industry A will not affect the supply curve of industry A because a fixed tax does not change the MC curve. (HINT: Focus on the marginal firms!)

8-9. Prove that if the supply curve is a straight line starting at the origin, supply elasticity always equals one.

SELECTED READINGS

BOULDING, K. E. *Economic Analysis* (3d ed.). New York: Harper and Bros., 1955, Chapter 27.

ROBBINS, L. "On the Elasticity of Demand for Income in Terms of Effort," *Economica*, June, 1930.

The following reading list is recommended to the student who is interested in pursuing the field of statistical supply curves:

FARNSWORTH, H. C. and JONES, W. O. "Response of Wheat Growers to Price Changes: Appropriate or Perverse?" *Economic Journal*, June, 1956.

GRILICHES, Z. "Estimates of the Aggregate U. S. Farm Supply Function," *Journal of Farm Economics*, May, 1960.

JOHNSTON, J. *Econometric Methods*. New York: McGraw-Hill Book Company, 1963.

NERLOVE, M. "Estimates of Elasticities of Supply of Selected Agricultural Commodities," *Journal of Farm Economics*, May, 1956.

chapter **9**

The Competitive Market

The first four chapters were devoted to the theory of demand. The four chapters that followed were concerned with the theory of supply. Since the share of the individual consumer in the market is infinitesimal, the consumer has no influence over the price and accordingly the market price plays the role of the independent variable in the theory of the consumer's behavior. Thus, the first four chapters rationalized the reaction of consumers to changes in market prices. If there are many producers, then the share of one individual producer is also negligible, and accordingly the market price also plays the role of the independent variable for the producer. Chapters 5, 6, 7, and 8 rationalized the reaction of producers to changes in market prices. In summary, the first eight chapters provide a theory that tells what quantity will be produced and what quantity will be bought at any given market price. There still remains the problem of determining the price in the market. This chapter will deal with this problem. In fact, the first nine chapters equip the reader with the tools required for analyzing problems arising in competitive markets for consumer's goods. In Chapters 10 and 11 we shall apply these tools to problems relating to excise taxes and agriculture.

THE MARKET PRICE

Before showing how the market price is determined at the point of intersection between supply and demand, one should be able to distinguish between a stable equilibrium and an unstable equilibrium. To illustrate this point, consider the following example: As far as its geographical location is concerned, a ball is in a stable equilibrium if placed at the bottom of a valley. Even if this equilibrium is upset by pushing the ball, there will be forces which will restore the original equilibrium. Next, let us place the ball on the top of a mountain. The ball cannot be claimed to be in a stable equilibrium because if pushed, there are no natural forces which will bring the ball back to its original position. To put it differently, being at the top of the mountain, the ball is in an unstable equilibrium.

Now, consider the market for a certain commodity. Let the demand curve for this commodity be denoted by D_0, and its supply curve by S_0, as indicated in Fig. 9-1. We claim that T, the point of intersection between the two curves, is a point of stable equilibrium. There, the price is P_0. At that price the quantity demanded is equal to the quantity supplied. This

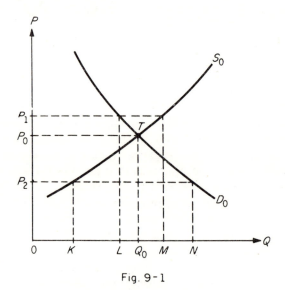

Fig. 9-1

quantity is denoted by Q_0. At point T consumers consume what producers produce. It can be readily seen that if the equilibrium is upset, by raising the price above P_0, say to P_1, producers will supply $0M$ units, but consumers will buy only $0L$ units. This will leave an excess quantity of LM units of output. Note that LM is the surplus per unit of time. In other words, unless producers start to lower their prices they will face a problem of a cumulative surplus. This surplus will give them an incentive to lower their prices. Thus, as long as the price is above P_0, there will be surpluses which will create incentives to reduce the price. This process of reducing the price will continue just until the price is P_0 at which point the two curves intersect with one another and Q_0 units of output are produced and cleared by consumers.

Next, consider any price below P_0, say P_2. There the quantity supplied is $0K$, while the quantity demanded is $0N$. The quantity supplied is short of the quantity demanded by KN units of output. This means that there are frustrated consumers who cannot get all they want at P_2. In their attempt to buy more than is available on the shelves, consumers will compete with each other by offering prices higher than P_2. Therefore, as long as there is a shortage in the market the price will be raised by unsatisfied consumers. This process will continue until the original price P_0 is restored.

Sometimes the government would fix the price at a level dictated by political considerations. Chapter 11 deals with a situation in which the government pegs the price at a level higher than the point of intersection between supply and demand. This is known as the agricultural price support program. In case the government enforces a price lower than the equilibrium price, the quantity demanded exceeds the quantity supplied, and the government must ration the limited supply among frustrated consumers. This has taken place during and in the post war periods.

DEMAND AND SUPPLY SHIFTS

When the demand curve shifts either rightward or leftward, the industry will move first along its short-run supply curve, and only after a period of adjustment is allowed will the industry operate at the point of intersection between the long-run supply curve and the new long-run demand curve.

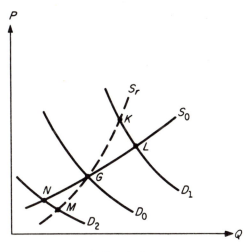

Fig. 9-2

Consider Fig. 9-2. Originally, the point of intersection between supply S_0 and demand D_0 is G. After demand increases, leading the demand curve to move rightward from D_0 to D_1, the industry expands along its short-run supply curve indicated by S_r. Thus, to the first approximation the industry operates at point K.

After a sufficient amount of time is allowed for adjustment, the industry returns to point L. Next, consider a decrease in demand leading to a leftward demand shift, say from D_0 to D_2. To the first approximation, the industry will contract by going from point G to point M, along the short-run supply curve. In the long run it will move from M to N.

In summary, demand shifts entail drastic price changes and mild quantity changes in the short run as compared with the long run.

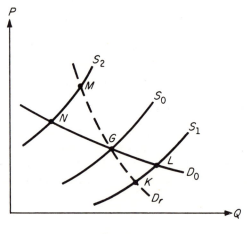

Fig. 9-3

Supply shifts are described in Fig. 9-3. Let supply increase, leading to a supply curve shift from S_0 to S_1. The industry expands along the short-run demand curve indicated by D_r. Thus, in the short run the relevant new point is K. But, after enough time elapses, consumers learn about the change and they substitute more intensively the relatively inexpensive commodity for other substitutes, until they are back on D_0, where the point of intersection between it and the new long-run supply curve is L. Similarly, following a decrease in supply leading to a leftward supply shift, say from S_0 to S_2, the industry will contract along the short-run demand curve denoted by D_r to point M. In the long run, the industry will move from M to N. As in the case of demand shifts, in the short run, prices change drastically and quantities mildly, compared with the long run.

A CHANGE IN TASTES

Let us assume that there is a change in tastes in favor of commodity A and against commodity B. It is recalled from Chapter 1 that this is equivalent to having a rightward shift in the demand curve for A and a leftward shift in the demand curve for B. This is illustrated in Fig. 9-4 and Fig. 9-5. To the first approximation, the prices of commodity A and commodity B, respectively, do not change. Thus, to the first approximation, there is a shortage of KL units of A and a surplus of MN units of B, as indicated in Figs. 9-4 and 9-5, respectively. This means that consumers will start to bid up prices of a commodity A by first offering premiums

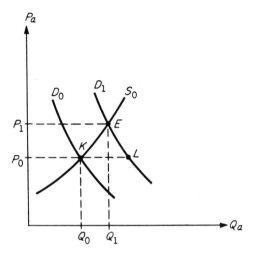

Fig. 9-4

which will eventually become a part of the new price. Producers of A will have an incentive to expand along their MC curves. But the aggregate MC is the supply curve of the industry. In order to expand, they will need more resources. Where will these needed resources come from? The answer

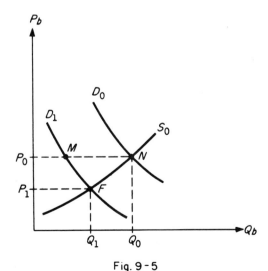

Fig. 9-5

is industry B. To the first approximation there is a surplus of MN units of commodity B. In order to get rid of this surplus, producers will offer concessions to less eager buyers of commodity B. In other words, producers of B will start to reduce prices and contract along their MC curves or along their aggregate MC curve, which is the supply curve of the industry. When contracting, they will lay off resources. Of course, in the short run they will lay off labor, raw material, and other variable inputs, but later on they will lay off less variable factors of production. These released resources will seek employment elsewhere. In other words, these released resources will look for the right signal which will be given by industry A. Industry A will offer, at least in the short run, higher wages. Producers of industry A will order more raw materials, coal, electricity, and other variable factors per unit of time. They will install more machines and other equipment in new buildings in the long run. Moreover, potential firms will now enter the industry.

All this is summarized by moving upward along the supply curve of A and downward along the supply curve of B. It is left up to the student to describe the short-run movements. In the long run, industry A will be at E which is the new point of intersection between supply and demand. At this point the price of A is higher and the quantity of A produced is larger. Industry B will be at point F, at which the price of B is lower and the quantity of B is smaller.

This is a good example of how the free enterprise economy is "automatically planned." Here the blessing of the free market is twofold. First of all, there is always a market mechanism which equates the price with the marginal cost. This is true because regardless of how the supply and demand curves shift, the price always tends to be at the point of intersection between supply and demand. But, since the supply is the aggregate marginal cost, this is equivalent to saying that the market mechanism automatically equates the price which is paid by the consumer with the marginal cost. This means that the consumer pays no more per loaf of bread than the extra cost of producing that loaf of bread. Secondly, there is an immediate and automatic response to the tastes of consumers. As illustrated above, if consumers want more of A and less of B, resources get the signal through the change in prices in favor of A, and they start to move from B to A. There is no need for a planning committee to tell so many workers, so many kilowatthours, so many tons of steel, etc., to move from industry B to industry A. It all happens in the market due to the fact that the right signals are given by both the expanding industry and the contracting industry. Thus, there is no need to waste energy on planning, because producers automatically respond to what consumers want. If you wish, this is a voting system where one dollar is one vote. When consumers vote for more A and less B, producers respond to this change in "public opinion" by shifting resources from B to A. This is what one might call an economy of consumer's sovereignty, as opposed to state sovereignty, or producer's sovereignty.

Consider now any planned economy, say, the Soviet Union, where there is state sovereignty. The Soviet citizens are governed by a political dictatorship and an economic dictatorship. It is not in the scope of this text to elaborate on political dictatorships, but, it is the role of this text to cast some light on the drawbacks of a planned economy which, in the case of the Soviet Union, happens to be regulated by an economic dictatorship. What will happen if Soviet consumers change their tastes against commodity B and in favor of commodity A? Let us assume that originally the two demand curves for commodity A and commodity B in the Soviet Union are D_0 in Fig. 9-4 and Fig. 9-5, respectively. Also let us assume that the planners decided to fix the price of A and B at P_0, and decided to produce Q_0 units of A and B, respectively. Now, after the change in tastes takes place, the demand for A shifts rightward and the demand for B shifts leftward. Then there is a shortage of KL units of A, and a surplus of MN units of B. But there is no immediate mechanism that shifts resources from industry B to industry A, because the prices of A and B, respectively, were fixed by the planners at P_0. Moreover, regardless of the surplus of MN units of B, the managers in industry B will continue to produce the same original amount of P_0N as indicated in Fig. 9-5, and they will even endeavor to increase production, because in the Soviet Union, the planners decided to tie premiums that are given to managers to the number of units produced rather than to the profit, which is considered evil there. Will the planners get the signal? Half of the signal they may get: they will become aware of the process of accumulation of B at a rate of MN units per unit of time. This is a typical *bottleneck* in a planned economy. But the other part of the signal is very difficult to detect, because there is no direct telephone line between the Soviet consumer and the planner.

While it is possible to estimate the magnitude of the surplus in the market for commodity B (MN in Fig. 9-5), the planner has no way of estimating the magnitude of the shortage which exists in the market for commodity A (KL in Fig. 9-4). Furthermore, even if the planner could provide an estimate of the order of magnitude of the shortage, he would have to solve another problem. How many units of labor, coal, raw materials, and machinery should move from industry B to industry A? In order to answer this question the planner will have to tell what the production functions and demand curves are in industry A and industry B. While it may be possible to provide a rough estimate of the respective production functions, the shapes of the new demand curves cannot be known. Accordingly, the planner cannot tell how many units of different factors, respectively, should be shifted from industry B to industry A.

Another drawback of a planned economy is a lack of incentives to shift resources from one industry to another. As indicated earlier, the incentive in a free exchange economy is provided by the fact that entrepreneurs in industry A start to receive higher prices. Thus, they tend to expand along their marginal cost curves. In order to expand, they have to hire more labor and use more capital. In industry B the price of one unit of output falls; thus, entrepreneurs tend to contract along their marginal cost curves. This is how the market mechanism provides an incentive for resources which are laid off in industry B to move to industry A. However, no such incentives exist in a planned economy.

In the planned economy, incomes of entrepreneurs are not related to prices or profits. Rather they are determined in a complex way by the physical volume of production. Thus, in spite of the surplus in the market for commodity B, managers have an incentive to continue to produce the same amount (Q_0) or even more. In a planned economy, resources will start to move from industry B to industry A only after the planner orders a certain shift in coal, electricity, raw materials, and labor. But, by the time the planner makes up his mind, a new demand shift will take place in the market and new bottlenecks will be created. Thus, the problem of the Soviet economy is insufficient mobility of factors of production and a lack of incentives at all levels. Moreover, in order to eliminate all incentives at all levels, the Soviet Union must pay very high salaries to planners who occupy offices and use other expensive services. Immediately after the revolution the problem of planning was not so complicated because there were relatively few needs to satisfy. The only thing the Soviet government had to do was to provide the bare minimum for the masses of workers who were busy constructing power stations, dams, and steel mills. But today, when more than the bare minimum is being provided, the problem of planning is far more difficult. There are many more commodities in the budget of the Soviet citizen, and he is allowed to change his tastes in favor of one commodity or another. There, the government decides how much the consumer can save. But the consumer is free to allocate his budget between finished goods and services as he wishes. However, there is no mechanism which quickly responds to the vote of the ruble. Instead of providing the right economic incentives, the planners in the Soviet Union apply administrative solutions which are like mild pills to a sick man.

In addition to the problem of improper allocation of resources, the planned economy suffers from ineffective use of resources. To be sure, Soviet economists are aware of this problem more than they are aware of the problem of misallocation. Professor E. Liberman of the Kharkov Engineering and Economics Institute published an article in *Pravda*, September 9, 1962, in which he criticized the ineffective use of resources in the Soviet economy. The following is the summary of his criticisms.

Presently, production targets for firms are set by the planning committees. The rewards are based on the degree of plan fulfillment. Overfulfillment is awarded by bonuses. It is clear that instead of encouraging the manager to do his best in the factory, such a system gives him an incentive to get low quotas. First of all, low quotas in the present assure low quotas in the future. The reason is that future targets are based on past assignments. Secondly, the lower the quota the easier it becomes to get higher rewards and bonuses by overfulfilling it. Professor Liberman also complained that the Soviet system does not welcome the introduction of new methods of production. Managers of firms refuse to try new technology. The reason is that trying new methods requires a diversion of effort away from current production. This endangers the fulfillments of quotas which are set by the planners. The third target of Liberman's criticism is poor quality. He points out that there is a special kind of relationship between quantity and quality: the poorer the quality, the easier it becomes to fulfill the quota. In the Soviet Union rewards are tied to quantity rather than quality, and so, managers concentrate on quantities and neglect the quality side.

We should be fair to Professor Liberman and mention the fact that in his article he outlined administrative remedies to cope with the problem of ineffective use of economic resources. It is important to note that one of Liberman's remedies was to replace the system in which incentives are tied to production targets by another system in which profits play a more important role. In fact, Liberman wrote about a "profitability-rate" which is the profit defined as total revenue, minus total cost, divided by the stock of capital. When advocating such a peculiar "rate of profitability," Liberman probably had in mind the need for saving capital. In other words, such a rate of profitability is expected to give managers an incentive to use the given resources more effectively, and to request less capital from the planner. Without becoming involved in a detailed argument, it seems that the planner can achieve the goal of prohibiting overuse of capital by simply raising the prices of capital items.

Professor Liberman did not dare to take the additional step which would give his idea of profit a more functional role in the Soviet economy. For the sake of simplicity, let us assume that Liberman advocates a system in which the rewards to firms are proportionately related to profit. Consider first a free exchange economy: when the demand for a certain commodity rises, the price also rises. In order to maximize profit at the new price, entrepreneurs have an incentive to expand along their marginal cost curves. In order to expand, firms hire more workers and use more services rendered by other factors of production. As we have shown, the opposite happens in the shrinking industry. Accordingly, in order for the profit to play a functional role in the Soviet economy, it must be linked with free markets in which prices of finished goods are determined at the

point of intersection between supply and demand. Furthermore, in order
to coax more resources into production, the expanding industry should be
allowed to offer them higher prices. Under such conditions, workers should
be allowed to move freely to industries that offer the highest wage rate.
This, of course, implies that firms that make coal, steel, electricity, and
other factors of production should be allowed to sell their products where
they can get the highest bid. Will the Soviet planners recognize the advantage of the free exchange market? Will they ever understand that profit
cannot play a functional role in an economy in which prices are pegged
and resources are not free to move? The author does not know the answer.

THE PROBLEM OF GROWTH

One can conceive of the following model of an economy: There are
many commodities that are currently produced there. For each commodity there is a demand function and a supply function. The price of
each commodity and its quantity supplied and cleared by the market is
determined at the point of intersection between supply and demand.
Growth can be looked upon as a simultaneous shift in the supply and
demand curve. Since our mind cannot analyze too many things simultaneously, let us apply a method of successive approximations. By
definition, commodities are either inferior and superior. We can divide
superior commodities between "just superior" and "luxurious" commodities.
A commodity is inferior if a consumer will buy less of it when his income
increases. All this is true under the assumption that all other things are
unchanged. If one wants to use economic terminology, then, when income
per capita rises, other things remaining equal, the demand for a superior
commodity increases, leading to a rightward shift in the demand curve,
while the demand curve for an inferior commodity shifts leftward. Note
that the aggregate demand curve for an inferior commodity may shift
rightward.

For example, consider the case where income elasticity is $-\frac{1}{2}$. On
the average, income per capita rises at a rate of 2 percent per annum
and the population growth at a yearly rate of 2 percent. Then, on the average the demand curve for each person will shift at a rate of $-\frac{1}{2} \times 2\% =$
-1%. But due to the growth of population it will shift 2 percent rightward. Accordingly, the net shift will be $2\% - 1\% = 1\%$, which is 1
percent rightward. Regardless of such a possibility, it is obvious that
demand curves for luxurious goods will shift rightward much faster than
demand curves for inferior goods and demand curves for superior goods
with relatively low income elasticity. It is also obvious that supply
curves of luxurious goods will shift to the right at a faster rate. This is
true because a rapid shift of the demand curve for luxurious goods to the
right entails higher prices. Higher prices mean that returns to entre-

preneurs in such industries are going to increase. This will give entrepreneurs an incentive to invest more in human capital. Moreover, it is
going to give entrepreneurs an incentive to invest more money in discovering new and better methods of production. But all this can be summarized by saying that the supply curve of luxurious or superior commodities with a relatively high income elasticity will follow the demand
curve shift to the right.

Other industries which are engaged in producing either inferior
commodities or superior commodities with relatively low income elasticity
will face a somewhat less pleasant situation. The demand curves that are
confronted by these industries will either shift leftward, not shift at all,
or shift rightward very slowly.

If the supply curve shifts only slightly over a period of time, prices
of these commodities will either fall, or rise only slightly. Marginal firms
in these industries will have to quit producing and other firms will have
to either contract or expand slowly.

Capital accumulation will be very negligible, or even negative, and
entrepreneurs will have little incentive to invest in new and better methods of production, knowing that in the future they may become the marginal firms of the industry. The least pleasant situation may be faced by
an industry which is confronted with a demand function with low income
elasticity as well as low price elasticity. This is an interesting case, and
unfortunately it is a real one. Agricultural commodities, when lumped
together, have these properties of low elasticities which give rise to the
farm problem. Since the farm problem is so important both economically
and politically, we will devote a full chapter to it later.

If the rate of growth is mild, we may have a situation where industries that make luxurious commodities expand by simply absorbing
the new addition to the labor force and by channeling the new savings in
their direction. Other industries may stagnate, or shrink slowly. But if
growth is very rapid, then expanding industries attract resources from
industries that are confronted with leftward shifting demand curves. So
far as the nonhuman resources are concerned, one can assume perfect
mobility between the two types of industries, because it is a minor problem
of shifting coal and other sources of energy, or raw materials from the
contracting to the expanding industry. But when it comes to human resources, perfect mobility cannot be taken for granted. It is admitted that
movement of labor is necessary only on the margin. But in order to assume
perfect labor mobility, one should assume that moving from the shrinking
to the expanding industry does not involve any social pain or monetary
loss. In addition to this, one should assume that information is perfect.
Most economists agree that labor mobility is not exactly perfect, in the
sense that wage differentials between expanding and contracting industries

are not wiped out overnight by an immediate influx of labor flowing toward the expanding industry. This is true because social and pecuniary losses are involved in moving from one geographical location to another, and also because information is imperfect.

Instead of arguing about the degree of imperfection concerning labor mobility, we should point out a positive policy aimed at improving mobility. Such a policy advocates providing more information through labor exchanges, providing better on-the-job training, as well as better job classification and aptitude tests. Such policy also advocates extending governmental loans to those who are relocating in order to help them during the transitional period of mobilization, because migrants usually have no collateral for borrowing from private banks.

PROBLEMS THAT MAY ARISE

Demand shifts may arise due to changes in tastes, changes in income, and changes in the price of other commodities. These problems were analyzed in Chapters 1, 3, and 4. We do not intend to repeat the analysis of demand shifts where the supply curve is incorporated into the model. If the supply curve is the same, then regardless of the cause of the shift, an increase in demand leading to a rightward demand shift will entail a larger quantity and a higher price, and a decrease in demand leading to a leftward demand shift will entail a smaller quantity and a lower price. This was illustrated in Fig. 9-2. Thus, in Fig. 9-2, the demand curve could have shifted rightward from D_0 to D_1 due to a change in tastes in favor of this commodity, a higher income if the commodity is superior, or the price of its close substitute rose; and finally it might have happened due to the elimination of a duty on its closest complementary good. Supply shifts are illustrated in Fig. 9-3. There, an increase in supply leading to a rightward supply shift could have resulted from a decline in the prices of resources, technological innovations, or simply because firms in the industry were investing intensively in better technology. Finally, the reader may have to analyze a problem where both curves are shifting simultaneously. In such a case, a method of successive approximation is recommended: shift one curve at a time.

PRICE DISPERSION

In competition, the market price tends to be set at about the same level regardless of geographical location. There are always economic forces that will tend to equate the prices in different geographical locations. For example, if it costs 1 cent to ship one orange from Florida to Chicago, then on the average the price differential between Chicago and Florida can only temporarily exceed 1 cent. For example, if, temporarily, the Chicago price is 13 cents and the Florida price is 10 cents, then there is an incentive to divert oranges away from the market in Florida to

Chicago. The net gain of shipping the first load to Chicago is 2 cents per orange. The process of shipping oranges to Chicago will lower the Chicago price and raise the Florida price just until the price differential amounts to 1 cent.

Price dispersion may arise due to the difference in service that is added to the product. For example, even though cleaners are competitive, one may charge you 25 cents per shirt while his neighbor charges 24 cents. The first cleaner may be relatively closer to a parking lot or a shopping center.

Price differentials due to the cost of transportation and heterogeneity of the service attached to the product are systematic. Unsystematic price differentials may arise due to a relatively high cost of obtaining information about the market, time spent being a major factor. If such a cost did not exist, then it would pay the consumer to call all the sellers in order to select the one who offers the lowest price. Thus, if information were absolutely costless, price dispersion of homogeneous commodities would be present only if heterogeneous services were attached to the product. In reality, however, information is not costless, and thus, consumers will devote only a limited amount of time to inquiring about the market prices. Stigler has shown that returns to obtaining information diminish very rapidly. For example, let sellers be divided into two groups, one in which sellers ask a certain low price, and one in which they ask a certain high price. Then, if only one seller is canvassed, the probability of paying the low price is 0.50. If two sellers are canvassed, the probability is 0.75. For canvassing four sellers, it becomes 0.9375.[1] Clearly, if the item is very expensive, it will take the canvassing of a relatively large number of sellers before the marginal cost of obtaining information is equated with its marginal gain. On the other hand, if the item is relatively cheap, the 10 cents that it costs to make one telephone call may exceed the expected reduction in price. Accordingly, price dispersion due to imperfect knowledge will be relatively low in the markets for expensive commodities and relatively high in markets for inexpensive commodities.

Note that price dispersion does not render our model of supply and demand unusable. The only revision that it needs is that the point of intersection of supply and demand determines the average market price rather than a unique market price. For example, an increase in supply leading to a rightward supply shift will lead to a lower average market price. This means that the various prices of the same commodity will be set at a lower level.

FUTURE TRADINGS

When we deal with nonperishables, the quantity supplied in a period

---

[1] G. J. Stigler, "The Economics of Information," *The Journal of Political Economy,* Vol. LXIX, June, 1961.

of time equals stocks carried into the period plus current production minus stocks carried out of the period. The decision on how much to carry out of the period will affect the price this period and the price next period: the larger the amount carried out of this period to next period, the smaller will be the supply in this period and the larger the supply next period. Accordingly, the higher will be the price this period and the lower will be the price next period. In other words, the price differential between this period and next period will be smaller, the larger the amount carried out. If the difference between the expected price next period and the price this period is larger than the marginal cost of storage, it pays producers to carry stocks out of this period to the next period. The marginal cost of storage is the extra cost of warehouses, loading, and interest charges minus the extra convenience of stocks per one additional unit of output stored.

Carrying out stocks from one period to the next tends to smooth prices over a long period of time. This is true because the amount carried out of this period is negatively related to the price differential between this period and the next.

Note that expected future prices are not usually equal to the prices that will exist in the future. However, there is statistical evidence indicating that expected future prices are unbiased estimates of prices that will exist in the future.[2]

JOINT PRODUCTS AT THE INDUSTRY LEVEL

Consider two joint products, such as beef and leather. If the two goods are produced in fixed proportions, then it is meaningless to speak about the conventional marginal cost of beef and the conventional marginal cost of leather, respectively, at the farm level. There is only one conventional marginal cost; that is the extra cost of producing one additional cow. In order to analyze the market for beef, we define one unit of beef as the quantity of beef obtained from one cow and one unit of leather as the quantity of leather obtained from one cow. If we accept these definitions, we can define the marginal cost of beef as the marginal cost of one cow minus the price of one unit of leather. (At this point the student is advised to review Chapter 7.) Let us now turn to the industry level. We can conceive of a supply curve of cows which is the aggregate marginal cost curve of cows. In order to obtain the supply curve of beef, we should subtract the price of one unit of leather from the price which is indicated by the supply curve of cows. Note, however, that at the industry level the price of one unit of leather is not fixed. In

[2] The student with some mathematical background will find L. Telser, "Future Trading and Storage of Cotton and Wheat," *Journal of Political Economy*, June, 1958, most interesting.

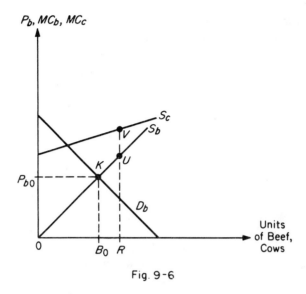

Fig. 9-6

fact, it is a function of the quantity of leather sold in the market as indicated by the demand curve for leather with which farmers are confronted. This is illustrated in Fig. 9-6 and Fig. 9-7.

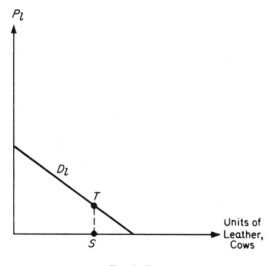

Fig. 9-7

In Figs. 9-6 and 9-7, the subscript c stands for cow, b for beef and l for leather. In Fig. 9-6, S_c stands for the supply curve of cows. Consider one point on it, say V. At point V, OR units of beef are produced. There the supply price of one cow (i.e., the marginal cost) is RV. (It is recalled again that OR cows must be produced in order to produce OR units of beef.) The problem is to find the relevant price of leather that should be subtracted from RV in order to obtain the supply price of one unit of beef. This price is derived from the demand curve for leather D_l in Fig. 9-7. There OS units of leather are equal to OR units of beef (and OR cows). As indicated by the demand curve D_l, the price per unit of leather there is the segment ST. Subtracting a segment ST ($= UV$) from RV in Fig. 9-6, we obtain a supply price RU which is the marginal cost of one unit of beef when OR units of beef are produced. Thus U is one point on the supply curve of beef. Applying this analysis to each point on S_c, we obtain S_b which is the supply curve of beef. The demand curve for beef is indicated by D_b in Fig. 9-6. The point of intersection between the supply curve of beef S_b and the demand curve for beef D_b is indicated by K, at which B_0 units of beef are produced at P_{b0}. It is left up to the reader to show that at K the marginal cost of producing one cow is equal to the price of one unit of beef plus the price of one unit of leather. It is also easy to show that an upward shift in D_l in Fig. 9-7 will give rise to a downward shift in S_b in Fig. 9-6, resulting in a larger production and a lower price per unit of beef. It is left up to the student to show that in that case the price per unit of leather will rise. The case where D_l shifts downward requires the same type of analysis.

In particular consider the case where a specific tax is imposed on leather. This is illustrated in Figs. 9-8 and 9-9. Imposing a specific tax

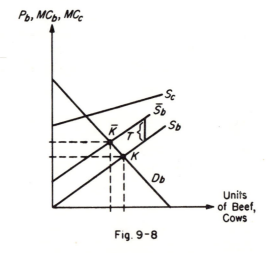

Fig. 9-8

of T dollars per unit of leather means that instead of receiving the market price as indicated by the demand curve D_l (Fig. 9-9), farmers will receive that price minus the tax T which is collected by the government. Accordingly, the new demand curve for leather with which farmers are

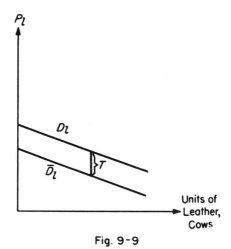

Fig. 9-9

now confronted is $\bar{D}_l$ which is lower than D_l by T.[3] Shifting the demand curve for leather downward by T dollars must shift the supply of beef S_b upwards by T dollars. This is true because originally the following held:

$$MC_b = MC_c - P_l$$

After the specific tax is imposed we have

$$\overline{MC}_b = MC_c - (P_l - T) = (MC_c - P_l) + T = MC_b + T$$

where $\overline{MC}_b$ is the aggregate marginal cost of beef (which is identical with the supply price of beef) after imposing the tax. Thus, the new point of intersection between the demand curve for beef and the supply of beef shifts from K to $\bar{K}$; that is, as a result of imposing a specific tax on leather, less cows will be produced and the price of beef will rise.

The case of an *ad valorem* tax is similar to the case of a specific tax.

SECONDARY EFFECTS

So far, we neglected to include secondary effects in the demand-shift supply-shift analysis. The following example will cast light on the nature of secondary effects.

Consider the markets for tea and coffee. The market for tea is represented by Fig. 9-10 and the market for coffee by Fig. 9-11. Supply and demand curves for tea and coffee in normal years are denoted by S_0 and D_0 respectively. Accordingly, the respective points of equilibrium in the two markets are A and B. Consider Prob. 9-3. Crops of coffee happened to be exceptionally good, and S_0 in Fig. 9-11 shifts rightward to S_1. To the

---

[3] An alternative approach is to shift the supply curve of leather upward by T dollars.

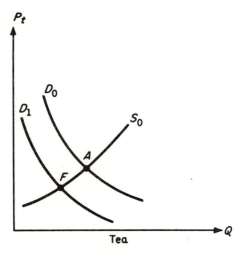

Fig. 9-10

first approximation, E is the new point of equilibrium in the coffee market. At E the price of coffee is lower. A lower price of coffee induces a leftward shift in the demand for tea which is a close substitute for coffee. In this analysis we ignore the income effect which is negligible. Thus, to the first approximation, the demand curve for tea shifts leftward, and the new point of equilibrium in the tea market is F. We have completed the first round, which concerns the first effect. The second effect will be to shift the demand curve for coffee leftward from D_0 to D_1 which is shown in Fig. 9-11. The new point of equilibrium will be G rather than E. But this

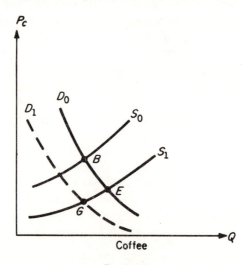

Fig. 9-11

in turn will tend to shift the demand curve for tea farther to the left (not shown in the diagram), and so this process will continue just until a new equilibrium will be achieved in both markets. Under normal conditions, secondary effects are weaker than first effects, tertiary effects are weaker than secondary effects, and so on.

PROBLEMS

In solving Probs. 9-1 to 9-8, you should start from an assumption that the market is in equilibrium. This equilibrium is upset as described in the problems. The disturbance brings about a shift in either the demand curve, the supply curve, or both. Indicate what is the nature of the shift by drawing a new curve. Then indicate what is the new market price and the new quantity at the new point of equilibrium.

9-1. The union of workers in industry A raises wages.

9-2. There is a change in tastes; People like more tea and less coffee.

9-3. Crops of coffee happened to be exceptionally good. Analyze the market for tea.

9-4. After hybrid corn was adopted by farmers, corn crops increased enormously.

9-5. The city of Chicago is going to increase the number of buses that are operated in the area. Analyze the market for cab services.

9-6. Due to the fact that the Suez Canal has been closed by Egypt, the cost of transporting oil via the sea has increased. Analyze the domestic oil market in a country where part of the oil consumption is supplied by domestic wells and part is imported from the East.

9-7. There is a severe frost in Florida. Analyze the market for oranges.

9-8. Duties on cars are eliminated in country X. Analyze the market for gasoline.

9-9. The *Walrasian stability condition* for a perfect market is based on the assumption that consumers would offer higher prices if at a given price the quantity demanded exceeds the quantity supplied. Producers would lower the prices they charge if at any given price the quantity supplied exceeds the quantity demanded. Accordingly, the Walrasian stability condition states that excess of quantity demanded over quantity supplied must be negatively related to the market price.

The *Marshallian stability condition* for a perfect market is based on the assumption that producers would increase production if at a given level of output the price indicated by the demand curve exceeds the price indicated by the supply curve. Producers would tend to lower the level of output if at a given level of output the price indicated by the demand curve is lower than the price indicated by the supply curve. Accordingly, the Marshallian stability condition states that excess of demand price over supply price must be negatively related to the quantity marketed.

Assume that the demand curve always has a negative slope. Let S and U stand for stable and unstable, respectively. Complete the following table:

Supply Curve	Stability Conditions	
	Walrasian	Marshallian
Has a positive slope.		
Has a negative slope, and cuts the demand curve from above going from left to right.		
Has a negative slope, and cuts the demand curve from below going from left to right.		

SELECTED READINGS

BOULDING, K. E. *op. cit.*, Chapter 7.

HICKS, J. R. *Value and Capital.* London: Oxford University Press, 1946, Chapter 10.

STIGLER, G. J. "The Economics of Information," *Journal of Political Economy,* Vol. LXIX, June, 1961.

TELSER, L. "Future Trading and Storage of Cotton and Wheat," *Journal of Political Economy,* June, 1958.

chapter **10**

Indirect Taxes

An excise tax is one in which a certain amount of money must be paid to the state on each unit of output sold in the market. Excise taxes are usually imposed on alcoholic beverages, gasoline, and commodities known as luxuries. Laymen sometimes say that the burden of an excise tax is borne by the consumer because producers can shift the tax forward to the consumer by asking him to pay a higher price. Laymen forget that consumers are free to buy less at a higher price, and by so doing, avoid paying part of the tax. There are other problems that the layman cannot answer very well. These are: (1) how does the excise tax affect the price of the taxed commodity? (2) how does it affect the welfare of producers and consumers? In this chapter, we shall gain insight into these issues by applying supply and demand analysis. The reader who is interested in price theory per se can omit this chapter without a loss.

TAXES IN GENERAL

The activities of the state are becoming increasingly important in developed countries. Everyone agrees that the army, the police, and other security agencies must be financed and run by the state. The majority of people agree that the post office and schools at all levels should be financed by the government. In some countries, especially in Western Europe, medical care and social security are nationalized. Why the government is becoming more involved in the economic life is a political issue. It will suffice to say that in Western democracies people voted for socialized medicine and public schools because they believe that each citizen is entitled to an equal amount of education and to medical services according to his needs. If you wish, people in the Western democracies believe in "halfway socialism," where the principle "from each according to his ability and to each according to his needs" applies only to four

171

important commodities: security, education, medical services, and social security.

Since so many of us do not like the term "half-way socialism," we often use the term *welfare state*.

In order to meet its bills, the government must impose taxes on the citizens. The state must employ workers, soldiers, teachers, and use other tangible resources in the process of providing the services previously mentioned. In other words, the government has to secure so many millions of man-days, so many million tons of steel, cement, and other raw materials, so many tons of coal, oil and so much electricity. The government has to channel a significant fraction of the national purchasing power into its account so as to be able to spend it on the needed resources. This the government does by imposing personal income taxes, corporation taxes, payroll taxes, excise taxes, and other taxes. Sometimes a tax is tied to a specific project. For instance, a specific payroll tax may be earmarked to finance a special fund. This fund might pay a fraction of or the entire old age retirement benefit for elderly people. An excise tax which is usually imposed on each unit of a certain product which is sold in the market may be earmarked for a special item in the budget of the state. For instance, an excise tax on gasoline may be imposed in order to finance the construction and maintenance of roads. Normally, however, taxes are not destined to finance one project or another. In what follows, we shall focus on excise taxes only. We shall assume that the commodities on which excise taxes are placed are made in a competitive market. We shall not inquire into the short-run effects of placing an excise tax on a certain commodity. The reason for this is that excise taxes are imposed by the government for long periods of time, and thus the short period of adjustment following the imposition of a new excise tax is of little practical interest. As far as the theory is concerned, the short run differs from the long run only in that supply and demand curves are less elastic in the neighborhood of their intersection point.

In Chapter 12 a special section will be devoted to imposing an excise tax on a monopolized commodity. Note also that there is a special tax which is difficult to classify, the *sales tax*. A sales tax boils down to imposing a certain fixed percentage tax on each purchase you make. For instance, if the rate of the tax is 5 percent, then if in the supermarket you buy commodities worth $10, you pay 5 percent of $10 which is 50 cents. This tax bears resemblance to a proportional tax on personal income. It is left up to the reader to show that if it is true that the rich save a larger fraction of their incomes, then a sales tax is regressive.[1]

[1] See section entitled "Interpersonal Comparison of Utility" in Chapter 2.

EXCISE TAXES

A Specific Tax and an Ad Valorem Tax.   A *specific tax* is one in which a certain sum of money must be paid to the state on each unit of a commodity which is sold in the market. The amount of money paid as a tax per unit does not change with either the price or the quantity. For instance, if a specific tax of $2 per bottle of whiskey is imposed, then $2 is paid to the government on each bottle sold regardless of whether the price of one bottle is $4, $6, or any other price.

An *ad valorem tax* is one in which a certain percentage of the price is paid to the state on each unit sold. For example, if an ad valorem tax of 50 percent is imposed on whiskey, then the tax on a $4 bottle is $2, and the tax on a $6 bottle is $3.

A Subsidy.   A specific subsidy is a specific negative tax. Here the government pays the producer a definite amount of money on each unit sold. An ad valorem subsidy is one in which the state pays the producer a certain percentage of the price of the commodity on each unit sold.

The Effect of the Tax on the Supply.   Placing a specific or an ad valorem tax on a commodity will shift the supply curve upward. Extending a specific or an ad valorem subsidy will shift the supply curve downward. Since the economic analysis is similar for the case of a specific tax and the case of an ad valorem tax, we shall illustrate only the case of a specific tax. A specific tax is more convenient to impose than an ad valorem tax. This stems from the fact that even though the price of one commodity tends to be unique, there arise geographical differences in the price of the same commodity due to the cost of transportation, and there are price differentials arising from quantity discounts and other factors.

Why does the supply curve shift upward after the tax is imposed? Consider the marginal cost curve of the firm. If, prior to imposing a specific tax of $2 the marginal cost at a certain level of production amounted to $7, then clearly, after imposing the tax the extra cost involved in producing one additional unit of output is $7 plus a tax of $2. This is true under the assumption that producers consider paying such taxes as variable costs. This analysis can be applied to any level of production; regardless of whether MC is $7, $2, or $20, after the specific tax is imposed the producer will have to pay an extra amount of $2 per each additional unit produced. That is, the MC of the firm shifts upward $2. But since each firm has to pay the same specific tax, the MC of each firm shifts upward $2; thus, the aggregate MC curve, which is the supply curve, shifts upward $2 as a result of imposing the tax. It is left up to the reader to show that a $2 subsidy will result in shifting the supply curve downward $2.

THE EFFECT OF THE TAX

Consider Fig. 10-1. Assume that a specific tax T is placed on commodity A. Prior to imposing the tax the original demand curve D_0 and supply curve S_0 intersected at E. The price was P_0 at which Q_0 units were produced per unit of time. After the tax, the supply curve shifts upward T dollars from S_0 to S_1. The new point of intersection is G at which the price is P_1 and output is Q_1. The government collects a revenue of Q_1 units times T dollars. Geometrically, T is equal to the segment indicated by FG. Q_1 is equal to a segment indicated by P_2F. Accordingly, the revenue collected by the government is the shaded rectangle area indicated by P_2FGP_1.

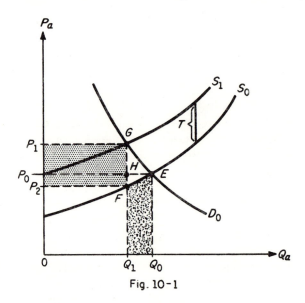

Fig. 10-1

Note that imposing the tax implies reallocation of resources. In order to cut down in production, a fraction of resources employed in the taxed industry have to be laid off. In Fig. 10-1 the extra resources that were needed in order to produce the extra output of Q_1Q_0 are laid off after the specific tax is imposed. In fact, the more elastic the respective demand and supply curves are, the larger the segment $Q_1 Q_0$ will be and the larger the dotted area below the MC curve will be.

Roughly speaking, the dotted area measures the dollar worth of variable factors that are laid off as a result of imposing the specific tax. These unemployed resources have to seek employment elsewhere, which may be unpleasant for human beings. Thus, the least that can be advocated is that a specific tax will be imposed on commodities with inelastic supply and demand curves so as to minimize the dotted area in Fig. 10-1. Also, the government should not shift the tax from one commodity to another too frequently, because this will force resources to be transferred endlessly from one industry to another.

A SUBSIDY

Consider the case where the government extends a subsidy of T dollars per unit of commodity B sold in the market. This is illustrated in Fig. 10-2. Originally, the point of intersection between supply S_0 and demand D_0 is E, at which the price is P_0 and the quantity produced and cleared is Q_0. After the subsidy is extended, the supply curve shifts

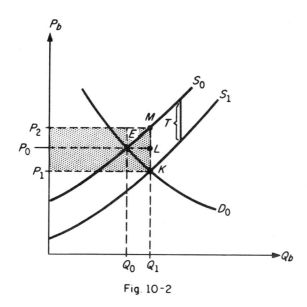

Fig. 10-2

downward by T dollars from S_0 to S_1. The new point of intersection between S_1 and D_0 is K. There, Q_1 units are produced. The cost of the program to the government is the shaded rectangle indicated by P_1KMP_2. In order to produce an additional output, which is indicated by the segment Q_0Q_1, firms in industry B will have to attract additional variable factors. The dollar worth of these additional factors is the area indicated by Q_0EMQ_1. Policy recommendations are comparable with the case of a specific tax.

THE PROBLEM OF INCIDENCE

Who bears the burden of the tax? Who benefits from the subsidy?

Laymen tend to think that the producer can load the burden of the tax on the consumer by simply shifting it forward to him. This can be done by charging him the original price plus the tax. This is another fallacy that can be exposed with the help of supply and demand. We have shown that producers always tend to operate in the neighborhood of the point of intersection of the price and the MC curve. The supply curve is the aggregate MC curve. Consider Fig. 10-1. The new market price is P_1. The new price, less tax, received by producers is P_2, and the quantity produced is Q_1. Note that Q_1 is the aggregate production of all firms. Each firm now maximizes its profit by producing a quantity as indicated by the new price of P_1 and by the new higher MC curve. Note that the tax T is equal to the segment FG. The burden of the tax is divided between consumers and producers as follows: Consumers pay a price P_1 which is by HG higher than the original price P_0. Producers receive a price after tax which is equal to P_2. Note that P_2 is lower than the original price P_0 by FH. Thus, the incidence of the tax is HG/T on consumers and HF/T on producers.

In the case of a subsidy, shown in Fig. 10-2, consumers pay a price P_1 which is LK dollars lower than the original price P_0 Producers get a price P_2 which is LM higher than the orignial price. The subsidy itself is T which is equal to KM. Accordingly, the incidence of the subsidy is LM/T on producers and LK/T on consumers.

Consider Fig. 10-1. For practical reasons the part of S_0 included between points E and F, and the part of D_0 included between points G and E can be considered as straight lines. Let the slope of D_0 be denoted by d and the slope of S_0 be denoted by s. Then, we have

$$d = \frac{GH}{HE} \qquad s = \frac{FH}{HE}$$

The incidence of the tax on the consumer is

$$\frac{HG}{T} = \frac{HG}{GF} = \frac{HG}{HG + FH}$$

Dividing the denominator and numerator by HE we obtain

$$\frac{HG}{GF} = \frac{HG/HE}{HG/HE + FH/HE} = \frac{-d}{-d + s} = \frac{d}{d - s}$$

Using the same procedure, we can prove that

$$\frac{FH}{T} = \frac{s}{d - s}$$

Note that the slope here is $\Delta P/\Delta Q$, which should not be confused with $\Delta Q/\Delta P$ appearing in the formula of elasticity.

Example: If $d = -1$ and $s = \frac{1}{2}$, then the burden borne by consumers is

$$\frac{-1}{-1-\frac{1}{2}} = \frac{1}{1.5} = \frac{2}{3}$$

or about 60 percent.

In this case, if originally the price was $100, a specific tax of $9 will be divided as follows: The new price paid by consumers will be

$$\$100 + \frac{2}{3} \cdot \$9 = \$106$$

The new price less tax received by producers will be

$$\$100 - \frac{1}{3} \cdot \$9 = \$97$$

If we multiply the numerator and the denominator of the expression $d/(d-s)$ by Q/P we obtain

$$\frac{HG}{T} = \frac{1/\eta}{1/\eta - 1/\epsilon}$$

Multiplying the numerator and the denominator by η gives

$$\frac{HG}{T} = \frac{1}{1 - \eta/\epsilon} = \frac{1}{1 + |\eta|/\epsilon}$$

Thus, if the supply curve is flat, ϵ approaches infinity and HG/T approaches one. Namely, the entire burden of the tax is borne by consumers. On the other hand, if the demand curve is flat $|\eta|$ approaches infinity and HG/T approaches zero. Here the entire burden is borne by producers.

Note that these formulas are valid only for small taxes. For example, in Fig. 10-1, the larger the tax, the larger the discrepancy between Q_1 and Q_0 and between P_1 and P_0. In addition to this, the larger the change in the quantity marketed, the wider the discrepancy between GH/HE and the slope of the demand curve and between FH/HE and the slope of the supply curve around point E.

THE INCIDENCE OF EXCISE TAXES IN REALITY

When excise taxes are imposed on commodities with relatively inelastic demand curves, a significant part of the tax is borne by consumers. Furthermore, it can be shown that under such circumstances the change in the quantity marketed is negligible. Accordingly, the government can absorb from consumers purchasing power which is slightly short of the quantity of the commodity marketed times the excise tax. For example, it is known that the demand curves for cigarettes and gasoline, respectively, are very inelastic. Thus, by placing a 4 cent tax on one gallon of gasoline, the Government can expect to collect from users of highways a revenue which is almost equal to the number of gallons sold prior to the imposition of the tax times 4 cents. In Fig. 10-3, the original point of intersection between the inelastic demand curve for gasoline and the infinitely elastic supply curve is E. Originally, the price is P_0 and the quantity marketed is Q_0. After a 4 cent tax per gallon is imposed, the horizontal

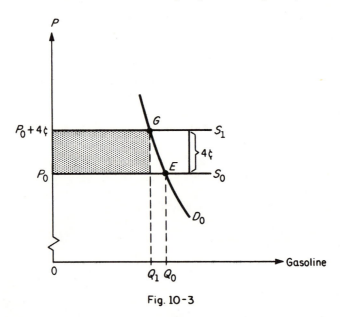

Fig. 10-3

supply curve shifts 4 cents upward, and the new point of intersection between the original demand curve and the new supply curve is G. Here, because the supply curve is flat, the burden of the tax is borne entirely by car drivers. But, due to the inelasticity of the demand curve, the new quantity marketed of Q_1 gallons is almost the same as the original quantity Q_0. Thus the inelasticity of the demand curve is equivalent to the statement that consumers of gasoline do not avoid paying the tax by diverting their purchasing power away from gasoline to other commodities. This is why excise taxes on cigarettes and gasoline are sometimes called "demand-absorbing taxes."

Imposing excise taxes on items for which demand is elastic leads to a significant decline in the quantity marketed. In other words, in the case of elastic demand curves consumers avoid paying a part of the tax by shifting purchasing power away from the taxed commodity to other goods. Accordingly, taxes which are placed on items with elastic demand curves are sometimes called "demand-shifting taxes." Since the demand for alcoholic beverages is probably elastic, imposing a tax on it is "demand-shifting."

ARE EXCISE TAXES REGRESSIVE?

The regressiveness or progressiveness of the excise tax depends on the income group which buys the taxed commodity. It is recalled that if a tax varies less than proportionately with personal income, the tax is regressive, and if it varies more than proportionately with income, the tax is progressive. Since the excise tax that the consumer pays is proportional to spending on the taxed commodity, the tax will be regressive if spending on the taxed commodity varies less than proportionately with personal income. Thus, taxes on cigarettes, gasoline, and alcoholic beverages are regressive, because in the United States spending on these items varies less than proportionately with income. Since these are the main items on which excise taxes are imposed, we conclude that in the United States excise taxes are generally regressive.

There are items such as cars on which the excise tax is likely to be progressive. Taxes on cars are ad valorem. We leave it for the reader to show that if income elasticity of cars is more than unity, then ad valorem taxes on cars are progressive.

ARE EXCISE TAXES GOOD?

What are the guiding principles that should be followed by the government when it imposes taxes? It appears that the majority of people agree that there are two guiding principles, one is called by economists the "benefits principle" and the other "ability-to-pay principle." According to the "benefits principle," the tax should be paid by those who benefit from the service. Moreover, the government should levy a tax which roughly amounts to the value of the service used. An example is a specific tax placed on gasoline. The revenue from this tax is earmarked for maintenance of roads. The reason for imposing such a tax is not hard to see. The administrative cost of collecting the fee from road users based on mileage traveled might be enormous. On the other hand, the administrative cost of collecting a specific tax placed on gasoline is relatively low. Moreover, it is realistic to assume that the usage of roads is proportional to the number of gallons burned. Of course, compact cars cover more mileage per gallon of gasoline, but this is offset roughly by the fact that compact cars cause less damage per one mile of road traveled. In summary, the excise tax which is placed on gasoline is justified on practical grounds.

What is the motive for imposing an excise tax on alcoholic beverages? The guiding principle here is probably a mixture of the "ability-to-pay principle" and "punishing-alcoholics principle." Alcoholics should be penalized only if they impose unpleasant effects on society. However, one finds it difficult to understand why the government penalizes a law-abiding citizen who takes a drink every once in a while without imposing any unpleasant effects on society. Moreover, imposing high excise taxes on alcoholic beverages provides an incentive to marginal persons to become actively engaged in all kinds of criminal activities such as moonshining. The elimination of incentives for crime is no less important than a strong police force. And so, it seems that instead of imposing high taxes on alcoholic beverages the government ought to penalize only those alcoholics who impose unpleasant effects on their neighbors.

Finally, excise taxes are imposed on "luxuries." A "luxury" has nothing to do with the definition of a luxurious commodity in Chapter 3. Whether one commodity is a "luxury" or a "necessity" is arbitrarily determined by the political system. For example, in 1960 ad valorem "luxury" taxes of 100 percent and more were placed on electrical appliances in Israel. These appliances are considered necessities in the United States. Those who advocate imposing "luxury" taxes justify it by applying the ability-to-pay principle. They claim that since "luxuries" are bought by wealthy persons, a "luxury" tax is in effect a progressive income tax. This argument neglects the possibility that there might be poor persons who are interested in buying the "luxuries." This is especially true when the time element is taken into consideration. For example, it is true that in 1950 only wealthy Israelies could afford to buy a refrigerator, and the government was justified in imposing heavy excise taxes on refrigerators. Due to the rapid growth of income per capita, consumers upgraded from iceboxes to refrigerators. Thus, in 1960 consumers who were most eager to buy refrigerators were penalized regardless of their ability to pay.

In summary, even though the guiding principle of imposing an excise tax on luxuries is the ability-to-pay principle, the tax does not achieve what is intended. In effect, it penalizes consumers who are eager to buy the taxed commodity without regard to their income.

Moreover, even if it can be shown that an excise tax is progressive, it still discriminates against one group of consumers. For example, the ad valorem 10 percent tax on cars gives rise to the following discrimination: Consider two families that earn the same income. The first family owns two cars, one for the husband and one for the wife. The second family owns only one car; the husband commutes by the train. Clearly, the tax on cars discriminates against the first family.

In addition to this distortion, there is a welfare loss to society as a whole. In Fig. 10-1 the area indicated by P_0P_2FE is the decline in the producer's surplus which is a loss to producers. The area indicated by P_1P_0EG is the decline in the consumer's surplus, which is a loss to consumers. Thus, total loss to the private sector due to the tax is the area indicated by P_1P_2FEG. But total gain is the rectangle P_1P_2FG which is the revenue collected by the government. This leaves the triangle GFE uncovered. This triangle is the excess of the loss over the gain. It is called a "dead-weight-loss," or simply welfare loss to society. This adds another argument to the case against excise taxes.

The problem of welfare loss will be discussed in detail in the Appendix to this chapter, and in Chapter 17.

PROBLEMS

10-1. As a result of imposing a tax of T dollars, the quantity produced has shrunk from Q_0 to Q_1. The dotted area is equal to $90,000,000. The share of labor in the variable cost is ⅓. Average annual wage rate is $3,000. How many workers will have to seek employment elsewhere as a result of this tax?

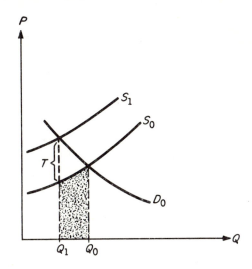

Prob. 10-1

10-2. By applying the relation $HG/T = 1/(1 + |\eta| /\epsilon)$ analyze the incidence of an indirect tax on consumers, under the following assumptions:

a) The demand curve is perfectly elastic.
b) The demand curve is perfectly inelastic.
c) The supply curve is perfectly elastic.
d) The supply curve is perfectly inelastic.

Answer questions 10-3 to 10-7 as being True, False, or Uncertain.

10-3. Currently, the market price is $10. Imposing a specific tax of $1 or an ad valorem tax of 10 percent, respectively, will result in the same new market price.

10-4. The proportion of the excise tax passed on to the consumer is greater, the smaller are the slopes of the demand and supply curves. (HINT: consider the case where the slope of the supply curve is equal to the slope of the demand curve.)

10-5. By raising the specific tax which is imposed on commodity A, the government will increase the revenue collected from this tax.

10-6. Rich people spend a smaller share of their income. This implies that imposing a 5 percent tax on the volume of sales is regressive.

10-7. In country A the government imposes specific taxes on both cars and gasoline. The government will lose revenue if it will eliminate taxes imposed on cars.

The following problem is designed for students with some knowledge of calculus.

10-8. A competitive industry consists of 50 firms, each with identical cost function:

$$C = Q^2 + 5Q + 36$$

The market demand function is

$$D = -10p + 575$$

Assume that the fixed cost of $36 is unavoidable in the short run. (a) Determine the functions of AC and AVC. (b) Determine the function of MC in the short and the long run. (c) Determine the supply function in the short and the long run. (d) Determine the price and quantity in equilibrium.

Supposing the government imposes a specific tax of $2.80 per unit of output. Determine the new cost functions and supply function. What is the new price paid by consumers and new quantity in equilibrium? What is the incidence of the tax on consumers? What is the incidence of the tax on producers? What is the revenue of the government?

SELECTED READINGS

DUE, JOHN F. *Government Finance, an Economic Analysis*. Homewood, Ill.: Richard D. Irwin, Inc., 1959, Chapters 17-19.

APPENDIX

WELFARE LOSS DUE TO SPECIFIC TAXES

Consider Fig. 10-1. As a result of imposing a specific tax T, the government is able to collect the rectangle area indicated by P_2FGP_1. Consumers lose an area of the consumer's surplus indicated by P_0EGP_1, and producers lose an area of the producer's surplus indicated by P_2FEP_0. Altogether, consumers and producers lose the area P_2FEGP_1 which exceeds the revenue collected by the government by the triangle indicated by FEG. Variable factors do not lose anything, because after a sufficient period of adjustment, variable resources that are laid off due to the tax will earn the dotted area indicated by Q_1Q_0EF elsewhere. Thus, the triangle indicated by FEG is a welfare loss to society. This measure of welfare loss should be taken with a grain of salt, because it calls for the assumption that the utility foregone per dollar paid by the private sector is equal to the utility gained per dollar spent by the state. Consider now Fig. 10-2. The cost of the subsidy to the government is the rectangle indicated by P_1KMP_2. The gain of consumers is P_0EKP_1. The gain of producers is P_0EMP_2. This leaves the uncovered triangle indicated by EKM as a "dead weight loss" to society.

Let us assume that the majority of people are ready to accept the assumption that in both the case of a specific subsidy and a specific tax, the utility foregone and gained by transferring one dollar, either from the private sector to the government, or from the government to the private sector, are equal. Then the triangle is one measure of the *undesirability* of a certain specific tax or subsidy. Let us adopt the notations

$$T^* = \frac{\Delta P}{P}$$

Where ΔP is the tax T, which is equal to the segment GF in Fig. 10-1, let

$$GH = \Delta P_d \qquad FH = \Delta P_s \qquad GF = \Delta P$$

Then we have

$$GF = \Delta P = GH + HF = \Delta P_d - \Delta P_s$$

But from the formulas of the elasticities we obtain

$$\Delta P_d = \frac{(\Delta Q/Q) \cdot P}{\eta}$$

and

$$\Delta P_s = \frac{(\Delta Q/Q) \cdot P}{\epsilon}$$

Thus,

$$\Delta P = \Delta P_d - \Delta P_s = \frac{\Delta Q}{Q} \cdot P\left(\frac{1}{\eta} - \frac{1}{\epsilon}\right)$$

and

$$\Delta Q = \frac{\Delta P}{P} \cdot Q \cdot \left(\frac{1}{1/\eta - 1/\epsilon}\right)$$

The area of the triangle in Fig. 10-1 is $\frac{1}{2} \times GF \times HE$, but $GF = \Delta P$ and $HE = \Delta Q$. Thus,

Area of triangle $GFE = \frac{1}{2} \cdot \Delta P \cdot \Delta Q$

$$= \frac{1}{2}\Delta P \cdot \Delta P \frac{Q}{P}\left(\frac{1}{1/\eta - 1/\epsilon}\right)$$

$$= \frac{1}{2}\frac{\Delta P \cdot \Delta P}{P \cdot P} \cdot (Q \cdot P)\left(\frac{1}{1/\eta - 1/\epsilon}\right)$$

$$= \frac{1}{2} \cdot T^{*2}(TR)\left(\frac{1}{1/\eta - 1/\epsilon}\right)$$

which means that the welfare loss is directly related to the square of the tax T^* and to total revenue. The relationship between the welfare loss and either η or ϵ is: If η is given, the larger ϵ is, the larger the welfare loss. If ϵ is kept unchanged, the larger $|\eta|$ is, the larger the welfare loss.

Sometimes we are justified in making the realistic assumption that the supply curve is flat, because we believe that in the long run the industry is governed by constant returns to scale, plus the assumption that for all practical purposes entrepreneurial services are unlimited. This means that ϵ is very large and $1/\epsilon$ is negligible. Thus we obtain

$$\text{Welfare loss} = \frac{1}{2}\,T^{*2} \cdot (TR) \cdot \eta$$

A rough guide for policy is one where the state should avoid imposing specific taxes on commodities with very elastic demand curves. A more detailed discussion will be found in the reading list. Note also that the formula for the welfare loss due to a subsidy is the same.

For the student who is interested in pursuing this area further, we recommend:

FRIEDMAN, M. *Price Theory, A Provisional Text*. Chicago, Ill.: Aldine Publishing Company, 1962, Chapter 3.

HOTELLING, H. "The General Welfare in Relation to Problems of Taxation and of Railway and Utility Rates," *Econometrica*, Vol. VI, July, 1938.

LITTLE, I. "Direct Versus Indirect Taxes," *Economic Journal*, Vol. LXI, September, 1951.

ROLF, E. R. and BREAK, G. F. "The Welfare Aspects of Excise Taxes," *Journal of Political Economy*, Vol. LVII, February, 1949.

AN ALTERNATE APPROACH

You will recall that we analyzed the problem of indirect taxes by assuming that the tax is an additional component of the marginal cost; thus it causes the supply curve to shift upward. An alternative approach is to assume that the marginal cost does not change, but instead, after the tax is imposed firms are entitled only to the net price. The net price is

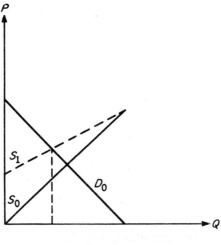

Fig. 10-4

the market price as indicated by the demand curve minus the tax. Choosing one approach or another is a matter of convenience.

For example, consider Figs. 10-4 and 10-5. An ad valorem tax of 40 percent is placed on commodity A. In Fig. 10-4 we shift the supply curve

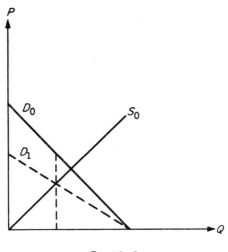

Fig. 10-5

upward, and in Fig. 10-5 we shift the demand curve downward by the tax. It can be seen from the diagrams that the results are the same.

Price Theory as Applied to Agriculture

Governments of developed countries spend significant fractions of their budgets on aid to agriculture. The American government, for example, spends more than 5 percent of its budget on aid to agriculture. The governments of developed countries are constantly engaged in finding ways of limiting the production capacity of the farm sector. The purpose of government aid to agriculture is either to increase income of farm people, or at least to maintain it at a reasonable level. In developed countries the per capita income of farm people is significantly lower than the per capita income of nonfarm people. In spite of government aid to agriculture, the average per capita income of farm people in 1960 in the United States was about 50 percent of the average per capita income in nonfarm areas. The low level of income in rural farm areas is known as the farm problem. The farm problem and government aid to agriculture will be the subjects of this chapter.

THE LOW INCOME ELASTICITY

The capacity of the human stomach is limited. In developed countries consumers spend diminishing fractions of their increasing income on food. In other words, the marginal propensity to consume food diminishes when personal income increases. The reason for this is that when people improve their standards of living, they tend to either spend more money on dining out, or to substitute better food for their plain fare. Beyond a certain point, when his income increases the consumer may begin eating in a fancy restaurant twice a week, or he may order prime steaks instead of hamburgers, but his physical food intake remains about the same. To illustrate this, consider a person whose annual income increases from $1,000 to $1,300 and his expenditures on food increases from \$300 to \$335. Notice that food does not include services of super-markets, cooks, etc. During the first year 20 percent of the additional income is spent on food; during the second year 10 percent of the additional food is spent on food; and during the third year only 5 percent of the additional income is spent on food. This is illustrated in Table 11-1.

TABLE 11-1

Year	Income	Expenditures on Food	Average Propensity to Consume Food	Marginal Propensity to Consume Food	Income Elasticity with Respect to Food
(1)	(2)	(3)	(4)	(5)	(6)
1	1,000	300	0.30		
				0.20	0.66
2	1,100	320	0.29		
				0.10	0.34
3	1,200	330	0.27		
				0.05	0.18
4	1,300	335	0.26		

You will recall that column 6 is obtained by dividing column 4 into column 5.[1] Econometric studies indicate that income elasticity with respect to food is in the order of magnitude of 0.10 to 0.20. It is recalled from Chapter 3 that income elasticity relates the shift in the demand curve to the change in the per capita income. Accordingly, an income elasticity of 0.20 means that if the income of a typical American increases 10 percent, his demand curve for food will only shift rightward 2 percent. If it were not for the population growth we would some day arrive at a point where the demand for food on the farm level would not shift at all. In summation, because the capacity of the human stomach is limited, income elasticity of food on the farm level is very low. This leads to the phenomenon that the demand curve for food shifts very slowly to the right over a period of time.

THE LOW PRICE ELASTICITY

Price elasticity with respect to food on the farm level is very low. It is recalled from Chapter 1 that price elasticity relates the percentage

[1] Let I denote income, F food, η_I income elasticity of food, and P the price of food Then

$$\eta_I = \frac{\Delta F/F}{\Delta I/I} = \frac{I}{F} \cdot \frac{\Delta F}{\Delta I} = \frac{I}{F \cdot P} \cdot \frac{(\Delta F) \cdot P}{\Delta I} = \frac{(\Delta F) \cdot P}{\Delta I} \bigg/ \frac{F \cdot P}{I}$$

which equals marginal propensity to consume food divided by average propensity to consume food.

change in the quantity demanded to the percentage change in the price. Accordingly, a low price elasticity indicates that consumers are not sensitive to changes in prices of food on the farm level. This insensitivity stems from two reasons: (1) food is essential, thus changes in its price do not affect its quantity demanded drastically; and (2) in developed countries people spend a relatively small fraction of their income on food, which reduces the sensitivity of consumers to changes in the price of food. Econometric studies show that price elasticity with respect to food on the farm level is in the order of magnitude of 0.20 to 0.25. The reader can already see for himself that such a low price elasticity creates a marketing problem. If the demand curve for food does not shift, then a 10 percent increase in the quantity of food will be cleared by the market only after price of food is cut down 40 percent!

THE SUPPLY SHIFT

In sharp contrast to the demand for food, the supply of food shifts rightward very fast. Recall that the supply curve shifts rightward owing to two reasons: (1) factors of production become cheaper; and (2) productivity on the farm increases. Farmers have benefited from cheaper factors of production at least to the extent that other industries have. For example, agriculture, like other industries, benefited from sources of energy that became cheaper with time. More important, due to new and better methods of production, productivity on farms has increased very rapidly during the lifetime of one generation. This change in productivity was mainly due to mechanization and electrification of farms: tractors, milking machines, and egg-washers are just a few examples. Farmers also benefited from biological changes in production, such as the hybrid corn. In addition to this, farmers learned to apply new chemicals such as weed killers and fertilizers. This revolution has not come to an end. It is still under way and will go on as long as technology changes. With it the supply curve of agricultural products will continue to shift very rapidly over to the right.

THE FARM PROBLEM

Over a period of time the supply of food shifts rightward very rapidly while the demand for food hardly shifts at all. The point of intersection between supply and demand becomes lower and lower which leads to the lowering of prices of agricultural products. Because of the low price elasticity of the demand curve for food, this also leads to a reduction of total farm revenue over a period of time. A farm problem would not arise if the reduction in farm revenue were accompanied by a more than proportionate reduction in farm population. (Why?) Reduction of farm population can be achieved through migration of farm families to the city. But farm out-migration is far from being sufficient. The reasons for this are:

1. Farm employees have imperfect knowledge about the labor market.

2. Entry into a unionized industry might be very difficult or even impossible.

3. There is the problem of retraining those who migrate to the city. Sometimes this arises because of old age, and in other cases it is the result of a lower level of schooling in rural farm areas.

4. It is very expensive for a family to migrate from a rural farm area to another area.

5. Before migrating, self-employed farmers have to liquidate their assets. This liquidation of property would usually involve heavy losses due to imperfections in markets for farm capital.

6. Farm people consider the codes of ethics in the city to be inferior. The insufficient farm out-migration is coupled with the known fact that the birth rate is higher in rural areas than in nonrural areas.

A NUMERICAL ILLUSTRATION

Let us create a theoretical model of the agricultural sector. For simplicity, assume that the supply curve is vertical and the demand curve has a price elasticity of $- \frac{1}{4}$. Originally, 100 million units of farm output are produced per annum and the market price is $10. Thus total revenue is $10 × 100 million = $1 billion. Assume that the share of labor is 50 percent; namely, total payments to labor amount to $500 million.[2] This is consistent with an assumption of 500,000 farm employees who receive an average income of $1,000 each. Assume also that average income in the nonfarm sector is $1,000. Let us assume that over a period of two years average income of nonfarm employees increases 2 percent. Also, let us simplify the analysis and assume that farm out-migration was sufficient enough to leave the farm labor force at the 500,000 figure. As we shall see in what follows, it was insufficient to equate the income of farm workers with the income of nonfarm workers. Recall that the shift of the supply curve of food to the right is faster than the shift in demand. For simplicity, assume that the supply curve has shifted 5 percent to the right, while the demand curve has not shifted at all.

Since we assumed a vertical supply curve, we can readily estimate the decline in the price of farm output as follows:

[2] This is consistent with a Cobb-Douglas production function in which the labor coefficient equals $\frac{1}{2}$.

Let the percentage change in the price of food be denoted by X. Then $5\%/X = -\frac{1}{4}$ and solving for X gives $X = -20\%$. Thus, the new price is 80 percent of \$10, that is, \$8, and the new quantity is 105 percent of 100 million, or 105 million units. The new total farm revenue equals \$8 × 105 = \$840 million. Assuming that the share of labor is still 50 percent, then total payments to labor amount to \$420 million. The average annual income per employee is

$$\frac{\$420 \text{ million}}{500,000 \text{ workers}} = \$840 \text{ per worker}$$

Recall that we assumed that average income of nonfarm employees increased 2 percent. It amounts to 102 percent of \$1,000, which is \$1,020. Thus, a 20 percent gap between the income of farm and nonfarm workers is created.

THE SOLUTION TO THE FARM PROBLEM

The solution to the farm problem is sufficient migration to cities. By definition, the production elasticity of labor is the elasticity relating the relative change in production to the relative change of labor. Let us make the realistic assumption that the production elasticity of labor in agriculture is $\frac{1}{2}$. Assume that 8 percent of farm workers are persuaded to migrate to the city.

Accordingly, production decreases 4 percent; instead of 105 million units it roughly amounts to 101 million units. (For simplicity we ignore the capital increase which would follow such a significant decrease in the labor force.) The new price of agricultural output is now \$9.3, and total farm revenue equals \$9.3 × 101 million = \$939 million. Total payment to labor amounts to \$469.5 million. The average annual income per employee is

$$\frac{\$469.5 \text{ million}}{460,000 \text{ workers}} = 1,021$$

which is about equal to the average earning of nonfarm workers.

This leads to the conclusion that a possible solution to the farm problem could have been more migration from the farm to the city. In spite of the difficulties involved in migrating to the city, it is possible to stimulate farm out-migration by providing farmers with better information about labor markets in the city, by helping those who migrate to retrain themselves for jobs in the nonfarm sectors, and by extending long term loans to those who leave agriculture in order to help them survive the transitional period. For political reasons, governments of developed countries do not attempt to cure the farm problem by stimulating farm out-migration. Instead, they are engaged in various programs of aid to agriculture that will be analyzed shortly. The most important forms of aid to agriculture are subsidy, price support, acreage control, crop quotas, and combinations of the above.

In what follows we shall discuss the programs of government aid to agriculture and a case study.

SUBSIDY

Originally, at the point of intersection of supply S_0 and demand D_0, the price is P_0 and the quantity demanded per unit of time is Q_0. The government decides to give farmers a subsidy of t dollars per unit of output, as indicated in Fig. 11-1. The cost of the subsidy to the government is the shaded rectangle indicated by P_2MLP_1. The gain of farmers is the additional producer's surplus, i.e., the area indicated by P_0KLP_1. The gain to

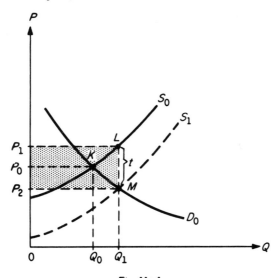

Fig. 11-1

consumers is the area indicated by P_0KMP_2. This leaves the uncovered triangle indicated by KML as a welfare loss, or what is known as the "dead weight loss" to society. If this program of subsidizing agricultural commodities could solve the farm problem, then it can be assumed that the welfare loss which is indicated by KML would be ignored. To be sure, such a program achieves the opposite of solving the farm problem, although in the short run this program helps to raise the income of farm employees. It raises the producer's surplus by the area indicated by P_0KLP_1. Also as indicated in Fig. 11-1, it gives rise to a larger agricultural production which increases from Q_0 to Q_1. In order to increase farm production, farm operators have to employ more labor, and if they face a rising supply curve of labor, they must raise farm wages in order to attract more workers to farms. Thus, in the short run, farm employees benefit from this program. But, the farm problem is not solved, because of the nature of the supply and demand shifts.

With or without a subsidy, the supply curve will continue to shift rapidly over to the right. This would incur a heavy loss to the government. In fact, the cost of this program to the government ($Q_1 \times t$ in Fig. 11-1) would increase proportionately to the growth of production. This flow of money ($Q \times t$) from the taxpayer to the farmer will hardly, if at all, compensate farmers for the loss in income. While the revenue from the subsidy ($Q_1 \times t = P_2 M L P_1$) increases over time, the revenue obtained in the market ($O Q_1 M P_2$) decreases over time due to the low price elasticity of demand. This will not continue for ever. When the subsidy amounts to more than the government can politically afford to pay, the government will make the payment of the subsidy conditional on the consent of farmers to a crop quota program. In such a program total output of each farmer is strictly restricted to a certain quota.

PRICE SUPPORT

According to this program, the government agrees to fix the price of farm output at a level which is higher than the market price, and to buy from farmers whatever surpluses are not cleared in the market. To illustrate this consider Fig. 11-2. There the market price is P_0. Now the

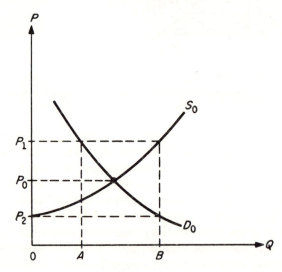

Fig. 11-2

government pegs the price at P_1. At that price, according to the demand curve D_0, only $0A$ units are taken by consumers. As indicated by the supply curve, $0B$ units are offered by farmers. Thus, a surplus of AB units of output is created in the market. This surplus is bought by the government. The purchasing of surpluses is a very expensive business. It involves costly operations such as loading, unloading, storage, spoilage, etc. Of course, the government can dispose of the surplus in foreign markets. Moreover, it can be extended as a gift to underdeveloped countries. If the proposition is free food or alternatively a pecuniary gift, then one suspects that underdeveloped countries would prefer the pecuniary gift with which they can develop their own agriculture.

The price support program involves a heavy loss to the government. The government has to accumulate the surpluses, which is a costly operation involving loading the surpluses, shipping, and storing them. Even if part of the surpluses can be dispensed in foreign markets, it is not without a loss. The price that can be secured abroad is significantly lower than the price at home. Furthermore, shipping of the surpluses overseas is at the expense of the government. In the long run, the price support program helps the rich and it works against the poor farmer. For the rich farmer who produces on large scale, the difference between the support price and the market price multiplied by output is a free gift from the government. The poor farmer may benefit from the program in the short run, but in the long run this program weakens the incentive to migrate to the city.

Another variation of the price support program is one in which the government guarantees farmers a price of P_1 (Fig. 11-2) and total output indicated by $0B$ is dumped in the market at a price of P_2. The cost of this program to the government is $0B \ (P_1 - P_2)$. Such a program is usually offered to farmers provided that they in return agree to a crop-quota program.

ACREAGE CONTROL

According to this program, farmers agree to cultivate only part of their land, say 80 percent. Note that this does not mean that 20 percent of the land capacity is going to become idle. The truth is that farmers will lay off their marginal lands, because they will try to minimize the loss in production capacity. As indicated in Fig. 11-3, if less land is available to farmers, their supply curve will shift leftward from S_0 to S_1. Recall that this program is based on the realistic assumption that the price elasticity of the demand curve D_0 is smaller than unity in absolute value. Thus, shifting the supply curve to the left will entail a larger total farm revenue. In Fig. 11-3, when the supply curve shifts from S_0 to S_1, the point of intersection between supply and demand changes from A to B.

At B, a smaller quantity Q_1 is produced but at a higher price, P_1. However,

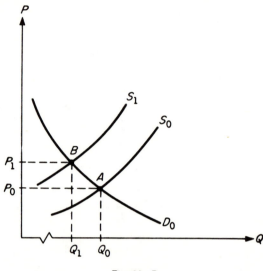

Fig. 11-3

since the demand curve is inelastic, the positive change in price dominates the negative change in quantity. Hence, total revenue at B is larger than total revenue at A. To illustrate this point assume that $\Delta Q = Q_1 - Q_0$ is -5% of Q_0. If $\eta = -\frac{1}{4}$ and X is the percentage change in price, then, $-5\%/X = -\frac{1}{4}$ and $X = 20\%$. Thus we have

$$Q_1 = 0.95 \cdot Q_0 \qquad P_1 = 1.20 \cdot P_0$$

Then the new total revenue is

$$TR_1 = Q_1 \cdot P_1 = 0.95 \cdot Q_0 \cdot 1.20 \cdot P_0 = 0.95 \cdot 1.20 \cdot Q_0 \cdot P_0 = 1.14 \cdot Q_0 \cdot P_0$$

But

$$TR_0 = Q_0 P_0$$

Hence

$$TR_1 = 1.14 \cdot TR_0$$

Namely, total revenue at $B(TR_1)$ is 14 percent larger than total revenue at $A(TR_0)$.

An acreage control program is impractical. Let us assume that to the first approximation the price rises to P_1. This higher price gives Mr. Smith an incentive to replace the idle land by other factors of production. For instance, he may use more fertilizers, irrigate a larger acreage of his land, and so on along the line. If Mr. Smith were the only smart farmer, then nothing has changed, but there are many smart farmers. In fact, one has to assume that they are all clever enough to prefer a larger income to a smaller income. Thus, all farmers will apply more fertilizers and other substitutes to land; as a result the supply curve will shift back toward its original position at S_0, and we are back where we have started.

Even if acreage control programs could be enforced in such a manner so as to really shift the supply curve significantly over to the left, this program involves a special welfare loss. This program requires laying off a significant percentage of farm lands. Since these idle lands have practically no alternative use elsewhere, it means that the farm problem is solved by forcing an important factor of production to become idle. A much better solution is the use of crop quotas which can achieve the same purpose of forcing production to decline without laying off an important resource.

CROP QUOTAS

The crop quota program is the most intelligent of those listed. It achieves the same purpose of shifting the supply curve leftward without laying off land which is specific to agriculture.

Thus it is preferred to the acreage control program. This program, however, has its own drawbacks, but, if properly handled, some of them can be eliminated. The first problem arising from instituting this program is: if quotas are imposed only on a few crops, then farmers will shift released resources from the crops under the program to crops which are not included in the program. For instance, if farmers agree to a 90 percent quota on corn, they will simply shift resources from corn to other crops such as barley and wheat. Thus, by solving the farm problem in the corn industry, they will immediately create a more serious problem in the wheat industry. This difficulty can be settled by imposing quotas on each and every crop.

Another problem is the weather. Even if a farmer plans his crops in advance, the weather can increase or decrease his harvest. Thus, if farmers happened to produce more than their quota allows them they may argue that they exceeded their quota because of exceptionally good weather.

Finally, and most importantly, quotas discriminate against the efficient farmer who cannot expand his scale of operations. Accordingly, it gives the right signal to the wrong guy. Normally one would expect the marginal farmer to migrate to the city; under the crop quota program the signal to out-migrate is given to the most efficient, or least marginal farmer.

The crop-quota program is illustrated in Fig. 11-4. Before the program is instituted, the market price is P_0 at which Q_0 units of agricultural output are cleared. After the program is instituted, farmers are

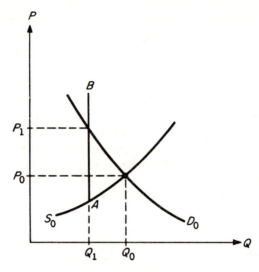

Fig. 11-4

restricted to the production of Q_1 units. Q_1 is a certain fixed percentage of Q_0. Let us assume that Q_1 is 90 percent of Q_0. Then if price elasticity is $-\frac{1}{4}$, the relative change in price which is $P_1 - P_0$ can be estimated as follows:

Let the percentage change in price be X. Then $-10/\%X = -\frac{1}{4}$, $X = 40\%$, and $P_1 = 1.40\,P_0$. Originally, total revenue is $TR_0 = P_0 \cdot Q_0$. After the crop quota program is effectively enforced, total revenue is equal to

$$P_1 \cdot Q_1 = 1.4 \cdot P_0 \cdot 0.9 \cdot Q_0 = 1.4 \cdot 0.9P_0 \cdot Q_0 = 1.26P_0 \cdot Q_0$$

Namely, if all crops are restricted to a 90 percent quota, this may increase total revenue by 26 percent. Note, finally, that after the program is effectively enforced, the new supply curve is S_0AB. This shape is justified by the fact that at prices which are higher than Q_1A only Q_1 can be produced.

A CASE STUDY: AGRICULTURAL POLICY DURING THE KENNEDY ADMINISTRATION

The Secretary of Agriculture in the Kennedy administration once noted that the U.S. Agriculture is half miracle and half mess. The miracle is the rapid rise in agricultural productivity. From 1920 to 1960 farm productivity per worker in the United States has quadrupled. The mess is the agricultural surpluses which are created by the price support programs. Orville Freeman's Agriculture Department spent about $7 billion per annum mainly on handling farm surpluses. This large-scale government aid to agriculture fails to solve the problem of poverty in rural farm areas: according to statistics published by the U.S. Government, average farm income per family in 1960 amounted to less than half the income per urban family. As indicated before, the problem of poverty in rural farm areas stems from the inelasticity of the demand curve and the spectacular shift in the supply curve rightward, due to a combination of better technology and a tremendous capital investment.

Such a rapid shift of the supply curve which is hardly followed by any shift of the inelastic demand curve gives rise to shrinking total farm revenue and, accordingly, low income per family. If a sufficient number of marginal farmers had out-migrated, the farm problem would have been solved, if not completely, at least partially. And there are many marginal farmers as indicated by government statistics.

For example, in 1960, 50 percent of total farm output was produced by the top 10 percent of farms. Such data clearly indicate that there are many small-scale farms which do not produce efficiently because of lack of capital and inability to manage it properly. In other words, there are many farms with relatively limited capacity and high average cost curves.

The price support program is sufficiently high to cover the average cost of the small farmer (where the cost does not include an element of alternative cost of the entrepreneur). For example, in 1963, the support price of corn was $1.25 per bushel. This gave many inefficient corn growers an incentive to remain on the farm with an income of less than $3,000, while urban families lived on average incomes of $6,000 and more. Had this price support program been abolished, a significant fraction of marginal farmers would not be able to cover total costs (excluding alternative payment to the entrepreneur) and would be forced to migrate to the cities.

Moreover, abolishing this program would release funds with which marginal farmers could have been retrained to become employees in the city. Note that the problem is twofold. In addition to weakening any incentive to migrate, as far as marginal farmers are concerned, this program provides an opportunity for the large-scale farmers to produce corn at a low average cost of 70 cents and get a price support of $1.25. No wonder that the efficient farmers could reap a free-risk bumper money crop year after year.

In most of the crops, the aid program was a combination of price support and acreage control. Acreage control failed to shrink the supply of corn!

Another interesting case study is wheat. The Kennedy administration inherited a combination of acreage control and price support in which farmers who agreed to divert a certain fraction of their lands away from wheat production were paid a support price of $1.25 per bushel. Raising the price artificially above $1, which was believed to be the market price, created enormous surpluses of wheat which cost the taxpayers hundreds of millions of dollars. The Kennedy administration was aware of the ineffectiveness of land restrictions as a device of shrinking the supply of wheat. By substituting fertilizers and other forms of capital for the diverted lands, farmers were able to produce as much or even more than they did prior to instituting the program. Of course, the incentive to produce more in spite of the acreage controls was provided by the support price. In order to cope with the problem of wheat surpluses, the Secretary of Agriculture suggested a combination of price support and a drastic control program. According to this program, the Department of Agriculture, in addition to telling each wheat grower how many acres he could plant, would tell him how many bushels of wheat he could market per acre. In return for agreeing to such a tight control on output farmers would receive a high support price of $2 instead of the $1.25 which they can get under the ineffective program of acreage control. The Department of Agriculture figured out that since the demand curve for wheat was probably inelastic, total revenue of wheat growers would be increased by restricting output. The administration thought that a price of $2 per bushel would clear the market without leaving any surpluses provided that the control is effective. But wheat farmers had to vote on either accepting the program or rejecting it. The American Farm Bureau Federation, the biggest organization of farmers in the United States, rejected the program because "freedom to farm" was, as they said, the most important issue. One can speculate, however, that what farmers really meant was freedom to produce without restrictions at a reasonably high support price. In other words, had the issue been the administration program versus producing at the market price which would be determined at the point of intersection of supply and demand, farmers would probably accept the drastic program of Secretary Freeman. Since farmers were convinced of their ability to get Congress to continue a program of price support and ineffective acreage control, they turned down the drastic program.

TWO POPULAR FALLACIES

When someone is in trouble, someone must be blamed. Laymen and petty politicians usually blame two groups for the farm problem: The first is the middleman, who "exploits" the farmer. The middleman simply leaves very little for the farmer. Thus, they say, if we could force the middleman to reduce his own fat share, the farmer could be left with a larger share. The second is the group engaged in producing capital goods. To make a long story short, the farm problem stems from the fact that farmers sell their output in a perfect market and buy their capital goods in a monopolized market.

It takes simple operations of supply and demand to expose the Achilles Heel of these popular fallacies. First of all, consider the problem of the middleman. When we speak about the middleman, we refer to those who are engaged in food processing, and transporting it from the garden to the supermarket.

These industries of processing and marketing food operate in markets that are either competitive, or nearly competitive. Recall that, roughly speaking, in a competitive market there are economic forces that tend to equate the price of a service to its marginal cost. The government could not possibly force the middleman to produce the same amount of services at a lower price. Trying to force him to produce at a price which is below the marginal cost would restult in a shortage of processing and marketing services. This is true because if a lower price is enforced, the marginal middleman would be forced out of the industry, and other middlemen would shrink the amount of services supplied as indicated by their marginal cost curves. Thus, the only way to go about this problem is to reduce the marginal cost of processing and marketing food. Let us now explain the concept of the *net demand curve*. In Fig. 11-5, D_g is the gross *demand curve*. Let this be the aggregate demand curve for tomatoes already on the shelves in the supermarket. Consider any point on this demand curve, say point A. At this point the quantity cleared by the market is Q_0, the

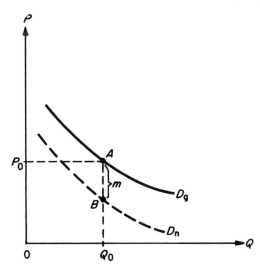

Fig. 11-5

price is $P_0 (= Q_0 A)$. Now, assume that the marginal cost of processing, transporting, and marketing tomatoes is $m = AB$; then the share of the farmer is the market price $Q_0 A$ minus the additional cost involved in processing, transporting, and marketing one additional tomato which equals $m (= AB)$. This leaves the farmer with a price of $Q_0 B = Q_0 A - AB$. Applying this analysis to each point on D_g we obtain D_n which is the *net demand curve*, or the demand curve on the farm level. It is left for the student to show that if m could be cut down, the net demand curve would shift rightward. It is admitted that such a rightward

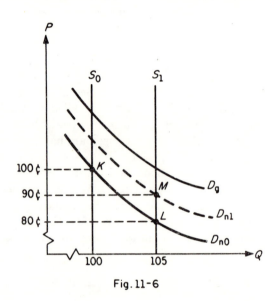

Fig. 11-6

shift is helpful, because, after all, the source of trouble lies in the fact that the gross demand curve D_g hardly shifts at all. Note, however, that in the twentieth century the industries engaged in transportation, food processing, and marketing underwent a tremendous technological and organizational progress. It is not in the scope of this chapter to survey the development of frozen foods, canned foods, gigantic supermarkets, etc. Most persons are aware of it. In spite of this progress, that is to say, in spite of the fact that middlemen industries are becoming more and more efficient, the farm problem has not been cured. In other words, the rightward shift of D_n is too negligible compared with the rightward shift of the supply curve. Like giving aspirin to a sick man, reducing the middleman costs is a relief, but not the solution to the problem. To summarize this problem, consider Fig. 11-6. There it is assumed that the gross demand curve D_g does not shift at all over a period of time. Originally, the horizontal supply curve S_0 intersects with the net demand curve D_{no} at point K. Note that the net demand curve is 20 cents lower than the gross demand curve. At point K, $Q_0 = 100$ units and net price received by farmers is 100 cents; thus, the original total revenue is $100 \times 100 = 10,000\cent$ or $100. Now, over a period of time, the supply curve shifts rightward from S_0 to S_1, which is a 5 percent shift. If price elasticity is estimated at $-\frac{1}{4}$, and the percentage change in price is denoted by X, then we have $5\%/X = -\frac{1}{4}$, and solving for X we obtain $X = -20\%$. Namely, if we assume no progress in the transportation, processing and marketing industries, the new point of intersection between supply S_1 and demand D_{no} is L, at which 105 units are sold for 80 cents a piece. The 80 cent figure is obtained by lowering the original price of 100 cents by 20 percent. Then, at L the new total revenue is equal to $105 \times 80 = 8,400\cent$ or $84. Thus, the dimension of the farm problem is in the order of magnitude of 16 percent reduction in total revenue. Let us make the *unrealistic* and extreme assumption that during that short period of time[3] the middleman costs were cut down by one-half. Namely, the real net demand curve is not D_{no}; rather it is D_{n1} which occupies a mid-position between D_g and D_{no}. We can see that D_{n1} is 10 cents higher than D_{no} and D_{n1} intersects with S_1 at M. At that point, net price received by farmers is 90 cents, and total revenue equals $105 \times 90 = 9,450\cent$, or $94.50. Even such a spectacular and hypothetical reduction in the marginal cost of middleman services could not completely cure the problem. The only thing it did was to change the order of magnitude of the farm problem from 16 percent to 5.5 percent.

Let us now turn to the second fallacy. The problem of monopoly and imperfect markets will be covered in Chapter 12. For our purposes it is sufficient to note that a monopolist can and usually does charge a price which is higher than the marginal cost.

Assume that farmers sell in a perfect market and buy in a perfect market. In other words, the markets for tractors, gasoline, seeds, fertilizers, farm machinery and equipment are perfectly competitive. The supply curve of agricultural output is S_0, and the demand curve facing farmers is D_0, as indicated in Fig. 11-7. The point of intersection between supply and demand is A. Now, assume that one day all industries which produce tractors, gasoline, fertilizers, and farm equipment become monopolized. This means that the price of resources purchased by farmers will be raised over night. This also means an upward shift in the supply curve of agricultural output. As indicated in Fig. 11-7, the supply curve shifts from S_0 to S_1. Recall that the supply curve is the horizontal sum of all marginal cost curves of all farmers. Since resources become increasingly more expensive, the marginal cost curve

[3] Assuming a 2.5 percent annual rate of growth implies that the period in question is about 2 years long.

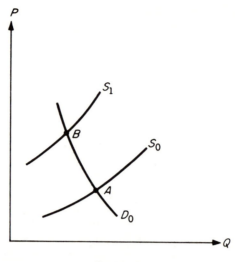

Fig. 11-7

of each farmer shifts upward and, accordingly, the entire supply curve moves upward. The new point of intersection between D_0 and the new supply curve S_1 is B. Since the price elasticity of D_0 is smaller than unity in absolute value, total revenue at B must be larger than total revenue at point A. It is left for the student to show that if at point B production is 5 percent less than it is at point A, and if price elasticity of D_0 is in the neighborhood of $-\frac{1}{4}$, then roughly speaking, total revenue at B is 14 percent higher than total revenue at A. As a result the agricultural industry benefits from securing its resources in a monopolized market.[4] The reason for bringing up this point is not to give monopolies credit. The evils of monopoly and imperfect markets will be discussed in the following chapter. Monopolies are undesirable socially. However, this fact does not give us license to arrive at the conclusion that monopolies can be blamed for the farm problem.

POLICY RECOMMENDATION

The United States Government spends more than 5 percent of its budget on artificially supporting the prices received by farmers. These programs weaken the incentives of farmers, and farm employees to migrate to the nonfarm sector. The reason for this situation is political rather than economic. In the United States, the urban and rural nonfarm population outnumbers the farm population. But due to the special political structure of the United States, the political power of farmers

[4] We assume that the share of labor is the same at points A and B.

is far larger than its share in the total population would suggest. Each state is represented by two senators. There are in the United States few states which are densely populated by urban and rural nonfarm people and a great number of states that are sparsely populated by rural farm people. Accordingly, the farm population is overrepresented by senators and representatives in the House. There are two reasons why those who represent agricultural states are not interested in stimulating the process of farm out-migration. First of all, farm people believe in solving the problem of poverty on the farm. Thus it is easier to extend relief on the farm than rescue in the city. Second, representatives and senators are aware that farm out-migration is, in fact, an exodus from the poor agricultural South to the rich industrial North. The result is a shrinking constituency that is of vast political importance to them.

An economist recommending a policy to cope with the farm problem must take this political background into consideration. For example, a price support without crop quotas is undesirable for taxpayers. It is inevitable that a support price will result in excess supply over demand, leading to large surpluses that must be purchased by the government with the money of the taxpayer. Most economists would probably agree that in order to save money to the taxpayer, a price support program must be combined with crop quotas in order to cancel surpluses. We have seen that since farmers were convinced of their ability to get Congress to continue a program of price support and ineffective acreage control, they turned down Freeman's program in a referendum. Many economists would recommend the gradual canceling of the current price support programs. They advocate that the billions of dollars that are currently spent by the U. S. government on handling surpluses should be gradually transferred to long-run goals such as raising the level of schooling in rural farm areas, providing necessary funds for retraining to farmers who want to migrate to cities, and providing loans that are necessary for the transitional period. Such a program will stimulate the process of farm out-migration and solve the problem of poverty in rural farm areas once and for all. Again the political obstacles on the way of achieving this economic program are enormous.

PROBLEMS

11-1. The government can effectively impose either an acreage control or production control program. If farmers have no preference, which program would you recommend?

11-2. Whatnot is the only commodity produced by farmers. In 1950, the production of whatnots reached a level of 1 million bushels, and the price per bushel was $1. From 1950 to 1955, the *vertical* supply of whatnots shifted 10 percent rightward. The demand curve ($\eta = -\frac{1}{2}$) did not shift at all. The share of labor is 50 percent of total revenue, and originally annual farm wage rate was $1,000. Estimate the farm wage rate in 1955. (Assume that the farm labor force has not changed over this period of time.)

11-3. In 1950 the production of whatnots amounted to 1 million bushels. The market price was $1, and the support price was $1.20. Assume a vertical supply curve and $\eta = -\frac{1}{2}$. (a) What is the additional quantity of whatnots that must be stored during 1950? (b) If, on the average, storage expenses are 30 cents per bushel, and if the surpluses are dumped in foreign markets at a price of 50 cents per bushel, how much would the program cost to the taxpayer in 1950?

11-4. Repeat Prob. 11-3, except that instead of a support price, a subsidy of 20 cents per bushel is given to the farmers.

11-5. If you were a farmer, would you be in favor of an agricultural policy according to which the government subsidizes fertilizers?

11-6. Do you agree with the following statement: "Farmers in underdeveloped countries should be opposed to receiving free food from the United States"?

SELECTED READINGS

COCHRANE, W. W. "Farm Prices: Myth and Reality," University of Minnesota Press, 1958.

FLOYD, JOHN E. "The Effects of Farm Price Supports on the Returns to Land and Labor in Agriculture," *Journal of Political Economy*, Vol. LXXIII, April, 1965.

GISSER, M. "Schooling and the Farm Problem," *Econometrica*, Vol. XXXIII, July, 1965.

GRILICHES, ZVI. "Research Expenditures, Education, and the Aggregate Agricultural Production," *American Economic Review*, Vol. LIV, December, 1964.

JOHNSON, D. G. "Forward Prices for Agriculture," University of Chicago Press, 1947.

———. "Comparability of Labor Capacities of Farm and Nonfarm Labor," *American Economic Review*, June, 1953.

———. "Policies and Procedures to Facilitate Desirable Shifts of Manpower," *Journal of Farm Economics*, Vol. XXXI, 1949.

SCHULTZ, T. W. *The Economic Organization of Agriculture.* New York: McGraw-Hill Book Company, 1953.

WILCOX, W. W. "The Farm Policy Dilemma," *Journal of Farm Economics*, Vol. XL, August, 1958.

chapter **12**

Monopoly

So far we have only discussed one market situation, which is known as pure competition. There are however, other market situations which will be the subject of this chapter. Before proceeding let us describe the most important market situations:

1. *Monopoly:* (e.g. telephone company) Where there is (a) difficulty of entry to the industry, (b) one seller, and (c) no close substitutes to the product or service. Both (b) and (c) imply a demand curve with finite elasticity.

2. *Oligopoly of Two Sorts:* Where the product is (a) homogeneous, (e.g., steel) and there is either (1) collusion or (2) a game theory problem, and (b) differentiated (e.g., soft drinks), and rivalry is generally non-price.

3. *Monopolistic Competition:* (e.g. retailing) Where there is (a) ease of entry and exit, (b) many sellers, and (c) a differentiated product, which implies a demand curve of finite elasticity.

4. *Pure Competition:* (e.g. agriculture) Where there is (a) ease of entry and exit, (b) many sellers, and (c) a homogeneous good. Both (b) and (c) imply an infinitely elastic demand curve.

This chapter is devoted to the problem of monopoly. Chapter 13 will be devoted to the problem of imperfect markets, i.e. oligopoly and monopolistic competition.

MONOPOLY

If product A is made by a sole producer, then product A is said to be monopolized, the producer is a monopolist and the firm is a monopoly. The monopoly is confronted with a single demand curve which is the demand curve for product A. It is recalled that in contrast to the monopoly, the competitive firm can produce any output without affecting the price of the commodity, because its share in the market is infinitesimal. In the case of monopoly, the firm has the whole market, and any change in the output made by the monopolist will change the price to the extent indicated by the demand function.

The monopolist can move along the demand curve in either direction, but he cannot deviate from the demand curve. By moving along the demand curve we mean either to lower the price and sell more or vice versa. He can produce so much output and find out from the market what price will clear his flow of output. Or, alternatively, he can set a price and find out what will be the maximum output cleared by consumers per unit of time.

THE OPTIMAL OUTPUT OF A MONOPOLIST

Consider a monopoly that faces a negatively sloped demand curve. At a price of $10 it can sell only one unit of output per unit of time; at a price of $9 it can sell 2 units of output per unit of time; at a price of $8 it can sell 3 units of output per unit of time, and so on. This is illustrated by column 1 and column 2 in Table 12-1. This information about the demand curve facing the monopolist is sufficient for the deriva-

TABLE 12-1

Q (1)	P (2)	TR (3)	TC (4)	Rent (5)	MR (6)	MC (7)
1	$10	$10	$10	$ 0	$10	$4
2	9	18	14	4	8	4
3	8	24	18	6	6	4
4	7	28	22	6	4	4
5	6	30	26	4	2	4
6	5	30	30	0	0	4
7	4	28	34	− 6	−2	4
8	3	24	38	−14	−4	4
9	2	18	42	−24	−6	4

tion of total revenue which is shown in column 3. The monopolist has to pay a fixed cost of $6 per unit of time. The extra cost per additional unit of output is $4. This provides the necessary information for the derivation of total cost in column 4 and marginal cost in column 7. The rent which is total revenue minus total cost is given in column 5. Marginal revenue which is extra revenue obtained from selling one additional unit of output is shown in column 6. For example, when production increases from one unit to two units (column 1) total revenue increases from $10 to $18 (column 3), and so extra revenue per one additional unit of output is $(\$18 - \$10)/(2 - 1) = \$8$. Column 5 clearly indicates that profit is *not* maximized where marginal cost equals the price. This occurs when 7 units of output are produced per unit of time; at that point rent is negative. In fact, if the monopolist had produced 7 units of output, he would incur upon himself a loss of $6 per unit of time. Rent is maximized where $MC = MR = \$4$. At a lower level of output MR is larger than MC. For example, when 2 units of output are produced per unit of time, MR amounts to $8 and MC equals $4; accordingly, an expansion of one unit increases rent by an amount of $\$8 - \$4 = \$4$. Thus it pays the entrepreneur to expand. The monopolist will expand just until he reaches the point where $MC = MR$. Beyond that point MC will exceed MR and it would pay him to cut down in production.

In summary, a monopoly will maximize its rent at the point where $MC = MR$. In this respect it is similar to a competitive firm. It differs from a competitive firm in another important respect. Its price is *not* identical with MR. Later we shall show that the discrepancy between the price and MR in the case of a monopolized industry gives consumers a cause for concern.

THE MARGINAL REVENUE OF A MONOPOLY

It is recalled that marginal revenue is defined as the change in total revenue per unit of change in total output, or the extra revenue obtained from selling one additional unit of output. It is also recalled that in the case of a competitive firm, the horizontal price line coincides with the marginal revenue curve, i.e., for a competitive firm the price is equal to the marginal revenue. In the case of a monopoly, where the demand curve is negatively sloped, the marginal revenue is below the price. If you are inclined toward a rigorous analysis, you are advised to review the last section of the first chapter, where you may find the answer to this problem. If not, apply your intuition. For a monopolist, expansion means lower prices. Thus, it is impossible to argue that the price of the monopolized item is the extra revenue obtained from selling an extra unit, because after all, the price that prevailed prior to selling an extra unit per unit of time is higher than the price that prevails after the expansion took place. We can gain an insight into the problem by considering Table 12-1, where the marginal revenue is derived from a negatively sloped demand curve. When the price is set at $9, marginal revenue is $8, when the price is $8, marginal revenue is $6, etc. Note that *total* revenue is maximized when marginal revenue stops taking on positive values and starts taking on negative values. This is obvious because a positive marginal revenue indicates that total revenue is growing while a negative marginal revenue indicates that total revenue is shrinking.

A GEOMETRICAL ILLUSTRATION

Geometrically, it can be shown that if the demand curve is a straight line intersecting with the price and the quantity axes respectively, then the marginal revenue is a straight line passing through the point of intersection of the demand curve and the price line, and the midpoint between the origin and the point of intersection between the quantity axis and the demand curve. In other cases the geometric derivation of the marginal revenue curve is more involved. The most important property of the marginal revenue curve, however, is that it lies below the demand curve and that it is negatively sloped. Other properties are secondary in their importance. Accordingly, we shall use straight lines to represent the demand curve.

As in the case of a competitive firm, the profit of the monopolist will be maximized when marginal revenue is equal to marginal cost. This occurs at point G in Fig. 12-1. If the monopoly is not regulated by the government, and if there is no political pressure applied, it will choose to operate at a price P_0 ($= Q_0 H$), as indicated by point G. This is the price at which $MC = MR$. Now, let us assume that the entrepreneur of the monopoly has never taken a course in economics. Then, why should he operate at H rather than, say, at K? Well, assume that he uses the *flexible markup* method and currently he operates at K. Then, since his motive is maximizing the profit, he will try to change the markup and see if he can increase the net profit. If he increases the markup, he will lose business. Moreover, he will get a smaller profit. But, if he expands, by lowering the markup, he will increase his profit. In fact, he will lower the markup just until the price is equal to P_0. He will stop there because trying to lower it even further will bring a smaller profit.

The profit of the monopolist is the shaded rectangle as indicated in Fig. 12-1. It is the quantity times the difference between the price and average cost.

Unlike the competitive firm, a monopoly maximizes its profit at a price which is higher than the marginal cost. We recall that perfect competition was praised mainly because it provides a mechanism which always tends to bring the price into level with the marginal cost. Thus, given the level of technology, the resources and the potential entrepreneurs, one can be sure that the price he pays for a good which is produced competitively cannot exceed its extra cost by much. Once there is a gap between the price and the extra cost, economic forces will be generated which will propel the market into a point where price is

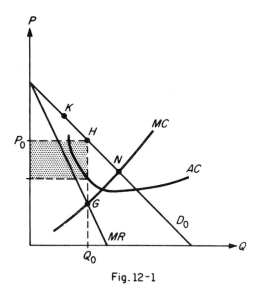

Fig. 12-1

again equal to MC. The "economic forces" are either new firms entering the industry, and/or the firms that are already in the industry producing more output. *In the case of a monopoly there are always forces which propel the monopolist to operate at a price which is above the marginal cost.* In Fig. 12-1 the price P_0 is GH dollars higher than the marginal cost. This gives modern societies a cause for concern because it simply means that consumers are exploited by monopolies.

The problem of welfare loss due to monopolies will be discussed in Chapter 17.

DEMAND CONDITIONS UNDER WHICH A MONOPOLY MAY EXIST

You will recall that a competitive firm has no appreciable influence over the price of the product it manufactures. On the other hand, a monopoly has an appreciable influence over the price of the commodity it manufactures. In fact, a monopoly can raise the price significantly by cutting down in production and vice versa. The monopolistic power is the power to change prices significantly without changing the level of production drastically. This does not mean that a monopolist will prefer to operate in a range of output where the demand curve is inelastic. On the contrary, a monopoly will avoid that range because an inelastic demand curve is equivalent to a negative marginal revenue.[1] This can be explained intuitively as follows: It was shown in Chapter 1 that in the case of an inelastic demand curve, the smaller the output, the larger

[1] Review the last section of Chapter 1.

the total revenue. Thus, if a monopoly is confronted with an inelastic segment of a demand curve, it pays the entrepreneur to decrease production just until it reaches a range of output where the demand curve becomes elastic. This is true because by shrinking production the monopoly increases its total revenue and decreases its total cost (by cutting down variable costs). Accordingly, the total effect is to increase profit. Once the monopolist is confronted with an elastic segment of the demand curve he will find the optimal point by a process of trial and error: increasing output will give rise to larger cost and larger total revenue and vice versa.

Theoretically, any firm facing a negatively sloped demand curve may be defined as a monopoly. In practice we apply the term monopoly only to a sole producer of a commodity which has no close substitutes. The electricity company is a typical monopoly. Even though the use of gas for cooking is a fairly good substitute for electricity, we find that substitutes for electricity in lighting are rather poor. On the other hand, consider a producer who enters the market with a new brand of cola. Theoretically, the producer of the new cola is a monopolist. He can raise the price of his product and still sell something in the market. However, his power to change the price is very limited; a small rise in the price will give many consumers an incentive to shift to other substitute colas which are available in the market. Thus, the monopolistic power of the new producer of cola is negligible, and, since colas are heterogeneous products, few consumers will continue to buy the relatively expensive cola. This is why the producer of cola is not purely "competitive." His demand curve, however, is very elastic.

Whether we should apply a model of a monopoly or a model of a competitive industry in the case of a cola depends on the purpose of the analysis. If we want to explain why there are small differences in the prices of the different colas, we must treat each brand of cola as a monopolized item. On the other hand, if we are interested in predicting the change in the cola price index resulting from placing a specific tax on all colas, we can assume a competitive market in which each producer faces an horizontal demand curve.

The cola industry is said to be governed by monopolistic competition which is characterized by product differentiation. Other products that are produced in monopolistic competition are beer, coffee, and the like. A very important aspect of monopolistic competition is advertisement. We shall discuss this problem in Chapter 13.

PRICE DISCRIMINATION

Quantity Discrimination.   If the monopoly makes a commodity that cannot be transferred from one consumer to another, it has an incentive to institute a policy of quantity discrimination. It will charge relatively high prices for small quantities and low prices for larger quantities. Such price setting is possible only if the product cannot be resold. This form of price discrimination cannot succeed if the product can be resold, because it will pay some one to buy large quantities and resell them at a small profit to consumers who need small quantities. Examples of products and services that cannot be resold are electricity and telephone services.

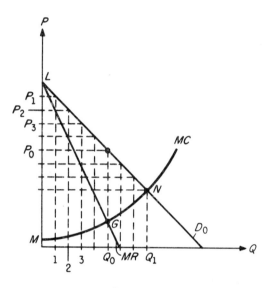

Fig. 12-2

If the monopolist decides to sell Q_0 units as indicated by point G, his producer's surplus would be the area bordered by the MR curve, the MC curve, and the price axis as indicated by LMG in Fig. 12-2. His net profit which is the shaded rectangle in Fig. 12-1 is equal to the producer's surplus minus payments to fixed factors (including the alternative cost of the entrepreneurial services). But, the monopolist may decide to charge the consumers more money by resorting to quantity discrimination. Accordingly, he will charge a price P_1 for the first unit, P_2 for the second unit, etc. Thus, the net additional gain on the first unit is the price minus the MC rather than MR minus the MC, and so on for the second and third, up to the last unit. Altogether the monopolist will now produce Q_1 units. (Why?) That is, the producer's surplus of the monopolist who institutes quantity discrimination is the area bordered by the demand curve, the MC curve and the price axis as indicated by LMN in Fig. 12-2. The monopolist has increased his profit by an area which is indicated by LGN. In reality if there are a million consumers, then if a price P_1 is set for the first unit, P_2 for the second unit and so on, the monopolist will sell the first million units at a price of P_1 dollars, the second million units at a price of P_2 dollars, etc. If public opinion objects to such practices, the monopolist who happened to be, say, an electricity company, may set only two prices, one for households and another for industries, which is a different case of price discrimination.

PRICE DISCRIMINATION BETWEEN TWO MARKETS

Monopolies may treat different markets differently. The most common practice is dumping commodities abroad at prices lower than the domestic price. Dumping is possible only if the difference between the domestic price and the price abroad is not larger than the cost of shipping the merchandise back home or if a tariff is placed on the imported commodity.

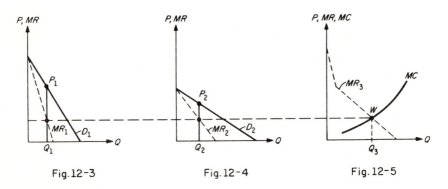

Fig. 12-3   Fig. 12-4   Fig. 12-5

Let the domestic demand curve and MR curve be D_1 and MR_1 in Fig. 12-3; the demand curve for the monopolized product abroad is D_2 and its marginal revenue is denoted by MR_2, as indicated in Fig. 12-4. The monopolist will maximize his profit when his marginal cost is equal to marginal revenue at home and marginal revenue abroad, respectively.

There are two stages in reaching maximum profit. First, the two marginal revenues have to be equated. For example, if $MR_1 = \$7$ and $MR_2 = \$4$, then it pays the monopolist to increase sales in the first market and decrease sales in the second market. The net gain from transferring the first unit from the second to the first market is $\$7 - \$4 = \$3$. However, since the marginal revenue curve has a negative slope, transferring output from the second to the first market will lower MR_1 and raise MR_2. It will pay the monopolist to continue transferring output from the second to the first market just until $MR_1 = MR_2$. For reasons we have already explained, the second stage is reaching the equality between MC and marginal revenues, i.e., $MC = MR_1 = MR_2$. Geometrically, this optimal point of production is obtained by deriving the aggregate MR curve. This is carried out in Fig. 12-5, where MR_3 is the aggregate MR curve. *Formally* the procedure of aggregating MR curves is identical with that of aggregating demand curves; thus we shall not elaborate on it. The MC curve intersects with the aggregate MR at W, at which point a total amount of Q_3 units of output is sold. This amount is divided between the two markets as indicated by their respective marginal revenue curves, i.e., the same marginal revenue which is equal to Q_3W prevails in each market. The quantity sold at home is Q_1 and abroad Q_2 and, of course, $Q_1 + Q_2 = Q_3$. Note that the domestic price P_1 is higher than P_2 which is charged abroad. But, in order to obtain the same marginal revenue of Q_3W in both markets, respectively, the monopolist must charge two different prices. In other words, P_1 is the only domestic price which will yield a marginal revenue of Q_3W at home, and P_2 is the only price which will yield the same marginal revenue of Q_3W abroad.

Examples of price discrimination are ample: doctors charge rich persons higher fees compared with poor persons. The explanation to this phenomenon is found in Figs. 12-3, 12-4, and 12-5. There, D_1 is the demand curve of the rich and D_2 is the demand curve of the poor for medical services rendered by doctors. The doctor maximizes his profit by charging the rich a price of P_1 and the poor a price of P_2. The demand curve of the rich is less elastic because he spends a smaller percentage of his income on medical services as compared with the poor. Note that the markets are separated; the poor person cannot resell an injection to the rich person!

Some movies are shown first to the most eager buyers at prices of $3 and more. After a few months, the movie is released to the neighborhood theaters at a price of $1 a ticket, for the less eager buyers.

In international trade, dumping is a prevalent practice. For example, a Fiat, the Italian manufactured automobile, is sold outside Italy at a lower price for an indentical model. This can be rationalized by assuming that the market for the Fiat car outside Italy is more elastic than it is at home. Dumping is most likely to take place if the market at home is protected.

Let the domestic market be denoted by the subscript 1, and the foreign market by the subscript 2. The monopolist will equate the marginal revenues in the two markets, that is $MR_1 = MR_2$. But,

$$MR_1 = P_1\left(1 + \frac{1}{\eta_1}\right) \qquad MR_2 = P_2\left(1 + \frac{1}{\eta_2}\right)$$

Thus,

$$P_1\left(1 + \frac{1}{\eta_1}\right) = P_2\left(1 + \frac{1}{\eta_2}\right)$$

If $|\eta_2| > |\eta_1|$ (and both demand curves are respectively elastic), then

$$\left(1 + \frac{1}{\eta_2}\right) > \left(1 + \frac{1}{\eta_1}\right)$$

but in order that the above equality will hold we must have $P_1 > P_2$. Namely, the monopolist will charge a higher price in the market where the demand curve is relatively less elastic.

CARTELS

Cartels are selling agencies. Usually a cartel is an organization of a large number of firms established for selling and promoting their product. In agriculture, cartels are usually called cooperatives. Thus, there are cooperatives for the common selling of different crops such as wheat and fruits. It is a common error to attach the tag of monopoly to all cartels. In fact, one can find many cartels which are not monopolies. The necessary condition for a cartel to become a monopoly is to be able to allot quotas to its members. Another important condition is that practically all producers will be organized in one cartel. If this is the case, then the cartel can move up along the demand curve by alloting smaller quotas and move down along the demand curve by alloting larger quotas. Thus, by moving up and down along the demand curve, the cartel will reach a point where it maximizes total profits for the industry as a whole. This total net profit will be divided among different producers according to a certain key, probably in direct proportion to the share of each producer in total production. Note that in practice it is rather difficult to organize a cartel that can exercise the power of a monopoly over the market. To illustrate this consider Fig. 12-1. Assume that MC is the aggregate MC curve of many small firms, or simply the supply curve of the industry. Next assume that all the firms decide to organize as a cartel. The cartel effectively enforces quotas, and by so doing the industry as a whole moves up along the demand curve from point N to point H, where the cartel maximizes its profit. But, recall that in the cartel each firm retains its individuality; hence it has a certain degree of independence. The firm has a tremendous incentive to go around the cartel and sell more than its quota. Unless the cartel is capable of imposing severe sanctions on firms that are not conforming, too many firms will sell more than their assigned quotas; thus, total output will increase, and price will decline until the industry will be back at the competitive point N. Accordingly, it is known that in agriculture the only cartel that has a monopoly power is the organization of growers of tobacco. Other cooperatives for selling grains and fruits have nothing to do with the monopoly. In fact, they promote competition by providing farmers with more information about the prevailing prices of different grains, both in the present and in the future.

We have seen that a cartel has little chance of becoming a monopoly. Its form of organization is too loose, and it cannot prevent its members from trying to benefit from the monopoly price and at the same time sell more than their quota allows them. In order for a cartel to become a monopoly, it needs a stronger form of organization.

INDIRECT TAXES

Recall that placing a specific tax on a product produced competitively results in a higher marginal cost curve. Since the supply curve in competition is the aggregate marginal cost curve, a specific tax leads to a higher supply curve which cuts the demand curve at a higher point and to the left of the original point of equilibrium.

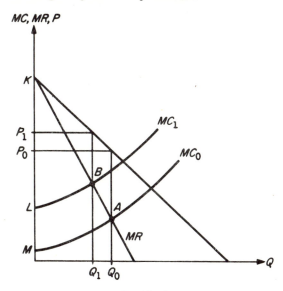

Fig. 12-6

In the case of monopoly, a specific tax leads to the same result. After the tax is imposed, the marginal cost curve shifts upward from MC_0 to MC_1. This is illustrated in Fig. 12-6. Originally the MC curve cut the MR curve at point A, to which point corresponded a quantity Q_0 and a price of P_0. The new marginal cost curve cuts the MR at point B, to which correspond a smaller quantity Q_1 and a higher price P_1. As a result, there is a once and for all adjustment: variable factors of production that were used in the production of the segment $Q_1 Q_0$ must seek employment elsewhere. The producer's surplus of the monopoly decreases from the area indicated by *KMA* to the area indicated by *KLB*.

PRICE LEADERSHIP

Consider the case where a certain identical product is made by many small firms and one large firm. It can be shown that this firm will in fact be a monopoly and a price leader. Total demand is D_0 in Fig. 12-7. Total supply *of all* small firms is S_0 in Fig. 12-7. Consider any price, say $0F$, in Fig. 12-7, which is denoted by $0K$ in Fig. 12-8. At that price the small firms together will supply *FG* units, but the demand will amount to *FH* units; thus, the excess demand will equal GH $(= FH - FG)$. This excess demand is the demand confronting the large firm. Accordingly, in Fig. 12-8, at a price of $0K$ $(= 0F$ in Fig. 12-7), a quantity of KL $(= GH$ in Fig. 12-7) will be demanded. This procedure can be applied to all relevant prices, and thus the demand curve D_f is obtained in Fig. 12-8. The mar-

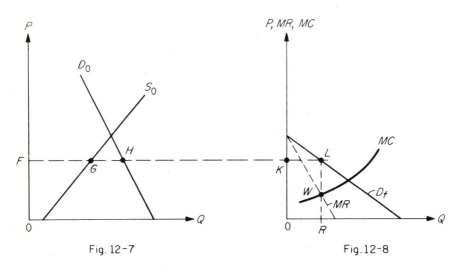

Fig. 12-7   Fig. 12-8

ginal revenue curve which corresponds to this demand curve intersects with the marginal cost curve of the large firm at point W, where the price is $0K$. This is the price which will be followed by all small firms. It is an equilibrium price, because as indicated before, the quantity demanded *FH* is equal to the combined quantity supplied at that price: the share of all small firms in production is *FG* in Fig. 12-7. The share of the monopoly (Fig. 12-7) is *GH*, which is equal to *KL* in Fig. 12-8. It is left for the student to show that if the government forces the monopolist to charge a price which equals its marginal cost, then the market price will be lower and a few marginal small firms will have to discontinue production.

AN IMPORTANT FORMULA

Consider Figs. 12-7 and 12-8. We have illustrated there how the demand curve confronted by a single firm is derived. If the demand confronting the firm is denoted by D_f, the supply of all other firms by S and the aggregate demand by D, we have

$$D_f = D - S$$

Let us assume that originally we have

$$D_{f0} = D_0 - S_0$$

and after the price changes by ΔP we have

$$D_{f1} = D_1 - S_1$$

Then, of course,

$$\underbrace{D_{f1} - D_{f0}}_{\Delta D_f} = \underbrace{D_1 - D_0}_{\Delta D} - \underbrace{(S_1 - S_0)}_{\Delta S}$$

Multiplying through by $P/(D_f \cdot \Delta P)$ we obtain

$$\frac{P \cdot \Delta D_f}{D_f \cdot \Delta P} = \frac{P \cdot \Delta D}{D_f \cdot \Delta P} - \frac{P \cdot \Delta S}{D_f \cdot \Delta P}$$

or

$$\frac{P \cdot \Delta D_f}{D_f \cdot \Delta P} = \frac{D \cdot P \cdot \Delta D}{D_f \cdot D \cdot \Delta P} - \frac{S \cdot P \cdot \Delta S}{D_f \cdot S \cdot \Delta P}$$

which is

$$\eta_{Df} = \frac{D}{D_f} \cdot \eta - \frac{S}{D_f} \cdot \epsilon$$

Where η_{Df} is price elasticity of the demand curve facing the firm, η is the price elasticity of the aggregate demand curve and ϵ is the price elasticity of the supply curve of all other firms. It is obvious that η_{Df} will be larger, the larger D/D_f and S/D_f are. In other words, the smaller the share of the firm, the flatter its demand curve. When D/D_f and S/D_f are very large, η_{Df} is also very large, and for all practical purposes, we are justified in saying that the demand curve is horizontal. To illustrate this, assume that the share of the firm is 1/1,000 of total production. Assume also that $\eta = -1$ and $\epsilon = 2$; then

$$\eta_{Df} = \frac{1,000}{1}(-1) - \frac{999}{1} \cdot 2 = -2,998$$

To be sure, in economics, $-2,998$ is very close to $-\infty$.

If as it is the case in Figs. 12-7 and 12-8, the share of one firm is fairly large, then η_{Df} is relatively small (in absolute value), and the firm is a monopoly.

THE WELFARE LOSS

Consider Fig. 12-9. If the monopolist were forced to operate at point S, we could claim that the industry is competitive in the sense that the price is equal to the marginal cost. Under such assumptions the consumer's surplus is KMS and the producer's surplus is MNS. But, when the monopolist behaves like one, he operates at the point of intersection between

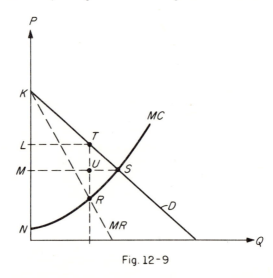

Fig. 12-9

MC and $MR(R)$. The consumer's surplus shrinks to KLT, the producer's surplus is $LNRT$. The monopolist extracts from consumers the rectangle $MUTL$. The triangle TRS is a welfare loss to society. Thus, even if the government imposed a fixed tax of $MUTL$ on the monopolist and returned it to consumers, there is still the welfare loss measured by the triangle TRS.

Welfare loss due to monopolies will be discussed in detail in Chapter 17.

A POLICY TO COPE WITH MONOPOLIES

In the case where monopolies provide services that are deemed to be essential to society, such as water, these services usually become public utilities. Ideally, public utility regulation should require that the price of the service rendered be equal to its marginal cost. In practice, the managements of public utilities tend to set markups similar to those in competitive industries. If you wish, setting the margins on public utility services bears resemblance to a cat-and-mouse game. Managers are given a wide discretion in the process of setting the price of the services. The lower limit is a price that will still allow for depreciation and net investment which is needed to meet the needs of a growing population. The upper limit is a high price that will not be tolerated by public opinion. If the mouse will become too bold and set the price too close to the upper limit, it will arouse the cat, which in this case is the Public Utility Commission. This political mechanism always keeps the entrepreneur of the public utility plant under the public eye.

Before advocating policies to cope with monopolies, we should discuss the conditions that give rise to the monopoly. Monopolies exist because potential rivals are excluded from production in one way or another. Many firms become sole producers of a product due to a patent. Prior to 1953, the United Shoe Machinery Company produced about 85 percent of the shoe machinery in the United States. This was due to a certain patent. This monopolistic power enabled the United Shoe Machinery Company to discriminate in rentals for the purpose of making a monopolistic profit. The court ordered the United Shoe Machinery Company to make its machinery available for sale and to cease discrimination which inhibited the entrance of new firms to the industry. In this case and similar cases where the patent is the source of monopoly, neither nationalization nor price regulation are desirable, the reason being that if we eliminate the monopolistic profit, we at the same time altogether eliminate the incentive to invent new methods of production, or new products. Thus, in order to stimulate new ideas, inventions must be patented. The only policy that we advocate here is that patents should expire after a reasonably short period of time. A reasonable period of time is one which will cover the extra cost of research. Extra cost of research includes, among other things, a sum of money which will compensate the inventor for his income foregone while working on the invention.

There are cases where monopolies arise because of capital requirements. For example, there are only three or four big car producers in the United States because it takes a tremendous investment in tangible capital to establish a car factory. Here, the small car producers are protected by the monopolistic price of General Motors. If the government enforced a lower price, it is possible that small car producers would not be able to break even, leaving General Motors as the sole producer of cars in the United States. Whether this is a desirable goal is a political issue that we leave for the reader to debate.

Economic history shows that there were cases where potential rivals were excluded from the market through temporary price cuts on the part of a monopolist or a group of oligopolists. Accordingly, cutting the price for the purpose of eliminating rivals should be illegal. There is, however, the danger that the courts will confuse between a permanent reduction in price due to a change in demand or production conditions, and a case of a temporary price reduction in order to eliminate a rival. If it is impossible to find a meaningful way of separating between the two types of price reduction, then the illegalization of price-wars may do the consumer more harm than good.

We have dismissed an issue worth a tome with one small section. The purpose was to give the reader the "flavor" of the problem, rather than to enter this complicated field.

PROBLEMS

Answer Probs. 12-1 to 12-7 as being True, False, or Uncertain.

12-1. A monopolist must not know the shape of his MC and demand curves in order to maximize his profit.

12-2. It is possible (in principle) to force a monopoly to produce at a point where price is equal to MC by taxing and subsidizing the monopolist at the same time without incurring any cost to the government.

12-3. If a fixed tax of $100,000 per annum is imposed on a monopoly, it will either close up, or continue to produce the same amount.

12-4. If a tax of 10 percent is imposed on its profits, the monopoly will cut down in production. (HINT: Draw the net profit curve as a function of production before and after the tax.)

12-5. U. S. Steel had to raise prices of steel in order to meet the new costs incurred by the new and better equipment. (HINT: Draw the MC curve before and after installing the superior equipment.)

12-6. A monopolist has no supply curve.

12-7. If the marginal cost curve of a monopolist is zero, regardless of the level of output, the monopolist will operate where the price elasticity of demand is -1.

12-8. Commodity X is produced by a monopoly. The monopoly is confronted with a negatively sloped demand curve at home and an infinitely elastic demand curve abroad. Currently the domestic price of X is higher than its price abroad. The government decides to impose a specific tax per unit of output sold by the monopoly at home. Analyze the domestic and foreign markets before and after the tax. A diagram will help. Assume that X can be shipped from the domestic market abroad, but not vice versa.

12-9. A monopolist considers setting a price in three separate markets.

Market	Price Elasticity
1	-2
2	-5
3	-4

What prices should be set in these markets if MC is always \$3?

12-10. The following is a demand curve confronting a monopoly:

Q	P
1	10
2	9
3	8
4	7
5	6
6	5
7	4

The marginal cost is always \$6. (a) What is the price set by the monopolist and the quantity marketed if the monopoly is not regulated? (b) Can the government force the monopoly to "behave competitively" by taxing and subsidizing it at the same time without a loss to the government? Justify your answer numerically.

12-11. The demand curve confronting the monopoly is like in Prob. 12-10. The monopolist operates two plants, A and B. The cost schedules of the two plants are:

Plant A		Plant B	
Q	TC	Q	TC
1	1	1	1
2	3	2	2
3	6	3	4
4	10	4	7
5	15	5	11

Determine the number of units that should be produced in each of the two plants in order to maximize profit.

12-12. The share of the large firm in total production is 1/10. The price elasticity of the market demand curve is -2, and the price elasticity of supply of all small firms is ⅓. What is the (relative) difference between the price and MC of the large firm?

chapter 13

Imperfect Competition

In this chapter market situations known as *oligopolies* and *monopolistic competition* are analyzed. The definitions of oligopoly and monopolistic competition were given in Chapter 12.

Oligopoly may arise because of various reasons. Let us cite a few examples: Ownership of a patent may give rise to market domination by a few firms. General Electric happened to own the patent of producing light bulbs. It allowed other small firms to use the patent for a fee and on condition that they did not exceed the quota allotted to them and followed the price set by General Electric. Thus, for all practical purposes, the market for light bulbs was shared by General Electric and a few other firms. General Electric's control of the market was eliminated only after the patent expired.

In other cases, the barrier to enter the industry is the requirement of huge initial investments in tangible capital. Millions of dollars must be raised in order to buy the equipment necessary to establish a firm in the aluminum industry. The fact is that entrepreneurs with the ability to raise huge funds are rare.

Entry into an industry which is dominated by a few firms may be prevented by economic warfare. Economic warfare consists of inflicting financial losses on rivals who may attempt to enter the industry. An example is the case where gasoline companies temporarily cut the prices below the average cost in order to discourage a new rival. Once the new rival is forced out of the industry, the price will again be fixed at the original level or even a higher level.

Finally, there is the case where oligopoly arises because of huge overhead costs. High overhead costs entail a high average cost curve for small levels of production, and a very low average cost curve for a large scale of production.

If this is the shape of the average cost curve, then the entry of a new rival may force some or all oligopolists to cut down in production and thus move up along the average cost curve. This may lead one or a few of them to leave the industry, and in the end the number of firms in the industry will not grow.

THE CASE OF A HOMOGENEOUS PRODUCT

In oligopoly the policy-maker of the firm must take into consideration a possible retaliation from other firms. Thus, if he cuts his price, he may in the short run attract many more customers, but other firms may declare a price war and cut their prices even further, thus gaining more customers to their product and so on along the line. Eventually the few firms that are in the industry will form a tacit merger or trust, where each firm will be allotted a certain fraction of total output. For example, an illegal merger of steel producers may decide to raise the price of steel by $6 per ton. Since it is illegal to conspire for the common purpose of limiting output, the head of this organization may call a secret meeting where the problem will be discussed between the different producers. Let us assume that steel producers will be convinced that the price elasticity is in the order of magnitude of -2. If the current price of steel is $60, then a $6 increase in price is consistent with cutting down production 20 percent. So as not to arouse the suspicion of the government, producers will independently raise the price of steel a few weeks apart. This is a case where antitrust laws may be very ineffective. They may be ineffective in the sense that it is very difficult to prove that there is collusion between producers. But even if it is possible to show collusion, due to the lack of sufficient data, it is very difficult to rule in the case. Thus, if raising the price of steel resulted from a leftward shift in the rising marginal cost curve, then raising prices was justified.

TABLE 13-1

Firm A		Firm B	
Quantity	MC	Quantity	MC
1	2	1	½
2	3	2	1
3	4	3	2
4	5	4	3
5	6	5	4
6	7	6	5
7	8	7	6
8	9	8	7

In the absence of anti-collusion laws, the few firms in the industry will tend to form a collusion and set a monopoly price. First, regardless of the price they set, oligopolistic firms will tend to divide output among themselves such that their respective marginal costs are the same. To illustrate this, consider a case of duopoly. The outputs and marginal cost schedules, respectively, of firm A and firm B are shown in Table 13-1. Let us assume that the entrepreneurs of the two firms made an agreement to peg the price at $10, at which marginal revenue equals $5. This is consistent with price elasticity of -2. At that price the market clears 10 units. Also, according to the agreement, firm A and firm B should share the market equally. Each of them will produce 5 units. This will not, however, be their final equilibrium.

The MC of firm A is $6 and the MC of firm B is $4. Firm B has an incentive to "bribe" firm A to transfer one unit of output from its quota to the quota of B. By foregoing the production of one unit firm A will reduce its cost by $6, and firm B will increase its cost by $5. Thus, between the two of them A and B will increase their combined profit by $1. How they will divide this extra profit will depend on their bargaining positions.

Saying that the oligopolists tend to equate their respective marginal costs is equivalent to saying that they have a meaningful aggregate MC curve. In Fig. 13-1 the marginal cost curve of firm A is denoted by MC_A and that of firm B by MC_B. In Fig. 13-2, the aggregate MC curve of the two firms is denoted by ΣMC. The aggregate MC curve intersects with

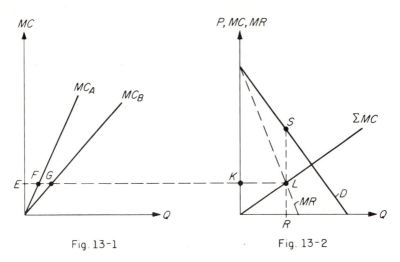

Fig. 13-1   Fig. 13-2

the MR curve at point L. Thus, the optimum combination for the industry is the quantity KL at a price of RS. KL in Fig. 13-2 equals EF plus

EG in Fig. 13-1. Thus, after the long-run adjustment takes place, a quantity EF is produced by firm A and a quantity of EG is produced by firm B, regardless of the original arrangement between them.

A *market-sharing cartel* is a market situation where a few firms which dominate the production of a homogeneous product agree to share the market according to some regional or any other arrangement. The above analysis indicates that if the sharing agreement prohibits transferring output from one firm to another, the combined profit of the member of the cartel is less than the possible maximum. If the management of the cartel is wise, it should allow firms operating at a low marginal cost to "bribe" firms operating at a high marginal cost to yield some of their quotas.

Note that the demand curve D in Fig. 13-2 is either the market demand curve or the net demand curve like D_f in Fig. 12-8. It is the market demand curve if small firms are excluded by an economic warfare or by an exclusive ownership of a patent. In economic jargon this case is known as closed oligopoly. There are cases, however, where a certain identical product is made by many small firms and a few large firms. Thus, if the market demand curve is D_0 and the supply curve of small rivals is S_0 in Fig. 12-7, the large firms are faced with D_f in Fig. 12-8. Thus, MC in Fig. 12-8 can be the aggregate MC of the oligopolists; and in absence of antitrust laws, oligopolists will tend to produce OR units of output at a price of RL. The share of the oligopolists in the market will be $KL(=GH)$ units of output in Fig. 12-8, leaving FG for the small rivals. If the oligopolists are threatened by antitrust laws one of them will become the price leader and others will follow him tacitly. For example, the leader may set a price of RL (Fig. 12-8). At that price small rivals will produce FG leaving GH ($=KL$) for the oligopolists (Fig. 12-7 and 12-8). The main problem will be to agree on the share of each oligopolist in total output. The technical problem of sharing the production of KL units may be resolved by tacitly agreeing to a certain geographical division of markets, or by adhering to a certain proportion that is accepted by all oligopolists. In fact, any allotment of the KL units (Fig. 12-8) can work out provided that each oligopolist can at least make the profit that he would have made without following the leader. The case where production is shared by many small firms and a few large firms is known as an open oligopoly. Examples of open oligopolies are abundant: In 1958, about 70 percent of steel was produced by the top four corporations, and this was the case in the tire industry. About 75 percent of flat glass was accounted for by four companies; other industries where a few firms dominated more than 70 percent of the market were aluminum, metal cans, and transformers.

PRICE LEADERSHIP IN OLIGOPOLY

Consider now a situation in which there is neither formal agreement nor a tacit collusion between the oligopolists. To simplify the analysis, consider an industry in which two firms dominate the production of a homogeneous commodity. Since the commodity is homogeneous a single price must prevail in the market. Assume that homogeneity gives rise to a 50-50 chance that a consumer will select either one of the two producers, denoted by A and B. In Fig. 13-3, D is the market demand curve, and d

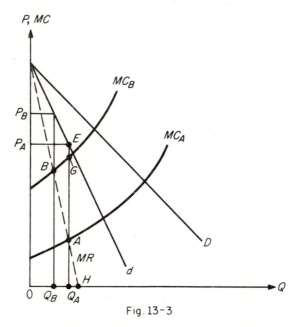

Fig. 13-3

(which is half the distance between D and the price axis) is the demand curve confronting each producer. The marginal cost curve of B, MC_B occupies a higher position than the marginal cost curve of A, MC_A. MC_B cuts marginal revenue, MR at point B and MC_A cuts MR at point A. Firm A would attempt to produce Q_A units and charge a price P_A. Firm B would attempt to produce Q_B units and charge a higher price, P_B. Clearly, the homogeneity of the product will preclude firm B from the market if it attempts to secure a price higher than P_A. Thus, firm B must follow the price set by A in the range extending from 0 to Q_A. The marginal revenue curve of B becomes the kinked line denoted by P_A EAH. It cuts MC_B at point G, and accordingly each of the two firms would produce Q_A units at a price of P_A. Firm A is known as the *price leader*. The case where MC_B cuts the line P_A E is left for the reader.

There are other possibilities of oligopolistic leadership. These possibilities are analyzed in the Mathematical Appendix.

GAME THEORY

In the case of collusion, the behavior of oligopolists is rational. They find a price which maximizes their aggregate profit, and then they share the profit so that each receives a profit equal to, or larger than, the profit that could be had without collusion.

Is there another rational solution short of collusion? There are situations where such a solution can be defined. This solution which is known as game theory is due to John von Neumann and Oskar Morgenstern.[1] Recall that in oligopoly the profit of the individual producer is determined not only by his behavior but by the behavior of other oligopolists as well. Let us now consider two duopolists, duopolist A and duopolist B. The behavior of each of them is divided into three strategies; let us denote the strategies open to duopolist A by A_1, A_2, and A_3 and the strategies open to duopolist B by B_1, B_2, and B_3. Strategies could be in the form of selling techniques, discounts given to customers, extra services performed while selling the product, and so on along the line.

Consider now Tables 13-2 and 13-3.

TABLE 13-2				TABLE 13-3			
	A's Profit (in $)				B's Profit (in $)		
	B_1	B_2	B_3		B_1	B_2	B_3
A_1	3	8	1	A_1	9	3	10
A_2	4	2	10	A_2	8	13	4
A_3	6	7	9	A_3	7	4	5

Table 13-2 shows the profits of A determined by his own and B's choice of strategy. For example, if he chooses strategy A_2 and B chooses B_3, his profit will amount to $10. Now, consider the following situation: duopolist A is going to select his strategy knowing that once he has chosen a strategy, duopolist B has three strategies open to him. Thus, if A chooses A_1, B will choose B_3 leaving A with $1. If A chooses A_2, B will choose B_2 leaving him with $2. Finally if A chooses A_3, B will choose B_1 leaving A with $6. Clearly A is going to choose A_3 which leaves him with the highest profit. By the same process of thinking B will choose

[1] John von Neumann and Oskar Morgenstern, *The Theory of Games and Economic Behavior*, Princeton, N. J.: Princeton University Press, 1954.

strategy B_1, and we arrived at a stable solution: at A_3B_1 duopolist A earns $6; by choosing either A_2 or A_1 he can only lose either $4 or $5. Thus A has no incentive to change his strategy. At A_3B_1, duopolist B earns $7. By changing his strategies to either B_2 or B_3, he will lose either $4 or $3. This is known as a *stable solution.*

Notice that although the combination of A_3 and B_1 is a stable solution, it is not the best solution. For example, the duopolists could form a collusion choosing strategies A_2 and B_2 yielding a joint profit of $15. Thus collusion could increase the profit of each of the duopolists by $1. In fact, sharing the extra profit of $2 from collusion is a matter that would be determined by bargaining. Accordingly, even if there is a stable solution, it probably is not a long-run solution. If the strategies of B are known to A, and vice versa, it would be unwise of them to play games while they can maximize their respective profits by forming a collusion.

The game can be played under the assumption that A cannot know what B's strategies are and vice versa. In other words, A has no idea of what Table 13-3 looks like. Then, if he chooses A_3, his profit will not go down below $6. If he chooses the remaining strategies, he takes the risk of reducing his profits to $2 or even to $1. Accordingly, if the assumption is made that duopolist A does not want to undertake any such risks, his choice would be A_3. By the same process, if duopolist B does not choose B_1, he takes the risk of earning only $4 or even $3. If B is against undertaking such risks, he would choose B_1, and we arrived at the same stable solution. If the duopolists are ready to gamble, the game is different. More important, here as in the previous game, the collusion is a possible solution and there is no reason why the duopolists should ignore it. Finally, it is possible to construct tables similar to Tables 13-2 and 13-3 where a stable solution cannot be found. This would lead to either indeterminacy or collusion as far as the behavior of oligopolists is concerned.

THE CASE OF A DIFFERENTIATED PRODUCT

If a differentiated product is made by a few firms, then the product is said to be produced by oligopoly. Examples are the industries producing cars, beer, soft drinks, and cigarettes. There are two market situations that should be considered here. One is where prices are flexible and rivalry is through altering prices as well as through advertising and changing the quality of the product. The other is known as nonprice rivalry. Here, the price is sluggish either because it is set by tradition or because the administrative cost of changing it is too high. An example is the industry of soft drinks: changing the price of one bottle from a dime to eleven cents would involve a very high cost, because of the necessity to readjust the soft-drink machines to the new price.

FLEXIBLE PRICES

Pure competitive firms never advertise. After all, why should farmers waste money on advertising if for all practical purposes they sell the same wheat. But, when it comes to beer, there are different flavors, and producers are each trying to convince the consumers that the taste of their particular beer is "just right." So far as the individual equilibrium is concerned, there is no difference between a monopoloy and an oligopoly producing a differentiated product. Like the monopoly, the oligopoly will operate where MC intersects with MR; thus, in both cases the firm is able to charge a price higher than the marginal cost. But there is the following difference: normally, the oligopoly producing a differentiated product is confronted with a relatively more elastic demand curve, or if you wish, a *relatively* flat demand curve. It is evident from the way the MR curve is derived that the flatter the demand curve, the closer to it is the marginal revenue curve. Accordingly, the price charged by a firm producing a differentiated product cannot be set too high above the marginal cost, and thus, the exploitation of the consumer is relatively small. The demand curve with which the oligopoly producing a differentiated product is confronted is not perfectly elastic because if the firm lowers the price of its product, it will win over many customers from other oligopolists, but not all of them. If the oligopoly raises its price, it will lose many customers to other oligopolists, but not all of them. For example, if Tareyton reduces

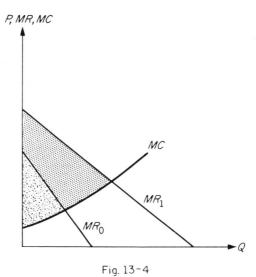

Fig. 13-4

the price of its cigarettes, it will attract a certain fraction of smokers of Kent and Pall Mall but not all of them. The reason is that there are differences in flavor, length, and filter that distinguish the various types of cigarettes from each other. Although these various types of cigarettes are heterogeneous, the element of substitution is quite strong and thus the absolute value of the price elasticity of each cigarette is very high. The higher the price elasticity, the closer the firm is to becoming competitive. The smaller the price elasticity (in absolute value), the closer the firm is to becoming a monopoly. This can be illustrated as follows:

$$MR = P\left(1 + \frac{1}{\eta}\right)$$

Then if $\eta = -5$, we have

$$MR = P\,(1 - \tfrac{1}{5}) = \tfrac{4}{5} \cdot P$$

Namely, marginal revenue is 80 percent of the price. If $\eta = -10$, we obtain

$$MR = P(1 - \tfrac{1}{10})$$

namely, marginal revenue is 90 percent of the price, and so on.

A serious problem that arises from oligopoly with a differentiated product is advertising. Since the products are differentiated, firms try to attract more customers by advertising. In economic terms, an oligopoly tries to change the tastes of consumers in favor of its product and against substitutes made by the other oligopolists. Thus, advertising boils down to spending money on shifting rightward the demand curve with which the firm is confronted. A rightward shift in the demand curve entails a rightward shift in the MR curve. It is recalled that the producer's surplus is the area bordered by the marginal revenue curve, the marginal cost curve, and the price axis. Assume that advertising is a fixed cost to the firm. This assumption will hold if advertising is carried out by putting ads in magazines and on TV. Following the shift in demand, the marginal revenue curve shifts rightward, say, from MR_0 to MR_1, as indicated on Fig. 13-4. Originally the producer's surplus was the dotted area. After the shift occurred, it increased by the shaded area. The net gain to the oligopoly is the shaded area minus the additional cost of advertising.

Advertising may entail an upward shift in the MC curve. For example, if the firm decides to advertise by inserting the product it makes in a fancy package that costs an extra amount of 10 cents per unit, then the marginal cost curve will shift upward 10 cents. The extra gain from advertising will be the area bordered by the price axis, MR_0 curve, MR_1 curve, and the old MC, minus the area between old MC and new MC. The gains of advertising may be dissipated because of retaliation of rivals. If a beer producer persuades the public to buy his beer instead of a competing brand, other oligopolists will retaliate by using the same kind of advertisement. This retaliation will shift his demand curve back toward its original

position leading MR_1 (Fig. 13-4) to shift toward MR_0. Thus, the effects
of advertising within the industry are canceled out. But advertising may
give rise to a gain by winning customers over from more remote substitutes. For example, if all beer producers advertise, the net effect on
each producer within the group is zero. But this advertising may gain
customers through incursions upon the markets of soft-drink producers.
In the long run, however, soft-drink producers will retaliate; and all extra
gains of advertising, within the industry and outside of it, will be dissipated. Since in the long run gains of advertising are dissipated, we must
answer the following question: *Is advertising a social waste?* In order to
answer this, one should be concerned with another issue; namely, *do we
want to have only one kind of cigarette, one make of car, and one type of
soft drink?* To be sure, in the market we vote democratically where each
dime is a vote, and a dollar is ten such votes. Accordingly it seems that
we have voted for a variety of cigarettes, cars, soft drinks, and all other
differentiated commodities that are made by oligopolies. Since we want
variety of cigarettes rather than one cigarette, we have to pay for advertising, because without it we cannot be informed about the differences
between various brands. It does not make any difference whether the
differentiation is "real" or "psychological," because the process of enjoy-
ment is psychological as well as physiological.

Notice, finally, that if a differentiated product is made by a small
number of oligopolists, altering the price by one oligopolist will affect the
demand curves of the others. To illustrate the process of price determination under conditions of product differentiation and price flexibility, con-

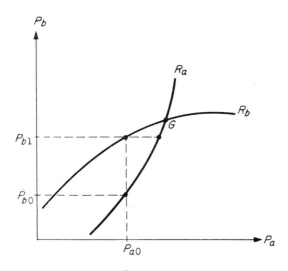

Fig. 13-5

sider the case of two duopolists, denoted by A and B. When B raises its price, the demand curve with which A is confronted shifts rightward and upward leading to a higher point of intersection between MC and MR and a higher price. Thus, a higher price of A's product leads to a higher price of B's product, and vice versa. The process which determines the equilibrium in the industry is illustrated in Fig. 13-5.

The horizontal axis represents the price of A and the vertical axis the price of B. R_a is the "reaction curve" of A telling what price A will set given the price of B. R_b is the "reaction curve" of B telling what price B will set given the price of A. If B sets a price of P_{b0}, A will set the price P_{a0} as indicated by R_a. In reaction, B will set a price of P_{b1}, and so on. This process leads us to G which is a point of stable equilibrium. At G, none of the duopolists has an incentive to change his price. It is easy to show that if R_a and R_b are interchanged, no stable equilibrium is attainable.

NONPRICE RIVALRY

As we indicated before, the price of a differentiated product may be fixed in the market either due to tradition and trade practices, or due to heavy costs involved in altering the price. Since the price is given, the oligopolist can only choose between different phases of the product, which is known as product variation. Product variation can be achieved through a change in the container of a soft drink, a change in color of the product itself, or a change in the contents of a newspaper. In what follows we shall use Chamberlin's model of nonprice rivalry.[2] In Fig. 13-6, the price is fixed at a level of $0E$. Two phases of the product are known to the producer. Denote them by X and Y. The average cost of phase X is denoted by X and that of Y by Y. Notice that the price line is not a demand curve with which the firm is confronted. How much will be demanded of each phase is determined by market conditions. Let us fix the market conditions and assume that if phase X is chosen, $0M$ units will be demanded, yielding a rent indicated by $FKLE$. (Why?) If phase Y is chosen, $0N$ units will be produced yielding a rent indicated by $GRSE$. (Why?) Clearly, the oligopolist will choose phase Y which yields the higher rent. If this rent is sufficiently high, entrepreneurs from outside may establish firms in the industry leading to smaller markets. In Fig. 13-6 this would mean a quantity smaller than $0N$ for phase Y and a quantity smaller than $0M$ for phase X. It is easy to show that if the new quantities are $0A$ for X and $0B$ for Y, the firm should discontinue production in the long run. Thus, so long as market conditions are unchanged, each oligopolist chooses

[2] Edward H. Chamberlin, *The Theory of Monopolistic Competition*, Boston, Mass.: Harvard University Press, 1958.

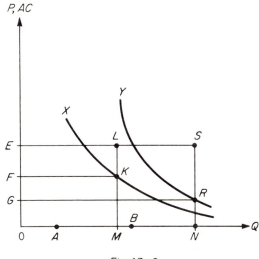

Fig. 13-6

the phase of product which maximizes his rent. Once market conditions change due to the entry of a new producer or the discovery of a new phase by one of the firms already in the industry, the firms in the industry must readjust to the new situation. Quantities corresponding to the various phases of production change, and, accordingly, some of the firms may find it advantageous to shift from one phase of the product to another. It is also possible that one or more firms will have to leave the industry.

The theory of advertising and nonprice rivalry is similar to product variation. Thus, in Fig. 13-6, X can represent the average cost curve of the product with a small selling cost. The quantity demanded is $0M$ and the rent is $FKLE$. Increasing the selling costs will shift the average cost curve to Y, and to the first approximation will increase sales from $0M$ to $0N$, thus increasing rent to $GRSE$. The change of MN is at least partially at the expense of other oligopolists who will react to it by increasing their own selling costs. Increasing the selling costs by other producers will reduce the quantity demanded in Fig. 13-6 to a quantity lower than $0N$, leading to a rent smaller than $GRSE$. This process leads to an equilibrium where the average cost (including selling costs) is very close to the fixed price.

MONOPOLISTIC COMPETITION

In monopolistic competition there are many sellers and ease of entry and exit. In this respect it is similar to pure competition. But, in contrast to pure competition, the product in monopolistic competition is slightly differentiated, which implies a demand curve of finite elasticity. Due to the presence of many close substitutes in the industry, the demand curve con-

fronting one firm in monopolistic competition is very elastic, and thus the
MC in equilbrium is very close to the price. Accordingly, the exploitation
of the consumer due to the divergence between the MC and the price is
relatively small. Like pure competition, monopolistic competition fosters
political freedom: the producer cannot force a low quality product upon
the consumer because of the existence of other producers. The employer
cannot mistreat the employee because of the presence of other producers
in the industry with whom the employee can work, and so on along
the line. Finally, by his decision to alter price and production, the
producer in monopolistic competition cannot appreciably affect other
producers. For example, if one retailer lowers the price in order to increase
sales, the result would be to decrease the demand for the services offered
by other retailers. But since there are hundreds of them, the reduction
in the demand confronted each of them separately will be negligible, and
it can be ignored for all practical purposes.

The individual equilibrium is achieved at the point of intersection
between MC and MR. Coming to the group equilibrium, it is very much
like in competition. If rent is relatively large on the average, and if this

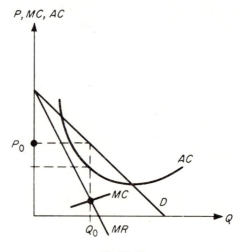

Fig. 13-7

rent is not a compensation for undertaking risk, then entrepreneurs from
outside the industry may enter the industry leading to a leftward shift in
the demand curves of all the firms in the industry. Firms whose demand
curves shift below the AC curve will discontinue production in the long
run, leaving in the industry firms with positive rents, and marginal firms.
The firm with positive rent, the marginal firm, and the firm leaving the
industry are illustrated by Figs. 13-7, 13-8, and 13-9, respectively.
Notice that while price equals AC in the case of the marginal firm, it is

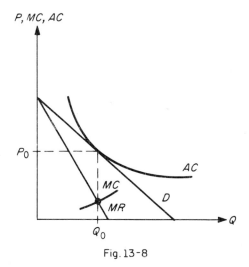

Fig. 13-8

higher than AC for the firm with positive rent. Having covered in detail the three noncompetitive market situations, we can now turn to other topics that are of interest in this chapter.

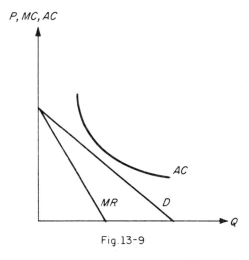

Fig. 13-9

ANTITRUST LAWS

Antitrust laws are passed after the public becomes concerned over the fact that many firms either merge or organize in trusts for the common goal of restricting production and raising prices above marginal cost. For example, the Sherman Antitrust Act was passed in the United States at the end of the nineteenth century. This act was designed to protect the American consumer from exploitation by big mergers and trusts that were formed in order to be able to employ monopolistic powers over consumers. Antitrust laws make it very difficult for small firms to combine. They give the government the right of breaking down big mergers.

It is not in the scope of this text to survey the history of antitrust laws. Also, it is not the role of this chapter to count all the advantages and drawbacks of such laws. However, the attention of the reader should be called to the complexity that may arise here. We refer, for example, to a case in which if many small firms combined, both marginal cost and average cost of the combined organization would be lower than the aggregate marginal cost and aggregate average cost of the competitive industry. This may be true where the management is becoming increasingly efficient, as in the case of increasing scales. Examples are railroad and telephone companies. In such cases, although the antitrust law may demand breaking up the company, society may be better off by allowing the merger to exist either as a public utility or a regulated monopoly.

Many devices are used by firms in order to eliminate competition and control the market. The holding company which acquires stocks of other companies is one way of controlling the industry. Another is the merger, which is a complete economic integration of two or more firms. Sometimes a merger can be achieved by buying the assets of the other firm. In the Congress, a firm which dominates the entire industry in order to eliminate competition is sometimes known as a *trust*. The Sherman Antitrust Law makes it illegal to monopolize a line of commerce, or to make contracts and conspire in order to restrict production.

One of the problems that arises here is how broad should the discretion of the courts be? For example, in 1911 when the Supreme Court ruled that the Standard Oil Trust should be dissolved, it also created a new doctrine which was named "the rule of reason." "The rule of reason" left a very broad discretion to the courts. According to this rule, restraints of trade are illegal only if the judge believes they will give rise to undesirable economic consequences. The main disadvantage of "the rule of reason" is that it does not define "undesirable economic consequences." As an example, the Carnegie Steel Company and the Morgan Steel Company united under the name of United States Steel Corporation. In 1920 they were cleared by the Supreme Court because it was believed that a larger scale in steel production would increase efficiency. Clearly, in the case of the United States Steel Corporation, the desirable effects of large-scale production made the merger legal. The judges probably believed that the large-scale effects were more important than the undesirable effects which may arise from the formation of a new giant in the steel industry.

In other cases the "rule of reason" could not help firms which tried to monopolize the market to evade the law. Perhaps, the most interesting case is that of Hartford Empire, which possessed the patents on glass-making machines. Hartford Empire restricted production of bottles by allotting bottlemakers strict quotas of production. This act increased monopolistic profits which were shared by Hartford Empire and the bottle-makers. The Supreme Court of the United States held that Hartford abused the patent grant. The company was put in receivership, and thus it had to give up its power to restrain the production of bottles.

Neither the Sherman Act nor the Clayton Act refer to price leader-ship. It is recalled that in case collusion is illegal, oligopolists would follow the price which is set by one firm. Price leadership is not a merger or a conspiracy to restrict production in the eyes of the law. The fact that pegging the price at a relatively high level gives rise to a smaller level of production is not caught by the antitrust laws. The only way to eliminate the monopolistic effects of price leadership is price regulation. In theory it is very simple: it boils down to equating the price of the product with the marginal cost of producing it. To be sure, in practice it is much more difficult.

THE MODEL OF KINKED DEMAND CURVE

Consider an oligopolist who believes that if he raises his price above the going market price, none of his rivals will imitate him, but if he lowers the price below the going market price, all of his rivals will follow and reduce their prices. Accordingly, above the going price the demand curve confronted by the individual oligopolist is very elastic, while below this price it has a low elasticity. In Fig. 13-10, the going market price is P_0,

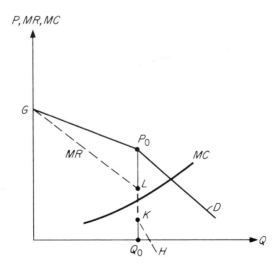

Fig. 13-10

at which there is a kink. Above the kink the demand curve is highly elastic; below it the elasticity of the demand curve is very low. The MR is smooth from point G to point L, there, because of the kink it falls to K and then it continues smoothly to H. This gives rise to price and quantity rigidities: the MC curve can shift up and down between K and L leaving the quantity fixed at Q_0 and the Price at P_0. Thus, this model is an attempt to rationalize price rigidities. There are two flaws in this model. First, this model implies that price rigidity is accompanied by quantity rigidity. In reality, this is not the case. Second, a good model of a kinked demand curve should be able to tell why the rigid price is set at one level and not another. There is nothing in this model that will explain why the kink was formed at one price and not another.

A NOTE TO THE READER

Oligopoly, at least in theory, can be rationalized by a wide variety of models, where each model is based on a specific mode of behavior. Some of the known models, such as *Cournot, Stackelberg, Collusion,* and *Market-sharing,* are discussed in the Mathematical Appendix.

PROBLEMS

13-1. Consider Fig. 13-3. Analyze the behavior of the duopolists under the assumption that MC_B cuts the line $P_A E$.

13-2. A certain industry is dominated by two firms. The commodity is homogeneous. Consumers are indifferent between buying from one duopolist or the other. Analyze the behavior of the duopolists under the assumption that their cost curves are identical.

13-3. The market for a homogeneous product is entirely dominated by three oligopolists. The industry is described by the following table:

Market Demand Curve			Producer (1)		Producer (2)		Producer (3)	
Q	P	MR	MC_1	TVC_1	MC_2	TVC_2	MC_3	TVC_3
1	20	20	1	1	3	3	5.5	5.5
2	19	18	3	4	5	8	5.5	11.0
3	18	16	5	9	7	15	5.5	16.5
4	17	14	7	16	9	24	5.5	22.0
5	16	12	9	25	11	35	5.5	27.5
6	15	10	11	36	13	48	5.5	33.0
7	14	8	13	49	15	63	5.5	38.5
8	13	6	15	64	17	80	5.5	44.0
9	12	4	17	81	19	99	5.5	49.5

Assume that only whole units can be produced. (a) How many units should each firm produce under collusion? Assume that none of the firms incurs fixed costs. (b) How many units should each firm produce if $FC_1 = \$10$, $FC_2 = \$10$, and $FC_3 = \$20$? Assume that the fixed costs are avoidable.

SELECTED READINGS FOR CHAPTERS 12 AND 13

BOULDING, K. E. *Economic Analysis* (3d ed.). New York: Harper and Bros., 1955, Chapters 29, 30, and 31.

CHAMBERLIN, E. H. *The Theory of Monopolistic Competition*. Boston, Mass.: Harvard University Press, 1958.

DEWEY, D. *Monopoly in Economics and Law*. Chicago, Ill.: Rand McNally and Company, 1964.

HARBERGER, A. C. "Monopoly and Resource Allocation," *American Economic Review*, Vol. XLIV, May, 1954.

HICKS, J. R. "The Theory of Monopoly," *Readings in Price Theory*, K. Boulding and G. Stigler, eds. Homewood, Ill.: Richard D. Irwin, Inc., 1952.

ROBINSON, J. *The Economics of Imperfect Competition*. London: The Macmillan Company, 1933.

STIGLER, G. J. *The Theory of Price*. New York: The Macmillan Company, 1966, Chapters 11, 12, and 13.

chapter **14**

The Theory of Distribution (Pricing of Factors of Production)

The following three chapters will be concerned with the theory of the markets for factors of production. In this chapter we shall consider the theoretical aspects of the market for factors of production. While the theory of supply of inputs is identical with the theory of supply of consumer goods, the theory of demand for inputs requires a new theory. The demand for resources is known as the *derived demand,* in the sense that it is derived from the demand for the final product. In Chapter 15 we shall focus on the market for labor, and in Chapter 16 we shall be concerned with some aspects of the capital market.

Traditionally, economists have divided all factors of production into three categories, namely, land, labor, and capital. A more recent approach is to reduce the three groups into two: labor and capital.

The modern trend is to subdivide capital into two categories: (1) tangible capital and (2) human capital. The reason for adopting this sub-classification is that tangible capital and human capital can compete in the market for loanable funds. For instance, consider a man who has graduated from high school and who must make a decision: He might like to invest in himself, i.e., acquire higher education and become, say, an engineer. Alternatively, he might start a small business of his own, which is an investment in tangible capital. It is obvious that these two forms of investment are competing alternatives. The decision, one way or the other, will depend on which of the two, human capital or tangible capital, is expected to be more profitable in the future.

Separating between the human agent and human capital is also useful when one wants to estimate returns to schooling. For example, if the average difference in the salaries of those who hold B.A. degrees and of those who hold M.A. degrees is $1,000 per annum, and if acquiring the M.A. degree requires one year of graduate study, then returns to schooling are $1,000 per annum per year of schooling at that level.

THE SUPPLY OF FACTORS OF PRODUCTION

The process of allocating factors of production between different industries was illustrated in Chapter 9. However, so far we have not used the demand for and supply of factors of production in the analysis. The theory of the supply of inputs is no different than the theory of the supply of a consumer item: it is defined as the aggregate marginal cost curve of producing the factor. For example, coal is a factor of production. The supply curve of coal at the economy level is obtained by horizontally totaling the marginal cost curves of all mines in the economy.

The supply of input facing the industry is derived by subtracting the aggregate demand curve for coal of all other industries from the aggregate supply curve of coal. This problem will be discussed in detail at the end of this chapter.

A special problem arises when the supply curve of labor is analyzed. The marginal cost of providing one hour of labor cannot be measured by money. The nonpecuniary extra cost of providing one additional hour of labor is a mixture of physical and mental fatigue plus the necessity to associate with colleagues who are not selectively chosen. To this one can add the amount of leisure time foregone which is also nonpecuniary. Thus, although the nonpecuniary marginal cost of labor cannot be measured in dollars, it probably increases in a certain range due to the fact that the marginal fatigue increases with the amount of labor rendered per unit of time.

The theory of the demand curve for a factor of production is quite complicated. One can approach it by using a simple model that explains why the demand curve for a factor is negatively sloped. Alternatively, one can apply a rigorous approach based on the theory of production. In order not to deprive students who are not rigorously inclined of the pleasure, we shall analyze the demand curve for factors of production at two different levels.

A DEMAND CURVE FOR A FACTOR OF PRODUCTION: A SIMPLE MODEL

You will recall from Chapter 7 that a decline in the price of a factor of production entails a downward shift in the MC curve and vice versa. Since the supply curve of a finished product is the aggregate MC curve, following a fall in the price of a factor, the supply curve also shifts downward. After the shift in supply occurs, the point of intersection between supply and demand shifts rightward and a larger output is produced. In order to produce more, entrepreneurs in the industry increase the quantity demanded for factors of production, including the one whose price has declined. This is known as the *expansion effect*. In addition to this, producers will use more of the factor whose price declined because it pays them to substitute this factor for other factors which are now relatively expensive. This is known as the *substitution effect*. In summary, following a fall in the price of a factor of production, producers will increase the quantity demanded for that factor due to the expansion effect and the substitution effect. This is why the demand curve for a factor of production is negatively sloped.

THE DEMAND CURVE FOR A FACTOR OF PRODUCTION: A RIGOROUS MODEL

The Competitive Firm Level.   It is recalled that if $A, B, \ldots, N$ are variable factors, then the firm is in equilibrium when the following holds:

$$\frac{P_a}{MPP_a} = \frac{P_b}{MPP_b} = \cdots = \frac{P_n}{MPP_n} = MC = P_x \ (P_x = MR)$$

where P_x is the price of the commodity which is made by the firm. Recall that in perfect competition the price of the good (P_x) equals the marginal cost. Accordingly, we obtain

$$\frac{P_a}{MPP_a} = P_x \qquad \text{and} \qquad P_a = MPP_a \cdot P_x$$

$$\frac{P_b}{MPP_b} = P_x \qquad \text{and} \qquad P_b = MPP_b \cdot P_x$$

$$\frac{P_n}{MPP_n} = P_x \qquad \text{and} \qquad P_n = MPP_n \cdot P_x$$

where A is labor, B is capital, and N is entrepreneurial services. We shall assume that factor N is fixed regardless of the time involved.

Assume that we start from a point of equilibrium where the price of factor B is equal to its $MPP_b \times P_x$, and the price of A is equal to its $MPP_a \times P_x$. Let us focus on factor A. Saying that $P_a = MPP_a \times P_x$ is equivalent to saying that in equilibrium the cost of one additional unit of input is equal to the value of the extra product of that unit of input. To illustrate this, assume that the price of the finished product P_x equals

$2, the marginal physical product of A (MPP_a) is 30 units of output, and the price of one unit of the factor is $60. Thus, we have $60 = 30 \times \$2$.

If the price falls below $60, say to $50, the firm will have an incentive to employ more labor (which is factor A). By employing one additional unit of labor the firm will have to pay an additional $50, but it will gain $60 = 30 \times \$2$. Thus, net profit will increase by $60 - \$50 = \$10$. When, however, more labor is added, MPP_a declines, and accordingly the value of the marginal product declines too. Let us assume that in this example after 5 units of labor are added, MPP_a falls to a level of 27 units of output. Then, the value marginal product of labor is $27 \times \$2 = \$54$. Still, it pays the firm to use more labor per unit of time because one additional unit of labor will give rise to a net gain of $54 - \$50 = \$4$. An equilibrium will be reached when MPP_a finally falls to a level of 25 units of output. There, $50 = 25 \times \$2$. At this point, it does not pay the producer to hire more labor, because using more labor will entail an even lower marginal physical product of labor. For example, if the producer hires 10 additional units of labor, the MPP_a will fall, say, to 21 units of output and the value marginal product of labor will fall to $21 \times \$2 = \$42$. Here the cost of the last unit of labor which is $50 is $8 higher than the value marginal product. Thus, it pays the producer to contract just until the cost of one additional unit of labor is exactly equal to the value of its marginal product. Accordingly, the demand curve for a factor of production is a locus of points that represent pairs of numbers, i.e., a price of a factor, and the corresponding quantity demanded. At each point the condition $P_a = MPP_a \times P_x$ for a factor A, etc., is fulfilled.

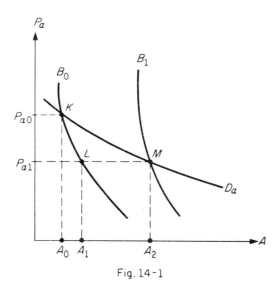

Fig. 14-1

The Demand for a Factor When all other Factors Are Kept Unchanged at the Firm Level. Assume that the competitive firm employs only three factors of production which are denoted by A, B, and N, where A stands for labor, B for capital, and N is entrepreneurial capacity which is fixed to the firm. Consider Fig. 14-1. When the price of labor is P_{a0}, A_0 units of labor are employed; also, at point K, B_0 units of capital are employed, and the following holds:

$$P_{a0} = MPP_{a0} \cdot P_{x0}$$
$$P_{b0} = MPP_{b0} \cdot P_{x0}$$

where P_{x0} is the price per unit of output.

Next the wage rate falls from P_{a0} to P_{a1}. In the short run capital cannot be varied, thus it is fixed at B_0. But labor can be varied, and since the new price P_{a1} is less than the value marginal product it pays the firm to hire more labor per unit of time. We recall that to the first approximation, the net gain coming from hiring one additional unit of labor will be $P_{x0} \cdot MPP_{a0} - P_{a1}$. But, as the firm will continue to hire more labor per unit of time, MPP_a will decline due to the law of diminishing marginal physical product. Finally, when an extra amount of $A_1 - A_0$ units of labor will be hired, the new MPP_a will have been reduced to the extent that the value marginal product of labor is equal to its new price. If we denote the new marginal physical product by MPP_{a1}, then when A_1 units of labor (and B_0 units of capital) are employed, we have

$$P_{a1} = MPP_{a1} \cdot P_{x0}$$

Thus, K and L are two points on a demand curve for labor (factor A), where capital is kept constant. Each point that belongs to this demand curve obeys the rule of logic, according to which the price of the factor of production (A) is equal to its value marginal product. We have denoted this demand curve which passes through K and L by B_0 because input B is kept constant at B_0 units of capital. We also recall that in this case B may stand for "all other factors."

The Demand Curve for a Factor When Other Inputs are Variable at the Firm Level. Let us now focus on B. Remember that we assumed dependence between MPP_a and the quantity of B employed and MPP_b and the quantity of A employed. Thus, when more of A is used in the process of production MPP_b rises. At point K the marginal physical product of B was MPP_{b0}, and there we had

$$P_{b0} = MPP_{b0} \cdot P_{x0}$$

But at point L more of A is employed; in fact, it has increased from A_0 to A_1. Thus at L the marginal physical product of B is larger than MPP_{b0}.

Let it be MPP_{b1}. Since the firm is competitive it exerts influence neither over the price of the goods P_x nor on P_b. Accordingly, at L we have

$$P_{b0} < MPP_{b1} \cdot P_{x0}$$

That is, the price of factor B is less than its new value marginal product. Thus, the firm has an incentive to increase the amount of capital services (B) it uses, and if enough time is allowed for adjustment, the firm will increase the use of B. But now, due to the very same law of positive dependence, when more of B is used, MPP_a rises, and thus the firm has the incentive to hire more units of input A. The firm will continue to hire more B and more A just until the new marginal physical products are $\overline{MPP}_a$ and $\overline{MPP}_b$ $(= MPP_{b0})$, respectively, where the following holds:

$$P_{a1} = \overline{MPP}_a \cdot P_{x0}$$

$$P_{b0} = \overline{MPP}_b \cdot P_{x0}$$

where

$$\overline{MPP}_b = MPP_{b0}$$

Let us assume that this occurs when A_2 units of labor and B_1 units of capital are employed—indicated by point M in Fig. 14.1. Thus, points K and M belong to a long-run demand curve for A which we denote by D_a. Along this demand curve, we require not only that the value marginal product of A will be equal to the price of A but also that the value marginal product of all other variable inputs will equal their respective prices.

Once we are at M, we can require that input B will be held constant at B_1 and obtain a short-run demand curve for labor (A) which we denote by B_1.

Consider point M. Assume also that factor N, which stands for entrepreneurial services, becomes variable in the sense that it can be increased in any desirable proportion. Furthermore, let the value marginal product of N equal its price. Under these assumptions the demand curve for A is a horizontal line passing through M, the reason being that if all factors are variable they can be increased in the same proportion. When factors A, B, and N are increased in the same proportion MPP_a, MPP_b, and MPP_m, respectively, do not change (Chapter 6). Thus, if N_0 is employed at point M, the same MPP_a will be obtained by employing $2A_2$ (and $2B_1$ and $2N_0$), or by employing $3A_2$ (and $3B_1$ and $3N_0$) and, in general, by employing KA_2 (and KB_1 and KN_0).

In summary, if all factors are variable, and assuming constant returns to scale, to each price of A there corresponds a horizontal line which is the long-run demand curve for A.

The Industry Level. The demand curve for input A of the industry as a whole is obtained by horizontally adding all demand curves of single firms. This demand curve is denoted by ΣD_a as indicated in Fig. 14-2. Thus, assume that currently the price of the product which is produced by the industry is P_{x0}, the price of the factor is P_{a0}, and as indicated in Fig. 14-2, the quantity demanded is ΣA_0 (i.e., the quantity demanded by the first firm at that price, plus the quantity demanded by the second firm at that price . . . plus the quantity of A demanded by the last firm

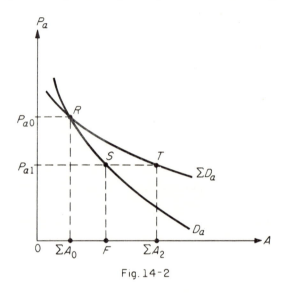

Fig. 14-2

at that price). When the price of A falls from P_{a0} to P_{a1}, all the firms in the industry will try to expand along the ΣD_a curve. However, since all of them will try to hire more labor (and more of B), all firms will produce more output. At the industry level a larger output would entail depressing the price of the good which is made by the industry. This price was denoted by P_{x0}. A lower P_x would lead to a shrinking value marginal product of factor A (and, of course, other factors). Thus, in order to bring the value marginal product of A into line with the new lower price of A, (P_{a1}) firms will not have to increase their demand for input A all the way from ΣA_0 to ΣA_2. Increasing it up to $0F$ units will suffice.

In Fig. 14-2, the relevant point which corresponds to P_{a1} is S rather than point T. Thus, the "real" demand curve passes through the original point R and point S. We denote this demand curve by D_a.

From now on, we shall refer to the D_a type curve when we consider the demand curve for a factor of production at the industry level. It should be noted that the demand curve at the industry level is the interesting one, because prices of factors of production, at least in the short run, are determined at the industry level.

It should be emphasized that in this analysis *prices of all other factors of production are kept constant along the demand curve for factor A*. In our example, we kept the price of factor B constant. But variables other than the price of other factors do change. Thus, in our example the quantity of factor B (capital) did change when more of A (labor) was employed. The price of the good which is made by the industry also changes. Accordingly, going down along D_a in Fig. 14-2 implied a lower P_x.

THE ELASTICITY OF THE DEMAND FOR AN INPUT

Consider the demand curve for factor A at the industry level. There are the following three rules of "common sense" relating to elasticity:

1. *The larger the degree of substitutability between A and other inputs (B in our example), the more elastic the demand for A*. Intuitively, it is obvious because if A and B are relatively good substitutes, a decline in the price of A will lead to substituting many units of A for B. In principle, if A and B were perfect substitutes, factor B would ultimately be replaced by factor A.

2. *The more elastic the demand for the finished good (X), the more elastic the demand for factor A*. When the industry hires more of a certain factor (and probably more of other inputs) it expands and accordingly P_x, the price per unit of output falls. If the demand curve for output is very inelastic, the price P_x will fall very rapidly. If it is elastic, it will fall slowly. But, when the price (P_x) falls rapidly, the value marginal product of A also shrinks rapidly, which means that the demand curve for A is relatively inelastic. But when P_x falls slowly, the value marginal product of A declines rather slowly, which means that the demand curve for A is relatively elastic.

3. *The more elastic the supply curves of other inputs, the more elastic the demand for factor A*. We shall now relax the assumption that the industry has no influence over the price of B. Instead we shall assume that the industry faces a rising supply curve of B. Let us begin with the substitution effect. When the price of factor A declines and the price of factor B is held unchanged, a certain amount of A is substituted for B. But, if the industry faces a rising supply curve of factor B, the decline in the demand for B will cause a decline in the price of factor B. With a lower price of factor B firms will tend to substitute a smaller amount of A for B compared with the amount of A substituted for B under a fixed price of B. Recall, however, that a fixed price of B would only exist if the supply curve of B is perfectly elastic. Thus, we conclude that the higher the elasticity of the supply curve of factor B, the larger the amount of A substituted for B resulting from a decline in the price of A, and accordingly the more elastic the demand curve for factor A. If factors A and B

are two complements (there are more than two factors), firms will use more of A and B and less of other factors. However, the less elastic the supply curve of B facing the industry, the more difficult it is to substitute A and B for other factors of production, and accordingly the less elastic the demand curve for factor A. This leads us to the same conclusion derived in the case of two substitutes. Coming to the expansion effect, we know that a decline in the price of factor A leads to a downward shift in the supply of the finished product. As a result, more of the finished product is produced and more of factors A and B are used in the process of production. If the industry is confronted with a positively sloped supply curve of factor B, then the price of B will rise as a result of the expansion effect, and the supply curve of the finished product will shift downward by less than it would under the assumption that the supply curve of B is perfectly elastic. Thus, the less elastic the supply curve of factor B with which the industry is confronted, the stronger the dampening effect of a higher price of B on the expansion, and the smaller the elasticity of the demand curve for factor A.[1]

DEMAND SHIFTS DUE TO A CHANGE IN THE PRICE OF ANOTHER FACTOR: A SIMPLE MODEL

Recall that prices of other inputs are kept constant along the demand curve for input A. In our example A happened to be labor, and B happened to represent "all other factors" of production, or simply capital. *How would D_a, in Fig. 14-2 shift as result of a change in the price of B?*

It is obvious that D_a, the demand curve for factor A will shift if P_b changes, since it is derived from assuming that the price of B is kept unchanged at P_{bo}. After the price of B changes, the industry will have a

---

[1] In some textbooks it is stated that the smaller the share of factor A in total cost, the less elastic the demand curve for A. This statement is true only under the assumption of fixed proportions between the factors of production. In the Mathematical Appendix, we shall prove that under constant returns to scale and a perfectly elastic supply curve of factor B the following holds:

$$E = - (K_b \cdot \sigma + K_a |\eta|)$$

where E is the elasticity of the demand curve for factor A, K_b and K_a are the respective shares of factors A and B in total cost, σ is the elasticity of substitution between the two factors, and η is the demand elasticity of the finished product. Differentiating E with respect to K_a (recall that $K_a + K_b = 1$) gives

$$\frac{\partial E}{\partial K_a} = \sigma - |\eta|$$

Thus, only if $\sigma < |\eta|$, is the above statement correct (because if $\partial E/\partial K_a < 0$, then $\partial |E|/\partial K_a > 0$). Under fixed proportions $\sigma = 0$, $\partial E/\partial K_a$ is negative and $\partial |E|/\partial K_a$ is positive. But if $\sigma > |\eta|$, the above statement is incorrect.

different demand curve for input A. To put it in different words, a change in the price of capital will entail a shift in the demand curve for labor. (And, of course, if one considers the demand curve for capital, a change in the price of labor will give rise to a shift in the demand curve for capital.)

Consider the case where there is a decline in the price of B. It is recalled from Chapters 7 and 8 that when the price of one factor, say factor B, falls, the marginal cost curve of each firm shifts downward (which is identical with a rightward shift). Accordingly, the supply curve also shifts downward and the industry produces more output than it did prior to the decline in the price of B. Thus, the industry as a whole is expanding. When each firm expands, it has a tendency to use more of all factors, including factor A. This is known as the *expansion effect*. But this is not the sole effect. We recall that if enough time is allowed for adjustment, and if we can assume that there is a certain degree of substitutability between factors of production, then the factor whose price falls will be substituted for other factors. Specifically, in our example factor A and factor B, which are labor and capital, can be assumed to be reasonable substitutes for each other. Thus, when the price of capital services declines, we should expect that entrepreneurs will substitute capital for labor. This is known as the *substitution effect*. Note that the substitution effect in production is comparable with the substitution effect in consumption.

In summary, when the price of factor B declines, two effects have to be considered:

1. *The Expansion Effect:* Following a decline in the price of input B the industry will expand, and in their attempt to increase production firms will have an incentive to employ more of factor A, which means that the demand curve for A (D_a in Fig. 14-2) will shift rightward.

2. *The Substitution Effect:* Since input B became relatively inexpensive, firms have an incentive to substitute B for A, i.e., to employ less units of A. This implies a leftward shift in the demand curve for A.

If the expansion effect dominates, then the demand curve for A will shift rightward. If the substitution effect dominates, then the demand curve for A will shift leftward. If more than two factors are used in the process of production, two factors or more may be complementary to each other. For example, machinery and gasoline are complementary to each other. If machinery, gasoline, and labor are the only factors that are used in the process of production, then resulting from a fall in price of machinery, producers will tend to use more machinery and also more gasoline. Both machinery and gasoline will be substituted for labor. Thus, the substitution effect (complementarity effect) will be to shift the demand curve for gasoline rightward and that for labor leftward. The expansion effect will be to shift these demand curves rightward. Note that in the case of complementary factors, the substitution effect (or rather complementarity effect) and the expansion effect shift the demand curve in the same direction.

You will recall from Chapter 5 that the substitution effect is defined for a fixed level of output. Thus, in the above example, in order to define substitution properly, we must keep output fixed at the level which existed prior to the decline in the price of machinery. After the price of machinery falls, producers have an incentive to use different proportions in producing the same output. They tend to divert labor away from production and replace it by using more machinery and gasoline.

It should be stressed again that even though labor and machinery cooperate in the process of production they are substitutes for each other. Moreover, in most of the cases there is a positive dependence between labor and capital in the sense that if labor is kept constant and more machinery is used, the *MPP* of labor increases.

Example: Analyze the market for input A in industry X after the price of input B rises. Assume that the factors are substitutes for each other and the substitution effect dominates the expansion effect. Here the *expansion effect* (contraction effect!) will be to shift D_A in Fig. 14-3 leftward, but the substitution effect will be to shift D_A rightward. Since we assumed that the substitution effect dominates, the *net* effect is a rightward shift from D_{A0} to D_{A1}, as indicated in Fig. 14-3. As a result, more units of A will be employed in the industry and the price of A will be higher. Note that we have not bothered to define the supply curve of A facing industry X. The reason for this is that we have already pointed out to the reader that the supply curve of a factor of production is formally de-

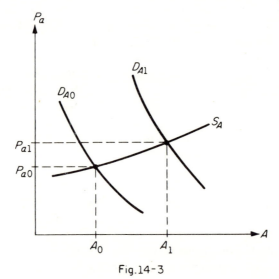

Fig. 14-3

fined as any supply curve of any finished good. But, the attention of the student is drawn to the fact that while the total supply curve at the economy level is positively sloped, the supply curve of input A facing one industry may be almost flat if the fraction of input A which is used by the industry is rather negligible. Thus, let A stand for labor, and assume that as a whole, industry X, uses only 1/1,000 of the total labor force in the economy. Intuitively, it is clear that under such circumstances the industry faces a supply curve of labor which is nearly horizontal. Under such circumstances, the fact that D_A shifts from D_{A0} to D_{A1} will result in employing more labor in industry X, and practically paying the same wage rate.

So far we have tacitly assumed that B is employed by industry X only. If B is employed by most of the industries in the economy, and if the substitution effect dominates in practically all of the industries, then other industries will shift their demand curve for A rightward. This, in turn, will mean that S_A in Fig. **14-3** will shift leftward because labor will be attracted to other industries as well as to industry X. However, when the entire economy is involved, it is more convenient to treat the problem at the economy level. Namely, assuming that the substitution effect dominates, a rise in the price of B will entail a rightward shift in the demand curve for A (for the whole economy!). But since the supply curve of A (again at the economy level) is positively sloped, the price of A will rise.

There are few cases where the supply curve of an input facing an industry is very inelastic. For instance, the supply of land is very inelastic as far as agriculture is concerned. In fact, for all practical purposes of analysis, it can be assumed that it is a vertical line.

DEMAND SHIFTS DUE TO A CHANGE IN THE PRICE OF OTHER FACTORS: A RIGOROUS MODEL

Consider one industry, say agriculture. Assume that in order to help farm labor, the government has decided to subsidize tractors. Whether farmers will benefit from it is yet to be analyzed. To the first approximation, more tractors will be used in farming. Given the same number of workers, each one will become more efficient, and so the marginal physical product of labor will increase. This is equivalent to saying that due to positive dependence between labor and tractors the marginal physical product of labor increases when more tractor services are used in farming. But, a lower price of services rendered by tractors will entail a rightward shift in the supply curve of agricultural output leading to a lower price per unit of agricultural output. The effect of a higher marginal physical product of labor is to shift the demand curve for farm labor upward (rightward) while the effect of a lower price per unit of output is to shift it downward (leftward). And the net effect is uncertain.

OTHER DEMAND SHIFTS

A Change in Productivity.   Consider first the industry level. In Chapter 7 we have shown that normally, a neutral increase in productivity will increase the MPP of all factors of production. Assume that all firms in Industry X benefit from this technological improvement. At each point on the demand curve for, say, input A, the following holds: $P_a = MPP_a \cdot P_x$, where P_a is the price of input A and P_x is the price per unit of output. You will recall that an increase in productivity entails a rightward shift in the supply curve of X; thus, the new supply curve of X intersects with the demand curve for X at a lower level. Whether the demand curve for input A will shift upward or downward will depend on which of the two dominates, the increase in MPP_a or the decline in P_x.

If industry X is the only one benefiting from the technological innovation; and if this is a relatively small industry, then it will hardly affect the price of the inputs that are employed by it, because the industry is confronted with very elastic supply curves of factors of production. However, if all industries in the economy benefit from a technological progress, then the analysis takes a different shape altogether. In such a case, the supply curves of finished goods of all industries will shift downward. Thus, prices of all commodities will decline. But, when all prices decline, one can say that on the average relative prices do not change. This is true because if P_x declines 10 percent and if the price index of all consumer goods also declines 10 percent, then the *relative* price of X is unchanged. In reality, you will find some commodities whose price declined by more than 10 percent and other commodities whose price declined by less than 10 percent. But for all practical purposes this problem can be neglected. To simplify the analysis, each time we attempt to analyze a problem at the economy level, we can make the assumption that there is one commodity in the economy and its price is always equal to $1. Thus, if the whole economy undergoes a process of a neutral technological progress, MPP_a rises, and $MPP_a \times \$1$ also rises. This means that the demand curve for factor A shifts upward. Note, however, that it takes a certain period of time for technological progress to develop. There is a good chance that during that period of time the supply curve of input A will also increase. Now, the price of A will rise over a period of time if the demand curve for A shifts rightward faster than the supply curve of A. There will be no change in the price of A if both curves shift rightward at the same rate, and P_a will decline if the supply curve of A shifts rightward faster than the demand curve for A. We shall return to this problem in the following chapter.

The attention of the student is drawn to the possibility of the so-called "labor-saving technological change," or "capital savings technological change," and so on. For example, a "labor saving technological change" may result in a lower marginal physical product of labor, but this is rather rare at the economy level.[2]

A Shift in the Demand for Output. Consider the case where the demand curve for output produced in a certain industry (X in our example) increases because of a change in tastes in favor of commodity X and against commodity Y. To the first approximation P_x will rise, and MPP_a × P_x will increase. Accordingly, the demand curve for factor A will shift upward. But, since the opposite occurs in industry Y, resources that are released by firms in industry Y will seek employment elsewhere. One such resource is factor A, and the supply curve of factor A in industry X will shift rightward. Whenever you analyze a problem of pricing a factor of production at the industry level, you should devote some thinking to other industries because there are many factors of production that are practically employed by all the industries in the economy. Labor is one example, and electricity is another.

MONOPSONY

Monopsony arises when there is a single buyer of a certain good. For example, monopsony in the labor market arises when there is a single buyer of labor in the market. Monopsony in the labor market, although it is rare, has important policy implication. In areas where labor is relatively immobile, and there is one or a few large firms, monopsony is important: it is the theoretical justification for minimum wage and collective bargaining.

In what follows we shall provide a logical framework to a case of monopsony with an eye on the labor market.

A firm in competition faces a horizontal supply curve of labor, or of any other factor of production. This stems from the fact that the share of the individual firm in the market for resources is negligible, and thus the firm cannot affect the price of the resource it uses by its decision to use more or less of it. In contrast to the firm in competition, the sole buyer of an input faces the aggregate supply curve of the input. Since the supply curve is positively sloped under normal conditions, the firm has to pay higher prices per unit of the resource if it wants to use more of it.

It is recalled from previous sections that an individual firm which secures a certain resource in a competitive market tends to equate the value marginal product of the resource with its market price. (The marginal revenue of the product is the price of the final output times the marginal physical product of the factor in the case of a competitive firm, and it is the marginal revenue times the marginal physical product

[2] See Appendix to Chapter 5.

of the factor in the case of monopoly.) In the case of monopsony, the firm will reach an equilibrium when it equates the marginal revenue product with the extra cost of one unit of the resource, which we shall call marginal factor cost. The reason for this was explained in previous sections.

In Table 14-1 we show a monopsony model in which the different functions are linear. For example, in column 4, the figure 3 is derived by taking $4 − $1 which is extra cost of labor to the firm and dividing it by 2 − 1 which is extra labor used. Columns 5 and 2 show the hypothetical marginal revenue product curve of labor. In equilibrium the firm will offer employment to 4 units of labor, because when 4 units are employed the marginal factor cost equals marginal revenue product which is $7. For reasons that were previously discussed, it does not pay the firm to employ either less than or more than 4 units of labor. In equilibrium, the wage of $4 is lower by $3 than the marginal factor cost of labor. The case of monopsony furnishes the only example in which more employment will be created by enforcing a minimum wage rate above equilibrium. For example, if the minimum wage rate of $5

TABLE 14-1

Supply of Labor		Total Cost of Labor (1) × (2)	Marginal Factor Cost	Marginal Revenue Product of Labor
Wage Rate (1)	Quantity of Labor Offered (2)	(3)	(4)	(5)
$1	1	$1	$	$10
2	2	4	3	9
3	3	9	5	8
4	4	16	7	7
5	5	25	9	6
6	6	36	11	5
7	7	49	13	4
8	8	64	15	3
9	9	81	17	2

is enforced, 5 units of labor will be employed. If a minimum wage rate of $6 is enforced, then 5 units of labor will actually find an employment. In summary, if the wage rate is raised to a new level between $4 and $7, employment will increase. Maximum employment will occur at a wage rate of $5.5. This is illustrated in Fig. 14-4. The supply curve of labor is S_L. The marginal factor cost curve MFC_L intersects the marginal revenue product of labor curve MRP_L at point G, where $MFC_L = MRP_L = $7. Thus 4 units of labor are employed at the wage rate of $4. Enforcing a minimum wage rate above \$4 but not higher than \$7 will increase employment. If a minimum wage of OR is enforced, then the new MFC is the kinked $RSTU$ intersecting MRP_L at E. Thus employment will increase from 4 units to OB units, provided that R is between \$4 and \$7.

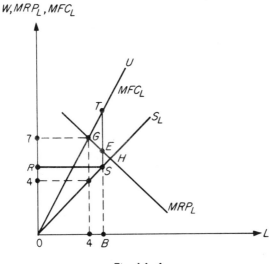

Fig. 14-4

We leave it for the reader to show that if ϵ is the elasticity of supply (S_L in Fig. 14-4), then $MFC_L = P(1 + \dfrac{1}{\epsilon})$ where P is the price as indicated by the supply curve. Since ϵ is positive, MFC_L is higher than S_L.

The case of monopsonies in labor markets may exist outside textbooks: In a small town there is a single hospital. Mobility of nurses is very limited. This is true because the decision to move or stay in the town rests with the husband, who earns most of the family income. Clearly such a situation gives rise to a positively sloped supply curve of nurses confronting the single employer in the region.

PRICING FACTORS OF PRODUCTION UNDER MONOPOLY

Consider a monopoly without influence over the price of an input, say labor. Then there is only one difference between the demand curve of a monopoly and the demand curve of a competitive firm. As shown before, the demand curve of a competitive firm satisfies the equality $P_a = P_x \times MPP_a$ Where P_a is the price of the factor, P_x the price of output, and MPP_a is the marginal physical product of the factor. In other words, in equilibrium the price of an input equals its value of marginal physical product. So long as $P_x \times MPP_a$ exceeds the price of the factor, it pays the firm to use more of the factor per unit of time because the excess of the contribution of the factor over its market price is a net addition to the profit. Under monopoly, the extra contribution resulting from adding one unit of input cannot be measured by the value of the marginal physical product, because under monopoly the price is not identical with marginal revenue. For example, if by increasing the employment of labor by one worker the monopoly increases production from 10 to 12 units of output and this leads to a reduction in the market price from $105 to $100, then marginal revenue equals $(1,200 - 1,050)/(12 - 10)$ = $75. The extra gross gain to the monopolistic firm is $MPP_a \times MR = 2 \times \$75 = \$150$. Clearly, if the cost of one unit of labor is $60 it pays the monopoly to hire more labor, just until $MPP_a \times MR$ equals $60. Note that this equality will be brought about both by decreasing the MPP_a due to the law of diminishing marginal physical product, and by lowering the marginal revenue when more output is produced. In the economic jargon $MPP_a \times MR$ is called the *marginal revenue product* as distinguished from the *value marginal product* denoting $MPP_a \times P_x$.

Consider the demand for factor A. The following will hold at each point belonging to the demand curve: $P_a = MPP_a \times MR$, where P_a is the price of the factor and MR is the marginal revenue. Since

$$MR = P_x \left(1 + \frac{1}{\eta} \right)$$

we obtain

$$P_a = MPP_a \cdot P_x \left(1 + \frac{1}{\eta} \right)$$

The analysis is similar to that applied in cases of competition, except that VMP is multiplied by the coefficient $1 + 1/\eta$ to take care of the monopoly power over the market.

If the monopolist is confronted with a rising supply of the factor, then, in equilibrium, $MFC = MPP_a \times MR$, where MFC is the marginal factor cost. If supply elasticity of the factor is denoted by ϵ, then $MFC = P_a(1 + 1/\epsilon)$, and in equilibrium we have

$$\underbrace{MFC}_{P_a(1 + 1/\epsilon)} = \underbrace{MPP_a \cdot MR}_{MPP_a \cdot P_x(1 + 1/\eta)}$$

THE SUPPLY OF AN INPUT FACING AN INDUSTRY

We have stated without proof that the smaller the share of an industry in a market for an input, the more elastic the supply curve of the input at the industry level. This can be illustrated as follows:

Consider Figures 14-5 and 14-6. Let D in Fig. 14-5 be the demand curve for input A of all the industries in the economy, except industry X. Let S in Fig. 14-5 be the supply curve of factor A at the economy (or "macro") level. Then, S_I, the supply of input A confronting industry X may be derived by figuring out the excess supply of factor A. For example, when the price of A is $0F$, the total supply is FH units of A, but the demand for A by all other industries amounts only to FG units. Thus, an amount of GH ($= FH - FG$) units of input A will offer to be employed in industry X at that price. The reader should note that expanding along the curve S_I in Fig. 14-6 means raising the price of factor A not only in industry X, but rather in the economy as a whole. Contracting along the S_I curve means a decline in the price of the factor throughout the economy. Thus, consider the case in Fig. 14-6 where the

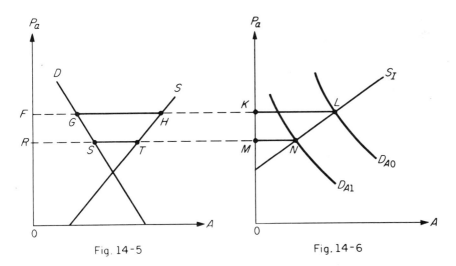

Fig. 14-5   Fig. 14-6

demand curve for A in industry X shifts leftward from D_{A0} to D_{A1}. The new point of intersection between the supply S_I and the new demand D_{A1} is N. Industry X now employs less units of input A. In fact, employment of factor A declined from KL units to MN units. These unemployed units are absorbed by the economy in the following manner: Trying to seek a market elsewhere, the producers of factor A will start to cut prices of A. By so doing they will induce other industries to employ more of A. In fact, as indicated by the curve D in Fig. 14-5, other industries will increase their demand for A from FG units to RS units. But, since the price of A is declining, producers (owners) of input A will shrink the quantity supplied from FH units to RT units.

Note that if all other industries in the economy increase their demand for input A, the demand curve D in Fig. 14-5 will shift rightward, but this in turn would mean that the supply of A facing industry X (S_I in Fig. 14-6) will shift leftward (upward). Likewise, an upward shift in the total supply S in Fig. 14-5 entails an upward shift in S_I in Fig. 14-6. Other shifts are left as an exercise for the student.

Let us adopt the following notations, relating to factor A:

$$OF = P_0, \quad FH = S_0, \quad FG = D_0, \quad KL = S_{I0}$$
$$OR = P_1, \quad RT = S_1, \quad RS = D_1, \quad MN = S_{I1}$$
$$\Delta P = P_1 - P_0, \quad \Delta S_I = S_{I1} - \overline{S_{I0}}, \quad \Delta S = S_1 - S_0, \quad \Delta D = D_1 - D_0$$

Then we have

$$S_{I0} = S_0 - D_0$$
$$S_{I1} = S_1 - D_1$$
$$S_{I1} - S_{I0} = S_1 - S_0 - (D_1 - D_0)$$
$$\Delta S_I = \Delta S - \Delta D$$

Multiplying through by $P/(S_I \cdot \Delta P)$ we obtain

$$\frac{P \cdot \Delta S_I}{S_I \cdot \Delta P} = \frac{P \cdot \Delta S}{S_I \cdot \Delta P} - \frac{P \cdot \Delta D}{S_I \cdot \Delta P}$$

Rearranging, we obtain

$$\frac{P \cdot \Delta S_I}{S_I \cdot \Delta P} = \frac{S \cdot P \cdot \Delta S}{S_I \cdot S \cdot \Delta P} - \frac{D \cdot P \cdot \Delta D}{S_I \cdot D \cdot \Delta P}$$

or

$$\epsilon_I = \frac{S}{S_I} \cdot \epsilon - \frac{D}{S_I} \eta$$

where ϵ_I is the elasticity of the supply curve facing industry X (S_I in Fig. 14-6), ϵ is the elasticity of supply of factor A in the economy (S in Fig. 14-5), and η is the elasticity of the demand curve of all other industries for A (D in Fig. 14-5).

To illustrate this, assume that A is labor, and the share of industry X in the labor market is one-tenth. Assume that $\epsilon = 1$ and $\eta = -2$. We can estimate the elasticity of supply of labor facing industry X as

$$\epsilon_I = \frac{10.}{1} \cdot 1 - \frac{9}{1} \cdot (-2) = 10 + 18 = 28$$

Relatively it is a very elastic supply curve. In order to increase employment of labor by 28 percent the wage rate will have to rise by only 1 percent. Accordingly, when you hear an economist say that "for all practical purposes" the supply curve of a factor of production facing an industry can be assumed to be flat, he really means that since the share of the industry in the total market of the input is rather small, the elasticity of the supply curve confronting the industry is probably in the order of magnitude of 20 or 30, and so on.

PROBLEMS

Answer problems 14-1 to 14-9 as being True, False, or Uncertain. In each of these problems you should restrict yourself to the supply of and demand for inputs at the industry level.

14-1. A rise in the price of farm machinery will entail a rise in land rentals. Assume that (a) the supply curve of land is a fixed vertical line, (b) the substitution effect will dominate the expansion effect, and (c) land and machinery are substitutes for each other.

14-2. Repeat Prob. 14-1, except that expansion effect dominates the substitution effect.

14-3. A monopolist can afford to pay wages below the market wage rate.

14-4. Normally, the demand curve for a factor of production is negatively sloped because both substitution effect and expansion effect lead to the same change in the quantity demanded.

14-5. The union of workers in industry A raises wages above the equilibrium rate. As a result, entrepreneurs in industry A will demand more capital services. Assume that (a) the substitution effect dominates, (b) labor and capital are substitutes for each other, and (c) monopsony does not exist.

14-6. Repeat Prob. 14-5, except that the expansion effect dominates.

14-7. Farm landlords will not benefit from a subsidy on fertilizers. Assume that the substitution effect dominates and that land and fertilizers are substitutes for each other.

14-8. Wages in industry A will rise in the short run if entrepreneurs invest in better equipment. (HINT: Wages are equal to the value marginal product which is the price of the product times the marginal physical product of labor.)

14-9. Repeat Prob. 14-8, in the long run. Assume that labor mobility is perfect.

14-10. A single hospital in a small town is the sole buyer of nurse-services. The supply curve of nurses is positively sloped. Nurses claim that enforcing a minimum wage rate would force the hospital to use more nurse-hours. By drawing the right diagram explain under what conditions this may be true.

SELECTED READINGS

BAUMOL, W. J. *Economic Theory and Operations Analysis*. Englewood Cliffs, N.J.: Prentice-Hall, Inc., Chapter 14.

FRIEDMAN, M. *Price Theory, A Provisional Text*. Chicago, Ill.: Aldine Publishing Company, 1962, Chapters 9, 10, and 11.

STIGLER, G. J. *op. cit.*, Chapter 14.

APPENDIX

THE COBB-DOUGLAS PRODUCTION FUNCTION

The Demand Curve for Factors of Production. At this point, the reader is urged to review the relevant parts in the Appendices to Chapters 5 and 6.

Consider the following production function of a certain firm:

$$Q = K \cdot A^\alpha \cdot B^\beta \cdot C^\gamma$$

recalling that

$$MPP_a = \alpha \frac{Q}{A}$$

Now, if $\alpha + \beta + \gamma = 1$, the firm is said to be governed by constant returns to scale. Thus, once the optimal proportion between A, B, and C is found, the demand curve for A is a flat line. To prove that this is true, consider a point at which this optimal proportion between the factors is maintained. At that point,

$$P_a = \alpha \frac{Q_0}{A_0} P_x \qquad P_b = \beta \frac{Q_0}{B_0} P_x \qquad P_c = \gamma \frac{Q_0}{C_0} P_x$$

If we increase all factors in the same proportion, say multiply them by K, output will also increase in the same proportion. Thus,

$$\alpha \frac{K \cdot Q_0}{K \cdot A_0} = \alpha \frac{Q_0}{A_0}$$

and so on for B and C. Since the firm has no appreciable influence over the price of the product it makes, the value marginal product is the same regardless of the scale of production.

In order to obtain a negatively sloped demand curve for a factor of production, we must assign to one of the factors the role of the fixed factor. Let C be the fixed factor. Assume also that A is labor and B is capital. You will find it interesting to generate a demand curve for factor A, first by keeping B constant, secondly, by allowing both A and B to vary when the price of A falls.

Consider the marginal physical product of a certain factor, say factor A. We recall again that

$$MPP_a = \alpha \frac{Q}{A}$$

Thus the value marginal product of A, which is denoted by VMP_a, equals MPP_a times the price per unit of output, which is denoted by P_x; namely,

$$VMP_a = MPP_a \cdot P_x = \alpha \frac{Q \cdot P_x}{A}$$

In equilibrium, $P_a = VMP_a$, that is,

$$P_a = \alpha \frac{Q \cdot P_x}{A}$$

Consider one industry, say industry X. If A units of A are employed there, then the absolute share of A is

$$A \cdot P_a = A\alpha \frac{Q \cdot P_x}{A} = \alpha \cdot Q \cdot P_x$$

Or, let the fraction of total cost that is being spent on A be denoted by K_a. Then

$$K_a = \frac{A \cdot P_a}{Q \cdot P_x} = \frac{\alpha \cdot Q \cdot P_x}{Q \cdot P_x} = \alpha$$

For example, if industry X produces 1,000 units of output per unit of time and the price P_x equals $1,000, then total revenue (which is equal to total cost) is $1,000,000 per unit of time. If $\alpha = \frac{1}{2}$, then the share of labor is $\frac{1}{2}$ (or 50 percent of the total), i.e., workers are paid $500,000.

We can now benefit from the Cobb-Douglas function, keeping in mind that it obeys all the required laws, such as diminishing MPP_a, and the law of dependence. Also, by imposing the condition that $\alpha + \beta + \gamma = 1$, it obeys constant returns to scale. Let us apply it to agriculture. Assume that the aggregate process of production in agriculture is represented by the function

$$Q = 1 \cdot A^{1/4} \cdot B^{1/4} \cdot C^{1/2}$$

where A is labor, B is capital, and C are all inputs that are fixed, or to put it differently, C is an input specific to agriculture. For our purposes, we can assume that C is land. Also, at the industry level, no harm will be done if we make the assumption that labor and entrepreneurial services are combined in one unit denoted by A. In what follows we are going to use convenient units even if they are not realistic. Let

$$A = 10 \qquad B = 10 \qquad C = 10$$

Thus

$$Q = 10^{1/4} \cdot 10^{1/4} \cdot 10^{1/2} = 10 \text{ units}$$

Let the price per unit of output be equal to $10; then, total revenue is equal to $10 \times \$10 = \$100$. Thus, we have

$$VMP_a = \frac{1}{4} \cdot \frac{10}{10} \cdot \$10 = \$2.5$$

$$VMP_b = \frac{1}{4} \cdot \frac{10}{10} \cdot \$10 = \$2.5$$

This is consistent with an assumption of 10 units of labor and capital priced at \$2.5 per unit respectively. As far as input C is concerned, we assumed that there are 10 units of land that cannot be varied. Thus, payments to landlords are residues. In this case total revenue is \$100, total payments to labor amount to \$25, and total revenue to capital is also \$25. Accordingly, the residue is $\$100 - (\$25 + \$25) = \$50$. Then land rentals are \$5 per unit. Let us make the realistic assumption that the industry faces horizontal supply curves of labor and capital, respectively. The industry can employ any amount of these two inputs. Consider a price support program, according to which the price of agricultural output is raised 20 percent (from \$10 to \$12). Then we have to solve the following set of equations:

$$\frac{1}{4} \cdot \frac{Q}{A} \cdot \$12 = \$2.5 \tag{1}$$

$$\frac{1}{4} \cdot \frac{Q}{B} \cdot \$12 = \$2.5 \tag{2}$$

$$Q = A^{1/4} \cdot B^{1/4} \cdot 10^{1/2} \tag{3}$$

Solving these equations we obtain $A = 14.4$ units, $B = 14.4$ units, and $Q = 12$ units of output. [You can check the following: $12 = (14.4)^{1/4} \times (14.4)^{1/4} \times 10^{1/2}$, and $\frac{1}{4}(12/14.4) \times \$12 = \$2.5$.] Thus, employment of variable factors increased 44 percent. As far as land rentals are concerned, we can estimate them as follows: the new quantity of agricultural output is 12 units and the new price is \$12, thus total revenue is \$144. Payments to labor amount to $14.4 \times \$2.5 = \$36$. The same holds for capital. Therefore the residue is $144 - 72 = \$72$. The new rental per unit of land is $\$72/10 = \$7.2$. Namely, landlords are the only persons benefiting from the price support program.

It is recalled that the Cobb-Douglas function has one specific drawback; namely, its elasticity of substitution between two factors takes on only one value. Thus, when a problem that involves a change in the relative price of a factor arises, one has to resort to another model. For example, consider the case where a subsidy is extended to farmers. The subsidy is paid on fertilizers.

Let A stand for labor and B stand for capital. Let σ stand for the elasticity of substitution between A and B; then the following formula can be proved:

$$\frac{\% \text{ change in } A}{\% \text{ change in } P_b} = K_b (\sigma - |\eta|)$$

This formula is true only for small changes in P_b. Note that this formula is derived under the assumption that η, the price elasticity of the commodity made by the industry, is negative.

Example: Assume that in agriculture $\eta = -\frac{1}{4}$ and $\sigma = 1.25$. Assume also that the share of capital in the total cost is 40 percent. Analyze the effect of a 5 percent *ad valorem* subsidy on capital.

Assume that the price of capital services will decline 5 percent. Then we have

$$\frac{\% \text{ change in } A}{-5\%} = \frac{4}{10} (1\frac{1}{4} - \frac{1}{4})$$

then,

$$\% \text{ change in } A = -5\% \cdot \frac{4}{10} = -2\%$$

chapter 15

The Labor Market

Payments to labor in form of wages and salaries account for about two-thirds of the national income in the United States. The importance of the labor market is more than this figure would suggest. The reason is that more than two-thirds of the families in the United States rely on wages and salaries as the main or only source of income. Since the welfare of so many people is related to wages and salaries, the labor market merits at least one chapter. No less important is the role of the union in the economy. Do unions lead in the determination of wages, or do they follow the market? These and other problems will be analyzed with the aid of supply and demand.

THE WAGE RATE

The wage rate is determined at the point of intersection between supply and demand for labor. For simplicity, assume that there is only one type of labor in the economy. Then, one can conceive of an aggregate demand curve for labor. At each point belonging to this demand curve the value marginal product of labor is equal to the wage rate. In Fig. 15-1, the wage rate is W_0, as indicated by the point of intersection between D, the demand curve for labor and S, the supply curve of labor. At this point of equilibrium L_0 units of labor are employed per unit of time. If the wage rate happened to be higher than W_0, then supply of labor would exceed the demand for labor in the economy. If wages are flexible, there will be immediate forces which will propel the labor market back to point N in Fig. 15-1, which is the point of intersection between supply of labor and demand for labor. An excess supply of labor means that so many workers are seeking jobs, but they cannot find one. These frustrated unemployed workers will start to offer labor services at a lower wage rate, which will depress the wage rate just until it is back at W_0. For example, if the wage rate happened to be W_1, then L_2 units of labor

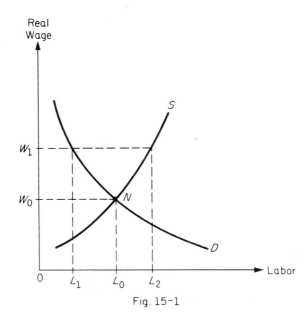

Fig. 15-1

will be offered, but only L_1 units of labor will find jobs. Unemployment will amount to the excess supply of labor, which is $L_2 - L_1$ units of labor. The unemployed will depress the prevailing wage rate in attempting to find jobs. This description of the forces operating in the labor market should not be taken literally. Usually the wage rate is sluggish to the extent that unemployed workers cannot put it downward, at least not in the short run. But, in the modern welfare state, unemployment entails an immediate automatic increase in the budgetary deficit of the government. If unemployment becomes severe, the government might use its discretionary powers and institute an easy-money policy as well as other fiscal policies which will generate a mild inflation. Thus, nominal prices of finished goods and services will start to rise, which in turn will depress the real wage rate.

If the wage rate happens to be below W_0 in Fig. 15-1, there will be a shortage in the labor market. This shortage will be cured by employers offering higher wages in order to attract scarce labor.

IDENTICAL WAGES FOR IDENTICAL WORKERS

Let us assume that there are only two industries in the economy, industry X and industry Y, that produce two different commodities and use different methods of production, yet use the same labor force. Assume also that working conditions are as pleasant in industry X as they are in industry Y. That is, the same nonpecuniary advantages and disadvantages exist in both industries. In other words, working conditions are similar to the extent that one does not care where he works so long as he gets the same salary. If this is the situation, then the wage rate in industry X is expected to be equal to the wage rate in industry Y. There will always be economic forces which will bring the wage rate in industry X into level with the wage rate in industry Y. Let us examine these economic forces which equalize wages under such conditions. The labor market of industry X is described in Fig 15-2 and the labor market of industry Y in Fig. 15-3. Consider the case where W_x, the wage rate in industry X is higher than W_y, the wage rate in industry Y. This is

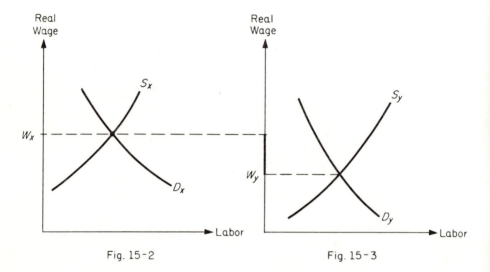

Fig. 15-2   Fig. 15-3

not a stable situation, because workers will start to move from industry Y to industry X. This is identical with saying that S_x in Fig. 15-2 will shift rightward while S_y in Fig. 15-3 will shift leftward just until the new lower wage rate in industry X will be equal to the new higher wage rate in industry Y. The incentive to move from industry Y to industry X stems from the fact that there is a difference in wages which is equal to $W_x - W_y$. So long as W_x is higher than W_y, there is an incentive to quit working in industry Y and find a job in industry X.

The attention of the student who intends to specialize in economics is drawn to the fact that there are "noneconomists" who discard economic analysis. Part of their criticism refers to economists who use cannons for killing flies. Economists probably deserve this part of criticism. But most of the criticism is devoted to showing that the theory does not explain reality. We had an opportunity to discuss this problem at the beginning of Chapter 12. We shall now discuss it again. The "noneconomists" claim that the theory is bad because we observe identical workers who receive different wages in different industries. For example, farm workers are paid less than nonfarm workers. So, why does one need a theory if blue collar workers in two different industries are paid differently? But the economists would react to this by saying that the theory is only a convenient framework to organize our thinking. Let us consider the above problem. First of all, the "color of the collar" is not the only measuring rod. Farm labor and nonfarm labor are not identical, at least because the level of schooling of farm employees is very low compared with the level of schooling of nonfarm workers. It is true, however, that even after one adjusts for the difference in the level of schooling, nonfarm wages are significantly higher than farm wages. Let us rationalize this by applying economic theory. Let Fig. 15-3 represent the labor market in farm areas and Fig. 15-2 represent the labor market in nonfarm areas. The difference between W_x and W_y measures the order of magnitude of the incentive to move from industry Y which is agriculture to industry X. To be sure, as the theory predicts, farm people do migrate to the cities. From 1940 to 1960, the farm labor force in the United States shrunk, not only as a percentage of the total labor force, but also in absolute members. (From 1910 to 1940, farm population had not changed in absolute numbers, but it had shrunk as a fraction of total population.) In summary, while a century ago about half of the American labor force was employed in agriculture, in 1965 only 7 percent of the labor force was employed on farms. In spite of this tremendous farm out-migration, farm incomes and wages remain relatively low. This is rationalized as follows: Over a period of time D_x, the demand curve for nonfarm labor shifts rightward rapidly. D_y, the demand curve for farm labor shifts very slowly, or does not shift at all. This tends to widen even further the wage differential indicated by $W_x - W_y$. The process of farm out-migration tends to close this wage differential, because migration of people from agriculture to other industries means that S_y in Fig. 15-3 shifts leftward while S_x in Fig. 15-2 shifts rightward. It should be noted that since the fraction of workers employed in agriculture is relatively small, equalizing W_y with W_x can be achieved mainly by shifting S_y leftward. Finally, we can summarize this by saying that the wage differential between the farm sector and the nonfarm sector persists due to insufficient farm out-migration. This conclusion enables the economist to advocate a policy to cope with the farm problem (see Chapter 11). On the other hand, those who refuse to rationalize economic phenomena are unable to recommend one policy or another! In the final analysis, the importance of the theory (and those who provide it!) will be determined by its ability to explain reality and help us to cope with economic problems.

Let us now turn to other problems relating to the labor market. We do not intend to cover demand for labor shifts due to changes in prices of other factors of production. This problem was covered in detail in Chapter 14.

EQUALIZING DIFFERENCES IN WAGES

Sometimes identical workers receive different wages even though labor mobility is practically perfect. Consider Fig. 15-2 and Fig. 15-3. It is possible that labor in industry X is identical with labor in industry Y. It is also possible that workers in industry Y are aware of the higher wages that are paid in industry X, and in addition they know that moving from industry Y to industry X is relatively inexpensive. Yet, the wage differential which is measured by $W_x - W_y$ persists. Moreover, one does not observe an "exodus" of workers from industry Y. This can be explained as follows: Assume that there are different working conditions in the two industries. In general there is more pleasure involved in working in industry Y as compared with industry X. It may be that Y is a "clean" industry while X involves work which is dirty. Or industry Y may be located in an area where the climate is nice and warm. Thus, let us arrange all the workers in Y according to their eagerness to move to industry X. The first worker is the one who is most eager to move to industry X; we can call him the "marginal worker." The second worker is the second most eager out-migrator . . . and so on to the worker who is least eager to move to industry X. The fact that no labor movement takes places from industry Y to industry X indicates that the "marginal worker" considers the convenience involved in working in industry Y as worth more than, or at least equal to the wage differential indicated by $W_x - W_y$. For instance, if X is the plumbing industry, W_x, the average wage of a plumber is currently $8,000, Y is the industry supplying clerical services, and W_y, the average wage rate of a clerk, is $6,000, one can say that the "marginal clerk" considers the convenience involved in being a "white collar" worker as worth at least $2,000 per annum. In other words, for the "marginal clerk," being able to wear a white shirt and a tie, plus avoiding manual labor, is worth at least $2,000. In this example, it is difficult to determine whether the equalizing difference in the wage rates arises from the low social prestige involved in being a plumber or from the convenience involved in doing clerical work.

Pilots receive higher wages partly because of the short working life involved. Namely, the salary of a pilot includes an equalizing element which "compensates" the pilot for the time when he will be grounded. Spies are paid fabulous amounts of money, mainly because their work is nerve-racking and involves a high risk of being imprisoned or shot. The average income of dentists is lower than the average income of physicians. It seems that at least part of the income differential can be explained by the fact that it takes only five to six years to become a dentist while it takes seven to eight years to become a physician. A difference of two years of training may mean a great loss of income due to two years' tuition and income foregone while attending the university. Note that here we make the assumption that it takes the same talent to become either a dentist or a physician. Finally, equalizing differences rationalize the fact that those who work the night shifts are paid better even though they are not better workers.

DIFFERENCES ARISING FROM NONCOMPETING GROUPS

Differences Arising From Natural Noncompeting Groups. People are different by nature. Some are born husky, others can hardly lift a shopping bag to the third floor. Some can memorize half of the Bible, others are not capable of memorizing the national anthem. Some people have guts and imagination, and make good salesmen; others are not as fortunate. Thus, differences in wages also arise from the fact that people are not equally talented. There are many examples that can be brought here. For instance, one cannot explain the difference between the salary of a professor and the salary of a clerk by equalizing differences. A professor does not have to check in and out at certain hours; he does not have to "kill" eight hours in the same office; he has a wide discretion in choosing his method of teaching and the material he wants to teach. What is more important, he can devote two hours a day to a small talk with his colleagues over a cup of coffee. The clerk does not enjoy life as much. He has to check in and out at a certain time. He can afford small talk with a friend only when the boss is not around—and this is not without risk. His job involves tedium, and he has almost no discretion whatsoever! As far as prestige is concerned, the average clerk probably has less of it in comparison with a professor of a university. If one were to assume identical labor, then one should expect the clerk to receive a higher salary in order to compensate him for the nonpecuniary inconveniences involved. On the other hand, professors should be paid very little, because their activities during the working day clearly indicate that their life is one long semivacation. But, in reality, professors are paid much more than clerks, the reason being that *the two groups are noncompeting!*

Let us go back to Fig. 15-2 and Fig. 15-3. Let D_x and S_x be the demand for and supply of services of professors. Let D_y and S_y be the demand for and supply of clerical services. Then, in spite of the fact that

W_x may be twice as high as W_y, there is no process of migration from the "clerical" industry to the industry which produces higher education. The reason is that those who are clerks are deprived for one reason or another from getting a degree which will certify them as professors. Note that there is probably some equalizing element in the relatively high salary of a professor, that is, an element of compensation for tuition and income foregone while attending the university as a student. But even after we adjust for this equalizing difference, the salary of an average professor still would be higher than that of an average clerk.

Differences between the salaries of movie stars and other "nonmovie stars" arise from noncompeting groups. Actress Elizabeth Taylor earns in one minute what most people make in one month, and perhaps in one year. Such a tremendous difference in salaries is not an equalizing factor, because what Miss Taylor does is not exactly tedious nor does it involve any inconveniences such as responsibility or nerve strain. The reason, however, for this difference is very simple: only a few girls can produce "services" that are similar to the services rendered by Miss Taylor.

Differences Arising from Artificial Noncompeting Groups. If you want to become a taxicab owner in New York City, you have to find an owner of a cab who is willing to sell you his medallion, which is the license to operate a cab in the city. The price of such a medallion is fabulous. The reason is that the municipal authority has restricted the number of medallions in face of a rising demand for taxicab services. Thus, the income of taxicab owners is relatively high in New York City. But in spite of the tremendous incentive on the part of identical labor to operate taxicabs in New York City, identical labor can be treated as a noncompeting group because there are artificial barriers to entry. Examples like this can be found in other areas. In fact, where there is a strong organization that exerts political influence on the local government, it is very likely that the local government will impose artificial barriers to entry. There are self-correcting political forces which will eventually eliminate these artificial barriers. Once the public becomes aware of the unjustified high prices that it pays, it will exert a counter political pressure attempting to eliminate the barriers.

Another form of imposing artificial barriers is through raising standards. For example, medical schools are known to turn down more than one-third of the applications to enter the schools. The official explanation of the American Medical Association is that this is necessary in order to maintain high standards. There probably is a grain of truth in this explanation, but it should be taken with a grain of salt, because one finds it difficult to believe that less than two-thirds of all applicants are good potential physicians.

The best that we can do here is to indicate that artificial barriers give rise to wasting human resources. The solution to this problem, however, lies in the realm of politics.

THE ROLE OF UNIONS

If the role of the union were strictly economic, then in a modern state there would be no need for unions. When we say modern state we refer to the *"welfare state"* where unemployed workers collect unemployment compensation, where information about jobs is available and labor mobility is almost perfect. In such a state the market mechanism will pay all workers according to their value marginal product, and one

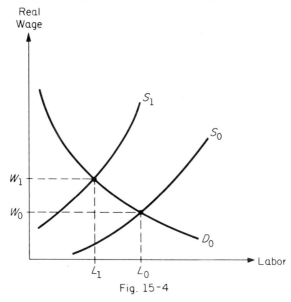

Fig. 15-4

cannot see what important economic role can be played by the union. In many countries the noneconomic role of the union is very important. Unions are engaged in educational programs and other cultural activities. They are also involved in on-the-job training programs as well as retraining those who are laid off.

Unions play an important *economic* role in cases where they can raise wages above the equilibrium rate. We have already indicated how unions can raise wages by imposing artificial barriers to entry. In economic terms this boils down to shifting the supply curve of labor in a certain industry leftward, and thus bringing the point of intersection between supply and demand into a higher level. This is illustrated in Fig. 15-4. By making it difficult to get a job in the industry, the union has shifted the supply curve of labor confronting the industry from S_0 to S_1. As a result, the wage rate is now at W_1. Note that the distortion in the labor market due to this act on the part of the union can be measured by $L_1 - L_0$ units of labor.

Strong unions do not have to resort to such methods. If the union can force employers to agree to pay a higher wage rate, say W_1 instead of W_0 in Fig. 15-4, then the market will take care of itself. When they are forced to pay higher wages, employers will lay off workers. As indicated by their demand curve for labor they will reduce employment from L_0 to L_1 units of labor.

It is obvious that if D_0 in Fig. 15-4 is very inelastic, the union demands to raise wages will lead to a relatively small change in employment. However, if D_0 is very elastic, the union wage demands will bring the management under pressure to lay off a significant fraction of the labor force. As an example, consider the railroad unions in the United States.

At the beginning of the century, trains were slow and 100 miles of travel was equivalent to one work day. The railroad unions managed to maintain this formula in 1960 even though in 1960 trains are much faster than they were in 1920. Thus, in 1960 a passenger train makes the 200 miles between Washington and New York in four hours. According to the old agreement this is equivalent to two days' pay. The engineer who operates the train collects two days' pay for half a day's work.

You will recall that the elasticity of D_0 in Fig. 15-4 depends mainly on the elasticity of the demand for the final product and the degree of substitutability between labor and capital. At the beginning of the century the demand for railroad services had a relatively low elasticity. Accordingly, the derived demand for labor had a low elasticity too, and unions could push wages upwards (by sticking to the 100 miles a day formula) without leading to a drastic reduction in jobs. When time elapsed, substitutes for railroad services were invented. The demand curve for services rendered by trains became very elastic because of the appearance of the truck and other substitutes. As a result, the derived demand for labor also became more elastic. One suspects that another reason why the demand for railroad workers became more elastic was increasing substitutability between labor and capital. For example, railroad companies could substitute capital for labor by introducing the diesel locomotives and laying off the firemen. Facing a more elastic demand curve and rising wages of engineers, firemen, and other workers, railroad companies laid off a significant fraction of its employees. For example, the Brotherhood of Locomotive Firemen and Engineers had some 130,000 members in 1920 and it had only some 80,000 members in 1960. In fact, had it not been for the featherbedding tactics of the unions, the figure for 1960 would be smaller. Before the diesel locomotive was invented, firemen were needed for shoveling coal. In the diesel, there is no coal and no need exists to shovel the nonexistent coal. But management had conceded to the strong Firemen's Brotherhood and agreed to keep firemen on the diesel loco-motives. The unions, of course, justify this type of featherbedding by claiming that firemen on diesel locomotives provide extra safety.

You should be aware of the possibility that sometimes unions raise the wage rate by not more than could have been achieved in the market without the union. In other words, they simply set the price of labor at the new point of intersection between supply and demand for labor.

When economists try to provide a theory regarding the wage behavior of unions, they refer to the long-run range. In the short run, a union can get away with a wage increase above the point of intersection between supply and demand without affecting the level of employment. This is true because in the short run, consumers will continue to consume the same flow of the final product even if the price is higher. Moreover, in the short run, capital cannot be substituted for labor which became relatively more expensive. The union is aware of the fact that in the long run, after sufficient time is allowed for adjustment, consumers will divert purchasing power away from the commodity whose price has risen due to a higher wage rate. Moreover, in the long run, management will substitute capital for labor. Thus, we are justified in making the realistic assumption that union leaders estimate the employer's long-run demand curve for labor. If the only interest of the unions were to achieve the high-est average wage rate for workers who retained their jobs in the industry, then the shape of the demand curve for labor would be of little interest to the union. The truth of the matter is that unions are sensitive to the number of workers who may lose their jobs as a result of a higher wage rate. This sensitivity is political rather than economic. It stems from the fact that as a political entity the union is interested in growth per se. Moreover, if the economy suffers from unemployment, the government will be concerned over the issue of higher wage rates that may cause a higher level of unemployment. In summary, the union will try to push the wage rate above equilibrium provided that it does not affect the level of employment significantly. For this, two conditions are necessary: The first is the ability to pass the increase in the wage rate on to the consumer. This can be done if the long-run demand curve for the final product is very inelastic. If the demand curve for the final product is elastic, firms will react to the higher wage rate by cutting down production through laying off labor and other variable factors of production. This is equivalent to saying that firms will not be able to pass the increase in wages on to the consumer. The second condition is a low degree of substitutability between labor and capital. If the degree of substitutability is high, then raising the wage rate above equilibrium will result in substituting capital for labor which will be diverted away from production. In summary, the long-run demand curve for labor is functionally related to the price elasticity of the demand curve for the final product and the degree of substitutability between capital and labor. The more elastic the demand curve for the final product and the larger the degree of substitutability between labor and capital, the more elastic the demand curve is for labor.[1]

Before one advocates policy, one has to determine whether unions play an important role in the economy. This can be achieved by comparing time series of wage rates of identical workers in unionized and nonunionized industries. If the wage differential of identical workers in unionized and nonunionized industries is negligible, no economic policy is called for. This means that unions facilitate rather than affect the labor market. Note that such a statistical comparison is meaningful only if we can assume that nonpecuniary advantages or disadvantages level off at the industry level.

GROWTH AND WAGE RATE

Let us now return to the macro level. It is recalled that if the supply curve of labor shifts rightward at the same rate as demand, then the real wage rate will not change over a period of time. The demand curve for labor shifts rightward due to rising marginal physical product of labor. Marginal physical product of labor increases due to the following:

1. More capital is available from year to year. Consumers save money and their savings are converted into investment in new capital. Other variables remaining the same, with more capital to cooperate with labor in production, marginal physical production of labor will rise. (The *ceteris paribus* is necessary here because if we do not assume the same amount of labor, and we assume constant returns to scale, then, say, over a period of five years, both labor and capital grow in the same proportion; and thus the marginal physical products of labor and of capital will not change.)

2. Due to better technology, productivity increases over time. We recall that normally a rise in productivity means a rise in marginal physical product of labor and other factors of production. Thus, a rise in marginal physical product of labor means an upward shift in the aggregate demand curve for labor. In backward countries, the aggregate demand

[1] Let K_b and K_a stand for the share of capital and the share of labor, respectively, in total cost. Let η stand for price elasticity of the demand curve for the final product and σ for the elasticity of substitution between labor and capital as defined in Chapter 5. Then it can be proved that the elasticity of the demand curve for labor η_A is

$$\eta_A = -\left(K_b \cdot \sigma + K_a \cdot |\eta|\right)$$

For proof see the Mathematical Appendix.

curve for labor does not shift rightward because of the *vicious circle of poverty*: In most of the underdeveloped countries income is entirely devoted to buying food for survival. Thus, saving is practically impossible because a significant saving may bring millions of people to the brink of famine. But without saving it is impossible to invest in tangible capital such as power stations and steel mills; neither is it possible to invest in "human capital" and technology so as to increase productivity. This is why underdeveloped countries are so dependent on foreign aid from the West. Why the West is willing to give aid is a different story!

Breaking this vicious circle of poverty by extending generous foreign aid to underdeveloped countries is only one side of the coin. There is no doubt that foreign aid to India has shifted the demand curve for labor over to the right in the past. Had the supply curve of labor not shifted, then the real wage rate of workers in India would have increased, because the new demand curve for labor would have intersected with the original supply curve at higher points. Unfortunately, however, the supply curve of labor shifts rightward very fast due to the "population explosion." In fact, there are countries where the rate of growth of the population is responsible for shifting the supply of labor fast enough to eliminate any gain from the shift in demand. Thus, underdeveloped countries should spend a significant fraction of their budgets for development and discovering methods to check the rate of growth of their populations.

In the United States the demand curve for labor shifts rightward faster than supply. It appears that the real wage rate rises at a rate of about one to two percent per annum. In Western Europe immediately after World War II, wages were very low. Even though many millions of people were killed during the war, many survived and with them a tremendous "know-how." Thus, one can say that potential productivity was there, and the only thing the Europeans needed was aid to invest in tangible capital. This aid was extended to them through the Marshall Plan, which shifted the demand for labor very rapidly to the right. On the other hand the rightward shift in the supply of labor was relatively mild. This is why real wages rose so fast in Western Europe, sometimes at a rate of 5 percent per annum and over.

LEISURE VERSUS OTHER GOODS

In Chapter 8, we discussed the backward bending supply curve of labor. It was explained that when the hourly wage rate rises, income increases; but the price of leisure rises too. Since leisure is a superior commodity, with more income the worker tends to buy more leisure, i.e., to work less. But at the same time, since the price of leisure rises, the worker tends to substitute other commodities for leisure.

Notice that a backward bending supply curve of the individual worker does not necessarily imply that the aggregate supply curve of all workers is backward bending; the reason being that even if the supply curve of each individual worker is backward bending, a higher wage rate may attract more people to join the labor force.

When over a period of time the aggregate demand curve for labor shifts more rapidly than the aggregate supply curve of labor, the wage rate rises. If for one individual worker or a group of workers it rises above the critical rate, the worker will tend to work less, i.e., to buy more leisure. This is why the working week and working day became shorter and shorter over the last two decades.

PROBLEMS

15-1. Self-employed workers (who on the average earn more money than hired workers) work a longer number of hours per year than do hired workers. Thus, this fact contradicts the assumption of a backward bending supply curve of labor. Do you agree?

15-2. A union succeeds in imposing a higher wage in industry A. Yet more workers are employed in that industry. Does this contradict the assumption of a negatively sloped demand curve for labor?

15-3. Mathematicians who are employed by private business earn more than mathematicians working for academic institutions. Explain.

15-4. A blue collar worker at International Harvester Company earns more money than my janitor. (NOTE: It takes one day to train a worker at International Harvester Company.) Explain.

15-5. It is very well known that, even after accounting for differences in training and education, farm workers are paid much less than workers in the nonfarm sector. Explain and suggest a policy to cope with this problem.

15-6. Presently a shortage of teachers exists. It is clear that raising the wages of teachers will eliminate this shortage. Assuming that the demand curve for teachers is a vertical line, what information would you need in order to recommend a proper wage rate.

15-7. Raising the level of schooling in rural farm areas in the United States will entail a higher marginal physical product of farm workers. Does this mean that farm wages will increase in the short run? (HINT: In equilibrium, wages = MPP of labor times the price of farm output.)

15-8. Repeat Prob. 15-7, except that the level of schooling is only raised in one state. Assume that the share of one state in total agricultural production is negligible.

SELECTED READINGS

BARTH, P. S. "Unemployment and Labor Forth Participation," *Southern Economic Journal*, Vol. XXXIV, January, 1968.

CARTER, A. M. *Theory of Wages and Employment*. Homewood, Ill.: Richard D. Irwin, Inc., 1959.

CHAMBERLIN, E. H. *The Theory of Monopolistic Competition* (7th ed.). Boston, Mass.: Harvard University Press, 1958, Chapter VII.

COHEN, S. *Labor in the United States* (2d ed.). Charles E. Merrill Books, Inc., 1965.

FRIEDMAN, M. and KUZNETS, S. "Income from Independent Professional Practice," New York, National Bureau of Economic Research, 1945.

HICKS, J. R. *The Theory of Wages*. New York: The Macmillan Company, 1957, Appendix.

MARSHALL, A. *Princples of Economics*. London: The Macmillan Company, 1952, Book VI, Chapters 3, 4, and 5.

APPENDIX

THE MARXISM THAT FAILED

You have probably heard the saying that if you did not happen to be a Marxist in your "teens" you had no heart, but if you remained a Marxist after you passed your "teens," you had no brains. It is important to devote a few pages to the problem, because in one-half of the globe Marxism is enforced as the only ideology. As we shall show later on, it is impossible to practice it.

Karl Marx (1818-1883) graduated from the faculty of law, and at the age of twenty-four he was the editor of a liberal newspaper. His articles were rebellious, and he was forced to leave Germany for England. There he worked together with Fredric Engels on the theory of "historical materialism." The works of Marx include *Capital*, where he tries to analyze the capitalistic system. Various parts of his philosophical approach can also be found in the *Manifesto of the Communist Party*. We shall not elaborate here on Marx' historical materialism according to which "the history of all hitherto existing society is the history of class struggles." Nor shall we go into detail here on the theory which claims that there are two structures in the development of societies throughout history; namely, the *substructure*, which is the social existence of men, and the *super-structure*, which is the consciousness of men. According to Marxism, the superstructure is determined by the substructure. These philosophical theories are attractive for some young people because they provide a simple formula that explains everything about human behavior. It is for this reason that adults find these theories naive and boring.

Let us turn to Marxian economics. Marx' starting point was the difference between the *value in use* and the *exchange value*. The *value in use* is the usefulness of the product to the person. This is a psychological phenomenon and is the reason that we exchange goods. But, according to

Marx, this is never the exchange value of the commodity. The exchange value is determined according to the quantity of labor or of working time which is necessary for the production of the goods. Thus, according to Marx if two hours of "congealed working time" are necessary to produce two *Kg* of iron, and two hours of "congealed working time" are also necessary to produce one hectoliter of wheat, then the exchange value of two *Kg* of iron is equal to the exchange value of one hectoliter of wheat. Even if it were true that labor is the only factor of production that counts, this theory of *the exchange value* is empty. This theory cannot solve even one minor problem relating to the market. For example, it is not capable of telling us how the market mechanism solves problems such as a change in tastes in favor of one commodity, or how much should be produced of each commodity.

But, let us leave this weak side of the theory and follow Marx further. Marx raises another question: We have seen that the value of commodities is determined solely by human labor contained in them. How is it possible for the manufacturer to obtain a greater value from his commodities than he has invested in them? Marx says that the value of labor is determined, like any other commodity, by the quantity of work needed to produce it. In his words "the value of labor power is the value of the necessities required to sustain its proprietor. The amount of necessities must be sufficient to maintain the working individual in his normal condition life." Again one can see that this theory is very vague because the "necessities" required to sustain the worker are not scientifically defined. According to Marx, labor is a commodity that has a value, but at the same time it has the ability to create other values because it is producing another commodity. The reason why the capitalists buy this commodity, labor power, is because of its peculiar essence; namely, the ability to produce other values. As a matter of fact, this essence is the reason why the labor power is exchanged. Marx calls this peculiar essence the *value in use* of the labor power.

Now Marx comes to the point where he explains why the capitalist is able to make profits and "exploit" workers. Suppose, says Marx, that the time needed to "produce" the labor power is four hours per day. These four hours are the congealed working time needed to "produce" this strange commodity; thus, it is the exchange value of the labor power. But the *value in use* of labor is its ability to produce other values. Let us assume that the value in use is, say, ten hours. Then, the capitalist pays workers only four hours per day, but he gets from them ten hours per day. Thus, the net profit of the capitalist per worker is six hours, which Marx called the *surplus value*. This, according to Marx, was the reason why capitalists tried to lengthen the working day of their employees.

Regardless of how you look at it, the Marxian economic theory does not make sense. There are too many Achilles heels that can be easily exposed. To begin with, if labor is the only factor of production, why do workers hire themselves out? By selling their product alone they can gain the *surplus value*. It is possible to have one silly worker who would like to exchange ten hours for four hours, but it is difficult to conceive of a possibility where all workers are silly: *all of them exchange ten hours for four hours!* The Marxian answer to this attack was the following: Labor is not "really" the sole factor of production. Capital, in the form of machines, equipment, and so on, is another factor of production. But, say the Marxists, capital was created by *labor* which lived in the past. This, however, is an altogether different proposition, because if this is the case, then it is possible that "capitalists" are exploiting those who are now among the dead. Note that in addition to these logical slips, Marxism is an empty theory. Suppose in one country or another a "Marxian economy" is established. Then this theory does not tell one how to pay workers. It is obvious that Marxism does not preach equality of wages, because different workers have different *values in use*, and a "fair" wage in such an economy should equal the worker's *value in use*, whatever this vague concept may be. Moreover, the theory does not provide a mechanism to compensate workers for nonpecuniary disadvantages; namely, it cannot solve the problem of equalizing differences which is solved so smoothly in the free labor market.

We have seen that in the free enterprise system, when consumers vote with their dollars for more of commodity A and less of B, the price of A rises, profits in industry A rise, and entrepreneurs raise the wage rate in order to coax more labor to the industry. Marxism does not provide such a mechanism. One can cite many more examples, but the point has been made. We can summarize it by saying that the free labor market allocates workers according to the principle that each worker gets paid according to his value marginal product. It is impossible to determine whether it is a just system, but it is the only system that can solve all these problems of equalizing differences in wages, or problems that arise from noncompeting groups. Also, this is one way of allocating labor according to the needs of consumers. Note that in Communist countries, wage rates are determined neither by any Marxian principle nor according to any principle of equality. We know that differentials in salaries are larger in Communist countries than in the Western democracies. For example, in Western countries an engineer may earn three times as much as a blue-collar worker. In Communist countries, an engineer may earn eight times as much money as an average worker. It is obvious that planners decided to pay engineers in the Soviet Union that much because of practical reasons: they thought that the economy needed many engineers and they had to provide the proper incentive. But they may well be wasting their resources because it is possible that they could have coaxed into engineering all those who have the required talents by paying them half of their present salary. Only the market has the mechanism which can determine the wage rate that will entice the right number of workers to one profession or another.

chapter 16

Capital and Interest

This chapter consists of two parts. Part I deals with the practical issues of capital budgeting. Part II deals with the theory of capital and interest. Part I is very important for students interested in the practical aspects of capital budgeting. Part II is very important for everybody.

PART I: CAPITAL BUDGETING

THE RATE OF INTEREST

If one wants to borrow money, he must pay interest. For example if Mr. Smith borrows $10,000 at 5 percent interest, he must pay the lender $500 annually. The sum of $500 is an annual payment to the lender who sacrificed present consumption worth $10,000. The lender had to be "bribed" to forego present consumption. The "bribery" in this example amounts to $500 per annum. The interest rate is the annual reward to the lender expressed either as a percentage (5 percent) or as a decimal (0.05) of the loan. For the time being we shall ignore the macro-problem of interest rate determination. We shall assume that the rate of interest is somehow determined by economic forces over which the individual, be he a consumer or a producer, has no influence.

FUTURE VALUES

Mr. Smith presently invests $100 in securities yielding 5 percent interest. The value of this investment one year hence is $100(1 + 0.05)$. For the same reason, if interest is compounded annually then two years hence its value would amount to $[100(1 + 0.05)]$ $(1 + 0.05)$ which is $100(1 + 0.05)^2$. The value of this investment n years hence is $100(1 + 0.05)^n$. In general, the value of a present investment of X dollars n years hence is

$$Y = X(1 + r)^n$$

where r is the going interest rate expressed as a decimal and compounded annually. Y denotes the future value of the investment.

Example: Marketing research indicates that consumers in Albuquerque will start to buy whatnots three years hence. The current cost of a whatnot producing plant is $1,000. Three years from now its cost is expected to amount to $1,300. If the going interest rate is 8 percent, should one construct the plant now or three years hence?

Solution: If one ties up presently $1,000 in a plant, he must lose 8 percent interest that he could have earned had he alternatively invested $1,000 in securities. Had he done so, the future value of his present $1,000 would be

$$Y = \$1,000 \ (1 + 0.08)^3 = \$1,000 \times 1.260 = \$1,260$$

Since $1,260 is less than $1,300, one should invest now $1,000

Example: The current cost of a certain bond redeemable for $100 three years hence is $79.36. What is the interest earned on that bond?

Solution:

$$100 = \$79.36 \ (1 + r)^3$$

$$\log \ (1 + r) = (\log 100 - \log 79.36) \ / \ 3$$

Thus,

$$r = 0.08$$

If a table of future values is available, then one has to calculate $100/79.36 = 1.26$. In the row corresponding to three years, the number 1.26 is found in the 8 percent column (see the appendix).

PRESENT VALUES

What is the present value of the income of $100 that would be realized three years hence? Assume that the rate of interest is 8 percent. In order to answer this question, suppose you try to sell your banker a promise to pay the bank $100 three years from now. The present value of such a promissory note is X dollars. If the banker would alternatively put the X dollars to work, it would grow by $(1 + 0.08)^3$ in a period of three years. Thus the banker would not pay you more than an amount of X dollars which if alternatively put to work could grow to $100. We have the following equation:

$$100 = X \ (1 + 0.08)^3$$

and

$$X = \frac{1}{(1 + 0.08)^3} \cdot 100$$

In general, the present value X of Y dollars n years hence is

$$X = \frac{1}{(1 + r)^n} \cdot Y$$

where r is the going interest rate. The expression $[1/(1 + r)^n] \cdot Y$ is known as the *discounted present value*, or simply the *present value* of Y.

Example: A shed is required for the production of whatnots. Half of its capacity is needed now and the second half will be needed five years from now. The going rate of interest is 5 percent. If the complete shed is constructed now its cost would amount to $10,000. If half of it is constructed now and the second half later, it would cost $5,300 per a half shed. The problem is how to time the investment.

Solution: The discounted present value of $5,300 five years hence at 5 percent interest is

$$X = \frac{\$5,300}{(1 + 0.05)^5} = \$5,300 \times 0.784 = \$4,155$$

Accordingly, the present cost of investing in a half shed now and in the other half five years from now is $5,300 + $4,155 = $9,455. It is less than investing $10,000 now in the complete shed.

THE COST OF CAPITAL

The alternative cost of services of capital per unit of time is depreciation plus the alternative rate of interest. Consider a machine which is purchased at a cost of $1,000. The economic lifetime of the machine is ten years. In order for the sum of $1,000 to be an investment in permanent capital, the owner of the machine must accumulate a fund, which will amount to $1,000 ten years hence. This is done by writing off an equal amount of X dollars at the end of each year, satisfying

$$X \cdot (1 + r)^9 + X (1 + r)^8 + \ldots + X (1 + r) + X = \$1,000$$

Thus,

$$X [(1 + r)^{10} - 1]/r = \$1,000$$

where r denotes the going rate of interest. Solving for X we obtain

$$X = \$1,000 \cdot r/[(1 + r)^{10} - 1]$$

where X may be considered as annual capital replacement. If we add to this interest payment foregone we obtain

$$\text{annual cost of capital} = \$1,000 \cdot r/[(1 + r)^{10} - 1] + \$1,000 \cdot r$$

In general, assuming an investment of $1, an economic lifetime of n years, and a rate of interest of r, the cost of capital per annum is

$$r/[(1 + r)^n - 1] + r$$

which is known as *capital recovery factor* (C.R.F.).

Example: A sum of $1,000 is invested in a machine whose lifetime is 10 years. The rate of interest is 5 percent. What is the annual cost of capital?

Solution:

$$r / [(1 + r)^n - 1] + r = 0.05 / [1 + 0.05)^{10} - 1] + 0.05 = 0.130$$

$$0.130 \times \$1,000 = \$130$$

and accordingly, the annual alternative cost of capital worth $1,000 is $130.

Capital recovery factor, like the factors converting future dollars to present worth and vice versa, is found in tables calculated for different values of r and n. Such tables for $r = 3$, 5 and 8 percent, and $n = 1, 2, \ldots, 10$ are shown in the appendix.

If a table for C.R.F. is not available, one can use a rule of thumb for approximation. According to this rule one has to apply $1/n + r/2$. For example, consider a comparison of C.R.F. with the rule of thumb for $r = 5$ percent and $n = 5, \ldots, 15$.

TABLE 16-1

n	5	6	7	8	9	10	11	12	13	14	15
C.R.F.	0.231	0.197	0.173	0.155	0.141	0.130	0.120	0.113	0.106	0.101	0.096
Rule of Thumb	0.225	0.192	0.168	0.150	0.136	0.125	0.116	0.108	0.102	0.096	0.092

BENEFIT COST ANALYSIS

Private entrepreneurs and governments judge the merits of an investment project by applying a simple benefit cost analysis. The benefit is the expected revenue per unit of time, pecuniary and in kind. The cost is simply the expected cost, such as the cost of labor and raw materials plus the expected cost of capital. The cost of capital per unit of time is obtained by applying the appropriate *capital recovery factors* to the various investments. Notice that different assets may have different economic lifetimes, and accordingly different C.R.F.'s should be used. Although this criterion is "suspiciously" simple, it is a very powerful test and widely used. The economic lifetime of an asset should not be determined by technical considerations only. In fact, due to technological inventions an asset may become obsolete five years from the time of investment, although technically it may live for as long as 10 years.

In deriving the formula for C.R.F., we assumed that the depreciation reserves earn the same rate of interest as the capital tied up in the project itself. Supposing, however, that the capital tied up is obtained from a loan at 6 percent interest, and the depreciation reserves accumulated in the sinking fund earn 5 percent. In that case we have

$$\text{C.R.F.} = 0.05/[(1 + 0.05)^n - 1] + 0.06$$

Sometimes the process of investment is extended over a long period of time, such as an investment in an orchard. If this is the case, the investment must be "transferred" through the future value factor to the point of time at which the investment starts to yield revenue. As an example consider Table 16-2, assuming that the investment starts to yield fruits at the beginning of the fourth year.

TABLE 16-2

Period	Investment	Future Value Coefficient, $r = 0.08$	Value of Investment at Beginning of Fourth Year
Beginning of 1st year	$1,000	1.260	$1,260
Beginning of 2nd year	500	1.166	583
Beginning of 3rd year	400	1.080	432
Total			$2,275

Thus, the total investment to which the C.R.F. should be applied is $2,275.

Example: Does it pay to sell an old machine capable of producing 9,000 whatnots per annum and replace it by a new machine capable of producing 11,500 whatnots annually? The value of the old machine in the market is $6,000. The cost of the new machine is $10,000. It takes the new machine five years to become old, and the going interest rate is 8 percent. The expected marginal cost per whatnot is 50¢, and the expected price is $1 apiece.

Solution: The extra investment of replacing the old machine by a new machine is $4,000 (= $10,000 − $6,000). The C.R.F. is 0.250, thus the extra cost of capital per year is 0.250 × $4,000 = $1,000. Next notice that marginal cost does not include the alternative cost of capital. Accordingly, the extra benefit, including a reward for capital, is 2,500 whatnots (11,500 − 9,000) times $0.5 (= $1.00 − $0.50), equals $1,250. This sum exceeds the extra cost of replacing the old machine. The old should be replaced by a new machine.

The basic assumptions underlying the benefit cost analysis on the annual basis, as underlined above, are the following:

1. The lifetime of the enterprise is unlimited.
2. The expected annual revenue and annual cost do not fluctuate drastically and do not reveal a trend to either increase or decrease over time.

If the investment is once and for all, and moreover, if revenues and costs are not the same in each year, then a way to determine the benefit cost ratio is to convert all future costs and investments into present values and add them together with the initial investment into a total present value of all costs and investments. This sum should then be divided into the total present value of all revenues, in order to obtain the benefit cost ratio.

Consider the following example (Table 16-3) in which an investment of $10,000 takes place at the end of the first year. This investment is once and for all, and it lives five years. The going interest rate is 5 percent.

TABLE 16-3

End of Year	Investment or Cost, Dollars	Revenue, Dollars	Discount Rate (Present Value Coefficient) Present-End of First Year	Discounted Present Value of Investment or Costs, Dollars	Discounted Present Value of Revenue, Dollars
1	$10,000		1.000	10,000	
2	1,000	7,000	0.952	952	6,664
3	3,000	8,000	0.907	2,721	7,256
4	7,000	6,000	0.864	6,048	5,184
5	2,000	4,000	0.823	1,646	3,292
6	5,000	5,000	0.784	3,920	3,920
Total				25,287	26,316

Thus, the benefit cost ratio is

$$\frac{\$26,316}{\$25,287} = 1.04$$

FUTURE RETURNS IN PERPETUITY

Let us define yield as total revenue minus total cost, where total cost does not include returns to capital. Supposing an asset is expected to yield I_1 dollars at the end of the first year, I_2 dollars at the end of the second year, and so on. Then V, the present value of future flows of income, can be expressed as

$$V = \frac{I_1}{1 + r} + \frac{I_2}{(1 + r)^2} + \frac{I_3}{(1 + r)^3} + \dots$$

We now prove that if $I_1, = I_2 = I_3 = \dots = I$, then $V = I/r$. Consider the series $1, R, R^2, \dots, R^n$, where R is any number. Then we define S as

$$S = 1 + R + R^2 + \dots + R^n$$

Multiplying through by R we obtain

$$S = 1 + R + R^2 + \dots + R^n$$

$$R \cdot S = \quad R + R^2 + \dots + R^n + R^{n + 1}$$

Subtracting one row from the other we get

$$S = \frac{1}{1 - R} - \frac{R^{n+1}}{1 - R}$$

If R is less than unity the expression $R^{n+1}/(1 - R)$ vanishes when n approaches infinity.

Let R stand for $1/(1 + r)$, which is less than unity. Then we have

$$V = -I + I + \frac{I}{1 + r} + \frac{I}{(1 + r)^2} + \cdots$$

$$= -I + I \cdot \left[1 + \frac{1}{1 + r} + \left(\frac{1}{1 + r} \right)^2 + \cdots \right]$$

$$= -I + I \cdot \frac{1}{1 - 1/(1 + r)} = -I + I \frac{1 + r}{r}$$

$$= -I + \frac{I}{r} + I = \frac{I}{r}$$

This completes the proof that the present discounted value of I dollars per annum in perpetuity is I/r. The present discounted value of one dollar in perpetuity is $1/r$.

Thus, one may find it convenient to define *a unit of tangible capital* as a "piece" of capital capable of producing a permanent income flow of one dollar.

PAYBACK PERIOD

A rule of thumb which is sometimes used to test the profitability of a project is known as the *payback* (or payout) *period*. For example, if it costs $6 million to establish a firm, and if the firm yields $0.5 million per annum, then the payback period is 12 years.

The payback period may be totally misleading. For example, it does not take into consideration the timing of future yields (Prob. 16-8) and it neglects the possibility that one of two enterprises with equal payback periods may live substantially longer.

INTERNAL RATE OF RETURN

The internal rate of return is defined as that rate of return which would equate the discounted present value of future yields to the cost of the investment. For example, what is the internal rate of return, i, on an investment of $285.7 which takes place at the beginning of the year, if the only expected yields are $100 one year hence and $200 two years hence?

$$\text{Solve: } 285.7 = \frac{100}{1 + i} + \frac{200}{(1 + i)^2}$$

Let the right hand member of this equation be denoted by X, then we go through a process of iteration (see Table 16-4).

TABLE 16-4

i	X	
0.04	281.2	low, try a lower i
0.02	290.2	high, try a higher i
0.035	283.4	low, try a lower i
0.025	288.0	high, try a higher i
0.03	285.7	

In this example, the internal rate of return is 3 percent.

Whenever the internal rate of return has to be determined for a project in which the yield alternates, a process of iteration must be employed. If the yield is I dollars in perpetuity, the determination of the internal rate of return boils down to solving $V = I/i$ where V is the cost of the investment, I is the expected annual income in perpetuity, and i is the internal rate of return.

The test of profitability is a very simple one: *The project should be accepted if the internal rate of return is higher than the going interest rate. The project should be rejected if the internal rate of return is lower than the going interest rate.*

As will be shown later, this rule is valid provided that the following two conditions are met:

1. Only one project is considered.
2. V and i are negatively related.

It is evident that if the yield is I dollars per annum in perpetuity, the curve relating V to i is a rectangular hyperbola. The curve relating V to i for $I = \$10$ is depicted in Fig. 16-1. Supposing the cost of the investment is $200. Then, the internal rate of return is 5 percent. If the going interest rate is 3 percent, this project should be accepted according to the above test. The true test, however, is to compare the present value of future yields at the going 3 percent interest rate with the cost of the investment. In our example the discounted present value of future yields is $333, and it exceeds the cost of investment of $200. Clearly this is a worthwhile investment, because assuming a perfect market, the project may be sold for $333 which is by $133 more than the cost of the project.

From the construction of Fig. 16-1 it is clear that if VV is negatively sloped, the internal rate of return test is in accord with the *true* present value test. The reason being that, as indicated by Fig. 16-1, if the interest rate is lower than the internal rate of return, then the discounted present value of future yields must exceed the cost of the investment.

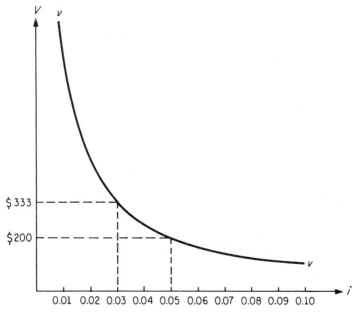

Fig. 16-1

But, consider a project in which the discounted present value of future yields is positively related to the interest rate. For example, consider an hypothetical project which yields $50 at the end of the first year, and $-$ $60 at the end of the tenth year. Table 16-5 describes how the discounted present value of this project rises with interest rate.

TABLE 16-5

i	0.01	0.02	0.03	0.04	0.05	0.06	0.07	0.08	0.09	0.10
$V$$	-4.8	-0.2	4.0	7.5	10.8	13.7	16.4	18.5	20.5	22.3

Supposing the cost of the investment is $18.5. Then, as indicated by Table 16-5, the internal rate of return is 8 percent. If the going rate of interest is 6 percent, the above test is misleading, because it tells us to accept the project. But as indicated by Table 16-5, at 6 percent interest rate, the discounted present value of the project is $13.7, which is less than the cost of $18.5.

Finally, consider two projects, say A and B, for which the cost of investment is the same, but the VV curves are different. This case is depicted in Fig. 16-2. We leave it for the reader to show that the internal rate of return test for profitability fails, if the problem at hand is to select only one out of the two projects.

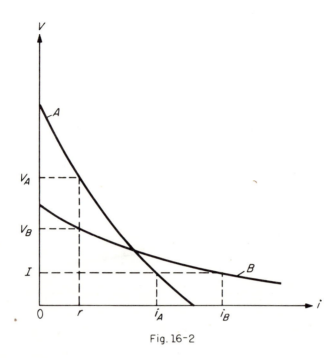

Fig. 16-2

PROBLEMS (See also the Appendix)

16-1. How many years would it take an investment of $100 to grow to $147 at a compounded 8 percent interest rate?

16-2. The lifetime of a superior structure is 10 years. Its cost is $10,000. The lifetime of an inferior structure is 5 years. Its cost is $7,000. If the rate of interest is 5 percent, would you prefer to invest once in a superior structure, or twice in an inferior structure?

16-3. Consider buying a machine which will last 4 years. After 4 years the machine disintegrates and it has no scrap value. Given the following table, does it pay to invest $22,000 in the machine, knowing that the going interest rate is 8 percent?

Time (1)	Expected Total Revenues, in Dollars (2)	Expected Costs, Excluding Interest and Depreciation, in Dollars (3)	(4)	(5)	(6)
end of year 1	$10,000	5,000			
end of year 2	8,000	3,000			
end of year 3	12,000	2,000			
end of year 4	7,000	4,000			
Total					

16-4. Prove that the C.R.F. $r / [(1 + r)^n - 1] + r$ can be expressed as $\dfrac{r (1 + r)^n}{(1 + r)^n - 1}$.

16-5. An asset whose lifetime is 10 years cost $10,000. The going rate of interest is 8 percent. (a) What is the sum that must be written off at the end of each year in order to obtain $10,000 ten years hence? (b) What is the C.R.F. and the annual cost of this asset?

16-6. Project A is expected to sell 100,000 whatnots annually at $1 apiece. The annual current cost of labor, electricity, maintenance, etc., is expected to amount to $60,000. The investment includes one asset at the cost of $100,000 and a lifetime of 10 years, and another asset at a cost of $80,000 and a lifetime of 5 years. The going interest rate is 5 percent. Calculate the benefit cost ratio of project A.

16-7. Two buildings have the same capacity. The rate of interest is 5 percent. Given the following information, in which of the two buildings would you prefer to invest?

	Alternative	
	A	B
Initial Investment, $	20,000	10,000
Lifetime, years	7	5
Maintenance per year, $	800	1,600

16-8. Determine the payback period of the following two projects. In which of them would you prefer to invest?

	Project A	Project B
Initial investment	$100,000	$100,000
Yield in year 1	70,000	10,000
Yield in year 2	20,000	70,000
Yield in year 3	10,000	20,000
Yield per annum in perpetuity, after the third year	10,000	10,000

16-9. If the VV curve in Fig. 16-1 is positively sloped, what should be the test of profitability.

16-10. Why does the test of internal rate of return fail in Fig. 16-2, when the problem is to select one out of two projects?

PART II: THE THEORY OF CAPITAL

There are many approaches to the theory of capital. Since we do not want to provide the student with an encyclopedia in price theory, we had to select only one approach. We shall follow the theory of capital as formulated by Frank H. Knight[1] and Milton Friedman.[2] We shall not discuss the relation between rates of return on real assets and financial assets which belong to macro-economics. Rather we shall limit ourselves to the relationship between the rate of interest and the market for factors of production, plus a note on the technical aspects of income inequality and Ricardian rent.

UNITS OF CAPITAL

DEFINITION: A unit of tangible capital is defined as a "piece" of capital capable of producing a permanent flow of one dollar. Note that the one dollar is yielded per a certain unit of time, say one year. Also, the one dollar is *net* income. This indicates that the flow of one dollar is net of replacement and maintenance payments.

When we speak about a "piece" of tangible capital, we refer to a combination of different "pieces" of, for example, machinery, equipment, buildings, and land which are combined *optimally* for the common purpose of producing a certain finished good. Also, one dollar is a real dollar. If the general price level doubles overnight, then tomorrow a flow of two nominal dollars will be equal to one real dollar today.

Thus, in what follows we shall refer to units of tangible capital where such a unit is a piece of capital capable of producing a permanent income flow of one dollar.

The Price of Capital. The present value of a permanent flow of I dollars is I/r. Thus the present value, or simply the price of our unit of tangible capital is $1/r$ where one dollar is being substituted for I.

Before analyzing the market for tangible capital, one should note that there is no market for human capital because human beings cannot be traded as pieces of capital. In principle, a man can apply the usual formula and find out what the present value of his future income is, but he cannot sell himself for that price. In fact, the only market for human capital is the market where slaves are traded. The price of a slave in a perfect market should be equal to the present value of the future flows of the net value of marginal product of the slave labor.

THE SUPPLY OF TANGIBLE CAPITAL

We recall that the units of tangible capital are defined as "pieces" of capital capable of producing permanent income flows of one dollar.

---

[1] F. H. Knight, "Capital and Interest," *Readings in the Theory of Income Distribution,* Fellner and Italey, eds., Homewood, Ill.: Richard D. Irwin, Inc.

[2] Milton Friedman, *Price Theory, A Provisional Text,* Chicago, Ill.: Aldine Publishing Company, 1962, Chapter 13.

Such units represent *stocks* of tangible capital. The supply curve of these stocks is defined as the aggregate marginal cost curve of tangible capital. Along this supply curve, the amount of human capital is kept unchanged. Also, we assume that the state of technology is unchanged. We claim that the supply curve of tangible capital as defined above is positively sloped due to the law of diminishing marginal physical product. This can be illustrated as follows: Consider a model economy whose aggregate production function is $Q = \sqrt{A \times B}$, where Q stands for consumer goods, A stands for labor, and B stands for *physical* units of tangible capital that should be *distinguished* from our units of capital. Our unit of capital is whatever combination of physical capital it takes to yield a permanent income flow of one dollar. It may take different amounts of *physical* units of capital, it all depends on the value marginal product of *physical* capital. In fact, we know that if labor is unchanged, then the marginal physical product of physical capital will decline if more of it is used. Since at the economy level the price of one unit of output can be defined to be one dollar, the value marginal product of physical capital will decline, or, alternatively, it will take more physical units of capital to produce a permanent flow of income of one dollar.

Let us illustrate this with our model. Assume that labor is fixed at 200 units and there are 50 units of *physical* capital, all per annum. Also, the price of one unit of output is one dollar. Then, it can be shown that the value marginal product of physical capital is one dollar. Here, one unit of *physical* capital is identical with our unit of tangible capital, because it yields a permanent income flow of one dollar. This is true under the assumption that in a perfect market, the rental is equal to the value marginal product. If the cost of one extra physical unit of capital is, say $10, then, since a physical unit is now identical with our unit, the marginal cost of producing one extra permanent dollar is $10. The $10 covers the present extra cost necessary to produce the extra machinery. Note that this is consistent with a rate of interest of 10 percent.

Next, let us increase the amount of capital from 50 physical units to 200 physical units, while keeping labor unchanged at its original level of 200 units. The value marginal physical product of physical capital is now 50 cents. Thus, the rental of one *physical* unit now amounts to fifty cents. Or, if you wish, on the margin it takes two *physical* units of capital to produce a permanent flow of one dollar. Accordingly, the marginal cost of one unit of tangible capital, as we have defined it, is now twice the amount of $10, namely, *$20*. This is consistent with a rate of interest of 5 percent.

Having illustrated why, when human capital (labor) and other things are unchanged, the supply curve of tangible capital is positively sloped, we can direct our attention to the demand for stocks of tangible capital.

THE DEMAND FOR TANGIBLE CAPITAL

Let us stress again that one unit of tangible capital is the complex of physical capital capable of producing a permanent flow of one dollar. Here, one can assume that the demand curve is either flat or negatively sloped. The assumption of a negatively sloped demand curve for capital is justified because when human capital and other things are unchanged, the larger the amount of tangible capital which is available, the smaller the value society attaches to one unit of tangible capital.

THE MARKET FOR THE STOCK OF CAPITAL

Let us bring the supply and demand for tangible capital together. This is illustrated in Fig. 16-3, where G is a long-run point of equilibrium. In our example, at point G, C_2 units of tangible capital are demanded

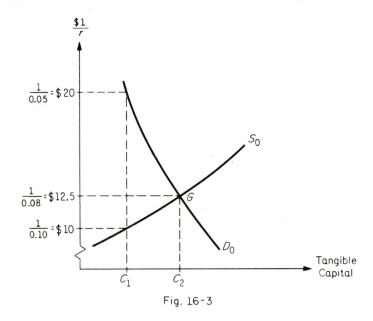

Fig. 16-3

and C_2 units are available. Thus, as long as human capital, the state of technology, and tastes do not change, the rate of interest (in this example) will be equal to 8 percent, which is consistent with a price of $12.5. As indicated by the demand curve D_0, if C_2 units of tangible capital are available, no net saving will take place because people are "happy" with C_2 units and, at a price of $12.5, they are not interested in either owning less tangible capital or owning more of it. Had people been interested in owning more tangible capital, they would start saving, i.e., give up consumption for the sake of buying more tangible capital. (At a rate of interest of 8 percent, they will have to give up consuming finished goods worth $12.5 in order to obtain one additional unit of tangible capital which is a permanent flow of one dollar.) Had people wanted to own less than C_2 units, they would avoid replacing their tangible capital and thus consume more.

Now consider the supply side. At point G there is no incentive on the part of manufacturers of factors of production to invest. At point G the market price is $12.5 and C_2 units of tangible capital are available. Had producers of producer's goods tried to increase the amount of tangible capital above C_2, the marginal cost would rise. Thus, if the marginal cost rises to $13, investors will lose half a dollar on each additional unit of capital they further produce. In other words, while it may cost $13 to produce one additional unit of tangible capital, demanders will only pay $12.5. Thus, at point G there is no incentive to undertake any net investment. For a similar reason, at point G there is no incentive to disinvest.

Let us now assume that only C_1 units are available. As indicated by the demand curve, if we could peg the rate of interest at 5 percent, i.e., raise the price of tangible capital to $20 apiece, owners of capital will be satisfied. What about producers of tangible capital? They will start to invest eagerly because while the extra cost of one additional unit of tangible capital is only $10, the market price is by assumption $20. In reality, manufacturers of factors of production will invest in new tangible capital, and in order to persuade owners of tangible capital to own more than C_1 units, they will offer to sell additional units at a price below $20. Accordingly, in the short run there will exist a certain rate of interest which takes on some value between 5 percent and 10 percent. At this short-run rate of interest, net saving will be equal to net investment. This is illustrated in Fig. 16-4. If the rate of interest is 5 percent, i.e., the price of tangible capital is $20, no net saving takes place. If the rate of interest is 10 percent, i.e., the price is $10, no net investment takes place. But, as indicated before, since there is a gap between the price which is consistent with no net saving and the price which is consistent with no net investment, saving and investment must take place. As indicated in Fig. 16-4, H is a short-run point of equilibrium. There the short-run price of capital is $(1/r)_0$ which is consistent with some intermediate rate of interest between 5 percent and 10 percent. At that rate of interest, saving S_0 is equal to investment I_0. Note that H exists only temporarily. To illustrate this, assume that at the beginning of the year, C_1 units of tangible capital are available, and saving and investment must therefore take place. As indicated by point H in Fig.

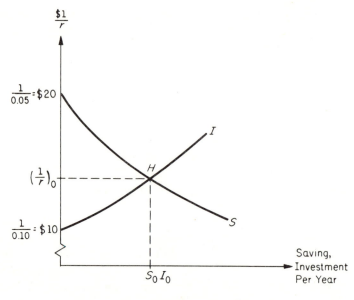

Fig. 16-4

16-4, saving per annum is equal to investment amounting to I_0 units. Thus, *roughly* speaking, after one year, tangible capital will increase from C_1 to $C_1 + r \times I_0$.

Let us focus on Fig. 16-3. When more than C_1 units are available, the range of possible prices of tangible capital is less than the range of $10 and $20. It now extends from $10 plus something to $20 minus something, and, of course, there are new saving and investment curves which correspond to the new situation. In fact, if we assume that "all other things," that is, human capital, the state of technology, and tastes do not change with time, then this process of investing will continue just until C_2 units of capital will be available. As indicated in Fig. 16-3, when C_2 units of capital are available, there is a price (in our example $12.5) at which the amount of stock of tangible capital demanded is equal to its quantity supplied, and thus, neither net saving nor net investment takes place.

The real picture is different from that. Over a period of time, the supply S_0 in Fig. 16-3 shifts rightward due to technological innovations; the demand D_0 also shifts rightward. This is true because when more human capital is available, the relative importance of tangible capital increases. Thus, in reality, the short-run point of equilibrium (point H in Fig. 16-4) is moving toward the long-run point of equilibrium (point G in Fig. 16-3). But point G is also moving. Thus, we have the following *moving* equilibrium: *The short-run equilibrium which is determined by saving and investment is moving toward the long-run equilibrium which is determined by the supply and demand for the stocks of tangible capital which is also moving.* At this point, we have entered the realm of macroeconomics.

SOME PROBLEMS OF TAXATION

In Chapter 10, we stated the case against excise taxes. The summary of the case is that excise taxes are undesirable because they discriminate against individuals on grounds of their tastes. This is as arbitrary as discriminating against an individual because of his political opinion. Next let us consider the corporate income tax. This tax discriminates against individuals who prefer the corporation to the partnership. The reason for this is that if you invest in a corporation you pay a double tax: first, you pay the corporate income tax, and then you pay the income tax on dividends. The corporation income tax gives rise to misallocation of capital: less capital is invested in incorporated in-

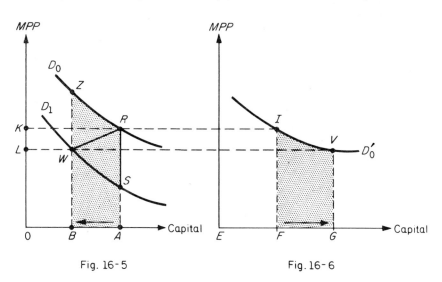

Fig. 16-5   Fig. 16-6

dustries than could have been without the corporate tax. To illustrate this, consider Figs. 16-5 and 16-6. Let D_0 in Fig. 16-5 be the *MPP* curve of the incorporated firms and D'_0 in Fig. 16-6 the *MPP* curve of the unincorporated industries. Note that in both diagrams capital is measured by the same unit, say a dollar's worth of capital. A dollar's worth of capital should not be confused with a piece of capital yielding a permanent $1. Also by assumption, the price of one unit of output equals one dollar.

In the absence of a corporate income tax, capital will be allocated between the two groups of firms so that the average marginal physical product of incorporated firms equals the MPP of unincorporated firms.[3] In our example, this occurs when $0A$ units of capital are invested in the incorporated firms and EF units of capital are invested in the unincorporated industries. The total amount of capital available in the economy is $0A + EF$.

Suppose the government imposes a corporate income tax equal to RS in Fig. 16-5. After the tax is imposed, curve D_0 in Fig. 16-5 is irrelevant for owners of capital. As far as they are concerned, D_1 is the relevant curve; we call it the *net* demand curve for capital. Prior to placing the corporate income tax, owners of capital invested in incorporated firms earned an average of AR dollars per annum per unit of capital. This was equal to FT ($= 0K$), which is the average annual return per unit of capital invested in unincorporated firms. But, after the tax is imposed, to the first approximation, owners of capital invested in incorporated firms would earn only AS dollars per annum per unit of capital. This would give them an incentive to transfer capital to unincorporated firms.

An alternative to shifting capital could be to dissolve the corporations and reorganize them as partnerships. Due to legal and technical considerations, a change of form from a corporation to a partnership is impractical. Thus, allowing enough time for adjustment, an amount of AB ($= FG$) units of capital will transfer from corporated industries to unincorporated industries. In our model, a new equilibrium is achieved when $0B$ units of capital are used by corporations while EG units are used by unincorporated firms. The new rate of return is $0L$ ($= BW = GV$), which is LK dollars lower than the original rate of return. The degree of the distortion in the economy may be measured by the shaded area in Fig. 16-5 minus the shaded area in Fig. 16-6. Roughly speaking, this amounts to the area of the triangle WRZ in Fig. 16-5.

If the corporate income tax is abolished, it should be accompanied by repealing the tax on capital gains. In the United States the tax is imposed on gains from assets owned more than six months. The rate is that of income tax but not higher than 25 percent. As a result, wealthy persons who derive their income mainly from ownership of stocks pay ridiculously low taxes on their income. Consider a person who has invested $1,000,000 in a corporation. The dividends coming to him amount to $50,000. If the investor were to add these $50,000 to his taxable income the marginal rate on it might very well reach 60 percent. Alternatively, these $50,000 may be invested internally in the corporation and thus increase the value of the stock by about $50,000. After a period of more than six months the stock may be sold at a gain of about $50,000,

---

[3] If there is a nonpecuniary advantage of investing in unincorporated firms, there would be a differential between the MPP in Figs. 16-5 and 16-6.

and the rate of the tax imposed on the gain is only 25 percent. Thus, this tax operates in the opposite direction of the corporate income tax: one hand of the government punishes owners of stocks through the corporate income tax while the other hand rewards them through the tax on capital gains. And so, we are led to the conclusion that the tax imposed directly on income is a better one: it is not based on the source of income or on the taste of the individual; rather, it is based on the "ability-to-pay" principle.

An important revision in income tax legislation should be considered: the progression of income tax penalizes those undertaking risky occupations. One feature of risky occupations is that they yield income that fluctuates from one year to the next. For example, consider two individuals; one earns $10,000 annually and the other earns $20,000 during the first year and nothing in the second year. Assume that the rate of the tax is 20 percent on $10,000 and 25 percent on $20,000. Accordingly, over the period of two years the first individual pays $4,000 and the second pays $5,000. The penalty for undertaking risk is $1,000 for the period of two years. Thus, those who pay more taxes than their *average* income suggests are brokers who facilitate trade in stocks and bonds and other entrepreneurs who promote both production and trade. It seems rather unwise to penalize this group of individuals who play an important role in our economy. The revised income tax should be one in which the rate of the tax is tied to the *average* income from a number of years rather than to annual income. The number of years used in the computation of the average should be determined by practical considerations. The administration of such a tax does not raise difficult problems. In our example, the first individual would pay $2,000 in each year. If a period of two years is used for taking the average, then the second individual would pay $5,000 in the first year and nothing in the second year. But at the end of the second year the government would mail him a check for $1,000 because his *average* annual income amounts to $10,000.

THE TECHNICAL ASPECTS OF INCOME INEQUALITY

In Chapter 15, we focused on the labor market. We have shown that differences in wages and salaries arise due to natural differences in talent and dexterity, artificial obstacles imposed on entry to a profession, and nonpecuniary advantages or disadvantages involved in performing one job or another. To this one may add differences in income arising from age. There is empirical evidence indicating that income from wages and salaries rises with age until it reaches its maximum at a certain age, and then it falls off. For example, consider Table 16-6.

TABLE 16-6

MEDIAN MONEY WAGE OR SALARY INCOME OF PRIMARY FAMILIES AND UNRELATED
INDIVIDUALS BY AGE, FOR 1950 AND 1960
(in dollars)

Age of Head	1950 (in 1960 prices)	1960
Under 35 years	4,065	5,377
35-44 years	4,680	6,344
45-54 years	4,615	6,256
55 years and over	3,728	4,719

SOURCE: Statistical Abstract of the United States, 1962, Table 447.

The data presented in Table 16-6 show that wage and salary incomes are maximized at the age bracket of 35 to 44 years. Beyond
that age income is a declining function of age. Another minor factor
giving rise to income differentials is the geographical location. In addition
to different nonpecuniary advantages or disadvantages that are associated with different geographical locations, the price level varies
slightly from one area to another. We expect that, *ceteris paribus*,
nominal wages of equal labor should be proportional to the consumer's
price index. This problem does not exist when real wages are considered instead of nominal wages.

We have shown that returns on capital are either in the form of
rentals, if the asset is rented out, or in the form of interest. For example,
an owner of an apartment building makes his income in the form of
rentals. The annual net rental is what is collected during the year from
the tenants minus depreciation and the cost of maintenance. We used
the term interest as referring to returns on loans, bonds, and stocks.
The reason is that even though interest and dividends differ technically,
they boil down to returns on invested capital. In fact, interest may be
viewed as annual net rental accuring to one dollar worth of capital.

Unequal distribution of capital among families gives rise to unequal distribution of income. It is a fact that, in most of the cases, million-
aires derive their income from property. Even though reliable data on the
distribution of capital among families is unavailable, it is known that
rent, interest, and dividends constitute a larger fraction of total income,
the higher the income bracket.

Finally, we have to dispose of another form of income, that is, rent,
as we have defined it in Chapter 6. The choice of the term rent is rather
unfortunate, because in the business world rent refers to what we termed
rental. A detailed discussion of rent is found in Chapter 6. In summary,
rent (profit) arises because of different degrees of risk involved in

different industries, monopoly power over a market, and natural or contrived restrictions on entry. Thus, we expect economic rents to be relatively higher in industries that involve high risks, provided that entrepreneurs are not gamblers. Accordingly, rent is unequally distributed among entrepreneurs and adds to the degree of inequality in our society.

THE MEASUREMENT OF INEQUALITY

There are few technical measures of income inequality. The best known measure of inequality is the Lorenz curve; other measures are the index of concentration and the standard deviation of income.[4] We cannot make absolute statements about inequality. At most we can say that if income is equally divided between families then absolute equality is achieved. At the other extreme, there is the case where one family receives the entire national income. This is known in theory as the case of absolute inequality. In between lies the real world. It appears that a meaningful way of describing the real world is a table in which families are ranked according to their incomes and all families are grouped into quintiles (or other convenient fractions). Each quintile is characterized by two figures. The first figure is the percentage of total income received by the specific quintile, while the second is the average income per family.

As an example, consider Table 16-7. In 1941 the lowest quintile of families received only 4.1 percent of the national income while the highest quintile received 48.3 percent. Another statement that can be made here is that the lowest 40 percent of families received only 13.6 of the national income and the highest 40 percent received 70.6 percent of the national income.

One can also learn from the Table 16-7 about the change in the

TABLE 16-7

Rank by Size of Income	Percent of Total Income Received			Average Income (in 1960 prices)		
	1941	1950	1960	1941	1950	1960
Lowest quintile	4.1	4.8	4.6	905	1,299	1,576
Second quintile	9.5	10.9	11.0	2,099	2,974	3,758
Third quintile	15.3	16.1	16.3	3,407	4,402	5,581
Fourth quintile	22.3	22.1	22.6	4,953	6,041	7,721
Highest quintile	48.3	46.1	45.5	10,851	12,612	15,588
Top 5 percent	24.0	21.4	20.0	21,351	23,451	27,368

SOURCE: Statistical Abstract of the United States, 1962, Table 443.

[4] See G. J. Stigler, *The Theory of Price*, New York: The Macmillan Company, 1966, Chapter 15.

degree of inequality over a period of time. While the relative share of the lowest quintile has not changed by very much from 1941 to 1960, the share of the highest 40 percent has diminished from 70.6 percent to 68.1 percent. The average incomes of the different groups are shown so as not to lose sight of the absolute changes. For example, in the period of 1941-1960 the share of the fourth quintile has changed by very little. However, average income of families in the fourth quintile has changed by $2,768.

A NOTE ON RICARDIAN RENT

Recall that the producer's surplus is total revenue minus payments to variable factors of production. Thus, it is a residue left for factors of production that are specific to the firm. The producer's surplus is due to the fact that one or more factors are fixed. Recall from Chapter 6 that if all factors are variable, then the marginal cost curve is horizontal and the producer's surplus is absent. The Ricardian rent in its pure form occurs when land is the only fixed factor. If there are more than one fixed factor, say land and entrepreneurial capacity, than the producer's surplus is a residue shared by both the landowner and the entrepreneur. This part of the producer's surplus accruing to land is known as the Ricardian rent; David Ricardo was the first one to notice that the price of land is determined by the price of agricultural commodities rather than the other way around.

The Ricardian argument is as follows: If land were a free resource, then the price of food would not rise as a result of the population growth. More land would be combined with labor and capital in order to produce more food at the prevailing price. But since land is limited, in the face of rising demand for food farmers must resort to cultivating more of the less fertile land and to applying more labor and capital to the fixed amount of land available to them. As indicated before, this results in a rising supply curve of food and, accordingly, higher prices. Thus, when the price of food rises, owners of fertile lands benefit from an increasing producer's surplus arising from the scarcity of land.

In 1871, Henry George advocated levying a single tax on the value of land.[5] The justification for the single tax on the value of land was that the Ricardian rent is a surplus which arises because of scarcity rather than an effort on the part of landowners. There is a flaw in this logic: a person inheriting a piece of capital earns an income for which he has not worked. Thus, by the same logic, a single tax must be levied on the value of inherited nonland property as well. It appears that the

---

[5] Henry George, *Progress and Poverty*, New York: Doubleday, Page & Company, 1925.

majority of people in the free enterprise economy would object to such taxes. Moreover, a single tax levied on the value of land is impractical because of the impossibility of separating the part in the producer's surplus accruing to land from the part accruing to other fixed factors. Finally, like incomes of owners of other factors of production, the Ricardian rent is an essential mechanism for allocating land optimally. If a single tax were imposed on owners of land, they would not have any incentive to shift land from one use to another in spite of a change in the tastes of consumers.

Notice, finally, that as in the case of other forms of capital, the value of land in a perfect market is determined by the formula

$$\text{Value of land} = \frac{\text{expected Ricardian rent}}{r}$$

with which the reader is already familiar.

SELECTED READINGS

FRIEDMAN, M. *Price Theory. A Provisional Text.* Chicago, Ill.: Aldine Publishing Company, 1962, Chapter 13.

GISSER, M. "On Benefit-Cost Analysis of Investment in Schooling in Rural Farm Areas," *American Journal of Agricultural Economics,* August, 1968.

HARBERGER, A. C. "The Incidence of the Corporation Income Tax," *Journal of Political Economy,* June, 1962.

HICKS, J. R. *Value and Capital* (2d ed.). London: Oxford University Press, 1957, Chapters XI, XII, and XIII.

PATINKIN, D. *Money, Interest and Prices* (2d ed.). Row, Peterson & Co., 1965

APPENDIX

A TABLE OF CAPITAL COEFFICIENTS

Interest Year	Future Value Coefficient $(1+r)^n$			Present Value Coefficient (Discount Rate) $1/(1+r)^n$			Capital Recovery Factor $r/[(1+r)^n - 1] + r$		
	3%	5%	8%	3%	5%	8%	3%	5%	8%
1	1.030	1.050	1.080	0.971	0.952	0.926	1.030	1.050	1.080
2	1.061	1.103	1.166	0.943	0.907	0.857	0.523	0.538	0.561
3	1.093	1.158	1.260	0.915	0.864	0.794	0.354	0.367	0.388
4	1.126	1.216	1.360	0.889	0.823	0.735	0.269	0.282	0.302
5	1.159	1.276	1.469	0.863	0.784	0.681	0.218	0.231	0.250
6	1.194	1.340	1.587	0.838	0.746	0.630	0.185	0.197	0.216
7	1.230	1.407	1.714	0.813	0.711	0.584	0.161	0.173	0.192
8	1.267	1.477	1.851	0.789	0.677	0.540	0.142	0.155	0.174
9	1.305	1.551	1.999	0.766	0.645	0.500	0.128	0.141	0.160
10	1.344	1.629	2.159	0.744	0.614	0.463	0.117	0.130	0.149

chapter **17**

General Equilibrium and Welfare Economics

PART I: GENERAL EQUILIBRIUM

Consumers pursue the goal of maximizing utility, subject to their income constraints which are derived from selling their labor and capital services to firms, and given the prices of goods and services in markets. Producers pursue the goal of profit maximization, given their production functions, and given either prices of goods and services in perfect markets, or demand schedules in imperfect markets. There are millions of consumers and producers operating in various markets for thousands of different commodities. Given the behaviors of consumers and producers, and given the goals pursued by them, do these economic agents live in harmony with each other, or do they live in eternal economic conflict? The purpose of the first part of this chapter is to show that although each economic agent independently strives to achieve his own goal, the economic system is simultaneously solved.

In what follows we shall first discuss the equilibrium of consumption, then the equilibrium of production, and finally bring consumers and producers together to the markets and show that a general equilibrium is achieved. For simplicity we shall assume that the economy is governed by perfect competition. This assumption can later be relaxed by introducing slight modifications into the structure of the model.

EQUILIBRIUM OF CONSUMPTION

Consider an economy consisting of n consumers and m commodities. Some of the commodities are primary goods such as labor. Consider a consumer who possesses only one primary commodity, say labor, and buys only two commodities in the market. Let the amount of labor be denoted by X_1, and the amounts of the two consumer's goods be denoted by X_2 and X_3. Their respective prices are P_1, P_2, and P_3. Supposing the maximum number of hours the consumer can sell per unit of time is $X_1^0 = 15$ hours. He possesses zero units of X_2 and X_3 respectively, namely $X_2^0 = 0$ and $X_3^0 = 0$. Let us assume that prices are $P_1 = \$3$, $P_2 = \$4$ and $P_3 = \$2$. The income of the consumer (per unit of time) is

$$M = \$3 \cdot 15 + \$4 \cdot 0 + \$2 \cdot 0 = \$45 \qquad (1)$$

This can be written in general as

$$M_i = \sum_{j=1}^{m} P_j X_{ji}^0 \qquad (2)$$

The subscript i denotes the ith consumer.

Supposing the consumer decides to sell only 10 hours of labor out of the 15 hours which he possesses. This means that he decides to possess only five hours of labor. To put it in realistic terms, the consumer decides to possess only five hours of leisure. Let us accordingly assume that he decides to allocate \$15 to labor (leisure), \$24 to X_2, and \$6 to X_3. We now have

$$M = \$3 \cdot 5 + \$4 \cdot 6 + \$2 \cdot 3 = \$45 \qquad (3)$$

In general, this becomes

$$M_i = \sum_{j=1}^{m} P_j X_{ji} \qquad (4)$$

where X_{ji} denotes the actual amount of commodity j consumed (or possessed) by consumer i after the exchange took place. In our example $X_{1i} = 5$, $X_{2i} = 6$, and $X_{3i} = 3$. X_{ji}^0 denotes the initial endowments: $X_{1i}^0 = 15$, $X_{2i}^0 = 0$, and $X_{3i}^0 = 0$.

The fact that the consumer cannot consume more than \$45 worth of goods and services is known as the *budget constraint*. If we subtract Eq. 1 from Eq. 3, we obtain the following convenient expression for the budget constraint

$$\$3 (5 - 15) + \$4 (6 - 0) + \$2 (3 - 0) = 0 \qquad (5)$$

The excess demand for labor, $5 - 15 = -10$, is negative. A negative excess demand indicates a sale. The excess demand for X_2 and X_3 is positive. It indicates a purchase.

The general form of the budget constraint for the ith consumer is

$$\sum_{j=1}^{m} P_j (X_{ji} - X_{ji}^0) = 0 \qquad (6)$$

Recall (Chapter 2) that in order to maximize his utility, subject to the budget constraint, the consumer must satisfy

$$\frac{MU_{1i}}{P_1} = \frac{MU_{2i}}{P_2} = \ldots = \frac{MU_{mi}}{P_m} \qquad (7)$$

These are $m - 1$ equations. Note that MU_{ji} $(j = 1, 2, \ldots, m)$ are not unknowns. Since utility is determined by the consumption of X_{ji} $(j = 1, 2, \ldots, m)$, MU_{ji} $(j = 1, 2, \ldots, m)$ is also determined by X_{ji} $(j = 1, 2, \ldots, m)$. Equation 7 shows that the consumer exchanges his primary goods, eg., labor, for other goods in order to maximize his utility. If labor is the first commodity, then Eq. 7 shows that in equilibrium, the marginal utility foregone from selling \$1 worth of labor must be equal to the marginal utility obtained from spending this dollar on good 1, or alternatively on good 2, and so on up to good m. Given the prices P_j $(j = 1, 2, \ldots, m)$, Eqs. 6 and 7 together constitute m equations which determine the quantities demanded X_{ji} for the various m commodities by the ith consumer. A more rigorous derivation of Eq. 7 is shown in the Mathematical Appendix.

EQUILIBRIUM OF PRODUCTION

Let us assume that there are h firms in the economy. Let the firms be denoted by the subscript g, i.e., $g = 1, 2, \ldots, h$. Consider the gth firm with the most general production function

$$F_g\left(X_{1g}, X_{2g}, \ldots, X_{mg}\right) = 0 \qquad (8)$$

Equation 8 is known as a *transformation* function. Recall that X_1, $X_2, \ldots, X_m$ are both inputs (primary goods) and outputs.[1] Thus, in the most general case the gth firm utilizes some of each of the inputs that are available in the economy in order to produce some of each of the goods that are bought by consumers. If X_{jg} is output it has a positive dimension, and if it is an input, it has a negative dimension. Clearly, if the firm produces an input, such as electricity, this input for that specific firm takes on a positive dimension.

Each firm pursues the goal of profit (rent) maximization. Let us denote profit by Π, then the profit of the gth firm is

$$\Pi_g = \sum_{j=1}^{m} P_j X_{jg} \qquad (9)$$

Profit should be maximized subject to the constraint of the transformation function (Eq. 8). We leave it for the reader to show that, since inputs take on negative dimensions and outputs take on positive dimen-

---

[1] While an input can be produced, such as electricity, a primary good is usually non-produced, such as land and labor.

sions, Eq. 9 boils down to total revenue minus total cost.

In order for the gth firm to reach profit maximization the following must hold

$$-\frac{\Delta X_{jg}}{\Delta X_{kg}} = \frac{P_k}{P_j} \begin{matrix} (k = 1, 2, \ldots, m) \\ (j = 1, 2, \ldots, m) \end{matrix} \tag{10}$$

where ΔX_{jg} and ΔX_{kg} are small changes in X_j and X_k by the gth firm. In equilibrium, Eq. 10 holds for any combination of two goods. The combination may be either a pair of outputs, a pair of inputs, or a mixed pair of an input and an output. Equation 10 shows that in equilibrium the marginal rates of substitutions between any two goods must be equal to their price ratio. Notice finally that although the maximal number of pairs is m^2; in fact only the $m - 1$ relations indicated by Eq. 10 are necessary in order to ensure that equilibrium is achieved. These $m - 1$ relations together with the transformation function make up a system of m equations with m unknowns. The unknowns are the X_{jg} ($j = 1$, $2, \ldots, m$). In other words, to solve the system is to determine the quantities demanded for inputs and the quantities of outputs supplied by firm g. A more rigorous derivation of equilibrium conditions is available in the Mathematical Appendix.

Let us now give Eq. 10 some economic meaning.

First, if the two goods are inputs the marginal rate of substitution is known as the *rate of technical substitution, RTS*. Consider two inputs, say X_1 and X_2. If all other inputs and all outputs are held constant then, as explained in Chapter 5, the firm must move along an isoquant (see Fig. 5-4) and roughly satisfy $- \Delta X_1 \cdot MPP_{x1} = \Delta X_2 \cdot MPP_{x2}$. But in order to minimize the cost of production the outlay line (Fig. 5-5) must be tangent to the isoquant; namely at the point of tangency (E_1, E_2, E_3, in Fig. 5-5) the slope of the outlay line P_1/P_2 must be equal to RTS:

$$RTS = -\frac{\Delta X_2}{\Delta X_1} = \frac{MPP_{x1}}{MPP_{x2}} = \frac{P_1}{P_2} \tag{11}$$

Another way of expressing this relationship is

$$\frac{MPP_{x1}}{P_1} = \frac{MPP_{x2}}{P_2} \tag{12}$$

The meaning of it is that if in equilibrium the firm shifts one dollar from spending on input X_1 to spending on input X_2, the level of output remains unchanged. Had this not been true it would pay the firm to shift money from one input to another, which contradicts the assumption that equilibrium has been achieved.

Second, consider the case where one good is an input and one good is an output. For simplicity assume that X_2 is an input and X_3 is an output. Recall from Chapter 14 that in equilibrium the value marginal product of each variable factor of production equals its market price. This is stated in our example as

$$MPP_2 \cdot P_3 = P_2 \tag{13}$$

$MPP_2 = \dfrac{\Delta X_3}{\Delta X_2}$ when all inputs and outputs, except X_2 and X_3, are kept constant. Recall also that in this formulation we agreed to assign negative values to inputs. For example, increasing X_2 from 4 units to 5 units becomes in the present model a change from -4 units to -5 units, which is an algebraic reduction. Thus it is legitimate to assign a minus sign to the marginal rate of substitution between X_2 and X_3, obtaining

$$-\frac{\Delta X_3}{\Delta X_2} = \frac{P_2}{P_3} \tag{14}$$

Third, if the two goods are outputs the marginal rate of substitution is known as the *rate of product transformation, RPT*. In order to simplify the explanation of this case, consider a firm employing only one factor of production, say X_2, and jointly producing two outputs, X_3 and X_4.

In Fig. 17-1 we show three product *transformation curves*, or *iso-*

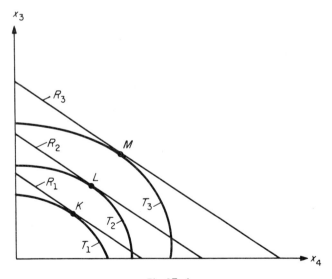

Fig 17-1

factor curves. A curve like T_1, T_2, or T_3 is generated by keeping the input X_2 constant at a certain level and producing various combinations of

X_3 and X_4. The concavity of the isofactor curves (from below) can be explained by assuming that in addition to X_2 which is used in the production of both X_3 and X_4, there is a certain fixed input employed in the production of X_3 and a certain different fixed input employed in the production of X_4. The firm is confronted with prices P_3 and P_4 over which it has no influence. Accordingly, the revenue function of the firm is $R = P_3 \cdot X_3 + P_4 \cdot X_4$. Following familiar routes of analysis we know that points like K, L, and M are optimal. These are points of tangency at which the firm maximizes revenue, given a fixed amount of input X_2. (Or minimizes the use of X_2 given a fixed revenue.)

Let us adopt the following notations: The marginal physical product of input X_2 with respect to output X_3 is MPP_{23}, and the marginal physical product of the same input X_2 with respect to output X_4 is MPP_{24}. Thus,

$$MPP_{23} = \frac{\Delta X_3}{\Delta X_2} \quad \text{and} \quad MPP_{24} = \frac{\Delta X_4}{\Delta X_2}$$

At tangency points such as K, L, and M the rate of product transformation is equal to the slopes of the revenue lines, that is,

$$-\frac{\Delta X_4}{\Delta X_3} = \frac{P_3}{P_4} \tag{15}$$

Ignoring the minus sign (which indicates that substitution takes place) and multiplying Eq. 15 by $(\Delta X_3 \cdot P_4)/\Delta X_2$ we get

$$P_4 \cdot \frac{\Delta X_4}{\Delta X_2} = P_3 \cdot \frac{\Delta X_3}{\Delta X_2} \tag{16}$$

or in different notations

$$P_4 \cdot MPP_{24} = P_3 \cdot MPP_{23} \tag{17}$$

This means that in equilibrium shifting one unit of the input X_2 from output X_3 to X_4, or vice versa, does not change total revenue. In other words, in equilibrium the value marginal product of input X_2 in the production of X_3 is the same as in the production of X_4. This makes sense, because if, for example, $P_4 \cdot MPP_{24}$ is higher than $P_3 \cdot MPP_{23}$, it would pay the firm to shift some of input X_2, which is tied up in the production of X_3, to the production of X_4.

EQUILIBRIUM OF MARKETS

Consider good j. The quantity demanded for good j by n consumers is

$$\sum_{i=1}^{n} (X_{ji} - X_{ji}^0) \tag{18}$$

Clearly, if the good is a typical consumer's good, such as bread, Eq. 18 is positive. If the good is primary, such as labor (leisure), Eq. 18 is negative.

Recall that there are h firms in the economy. Unlike consumers, firms do not possess initial amounts of primary factors. They are engaged in the process of transforming flows of inputs into flows of outputs.

The amount of good j supplied by h firms is

$$\sum_{g=1}^{h} X_{jg} \tag{19}$$

Clearly if good j is an output, Eq. 19 is positive, and if it is an input, Eq. 19 is negative. In fact, if good j is strictly an input then Eq. 19 is the aggregate demand for an input.

Equilibrium in the market is attained when the market is cleared, namely when quantity demanded is equal to quantity supplied. For example,

$$\sum_{i=1}^{n}(X_{ji} - X_{ji}^{0}) = \sum_{g=1}^{h} X_{jg} \tag{20}$$

GENERAL EQUILIBRIUM

Let us count the number of equations and unknowns:
Equilibrium of consumption:

$$\underbrace{\frac{MU_{1i}}{P_1} = \frac{MU_{2i}}{P_2} = \ldots = \frac{MU_{mi}}{P_m}}_{m-1 \text{ equations}} \qquad i = 1, 2, \ldots, n$$

$$\sum_{j=1}^{m} P_j (X_{ji} - X_{ji}^{0}) = 0 \qquad i = 1, 2, \ldots, n$$

Equilibrium of production:

$$-\frac{\Delta X_{jg}}{\Delta X_{1g}} = \frac{P_1}{P_j} \qquad \begin{array}{l} j = 2, 3, \ldots, m \\ g = 1, 2, 3, \ldots, h \end{array}$$

$$F_g (X_{1g}, X_{2g}, \ldots, X_{mg}) = 0 \qquad g = 1, 2, \ldots, h$$

Equilibrium of markets:

$$\sum_{i=1}^{n}(X_{ji} - X_{ji}^{0}) = \sum_{g=1}^{h} X_{jg} \qquad j = 1, 2, \ldots, m - 1$$

There are only $m - 1$ market equations. To understand this intuitively, consider the consumer in our example. He has three commodities in his budget. Let us assume that these commodities are labor, bread, and wine. If the consumer has already decided to sell so many hours of labor and buy so many loaves of bread, he does not have to make a decision as to how many bottles of wine he should buy. The budget which is left divided by the price of wine automatically gives the quantity demanded for wine.

Counting the equations we have

Equilibrium of consumption	$(m - 1) \cdot n + n$
Equilibrium of production	$(m - 1) \cdot h + h$
Equilibrium of markets	$(m - 1)$
Total	$m \cdot n + m \cdot h + m - 1$

Counting the variables we have m goods demanded by n individuals which we have denoted by X_{ji}. These are $m \cdot n$ unknowns. There are h firms, supplying or demanding the m goods denoted by X_{jg} and thus giving rise to $m \cdot h$ unknowns. Finally there are the m prices denoted by P_j. Altogether there are $m \cdot n + m \cdot h + m$ unknowns, exceeding the number of equations by one.

This is not surprising. Recall that microeconomics concerns itself with relative prices rather than with absolute prices. If money does not exist, then doubling all nominal prices leaves the economy unchanged in real terms. The exchange ratios among the various goods and services also remain unchanged. For example, the consumer who sells labor in order to buy bread and wine would not change his behavior if one morning he wakes up and finds out that prices of labor, bread, and wine have doubled. The exchange ratios between labor, bread, and wine would remain unaltered, and, accordingly, the consumer would not change his behavior. In fact, we can select arbitrarily one good, bread, and define all prices as exchange ratios relative to bread. Then bread is called the *numéraire*. If the price of bread is P_2, we divide the set of prices P_1, P_2, and P_3 by the price of the numéraire and obtain a new set of relative prices, namely $\dfrac{P_1}{P_2}, 1, \dfrac{P_3}{P_2}$. The same is true with respect to firms. Doubling all prices would leave Eq. 10 unaltered, and thus all firms would continue to do exactly what they used to do prior to the doubling of the price level. In summary, by selecting a numéraire we reduce the number of unknowns to $m \cdot n + m \cdot h + m - 1$, and the system can be solved for all the unknowns. Such a *non-monetary* system solves for *relative prices* (exchange ratios). In order to determine the absolute price level, namely the nominal price of the numéraire, the monetary sector must be integrated with the real sector. But this is the point where microeconomics gives way to macroeconomics, and accordingly this topic is not in the realm of this chapter.[2]

[2] The reader should be warned that counting equations and unknown is *not* sufficient; a difficult *existence* and *uniqueness* problem remains.

PART II: WELFARE ECONOMICS

Welfare economics considers economic policies that can lead to an improvement in economic welfare. An improvement in economic welfare is achieved when either all individuals in society are better off, or at least some individuals are better off and none are worse off. If a certain economic policy leads to an improvement of welfare of some individuals and deterioration of welfare of others, then unless the second group is compensated so that its members are as well off as they were prior to the initiation of the new policy, it cannot be claimed that welfare improvement has been achieved. Recall from Chapter 2 that interpersonal comparison of utility is impossible. This is why the *compensation principle* must be incorporated into the theory of welfare economics.

WELFARE OF EXCHANGE

Consider two consumers, 1 and 2 who have only two commodities in their budgets, X and Y. Consumer 1 is initially endowed with X_1^0 units of X and Y_1^0 units of Y. Consumer 2 is initially endowed with X_2^0 units of X and Y_2^0 units of Y. If we rotate the graph of consumer 2 $180°$ clockwise about its origin and bring the graph of 2 together with the graph of 1, we obtain the Edgeworth box diagram. This diagram is shown in Fig. 17-2. Point K represents the original endowments of the two consumers. U_1 and U_2 are the indifference curves of 1 and 2, respectively, passing through point K. Let us denote the marginal rate of commodity substitution by RCS. Recall from Chapter 2 that RCS measures the marginal rate of substitution of one good for another along the indifference curve. From Fig. 17-2 it is evident that $\Delta Y_1 / \Delta X_1$ exceeds $\Delta Y_2 / \Delta X_2$. Consumer 1 can forego ΔY_1 and add to his consumption ΔX_1, thus moving along his indifference curve from point K to point L. At point L he is as well off as he was at point K. Consumer 2 can forego the consumption of ΔX_2 and add to his consumption ΔY_2, thereby moving from point K to point M. At point M he is as well off as he was at point K. If 1 moves from K to L and 2 moves from K to M, both consumers are left with "free" LM units of X. They can move to any intermediate point such as N. At point N both consumers are better off. Each has moved to a higher indifference curve. Accordingly the inequality of the marginal rates of substitution led consumer 1 to trade Y to consumer 2 in exchange for X. As long as the RCS of one consumer differs from the RCS of the other it is worthwhile to continue trading and thereby climbing the utility hill. Supposing 1 and 2 finally reach a point, such as S, where their indifference curves are tangent to

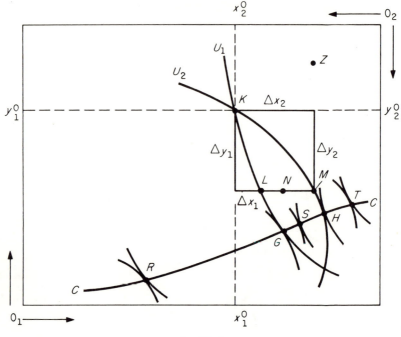

Fig. 17-2

each other. At point S the RCS of 1 and 2 is the same. Moving away from point S must lead to a welfare deterioration of at least one of the consumers. The curve CC, known as the *contract curve*, is the locus of all tangency points such as R, G, S, H, and T. If 1 and 2 are at any point, such as K, which does not belong to the contract curve, it pays both of them to move through exchange to the contract curve. Note, however, that not every point on the contract curve is preferred to a point such as K. Only points that lie on the contract curve between G and H are preferred to point K. But the point has been made: If the marginal rates of commodity substitution of Y for X are not the same for the consumers, both consumers will upgrade their utility by exchanging commodities just until the marginal rates of commodity substitution are the same. Where, on the contract curve between G and H, the two consumers will settle depends on their bargaining positions. In summary, equilibrium of exchange between any two consumers trading in any two commodities occurs when

$$RCS_1 = RCS_2 \qquad (21)$$

WELFARE OF PRODUCTION

Consider a case where a firm endowed with inputs A and B produces two commodities X and Y. A similar case is one in which two firms, are endowed with inputs A and B. One firm produces X and the other produces Y.

The initial endowment is indicated by point G in the Edgeworth box diagram in Fig. 17-3. Thus, initially A_x^0 units of A and B_x^0 units of B

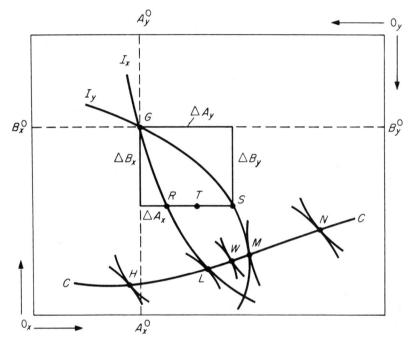

Fig. 17-3

are tied up in the production of X, and A_y^0 units of A and B_y^0 units of B are tied up in the production of Y. I_x and I_y are the isoquants of X and Y passing through point G. Recall that $\Delta B_x / \Delta A_x = - MPP_{ax} / MPP_{bx}$ and $\Delta B_y / \Delta A_y = - MPP_{ay} / MPP_{by}$. It is clear from Fig. 17-3 that

$$RTS_x = \frac{\Delta B_x}{\Delta A_x} > \frac{\Delta B_y}{\Delta A_y} = RTS_y$$

accordingly,

$$\frac{MPP_{ax}}{MPP_{bx}} > \frac{MPP_{ay}}{MPP_{by}}$$

Intuitively, this inequality indicates that on the margin, input A is relatively more productive in the production of X, and input B is relatively more productive in the production of Y. Hence, more A and less B should be used in the production of X, and vice versa in the production of Y. One can see the benefit of factor substitution from observing that while $\Delta B_x = \Delta B_y$, ΔA_y exceeds ΔA_x. For example, suppose $\Delta B_x = \Delta B_y = 3$, $\Delta A_y = 4$, and $\Delta A_x = 1$. By moving from point G to point R, the producer of X releases 3 units of B and absorbs 1 additional unit of A. By moving from point G to point S, the producer of Y releases 4 units of A and absorbs 3 additional units of B. At points R and S the production of X and Y, respectively, remains at the previous level, but RS ($= 3$) units of A are unused. The 3 units of A may be added to the production of both X and Y. This is achieved by moving to an intermediate point such as T. As in the case of consumption, if the marginal rate of technical substitution (RTS) in producing X is not equal to the marginal rate of technical substitution in producing Y, the production of both X and Y can increase through factor substitution. The equilibrium of production is achieved when the two marginal rates of technical substitution are equal. The RTS of X and Y are equal when the isoquants of X and Y are tangent to each other. In Fig. 17-3, H, L, W, M, and N are such points of tangency. The contract curve is the locus of all tangency points. Any point on the contract curve between L and M is preferred to G. W is an example. The requirement that the marginal rate of technical substitution in the production of any two goods in equilibrium be equal can be formally stated

$$RTS_x = RTS_y \tag{22}$$

It is an easy matter to construct an Edgeworth box diagram for two firms denoted by α and β producing the same good, X. The analysis is formally identical with the case of two different commodities. The result is that both firms will prefer to be on the contract curve, namely

$$RTS_x\,(\alpha) = RTS_x\,(\beta) \tag{23}$$

The reader can verify for himself that the theory of consumption welfare is formally identical with the theory of production welfare. In fact, if the two consumers are viewed as two plants producing utility, the theory is exactly identical.

THE PRODUCTION-POSSIBILITY CURVE

Consider Fig. 17-3 again. The contract curve CC is a locus of maximum production points. Given the initial endowment of inputs, and given the level of production of the other good, the maximum production of a good is found on the contract curve. For example, if the level of the other good, Y, is represented by the isoquant I_y, then a point outside the contract curve, such as G, does not yield maximum production of X. At point M the production of Y is the same but that of X is higher, because the isoquant of X which is tangent to I_y at point M occupies a higher position than I_x. The *production possibility curve*[3] in Fig. 17-4 is obtained

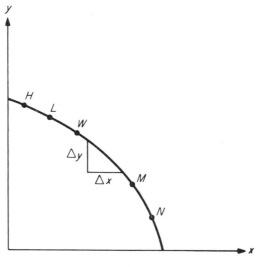

Fig. 17-4

by mapping the contract curve from the Edgeworth box diagram in Fig. 17-3 to a diagram in which the axes are the two outputs. The production possibility curve known also as the transformation curve is concave from below. This may be true either due to the fact that there are specific factors of production which are tied up in the production of X and Y, or alternatively, this may be true under the assumption of constant returns to scale, coupled with the assumption that one final good is capital intensive and the other is labor intensive. This means that as the firms keep on shifting resources from the production of Y to the production of X, on the margin more Y must be diverted away from production in order to produce an extra unit of X. It is left for the reader to show that points to the right of the transformation curve are unattainable. Points to the left of the production possibility curve are inefficient, in the sense that given the inputs, less than the maximum output is produced. Recall that the marginal rate of product transformation in production is denoted by RPT. The RPT in Fig. 17-4 is more sophisticated than the RPT described in conjunction of Fig. 17-1. In Fig. 17-1 the assumption was made that a single input is used in the production of

[3] The *production possibility curve* is known also as the *production possibility frontier* or the *transformation curve*.

two outputs. In Fig. 17-4 we assume that two inputs are used in the production of two outputs. On the margin, the firm can decrease Y by ΔY and increase X by ΔX by diverting either factor A or factor B from the production of Y to the production of X. We have two alternatives (or a combination of both):

$$\Delta Y = MPP_{ay} \cdot \Delta A$$
$$\Delta X = MPP_{ax} \cdot \Delta A$$

Thus,

$$RPT = \frac{\Delta Y}{\Delta X} = \frac{MPP_{ay}}{MPP_{ax}}$$

or,

$$\Delta Y = MPP_{by} \cdot \Delta B$$
$$\Delta X = MPP_{bx} \cdot \Delta B$$

Thus,

$$RPT = \frac{\Delta Y}{\Delta X} = \frac{MPP_{by}}{MPP_{bx}}$$

Consider now two firms, α and β. The transformation curves of α and β are shown in Fig. 17-5a and Fig. 17-5b. Since ΔX can be arbitrarily

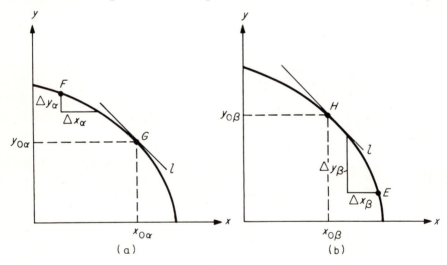

Fig. 17-5

determined, let $\Delta X_\alpha = \Delta X_\beta = 1$. It is clear from the way the diagram is drawn (point E in Fig. 17-5(b) and F in Fig. 17-5(a)) that

$$RPT_\alpha = \frac{\Delta Y_\alpha}{\Delta X_\alpha} < RPT_\beta = \frac{\Delta Y_\beta}{\Delta X_\beta}$$

This inequality indicates that diverting away from production one unit of X by firm β in order to be able to increase production by ΔY_β, and at the same time, diverting ΔY_a from the production by firm a in order to increase the production of X by an extra unit, results in producing the same amount of X but a larger quantity of Y. In fact, the net increase in the output of Y is $\Delta Y_\beta - \Delta Y a$. The point is that so long as the marginal rates of product transformation, of any two firms producing any two commodities, are not equal, total output of at least one good can increase through transformation. Accordingly, the condition for maximizing production by all firms is equality of all the marginal rates of product transformations. Formally

$$RPT_a = RPT_\beta \tag{24}$$

THE WELFARE OF CONSUMERS AND PRODUCERS

The transformation curves of all the firms in the economy can be aggregated. The aggregation is carried out under the assumption that there is some mechanism in the economy which induces all the firms to equate their RPT's. To illustrate this, consider a certain RPT represented by a line l in Fig. 17-5. Line l has the same slope in Fig. 17-5(a) and Fig. 17-5(b). At this slope (RPT), firm a produces the combination of X and Y represented by point G, and firm β produces the combination represented by point H. The aggregate production possibility curve (not shown in Fig. 17-5) contains a point at which the slope is l, output of X is $X_{0a} + X_{0\beta}$ and output of Y is $Y_{0a} + Y_{0\beta}$. However, indifference curves of consumers cannot be aggregated. This is due to the ordinal nature of utility. Fortunately, we are interested in marginal rates of substitution rather than in the entire indifference map of each consumer. Consider any consumer. Let his indifference map (dashed axes) be imposed on the aggregate transformation curve in Fig. 17-6. It can be shown that if the marginal rate of commodity substitution RCS is different from the marginal rate of product transformation RPT, welfare of this consumer can be improved through transformation. For example, consider point R_1. There the slope representing RCS is the line K and the slope representing RPT is l. Clearly since RCS is not equal to RPT, giving up the consumption of one unit of Y will release resources sufficient to produce an extra amount of X, which is more than the extra amount of X necessary to compensate the consumer. To put it in technical terms, the extra amount of X which can be produced with the resources released from the reduction in the production of Y exceeds the extra amount of X which must be given to the consumer in order to leave him on the same indifference curve U_1. Thus, if the consumer happens to be at point R_1 at which RCS is not equal to RPT, his utility will increase through technological transformation. This process of transforma-

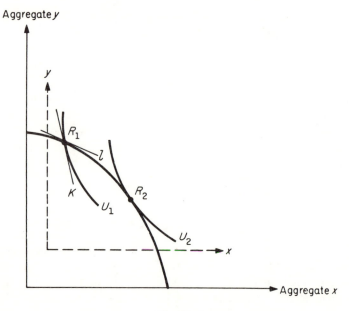

Fig. 17-6

tion whereby (in this example) the production of X expands and the production of Y shrinks should continue just until point R_2 is reached. At point R_2 the indifference curve U_2 is tangent to the transformation curve. The marginal rate of commodity substitution in consumption is equal to the marginal rate of product transformation in production. Trying to move away from R_2 in either direction would lead to a situation where the marginal transformation pushes the consumer down the utility hill. Thus, tangency between the indifference curve and the transformation curve is required for attaining maximum utility. Formally, this is stated

$$RCS = RPT \tag{25}$$

PARETO OPTIMALITY

An economic situation is defined as *Pareto optimal* if no individual can increase his welfare without adversely affecting the welfare of at least another individual. As shown above, if equalities (Eqs. 20 through 25) are satisfied, any deviation from these equalities must lead to a welfare reduction.

Let us now summarize the five conditions that must be satisfied in order to achieve Pareto optimality:

1. The marginal rates of commodity substitution between any two goods for any two consumers are equal.

$$RCS_1 = RCS_2 \tag{21}$$

2. The marginal rates of technical substitution between any two inputs in the production of any two goods are equal. This is true regardless of whether the two goods are jointly produced by one firm or separately produced by two firms.

$$RTS_x = RTS_y \qquad [22]$$

3. The marginal rates of technical substitution between any two inputs in the production of a single commodity is equal for any two firms.

$$RTS_x (\alpha) = RTS_x (\beta) \qquad [23]$$

4. The marginal rates of product transformation between any two goods is equal for any two firms.

$$RPT_a = RPT_\beta \qquad [24]$$

5. The marginal rate of commodity substitution and the marginal rate of product transformation between any two goods must be equal for all consumers and all firms.

$$RCS = RPT \qquad [25]$$

COMPETITION AND WELFARE

The law of the "Invisible Hand" can now be proved. Recall from other courses in economics that Adam Smith was the father of the famous dictum claiming that each individual, by pursuing his own selfish economic goals, is led, as if by an *invisible hand,* to attain the maximum welfare for society as a whole. In this section we prove that if the economy is perfectly competitive, then the law of the Invisible Hand is true in the Pareto optimality sense. In what follows the knowledge of previous chapters is taken for granted.

(a) In order to maximize utility, the consumer allocates his budget among various goods and services such that the marginal rate of commodity substitution equals the price ratio of any pair of commodities. That is,

$$RCS = \frac{P_x}{P_y} \qquad (26)$$

Here Y and X represent any possible pair of commodities. Price uniformity in competition guarantees the equality of all the RCS's.

(b) Consider the marginal rate of technical substitution between any two inputs, A and B, in the production of any output, say X.

$$RTS_x = \frac{\Delta B_x}{\Delta A_x} = -\frac{MPP_{ax}}{MPP_{bx}} = -\frac{MPP_{ax}}{MPP_{bx}} \cdot \frac{P_x}{P_x} = -\frac{P_a}{P_b}$$

This is true due to the principle of equating the value marginal product of inputs to their market prices. We can derive the same relation for commodity Y. Then,

$$RTS_x = -\frac{P_a}{P_b} \left. \right\}$$
$$RTS_y = -\frac{P_a}{P_b} \left. \right\} \tag{27}$$

The uniformity of prices of inputs in competition guarantees the equality of RTS_x with RTS_y.

(c) Consider two firms, α and β. In competition the rates of technical substitutions are equal by the same argument used in (b).

$$RTS_x(\alpha) = RTS_x(\beta) = -\frac{P_a}{P_b}$$

The uniformity of input prices is crucial here as in (b).

(d) Recall that going along the transformation curve,

$$RPT = \frac{\Delta Y}{\Delta X} = \frac{MPP_{ay}}{MPP_{ax}} = \frac{MPP_{by}}{MPP_{bx}} \tag{28}$$

Competitive firms produce where the price is equal to the marginal cost.

$$P_x = MC_x = \frac{P_a}{MPP_{ax}} = \frac{P_b}{MPP_{bx}} \tag{29}$$

$$P_y = MC_y = \frac{P_a}{MPP_{ay}} = \frac{P_b}{MPP_{by}} \tag{30}$$

Dividing Eq. 29 by Eq. 30,

$$\frac{P_x}{P_y} = \frac{MPP_{ay}}{MPP_{ax}} = \frac{MPP_{by}}{MPP_{bx}} \tag{31}$$

Equation 28 together with Eq. 31 gives

$$RPT = \frac{P_x}{P_y} \tag{32}$$

Price uniformity in competition guarantees the equality of RPT's for any pair of firms,

$$RPT_\alpha = RPT_\beta = \frac{P_x}{P_y} \tag{33}$$

(e) Equations 26 and 33 together are

$$RPT = RCS = \frac{P_x}{P_y} \tag{34}$$

In competition, price uniformity guarantees that the price ratio of any pair of goods is the same for consumers and producers.

WELFARE AND TAXES

The problem of indirect taxes was discussed in Chapter 10. All that remains now is to show the effects of indirect taxes on welfare. Let us assume that there are only two goods in the economy, X and Y. Each of these commodities is produced competitively. Using the technique of Fig. 17-6, where indifference curves represent slopes at points of tangency, we draw the aggregate transformation curve and an indifference curve U_2 in Fig. 17-7. The indifference curve U_2 is tangent to the trans-

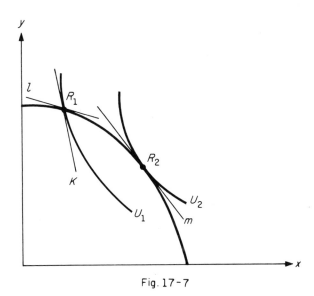

Fig. 17-7

formation curve at point R_2. At this point of tangency, the slope which is represented by the line m is

$$RPT = RCS = \frac{P_x}{P_y}$$

Following Chapter 10, the government imposes a tax of T dollars per unit of output X. Let us continue to denote the price net of the tax by P_x. This is the price received by producers of X and accordingly this is the price which is relevant for them. The price paid by consumers is $P_x + T$. The marginal rate of product transformation in production is no longer equal to the marginal rate of commodity substitution in consumption:

$$RCS = \frac{P_x + T}{P_y} > RPT = \frac{P_x}{P_y} \tag{35}$$

In order to find a new point of equilibrium after the tax is imposed, we start moving leftward along the transformation curve. We finally reach the point R_1 at which the line l is tangent to the transformation curve. The line l represents the slope $RPT = \dfrac{P_x}{P_y}$. The line k which is tangent to the indifference curve U_1 at point R_1 represents the slope $RCS = (P_x + T)/P_y$. Thus, the diversion of RCS from RPT forced consumers to shift from a high level of utility U_2, to a lower level of utility U_1. The gap between RCS and RPT was caused by the indirect tax which led to a diversion of the price ratio confronting consumers from the price ratio confronting producers. The fact that the slope of l differs from the slope of m shows that the price of X (relative to the price of Y) facing the producer has declined. Accordingly, the price paid by consumers has increased, but not by the full amount of the tax.

Before departing we should stress the point that the tax does not change the shape and position of the transformation curve. This becomes realistic if we think of X and Y as strictly consumption goods for which a certain fraction of national resources is earmarked. The revenue of the tax is spent on the remaining resources in the production of defense services.

WELFARE AND MONOPOLIES

Suppose that commodity X is produced by a monopoly and commodity Y is produced competitively. The reader can easily show that a monopolist combines factors of production efficiently in the process of production. In other words, rule 2 of Pareto optimality is not violated under monopolistic production. Consider any of the inputs used in the production of X and Y, say input A. Firms producing Y equate the *value marginal product* of A with the price of A while the monopoly equates the *marginal revenue product* of A with the price of A. This may be written as follows:

In competition $MPP_a \cdot P_y = P_a$

Under monopoly $MPP_a \cdot MR_x = P_a$

Thus, since P_a is uniform for all firms,

$$MPP_{ay} \cdot P_y = MPP_{ax} \cdot MR_x$$

But since $MR_x < P_x$, then,

$$MPP_{ay} \cdot P_y < MPP_{ax} \cdot P_x$$

and, rearranging the last inequality, we get,

$$\frac{MPP_{ay}}{MPP_{ax}} < \frac{P_x}{P_y}$$

But, for consumers, the marginal rate of commodity substitution equals the price ratio. That is,

$$RPT = \frac{MPP_{ay}}{MPP_{ax}} < \frac{P_x}{P_y} = RCS$$

To put it more rigorously,

$$RPT = \frac{MR_x}{P_y} = \frac{P_x\left(1 + \frac{1}{n}\right)}{P_y} < \frac{P_x}{P_y} = RCS$$

We can use Fig. 17-7 to demonstrate the position of the monopoly. RPT is a slope represented by line l. RCS is a slope represented by line K. RPT, the marginal rate of product transformation at point R_1, is smaller than RCS, the marginal rate of commodity substitution at the same point. We leave it for the reader to show that the government can increase the welfare of consumers by subsidizing the monopolized commodity. In summary, monopolies reduce the economic welfare of society by creating a gap between RPT and RCS. This can be corrected by "forcing" the monopolist to behave competitively. This is illustrated in the solution to Prob. 17-5.

WELFARE AND MONOPSONIES

Consider a case in which a firm producing output X uses two factors of production, A and B. The firm faces a positively sloped supply curve of input A, i.e., the firm enjoys a monopsonistic position in the market for input A. In the market for A the supply elasticity is $\epsilon > 0$. The firm has no influence over the price of factor B or the price of output. Recall from previous chapters that the firm would employ inputs A and B such that the marginal factor cost of A equals the value marginal product of A and the price of B equals the value marginal product of B. This can be written as

$$P_x \cdot MPP_{ax} = P_a\left(1 + \frac{1}{\epsilon}\right) \tag{36}$$

$$P_x \cdot MPP_{bx} = P_b \tag{37}$$

Dividing Eq. 36 by Eq. 37,

$$RTS_x = \frac{MPP_{ax}}{MPP_{bx}} = \frac{P_a\left(1 + \frac{1}{\epsilon}\right)}{P_b} \tag{38}$$

Consider a firm in industry Y which sells its output and buys its inputs in competitive markets. There

$$P_y \cdot MPP_{ay} = P_a \tag{39}$$

$$P_y \cdot MPP_{by} = P_b \tag{40}$$

Equation 39 divided by Eq. 40 gives

$$RTS_y = \frac{MPP_{ay}}{MPP_{by}} = \frac{P_a}{P_b} \tag{41}$$

Equations 38 and 41 together are

$$RTS_y = \frac{P_a}{P_b} < RTS_x = \frac{P_a \left(1 + \frac{1}{\epsilon}\right)}{P_b} \tag{42}$$

The reader can easily show that the inequality of the marginal rates of technical substitution induces the two firms to be at a point like G in Fig. 17-3 rather than at a point like W on the contract curve. This is a deviation from rule 2.

If one of two firms in the X industry enjoys monopsonistic position in the market for A, while the other firm does not, and if both firms sell output and buy B in competitive markets, the analysis is similar to the previous case. Denoting the first firm by α and the second by β, then,

$$RTS_x \, (\beta) = \frac{P_a}{P_b} < RTS_x \, (\alpha) = \frac{P_a \left(1 + \frac{1}{\epsilon}\right)}{P_b} \tag{43}$$

which is a deviation from rule (c).

SUMMARY

Pareto optimality should be taken with a grain of salt. For example, we should not jump to the conclusion that production under competition is always preferred to monopoly. An enlightened monopolist may accumulate substantial funds and apply them to technological research at a scale which cannot be attained under competition. Moreover, by either regulating the price charged by the monopolist or subsidizing and taxing the monopolist simultaneously, the government can substantially reduce the welfare loss to society.

In judging the merits of various ways of imposing taxes, we sometimes ignore Pareto optimality altogether. The outstanding example is income tax. Although taxes imposed on income cause welfare losses (Prob. 17-3), income taxes have been accepted by practically all countries. Here, the ability-to-pay principle, which is political, outweighs economic considerations. On the other hand, Pareto optimality may help us to favor a general sales tax (imposed as a fixed percentage on consumption) to excise taxes imposed at different rates on a variety of goods chosen arbitrarily by the government. Pareto considerations exclude cases like the excise tax on gasoline which is a practical substitute for levying the fee from road-users.

There are other cases in which Pareto arguments could make more sense than non-economic arguments that usually are drafted. For example, enforcing a minimum wage rate in an area in which the local labor force is dominated by a monopsony is usually based on social justice. But Pareto optimality, which in this case could claim that monopsony reduces the welfare of society as a whole, not only of laborers, may be more effective in bargaining.

Finally, Pareto criteria tell us nothing about the distribution of income. For example, consider Fig. 17-2. The starting point is K which represents a certain initial distribution of goods between the two individuals. Pareto criteria show that *given this initial distribution* both individuals will benefit from moving to any point between G and H on the contract curve. Supposing the government redistributes income of the two individuals so as to move them from point K to point Z. Pareto criteria are not capable of telling whether this is good or bad. Consumer 1 will benefit and consumer 2 will suffer from such a redistribution of income. Moreover, the government can obtain the means for redistributing income by inflating the economy, thus raising all prices equi-proportionately and leaving price ratios unchanged. The only thing Pareto criteria can tell us is that the two individuals will find a segment on the contract curve where each point is preferred to Z. But the impossibility of inter-personal comparison of utility prohibits us from telling whether the gain of utility from moving from K to Z for consumer 1 exceeds the loss of utility for consumer 2 or vice versa.

EXTERNAL TECHNICAL ECONOMIES AND DISECONOMIES

In general, the marginal rate of product transformation is the same for society and for a single firm, or one industry. There are cases in which this is not true. For example, consider the paper industry which discharges pollution into the water. When less paper is produced, resources are released. Let us make the assumption that these resources are absorbed by other industries which do not pollute the water. The private transformation curve does not reveal the extra "output" which, resulting from this transformation is created by the recreation industry. In Fig. 17-8 the RCS (line g) equals the private RPT at point A. In absence of governmental interference the economy will operate at point A. The transformation curve of society does not coincide with the private curve.

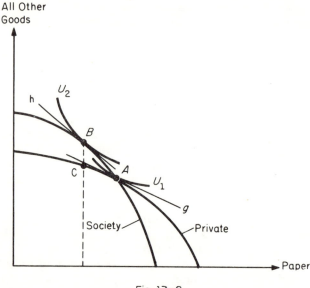

Fig. 17-8

This situation reflects the fact that the output gain to society per unit of paper diverted away from production is more than extra output the private sector can produce with the released resources. The RCS (line h) equals the RPT of the social transformation curve at point B. A higher level of welfare is attained at point B. In order to move from point A to the higher point B, the government should impose an excise tax on paper and increase it just until point C is attained.

PROBLEMS

17-1. Show that if the transformation curve in Fig. 17-7 is linear, then the price of X received by producers does not change as a result of the tax. Who bears the burden of the tax?

17-2. Roughly speaking, a subsidy of $S(=T)$ dollars per unit of X would lead to the same welfare loss as a tax of T per unit of X. Do you agree?

17-3. Show that a tax on income leads individuals to deviate from Pareto optimality. HINT: (a) Assume that X is leisure and Y is all other goods. (b) P_x is the wage rate. (c) Show that RPT is the marginal physical product of labor. (d) Employers pay labor a wage rate P_x equal to the value marginal product of labor.

17-4. Show that a monopolist combines factors of production efficiently, that is, if X is output and A and B are any two inputs, then for the monopoly (as for any other competitive firm) $RTS_x = -P_a / P_b$.

17-5. Show that the government can shift the economy from point R_1 to the optimal point R_2 in Fig. 17-7. Assume that initially X is produced by a monopoly and Y is produced by a competitive industry. The economy operates at point R_1. The government extends a subsidy per unit of X and in order to cover the cost of this subsidy the government imposes a fixed tax on the monopolist.

17-6. Show that price discrimination leads to a reduction in welfare. Assume that commodity X is made by a monopolist while commodity Y is produced competitively. Assume that consumers are divided into two groups, 1 and 2. The monopolist discriminates against group 1. By using an Edgeworth diagram similar to Fig. 17-2, show that point K, rather than S, represents the allocation of goods among consumers.

17-7. Commodity X is produced competitively in economy 1 and economy 2. The variable factor A is used in the production of X in both economies. The government of economy 1 imposes a duty of $\$U$ per unit of X imported from economy 2 to economy 1. For simplicity assume that the cost of shipping either commodity X or factor A between the two economies is negligible. Show that this gives rise to a loss of welfare.

chapter **18**

Linear Programming

A NON-MATHEMATICAL INTRODUCTION

In most cases only a finite number of separate processes of production are known to the entire firm. If we were not interested in the firm per se, but rather in all the firms in the industry, it would be convenient to pretend that the technology of the firm can be summarized by a single relation known as the production function. However, when it comes to a specific firm which can produce something like five joint products by applying several separate processes of production, pretending that the processes of production are summarized by a single production function is of no help.

Linear programming deals with finding optimal solutions to problems that are governed by linearity. The nature of these problems and why the calculus is incapable of solving them will become clear in the course of this chapter. For the time being it is sufficient to describe the linear program as a problem in which profit appears as a linear function of various processes. This is known as the objective function. Profit has to be maximized subject to several side conditions. These side conditions, or constraints, take on the form of linear inequalities.

A mathematical solution to the linear program problem was not available until World War II.[1] During World War II, a group headed by Marshall K. Wood was involved in analyzing the problem of resource allocation for the United States Air Force. In 1947, George B. Dantzig, a member of that group, formulated the linear programming problem and developed a mathematical technique known as the simplex method for maximizing or minimizing the objective function.

Earlier, in 1945, George J. Stigler used another technique to solve the least cost balanced diet that can be formulated as a linear programming problem.

---

[1] The Russian economist, Kantorovich, started to work on linear programming in 1939.

Dantzig's technique and the postwar development of electronic computers rendered linear programming a very important tool in business and economics. Today linear programming is widely used in solving problems of resource allocation in almost all industries. It is especially important in solving problems of resource allocation, blending, animal feeding, transportation, and timing inloads and outloads in warehouses.

The purpose of this chapter is limited to serve as an appetizer for the reader. Studying linear programming takes about one semester, and thus the student who acquires some appetite for linear programming should either take a course in linear programming, or read one of the many texts on the subject.

In what follows we shall formulate *simple* linear programs, and solve them by use of geometry, hoping that such a procedure will help to create in the mind of the student the "right" image of linear programming, and give the reader some of the flavor of operations research.

BASIC CONCEPTS

The basic concepts of linear programming will be introduced by considering an example.

There are three factors of production, A, B, and C, used in the production of two commodities, X and Y. Let us assume that it takes 1 unit of A, 1 unit of B, and 4 units of C to produce 1 unit of X. It takes 2 units of A, 1 unit of B, and 1 unit of C to produce 1 unit of Y. This information can be summarized by the accompanying input-output table:

Table 18-1

X	Y	
1	2	A
1	1	B
4	1	C

Also, Table 18-1 shows two *processes of production*. Sometimes a process of production is called an activity. Each of the two columns in Table 18-1 represents a process of production. The phrase *process of production* tells us what combination of inputs it takes to produce a certain level of output.

When discussing processes of production, the following should be clear:

1. The processes X and Y can be two separate activities employed in the production of the same commodity. For example, let the firm in our example be engaged in the production of whatnots. Let A stand for labor, B for land, and C for capital. If process X is used, it takes 1 unit

of labor, 1 unit of land, and 4 units of capital to make one whatnot. If process Y is employed, it takes 2 units of labor, 1 unit of land, and 1 unit of capital to produce one whatnot.

2. Each process of production is governed by *fixed proportions* and *constant returns to scale*. *Fixed proportions* means that if process X is employed, then the proportion of labor to land is 1 and the proportion of capital to land is 4. These proportions cannot change. For example, if whatnots are planted on 2 units of land, then 2 units of labor and 8 units of capital must be employed in the process of production. Constant returns to scale imply that if 2 units of labor, 2 units of land, and 8 units of capital are employed, then two whatnots are forthcoming. In general, if $K \cdot 1$ units of labor, $K \cdot 1$ units of land, and $K \cdot 4$ units of capital are employed, then K whatnots are produced.

3. The processes are *independent* of each other. Independence means that changing the level of activity X neither requires a change in the level of Y, nor does it give rise to such a change, and vice versa.

The assumptions of constant returns to scale, fixed proportions, and independence lead to linearity. Linearity means that we can formulate the process of production by adding as many units of X to as many units of Y, without squaring X, or taking logarithms.

Divisibility is another assumption made here. Divisibility implies that the firm can produce fractions of units. For example, if the firm decides to produce 2.5 whatnots by employing process X and 3.2 whatnots by employing process Y, then the activities are as indicated by Table 18-2. The assumption of divisibility may be relaxed in the solution of specific problems.

Table 18-2

X	Y	
2.5	6.4	A
2.5	3.2	B
10.0	3.2	C

It is given that profit per unit of X is $15 and profit per unit of Y is $20. The reader can verify that this is consistent with an assumption that the firm faces a market in which the price per whatnot is $30. The firm is confronted with prices of variable inputs such that the average variable cost per unit of process X is $15, and the average variable cost per unit of process Y is $10. Profit in this context does not consider fixed costs. In fact the firm would break even only if the total profit would be equal to, or exceed, the capital recovery value of factors B and C plus the salary paid to factor A.

Let us denote profit by π, then the profit function becomes

$$\pi = 15\,X + 20\,Y$$

This function is called the *objective function*. Here linearity is made possible by the assumption of perfect competition. If we relax the assumption of a perfectly competitive market for whatnots and variable inputs then the objective function would take on the form of a non-linear function, leading to non-linear programming.

Finally, let us assume that not more than 14 units of A, 8 units of B, and 24 units of C are available to the firm. Then, if X units are produced by employing process X, and Y units are produced by employing process Y (X whatnots are made through process X and Y whatnots are made through process Y), the following are the *constraints* by which the firm must abide:

$$1 \cdot X + 2 \cdot Y \leq 14$$
$$1 \cdot X + 1 \cdot Y \leq 8$$
$$4 \cdot X + 1 \cdot Y \leq 24$$

The problem is to maximize profit subject to the above constraints. Formally the linear programming problem can be stated as
Maximize:

$$\pi = 15 \cdot X + 20 \cdot Y$$

Subject to:

$$1 \cdot X + 2 \cdot Y \leq 14$$
$$1 \cdot X + 1 \cdot Y \leq 8$$
$$4 \cdot X + 1 \cdot Y \leq 24$$
$$X \geq 0$$
$$Y \geq 0$$

where the last two constraints ensure that activities are used only at positive levels.

ALLOCATION OF LIMITED RESOURCES

The above example is a typical problem of allocating limited resources among several processes of production. The allocation of limited resources should be optimal, that is, it should lead to profit maximization. The limited resources on the farm are usually land and water. In the short run, tractor capacity may also become a limiting factor. In industry, the limited resources may be either machine time, the plant size or space available in warehouses. But, regardless of the technical nature of the limited resources and the process of production, the solution to the problem can be accomplished by applying linear programming.

Let us now consider the geometrical solution of the problem. We start with the inequality $X + 2Y \leqq 14$. The line AA in Fig. 18-1 represents the equality $X + 2Y = 14$. We leave it for the reader to show that the region to the left of (or below) AA represents the inequality

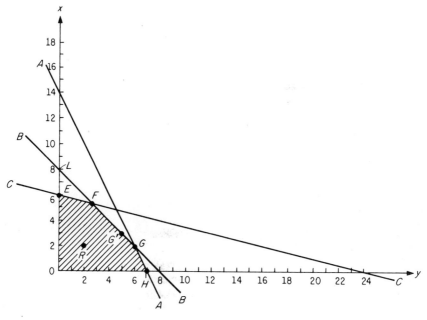

Fig. 18-1

$X + 2Y < 14$. This region plus the line AA represents the inequality $X + 2Y \leqq 14$. Thus, if A were the only limitation, then the region to the left of AA and AA would be the *feasible region* of production. Attempting to produce combinations of X and Y represented by points in the region to the right of AA would not be feasible because production would take more than is available of input A. If we add the limitation of input B, then the feasible region becomes the region to the left of, and including, LGH. Finally, if the limitation of input C is added, the feasible region becomes the region to the left (and including) $EFGH$. Since we limited ourselves to positive levels of production, the feasible region becomes the shaded region bordered by $0EFGH$, including the border. It is evident from Fig. 18-1 that the point of maximum profit must lie on the frontier of the feasible region. Recall that both X and Y are profitable. Then, logically one can find points on the frontier which yield more profit than any point inside the region such as point R. This is true because moving away from point R, either rightwards or upwards, or both, implies an increased production of either X, or Y, or both. Recall

that the assumption of constant returns to scale and competition elimi-
nates the presence of either diminishing or increasing returns to scale,
diminishing prices of output, or rising prices of variable inputs. Accordingly, such a movement away from R towards the frontier, as described
above must lead to increasing profits.

The problem of linear programming boils down to locating the
optimal point on the frontier, indicated by $EFGH$. It is very likely that
the optimal solution would be a *corner*, such as point E, F, G, or H. The
simplex method is an iterative process which tells how to reach the
optimal point step by step. The steps, however, are not taken at random.
The rule of taking the next step is such that profit must increase with
it. This guarantees that the optimal point will be discovered in a *finite*
number of steps.

Leaving the simplex method for textbooks specializing in linear
programming, let us describe the geometrical solution.

The profit function of the firm in our example is $\pi = 15X + 20Y$.
One can imagine an infinitely large number of isoprofit lines corresponding to the profit function. Only three such isoprofit lines are illustrated
in Fig. 18-2. These are $\pi_1 = \$80$, $\pi_2 = \$150$, and $\pi_3 = \$300$.

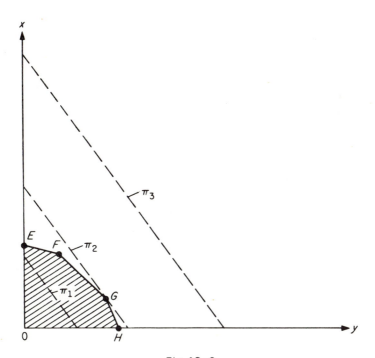

Fig. 18-2

Supposing we start to move rightwards from π_1 to higher isoprofit lines. We seek the highest isoprofit line which contains at least one feasible point. The isoprofit denoted by π_2 is the highest such line containing a feasible point. The feasible point is the corner denoted by G. This is known as *a corner solution*. The point G yields the maximum profit.

The solution may not be a corner solution. For example, supposing the isoprofit lines happen to be parallel to the segment FG. In that case, the points which lie on this segment, including the corners F and G, are optimal. This implies that each of the points belonging to the optimal segment must yield the same profit.

The reader can imagine a situation in which the profit of X increases. This would lead to a counterclockwise rotation of the isoprofit lines. If the increase in the profit of X is substantial, F will become the corner tangency point, leading to a decline in the production of Y and a rise in the production of X. This in turn would lead to increasing the demand for input C and reducing the demand for input A.

We leave it for the reader to show that at point G the firm produces 2 units of X and 6 units of Y. Accordingly the maximum profit amounts to $\$150 = 2 \cdot \$15 + 6 \cdot \$20$.

Notice finally that input C is not exhausted in the process of production. You should find it instructive to show that only 14 units of input C are used up in the process of production. Accordingly, input C is a free input for the firm. The firm would not pay money for additional units of C, because such a purchase would only increase the number of idle units of C.

SHADOW PRICES AND DUALITY

Shadow prices are fancy names for marginal revenue products. Accordingly, the shadow price of an input is determined by first reaching the optimal combination of processes yielding maximum profit. The second step is to decrease by one unit the use of the input whose shadow price we want to determine. By definition of optimality this must lead to a reduction in the profit. This change in profit is the shadow price, or simply the marginal revenue product of the input.

What is the shadow price of input A? If we reduce A by one unit the first constraint becomes $X + 2Y \leqq 13$. The line represented by $X + 2Y = 13$ would be parallel to AA. It would cut the line BB at point G' shown in Fig. 18-1. At point G' the firm would produce 3 units of X and 5 units of Y, and the new profit would be $\$145 = 3 \cdot \$15 + 5 \cdot \$20$.

Thus shadow price of $A = \dfrac{\$145 - \$150}{13 - 14} = \$5$.

We leave it for the reader to show that the shadow price of input B is \$10. In the event you take a course in linear programming, you will find out that shadow prices may be obtained by solving the *dual problem*, namely,

Minimize:

$$14 \cdot U + 8 \cdot V + 24 \cdot W$$

Subject to:

$$1 \cdot U + 1 \cdot V + 4 \cdot W \geqq 15$$
$$2 \cdot U + 1 \cdot V + 1 \cdot W \geqq 20$$
$$U \geqq 0$$
$$V \geqq 0$$
$$W \geqq 0$$

The solution must be $U = \$5$, $V = \$10$, and $W = 0$, where U, V, and W are the shadow prices of A, B, and C. Solving the dual problem is superfluous because once the optimal solution is available, shadow prices are easily derived from it.

THE SUPPLY CURVE

Let us consider now the supply of X. Assume that X and Y are two different commodities. We have specified before that A, B, and C are fixed inputs. The firm is stuck with 14 units of A, 8 units of B, and 24 units of C. The profit per unit of Y is \$20 and we shall assume that this profit does not change. Let us assume that it takes \$15 in order to pay for variable inputs which are required for the production of one additional unit of X. Consider now a market situation in which the price of X rises. If the price of X is between \$0 and \$15, the profit per unit of X is negative. Accordingly the firm would produce 7 units of Y as indicated by point H in Fig. 18-1. Output of X would be zero.

Moving from H to G along the AA line, the firm gives up one unit of Y for 2 units of X. Thus, if the profit per unit of X is \$10, then the firm foregoes \$20 by giving up 1 unit of Y, but it regains the same amount because two additional units of X yield $\$20 = 2 \cdot \$10$. Since the average variable cost of X is \$15, the entrepreneur would be indifferent between points H and G only if the price of X is \$25.

Moving from G to F along the BB line, the firm gives up one unit of Y for 1 unit of X. Thus, in order for the entrepreneur to be indifferent between G and F, the profit per unit of X must be equal to the profit per unit of Y. Accordingly, the profit per unit of X must be \$20. This implies that the price per unit of X must be \$35.

Moving from F to E along the CC line, the firm gives up one unit of Y for $\frac{1}{4}$ of a unit of X. In order for the entrepreneur to be indifferent between points F and E, the profit per unit of X must be \$80. Thus, the gain of $20 = 0.25 \cdot \$80$ is equal to the loss of $20 per one unit of Y diverted from the process of production. The price of X must be $95. The price of X may continue to rise, but the firm will continue to make 6 units of X. This is summarized in Table 18-3.

TABLE 18-3

Corner	Y	X	Proft Per Unit of Y (dollars)	Profit Per Unit of X (dollars)	Price of X (dollars)
H	7	0			
			20	10	25
G	6	2			
			20	20	35
F	2⅔	5⅓			
			20	80	95
E	0	6			

The resulting supply curve of X is shown in Fig. 18-3. This is a step-shaped supply curve denoted by $OEFGHIJ$. It is likely that in reality most of the supply curves of firms are step-shaped. When aggregated, however, they give rise to the industry supply curve which may assumed to be smooth for all practical purposes.

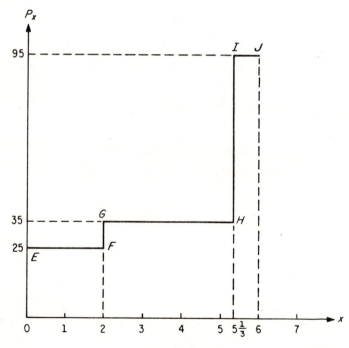

Fig. 18-3

Moreover, one can easily show that the step-shaped supply curve behaves like smooth supply curves. Thus, a fall in the prices of variable factors would lead to a downward shift in the step-shaped supply curve, and vice versa.

LEAST COST COMBINATION OF INPUTS

There are many economic problems in which the process of profit maximization can be broken down into two parts: (a) determining the expansion path of the firm and (b) locating the optimal point on the expansion path. One example is the problem of feeding animals. The first problem is to determine the least cost combinations of feeds subject to specific diet constraints. These constraints specify the *minimum* amount of each of many nutrients that must be fed to the animals per unit of time. This is a linear programming problem. The second problem is to find the optimal period of time beyond which it does not pay to keep the animal. The law of diminishing marginal physical product guarantees the existence of such a point. The problem is to maximize the present value of the revenue minus the cost.

In general, the problem may be one in which there are n varieties of grains. Each grain contains m (or less) nutrients. The animals must be fed at least a certain amount of each nutrient per unit of time. These are the constraints. Given the prices of the grains with which the farm is confronted, the least cost combination of grains is to be found.

A similar problem is one in which a manufacturer wants to blend various alloys each containing a certain percentage of copper, tin, and zinc. The desired blend should contain a certain proportion of copper, tin, and zinc. If the firm considers 10 alloys whose prices are given in the market, then the problem is to find the least cost blending of these alloys into the desired blend. Since this minimization problem is subject to 3 constraints, the optimal solution would be to blend three alloys into the desired alloy. The solution would select the three alloys and indicate the proportion at which each of the three alloys would enter the blend.

Consider now the following hypothetical problem: A farmer has to find the least cost combination of two grains, X and Y. The contents of the grains are shown in Table 18-4. The animal must be fed per day at least 9 units of nutrient A, 5 units of nutrient B, and 16 units of nutri-

TABLE 18-4

Grain Nutrient	X	Y
A	1	3
B	1	1
C	8	2

ent C. Accordingly, the constraints are

$$1 \cdot X + 3 \cdot Y \geqq 9$$
$$1 \cdot X + 1 \cdot Y \geqq 5$$
$$8 \cdot X + 2 \cdot Y \geqq 16$$

In Fig. 18-4, the first inequality is denoted by AA, the second by BB, and

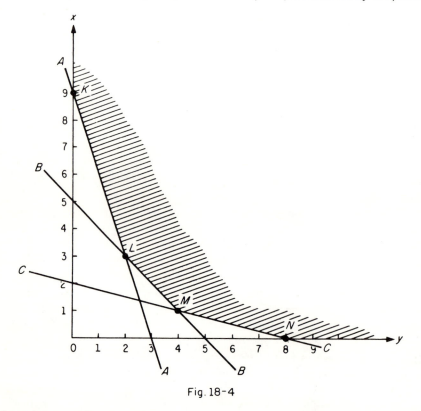

Fig. 18-4

the third by CC. The difference between Fig. 18-1 and Fig. 18-4 is that in Fig. 18-1 the feasible region lies to the left of the frontier, while in Fig. 18-4 the feasible region lies to the right of the frontier.

Supposing the farmer is confronted with a market in which the price of X is \$4, and the price of Y is \$6. Then, the problem is
Minimize:

$$TC = 4 \cdot X + 6 \cdot Y$$

Subject to:

$$1 \cdot X + 3 \cdot Y \geqq 9$$
$$1 \cdot X + 1 \cdot Y \geqq 5$$
$$8 \cdot X + 2 \cdot Y \geqq 16$$
$$X \geqq 0$$
$$Y \geqq 0$$

where the last two inequalities ensure that X and Y are non-negative.

The problem is solved by selecting the lowest isocost line which contains at least one feasible point. In Fig. 18-5 only 3 isocost lines are

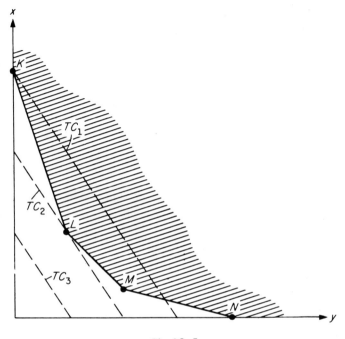

Fig. 18-5

shown. These are $TC_1 = \$36$, $TC_2 = \$24$, and $TC_3 = \$12$. TC_2 is the lowest isocost line containing at least one feasible point. This point, which is denoted by L, is a corner tangency point. If the price of Y would decrease relative to the price of X, such that the isocost lines would rotate counterclockwise until they are parallel to the segment LM, then the least cost combination would be any point on the segment LM, including the points LM. A further reduction in the relative price of Y would lead to switching the point of tangency from L to M. As indicated by Fig. 18-5, the farmer would substitute grain Y for grain X.

At corner L, $X = 3$ and $Y = 2$. Accordingly the cost is $\$24 = \$4 \cdot 3 + \$6 \cdot 2$. The animal is fed 9 units of nutrient A, 5 units of nutrient B, and 28 units of nutrient C. The requirement of A and B are just satisfied. The requirement of C is oversatisfied. In fact, the animals are fed 12 units of nutrient C in excess of the required minimum.

Shadow prices in cost minimization problems provide additional information about the constraints. The shadow price of a constraint, such as nutrient A, is determined by first reaching the optimal solution, and then changing the constraint by one unit. By definition of optimality this must lead to a change in total cost. This change in total cost is the shadow price. In our example, the least cost combination of resources is achieved at point L ($X = 3$ and $Y = 2$). There, total cost amounts to $24. Lowering the minimal use of nutrient A by 1 unit, from 9 to 8, would lead to a new point where $X = 3.5$ units and $Y = 1.5$ units. We leave it for the reader to locate this point in Fig. 18-5. The new cost amounts to $23 ($= \$4 \cdot 3.5 + \$6 \cdot 1.5$). Thus,

$$\text{Shadow price of nutrient } A = \frac{23 - 24}{8 - 9} = \$1.$$

The reader should find it easy to calculate the shadow prices of nutrients B and C.

TRANSPORTATION PROBLEMS

Transportation problems fall into the class of cost minimization. To illustrate the formulation of transportation problems, consider the following problem:

A homogeneous product is produced in $i = 1$, 2, 3 origins. The respective quantities produced are q_1, q_2, q_3. There are $j = 1$, 2, 3, 4 shipping destinations. The respective quantities demanded in the shipping destinations are d_1, d_2, d_3, and d_4. The amount that goes from origin i to destination j is X_{ij}. Supply equals demand, that is, $\sum_i q_i = \sum_j d_j = Q$. Q is the total quantity produced. The cost of shipping one unit of output from origin i to destination j is C_{ij}. The linear programming problem is Minimize:

$$\sum_{i=1}^{3} \sum_{j=1}^{4} C_{ij} X_{ij}$$

Subject to:

$$\sum_{j=1}^{4} X_{ij} = q_i \qquad i = 1, 2, 3$$

$$\sum_{i=1}^{3} X_{ij} = d_j \qquad j = 1, 2, 3, 4$$

$$X_{ij} \geq 0 \qquad i = 1, 2, 3 \qquad j = 1, 2, 3, 4$$

Although the transportation problem may be solved by applying the simplex method, special methods for solving such problems are available.

WAREHOUSE PROBLEMS

Consider a warehouse with a capacity to store A units. In each period of time the purchase price equals the selling price. The costs of the various activities are:

Storage .... a dollars per unit
Buying or Selling ..... b_t dollars per unit
Unused capacity ...... c dollars per unit.

Let us adopt the following notations:

Selling stock W
Storing stock X
Buying stock Y
Unused capacity Z

where W, X, Y, and Z denote quantities. The stock carried over from the previous time period, plus the stock bought presently, minus the stock sold must equal the stock presently stored:

$$X_{t-1} + Y_t - W_t = X_t$$

Shifting the X_t to the left we get

$$X_{t-1} + Y_t - W_t - X_t = 0$$

And, to this we add the capacity equation

$$X_t + Z_t = A$$

Let us agree to assign minus signs to the costs of storage, unused capacity, and buying stocks. The selling price is assigned a positive sign. We have to solve the following problem, under the assumption that $t = 1, 2, \ldots, n$, Maximize:

$$\sum_{t=1}^{n} -a \cdot X_t - b_t \cdot Y_t - c \cdot Z_t + b_t \cdot W_t$$

Subject to:

$$X_{t-1} + Y_t - W_t - X_t = 0 \qquad t = 1, 2, \ldots, n$$
$$X_t + Z_t = A \qquad t = 1, 2, \ldots, n$$

The initial stock, X_0, must be known in advance. The formulation of other problems, such as *production planning* and *paper trim* are available in linear programming textbooks.

LEONTIEF MODEL

In his famous book, *The Structure of American Economy* (Oxford University Press), Wassily W. Leontief developed the input-output model of the macro-economy. The Leontief model serves as a convenient summary of the economy broken down into its sectors. It sheds light on interindustry relations and it provides a tool for forecasting the future demand for inputs such as electricity, water, and so forth. The main advantage of the Leontief model is its simplicity. It is so simple that it lends itself easily to empirical work. The main drawback of the Leontief model is its basic underlying assumption of fixed proportions between inputs and outputs. If a crude assumption of fixed proportions cannot be substantiated, then the predictive ability of Leontief's model is in doubt.

Consider an economy with m sectors. Let x_j stand for the total output of sector j. The flow of output from sector i to sector j is written as x_{ij}, where $i = 1, 2, \ldots, m$ and $j = 1, 2, \ldots, m$. In fact, x_{ij} is an output when it leaves sector i and it becomes an input reaching sector j. The various sectors also use primary factors of production such as imports, governmental services (in the form of net indirect taxes), and labor services measured in wages.

In equilibrium each sector must satisfy the final demand for its product as well as demands of other sectors, that is,

$$x_i = x_{i1} + x_{i2} + \ldots + x_{im} + y_i \qquad i = 1, 2, \ldots, m$$

where y_i denotes the final demand of good X_i by consumers.

We may write it as

$$x_i - x_{i1} - x_{i2} - \ldots - x_{im} = y_i \qquad i = 1, 2, \ldots, m$$

Let us define the input-output coefficient as

$$a_{ij} = \frac{x_{ij}}{x_j}$$

Then, $x_{ij} = a_{ij} x_j$ and the Leontief system becomes

$$x_i - a_{i1} \cdot x_1 - a_{i2} \cdot x_2 - \ldots - a_{im} \cdot x_m = y_i \qquad i = 1, 2, \ldots, m$$

Given the estimates of a_{ij}, $i = 1, 2, \ldots, m$, $j = 1, 2, \ldots, m$, and given the forecast of future y_i, $i = 1, 2, \ldots, m$, the Leontief model becomes a system of m linear equations with m unknowns. Solving for the unknowns x_j, $j = 1, 2, \ldots, m$, we obtain the forecast of the future demand for the m products. Given the primary input-output coefficients, such as the labor-output coefficient, one can forecast the future demand for labor by multiplying these coefficients by the corresponding levels of output.

NONLINEAR PROGRAMMING

Linear programming excludes the case of imperfect markets. To assume that prices of inputs and outputs are unaffected by the behavior of the firm is to assume perfect competition. To give a single example, the profit function in Fig. 18-2 was $\pi = 15X + 20Y$. But, suppose the firm sells output X in a perfect market, and output Y in an imperfect market, such that the profit of Y is a declining function of Y as follows:

Profit per unit of $Y = 40 - 0.5Y$

which means that the profit of Y decreases by \$0.5 per each additional unit of Y sold.

The profit function of the firm becomes

$$\pi = 15X + (40 - 0.5Y) \cdot Y \qquad \text{or} \qquad \pi = 15X + 40Y - 0.5Y^2$$

The isoprofits of this profit function are nonlinear and methods other than the simplex procedure must be employed in order to locate the optimal point.

If the process of production is governed by fixed proportions, constant returns to scale and independence (between activities), the constraints remain linear. But if the firm sells at least one of its outputs in a monopolistic market, then the isoprofit curves are nonlinear. This situation is illustrated in Fig. 18-6a. The highest isoprofit curve contain-

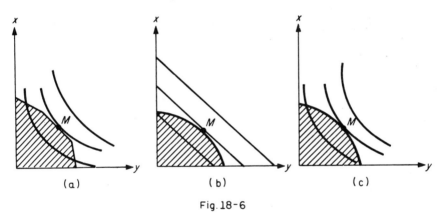

Fig. 18-6

ing at least one feasible point is tangent to the frontier of the feasible region at point M. Notice that unlike in the linear case, the point of tangency is not necessarily a corner. Only by accident could a corner become a tangency point.

A firm may be selling its outputs in a perfect market as well as buying its variable inputs in a perfect market. Thus, its isoprofit curves are linear. But if the process of production is governed by decreasing returns to scale and/or dependence (between activities), then the constraints are nonlinear. This situation is depicted by Fig. 18-6b. Here the highest isoprofit line is tangent to the nonlinear frontier of the feasible region at point M.

Finally, the case in which both the constraints and the objective function are nonlinear is depicted in Fig. 18-6c.

In the above three cases the optimal solution has been found on the frontier of the feasible region. But once we relax the assumption that the objective function is linear this must not be the case. In Fig. 18-7 the

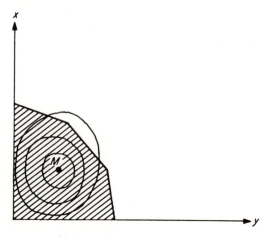

Fig. 18-7

profit function generates closed isoprofit curves that lie inside each other. The peak of the hill-shaped function is point M. This point lies inside the feasible region.

Unlike linear programming in which the simplex method prevails, in the field of nonlinear programming there are various methods of reaching the optimal solution, among which the family of the *gradient methods* is the one most commonly used. Most of the real problems of nonlinear programming fall into the class illustrated by Fig. 18-6a and Fig. 18-7.

PROBLEMS

18-1. At point G in Fig. 18-2, the firm produces ———— units of X and ———— units of Y.

18-2. By investigating the marginal rates of substitution between X and Y along the lines CC, BB, and AA in Fig. 18-1, show that it pays the entrepreneur to move from E to F and from F to G, but it does not pay to continue moving from G to H.

18-3. Show that at point G in Fig. 18-2 only 14 units of C are employed by the firm.

18-4. Calculate the shadow price of input B in Fig. 18-2.

18-5. What is the shadow price of input C in Fig. 18-2?

18-6. Draw the supply curve of X (Fig. 18-3) under the assumption that prices of variable factors of production fall, leading to a reduction in the average variable cost of X from \$15 to \$5.

18-7. Consider Fig. 18-5. At what price of Y would the farmer be indifferent between points L and M?

18-8. Calculate the shadow prices of nutrients B and C in Fig. 18-5.

Answers

CHAPTER 1

1-1. Plus 5 percent. **1-2.** -30 percent. **1-3.** TR will decline by about 13 percent. **1-4.** No change. **1-5.** TR will increase by 3 percent. **1-7.** Bad. **1-8.** Farmers should be indifferent under the assumption that the cost is the same. **1-9.** Yes. By -10 units.

CHAPTER 2

2-1. (a) 2 utils. (b) No. (2) HINT: If the marginal utility is a constant, then the marginal gain from transferring a dollar from C to A is a constant too. **2-4.** Show that there is a gain of 5 utils from transferring the last dollar in a certain direction! **2-5.** HINT: Assume that there is relationship between the price of the "prestige commodity" and its MU.

CHAPTER 3

3-1. $-\frac{1}{4}$. **3-2.** -2 percent. **3-3.** 30 percent. **3-4.** Superior or "Giffen." **3-5.** HINT: Try to rationalize it by assuming first of all that meat is inferior and then by assuming that meat is superior. **3-6.** $1\frac{3}{4}$ percent. **3-10.** 3.

CHAPTER 4

4-1. F. **4-2.** F. **4-3.** T. **4-4.** U. **4-5.** T. **4-6.** HINT: In England cream is added to tea as well as to coffee. **4-7.** HINT: Assume that the decline in the price is not due to the fact that compact cars are now fashionable!

CHAPTER 5

5-1. (a) 0.95. (b) 0.24. (c) 0.48. (d) 0.24. (g) Production will double. **5-2.** 0.50.

CHAPTER 6

6-1. (a) and (b) HINT: Review the definition of a competitive firm. (c) HINT: How will the AC curve shift? (d) HINT: How will the MC curve shift? **6-2.** F. **6-3.** T. **6-4.** F. **6-5.** T. **6-6.** F. Compare a cost of $2 with $0.74. **6-7.** T. Compare a cost of $0 with $0.74.

CHAPTER 7

7-1. (b) HINT: MC is functionally related to the price of labor and MPP of labor. **7-2.** 2 units. **7-3.** HINT: Assume that the producers of whatnots consider taxes as costs. **7-4.** (a) \$10. (b) Expand. (c) \$12. **7-5.** $MC = 0.833 - 1.666\ Q$.

CHAPTER 8

8-1. 30 percent. **8-2.** $\epsilon = 2$. **8-3.** About 2 cents. **8-4.** Using $Q_0 = 100$ and $P_0 = 10$ for estimating ΔQ, we obtain $\Delta Q = 20$ units. The additional producer's surplus is roughly \$110. The additional total variable cost is \$210. **8-5.** T. **8-6.** F. **8-7.** T. **8-8.** HINT: Focus on the marginal firms.

CHAPTER 9

9-1. Higher price and lower quantity of product A. **9-2.** Price of tea rises, and more tea is consumed. **9-3.** Ignore income effect. Less tea will be consumed at a lower price. **9-4.** The price of corn fell. **9-5.** Ignoring the income effect, cabs will supply less services at a lower price. **9-6.** More domestic oil will be supplied at a higher price. **9-7.** Prices will be higher, quantities smaller. **9-8.** More gasoline will be bought at a higher price.

CHAPTER 10

10-1. 10,000. **10-3.** F. **10-4.** F. **10-5.** U. **10-6.** T. **10-7.** U. **10-8.** $P_0 = 20$, $Q_0 = 375$. $P_1 = 22$, $Q_1 = 355$. Incidence = 71.4%. Government revenue = 944.

CHAPTER 11

11-2. \$880. **11-3.** (a) About 100,000 bushels. (b) \$100,000. **11-4.** The cost per year is \$200,000. **11-5.** HINT: Analyze the supply shift. **11-6.** HINT: Analyze the domestic market for agricultural output and the effect of cheap food on the income of farmers in underdeveloped countries.

CHAPTER 12

12-1. T. **12-2.** T. **12-3.** T. **12-4.** F. **12-5.** F. **12-6.** T. **12-7.** T. **12-9.** $P_1 = 6$, $P_2 = 3.75$, and $P_3 = 4$. **12-12.** 4.5%.

CHAPTER 13

13-3. (a) 3, 2, 3. (b) 4, 3, 0.

CHAPTER 14

14-1. T. **14-2.** F. **14-3.** F. **14-4.** T. **14-5.** T. **14-6.** F. **14-7.** T. **14-8.** U.

CHAPTER 15

15-1. It is not true. **15-2.** HINT: Shift the demand curve of labor. **15-3.** and **15-4.** HINT: What are the nonpecuniary advantages involved? **15-6.** Supply elasticity of services rendered by teachers. **15-8.** Farm wages will rise.

CHAPTER 16

16-1. 5 years. **16-2.** Once. **16-5.** a) \$690. **16-6.** 1.093. **16-7.** B is by \$350 cheaper per year.

CHAPTER 18

18-1. 2 units of X and 6 units of Y. **18-4.** \$10. **18-5.** \$0. **18-7.** \$4. **18-8.** \$3, \$0.

Review Problems

1. A and B are the only two commodities in my budget. Currently, I consume 20 units of A and 30 units of B per unit of time. The price of A is $4 apiece, and the price of B is $6 apiece. My income is ———. If the price of B rises from $6 to $8, my apparent real income will change by $\pm$ $———. Why?

2. Your income has decreased 10 percent and your income elasticity with respect to milk is -2. By how much will you increase or decrease the consumption of milk? Assume that the price of milk does not change.

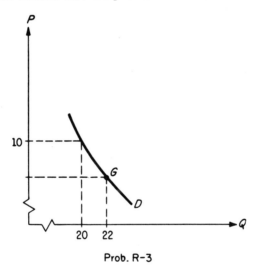

Prob. R-3

3. Price elasticity is $-\frac{1}{2}$. Estimate total revenue at point G on the accompanying graph. Use the original price and original quantity in your estimate.

4. Your income has increased 20 percent. Your income elasticity with respect to potatoes is $=\frac{1}{4}$. By how much will you increase or decrease the consumption of potatoes? Assume that the price of potatoes does not change.

5. The price of rice in country A rises due to bad crops of rice. Analyze the market for wheat. Assume that (a) wheat and rice are substitutes for each other, (b) wheat is inferior, and (c) the income effect dominates the substitution effect.

Draw two diagrams. Is assumption (c) necessary?

6. The Italian Fiat is sold at a lower price outside Italy. Explain by drawing the right diagrams.

7. How will the price of land change as a result of a subsidy on fertilizers? Assume that the expansion effect dominates, and the supply of land at the industry level is vertical. Also assume that land and fertilizer are substitutes for each other.

8. Assume a perfectly competitive industry. The industry is confronted with flat supply curves of inputs. The price elasticity of the final output is $-\frac{1}{4}$. The elasticity of substitution between factors A and B (the only two inputs) is 1.25. By employing the proper relations, indicate the effects of a 5 percent decline in the price of A on the quantity demanded for A and on the demand for B. The share of factor A is 40 percent of the total cost. The process of production is governed by constant returns to scale.

9. You are the producer of a certain product A which is sold in a perfect market. Currently you produce 100 units per month. If you were to produce 107 units, the extra costs would be labor $30, raw materials $20, electricity $7, and other items $13. Should you increase production if product A sells for $12 apiece? Why?

10. In country A, electricity is monopolized. Households pay a higher price per kilowatthour than factories. Explain by drawing the right diagram.

11. Assume that the world demand elasticity for tin is -3, and Bolivia produces $\frac{1}{4}$ of the world's tin. What is the highest (algebraic) value of the elasticity of demand for Bolivia's tin? A diagram and a formula will help.

12. $Q = (A \cdot B)/2$ is a production function. Estimate MPP_b, when A $= 4$ units, $B = 5$ units. (HINT: Increase B by one unit!)

13. How will the demand curve for labor (at the industry level) change as a result of a decline in the price of machinery? Assume that the substitution effect dominates the expansion effect, and machinery and labor are substitutes for each other.

14. How will the price of tea change as a result of a decline in the price of coffee? Assume that tea and coffee are substitutes for each other and tea is an inferior commodity.

15. Under what conditions will a prestige commodity have a positively sloped demand curve?

16. Mr. Smith uses A and B as substitutes. Originally, $MU_a = 30$ utils, $MU_b = 21$ utils, $P_a = \$10$, and $P_b = \$7$. If the price of A decreases 40 percent, what will Mr. Smith do? (Supplement your answer numerically.)

17. Again, Mr. Smith uses A and B as substitutes. Originally, $MU_a = 25$ utils, $MU_b = 30$ utils, $P_a = \$5$, and $P_b = \$6$. If the price of A doubles, what will Mr. Smith do? (Supplement your answer numerically.)

18. If the government will impose a specific tax on oranges, the price of lemons will increase. Do you agree?

19. How will the price of butter change as a result of a decrease in the price of bread? Assume that bread and butter are complementary to each other and butter is superior.

20. How will the aggregate demand curve with respect to commodity A shift over one year as a result of 8 percent growth in national income? The population grows at a rate of 4 percent per annum. Income elasticity with respect to A is estimated at -1.

21. The test of internal rates of returns fails when (a) more than one project are considered and (b) the present value (V) and interest rate (i) are positively related. Explain by drawing the proper diagrams.

22. Is the following statement true? "The price of A will increase by 20 cents as a result of a 20 cent increase in the marginal cost of A."

23. The effect of imposing a fixed tax of $100 (per annum) on monopolist A would be to cut down his production. Do you agree?

24. Let A and B be substitutes for each other. A decline in the price of A must entail a decline in the price of B. Do you agree?

25. Over a period of time the demand curve has not shifted at all. Its price elasticity is $-\frac{1}{2}$. The vertical supply curve has shifted rightward 10 percent. By how much has total revenue declined?

26. Currently monopolist A produces 80 units per unit of time. If the information in the following tabulation is reliable, monopolist A should expand. Do you agree?

Production	Total Costs	Price
80	$58	$15.0
100	$68	$12.2

27. The marginal cost curve of a monopolist is also his supply curve. Do you agree?

28. "Farmers as a group should be opposed to technological improvements. But it always pays the individual farmer to use the best technology available." Evaluate. (Use demand and supply curves in your analysis.)

29. In country A, the wage rate of all workers was effectively raised by unions. Must this entail a rise in the rate of unemployment?

30. A consumer spends his entire income on two commodities, X and Y. His demand curve for X is inelastic. The price of X rises. Will he consume more or less units of Y?

31. A consumer spends his income of $260 on two commodities, X and Y. He currently buys 20 units of X and 30 units of Y. At this combination his marginal utilities are $MU_x = 20$ and $MU_y = 25$. The price of X is $4. Will the consumer increase his utility by raising his consumption of X?

32. The only commodities in the budget of a consumer are X and Y. The consumer receives a present of three units of X which he cannot sell in the market. (a) What will the shape of the new budget line be? (b) Under what conditions would his utility increase if he could sell the present in the market? (Apply indifference curve analysis.)

33. A monopolist buys factor A in three separate markets. The elasticities of the supply curves, respectively, are constants. Complete the accompanying table.

Market	Supply Elasticity	Price of Factor
1	½	$2
2	⅕	————
3	2	————

34. A factor of production is used by a monopsony and many small rivals. Consider the accompanying tables. What will be the price of the factor and the quantity of the factor used by the monopsony and the small rivals, respectively?

Price of the Factor	Supply of the Factor	Demand (for the factor) of Small Rivals
$10	15	7
9	14	8
8	13	9
7	12	10
6	11	11
5	10	12

Quantity of the Factor Used by the Monopsony	Marginal Value Product
3	$14
4	13
5	12
6	11
7	10
8	9

35. The only variable factor of production is A. Analyze the effect of a subsidy on the MC curve under the assumption that the subsidy is a specific amount given (a) per unit of output and (b) per unit of the variable factor.

36. Commodity X is produced by a monopoly. The monopoly is confronted with a negatively sloped demand curve at home and an infinitely elastic demand curve abroad. The two markets are separated and currently the domestic price of X is higher than its price abroad. The government decides to impose a (specific) tax per unit of output sold by the monopoly at home. Analyze the domestic and foreign markets before and after the tax. A diagram will help.

37. Commodity X is produced by a monopoly. Currently the domestic price of X is higher than its price abroad. The government decides to extend a subsidy per each unit of X exported. Analyze the domestic and foreign markets before and after the subsidy. Assume that the two markets are separate and there is no retaliation.

38. Do you agree with the following statement? "When the marginal physical product of factor A diminishes, the marginal physical product of factor B is always positive."

39. A certain firm produces and sells product X in a competitive market. Factor A which is bought in a competitive market is the only variable factor of production. It is given that the firm is in equilibrium, the price of A is $3, the price of X is $9, the firm uses 9 units of A in order to produce 3 units of X. Calculate the marginal physical product of A and the elasticity of production at the point of equilibrium.

40. Growers of vegetables in country A form a cartel. By using government power the cartel has organized in it all farmers who grow vegetables. Analyze the following alternative forms of marketing. (a) All members of the cartel agree to sell vegetables to the cartel at a low selling price set by the management of the cartel. The management sells the vegetables to wholesalers at a higher price. The profit of the cartel is divided among farmers. By drawing a diagram show what should the two prices be in order to maximize the profit of farmers. (b) The government agrees to absorb (and destroy) any surpluses at a guaranteed minimum price. The guaranteed minimum price is lower than the wholesale price in part (a). There is no limitation on production. (c) The same as (b) except that the government agrees to absorb only a limited quantity of vegetables at the guaranteed minimum price.

41. Commodity X is produced by a cartel. The government protects the cartel by administratively excluding imports of X. Assume that the cartel has no influence over the price of X in the world market. Analyze the effect of lifting the prohibition on imports of X under the assumption that (a) export of X exists and (b) export of X does not exist.

42. Around the point of intersection between supply and demand the slope of demand is -2, and the slope of supply is 3. What is the burden (in percent) of a specific tax which is borne by producers?

43. The share of the large firm in total production is $\frac{1}{10}$. The price elasticity of the market demand curve is -2, and the price elasticity of supply of all small firms is $\frac{1}{3}$. What is the (relative) difference between the market price and MC of the large firm? Assume that the large firm is in equilibrium.

44. Do you agree with the following statements. (a) The own-price elasticity of demand for a commodity must always equal or exceed, in absolute value, the marginal propensity to consume of that commodity. (b) If the United States exports one tenth of its coal, the elasticity of supply of domestic coal being unity, the elasticity of supply of U.S. coal exports must be at least 10. (c) Commodity X is sold in a competitive market. The own-price elasticity of demand for factor A derived from industry X must be less than the price elasticity of the aggregate demand for X, provided that factors of production are used in fixed proportions. Assume constant returns to scale. (d) The own-price elasticity of demand for factor A derived from industry X will be more elastic, the larger the share of factor A in the total costs of the industry in question. Assume constant returns to scale. (e) The price elasticity of demand for a good will be higher, when the income elasticity of demand for that good is higher. (f) Food and "all other commodities" cannot be complements. (g) A falling marginal cost curve implies that marginal cost is below average cost.

45. A 10 percent tax on coffee leads to a 6 percent increase in the quantity of tea consumed. What would be the effect of a 10 percent tax on tea on the consumption of coffee? Ignore income effects and assume that consumers spend twice as much money on coffee as they do on tea.

46. As soon as the cartel was formed, all the members of the cartel agreed to discontinue the production of the largest firm in the cartel. Can you rationalize it?

47. "Abolishing the corporation income tax will lead to a movement of capital from the noncorporate industries to the corporate industries." Evaluate.

48. "The average cost curve of the leading firm (that shares 20 percent of the market for X) is *constant* at $2. All other small firms are competitive and their supply curves are positively sloped. The price set by the leading firm cannot exceed $2.50 if the elasticity of the demand for X is 1." Do you agree?

49. Will a premium pay for overtime work reduce the amount of labor supplied? Assume that the supply curve of labor is backward bending.

50. A firm in perfect competition mines coal. The firm uses a digging machine that runs on part of the coal that is mined. What is the numerical value of the marginal physical product of the input coal?

Mathematical Appendix

Let $Q = f(P)$ be a demand function. Price elasticity was defined as

$$\eta = \frac{\Delta Q/Q}{\Delta P/P} \tag{1}$$

By rearranging it we obtain

$$\eta = \frac{\Delta Q \cdot P}{\Delta P \cdot Q} \tag{2}$$

If the demand function is differentiable, we can write

$$\lim_{\Delta P \to 0} \frac{\Delta Q}{\Delta P} = \frac{dQ}{dP} \tag{3}$$

Thus price elasticity is

$$\eta = \frac{dQ \cdot P}{dP \cdot Q} \tag{4}$$

You will recall that under normal conditions the demand curve is negatively sloped. As indicated in Eq. 4, this stems from the fact that the slope of the curve dQ/dP is negative. Let $X = \log P$ and $Y = \log Q$, then $P = e^x$.

$$\frac{d(\log Q)}{d(\log P)} = \frac{dY}{dX} = \frac{dY}{dQ} \cdot \frac{dQ}{dP} \cdot \frac{dP}{dX} = \frac{1}{Q} \cdot \frac{dQ}{dP} \cdot e^x = \frac{dQ}{dP} \cdot \frac{P}{Q} \tag{5}$$

Making use of Eqs. 4 and 5 we obtain

$$\eta = \frac{d(\log Q)}{d(\log P)} \tag{6}$$

The following is a demand function with constant elasticity:

$$Q = K \cdot P^\eta \qquad (\eta = \text{constant}) \tag{7}$$

355

Taking the logarithms of Eq. 7 gives

$$\log Q = \log K + \eta \log P \tag{8}$$

Differentiating Eq. 8 gives

$$\frac{d\ (\log Q)}{d\ (\log P)} = \eta \tag{9}$$

This proves that η in Eq. 7 is the price elasticity.

THE AGGREGATE DEMAND CURVE

Let the price be held at P_0. At that price, the aggregate quantity demanded is Q. Let Q_1 be the quantity demanded by the first consumer, Q_2 the quantity demanded by the second consumer, and so on, all at P_0. Then,

$$Q = Q_1 + Q_2 + \cdots + Q_n \tag{10}$$

Differentiating with respect to P gives

$$\frac{dQ}{dP} = \frac{d(Q_1 + Q_2 + \cdots + Q_n)}{dP}$$

and so

$$\eta = \frac{P_0}{Q} \cdot \frac{dQ}{dP} = \frac{P_0}{Q} \cdot \frac{d(Q_1 + Q_2 + \cdots + Q_n)}{dP}$$

$$= \frac{P_0}{Q} \cdot \left(\frac{dQ_1}{dP} + \frac{dQ_2}{dP} + \cdots + \frac{dQ_n}{dP} \right)$$

$$= \frac{Q_1}{Q} \cdot \frac{P_0 \cdot dQ_1}{Q_1 \cdot dP} + \frac{Q_2}{Q} \cdot \frac{P_0 \cdot dQ_2}{Q_2 \cdot dP} + \cdots + \frac{Q_n}{Q} \cdot \frac{P_0 \cdot dQ_n}{Q_n \cdot dP}$$

$$= K_1 \cdot \eta_1 + K_2 \cdot \eta_2 + \cdots + K_n \cdot \eta_n \tag{11}$$

where K_1 is the relative share of the first consumer, η_1 is the price elasticity of the demand curve of the first consumer, and so on. Equation 11 holds only if the demand curves are differentiable.

You will find it instructive to show that if the demand curve is linear, say $Q = a \cdot P + b$ (a is negative) then

$$\eta = \frac{a \cdot P}{a \cdot P + b}$$

Accordingly, at the point of intersection with the price axis $\lim \eta = -\infty$; and at the point of intersection with the quantity axis, $\eta = 0$.

THE RELATIONSHIP BETWEEN η AND MR

Let total revenue be denoted by R. You will recall that marginal revenue is the change in total revenue per one unit change in the quantity demanded. This is denoted by $\Delta R/\Delta Q$. If total revenue is a differentiable function of the quantity demanded, we can write

$$\lim \frac{\Delta R}{\Delta Q} = \frac{dR}{dQ} \text{ when } \Delta Q \longrightarrow 0 \tag{12}$$

where $R = P \cdot Q$ is the function which relates total revenue to the quantity demanded. By differentiating it we obtain

$$\frac{dR}{dQ} = \frac{d(P \cdot Q)}{dQ} = P + Q\frac{dP}{dQ} = P \cdot \left(1 + \frac{Q \cdot dP}{P \cdot dQ}\right) = P\left(1 + \frac{1}{\eta}\right) \tag{13}$$

We made use of Eq. 13 in Chapter 1, where we established rules relating to the functional relationships between price elasticity and total revenue when moving along a demand curve. You will recall also that Eq. 13 was useful in proving certain theorems concerning the behavior of monopolies.

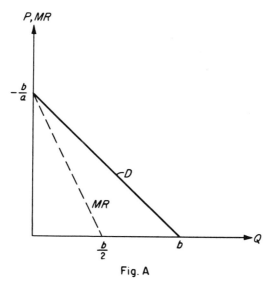

Fig. A

Consider a linear demand curve (Fig. A) whose function is $Q = aP + b$, where a is negative. This demand curve intersects with the quantity axis at $Q = b$ and with the price axis at $P = -b/a$. Total revenue is obtained by multiplying the quantity demanded by the price, that is,

$$R = Q \cdot P = aP^2 + bP \tag{14}$$

Substituting $(Q - b)/a$ for P in Eq. 14 gives

$$R = a\frac{(Q - b)^2}{a^2} + b\frac{Q - b}{a} = \frac{(Q - b)^2 + b(Q - b)}{a}$$

$$= \frac{(Q - b) \cdot Q}{a} = \frac{Q^2}{a} - \frac{b}{a}Q \qquad (15)$$

Differentiating Eq. 15 with respect to Q gives

$$MR = \frac{dR}{dQ} = \frac{2}{a}Q - \frac{b}{a} \qquad (16)$$

Equation 16 indicates that MR is linear too. For $Q = 0$, $MR = -b/a$, and for $MR = 0$, $Q = b/2$. In other words, the demand curve and the MR curve cut the vertical axis at the same point; the demand curve cuts the horizontal axis at $Q = b$ and the MR curve cuts the horizontal axis at the midpoint between $Q = b$ and $Q = 0$. This is illustrated in Fig. A.

NOTES TO CHAPTERS 3 AND 4

THE NOTATIONS OF ELASTICITIES

Consider a consumer who has only three commodities in his budget, X, Y, and Z. Let X, Y, and Z stand also for the quantities demanded for these commodities respectively. If I is nominal income, then

$$X = F(P_x, P_y, P_z, I) \qquad (17)$$

is the demand curve for X.

Note that Eq. 17 is homogeneous of degree zero in P_x, P_y, P_z, and I. That is, if P_x, P_y, P_z, and I are multiplied by K, X will not change $(X_1 = K^0 X_0 = 1 \cdot X_0 = X_0)$. To put it in other words, the quantity demanded for X does not change if nominal income and all prices are increased proportionately.

Let us assume that all partial derivatives of the first order exist. Then price elasticity, cross elasticity, and income elasticity are defined as

$$\text{Price elasticity} = \eta = \frac{\partial X}{\partial P_x} \cdot \frac{P_x}{X} \left[= \frac{\partial(\log X)}{\partial(\log P_x)} \right] \qquad (18)$$

$$\text{Cross elasticity} = \eta_{\overline{XP}_y} = \frac{\partial X}{\partial P_y} \cdot \frac{P_y}{X} \left[= \frac{\partial(\log X)}{\partial(\log P_y)} \right] \qquad (19)$$

$$\text{Income elasticity} = \eta_{XI} = \frac{\partial X}{\partial I} \cdot \frac{I}{X} \left[= \frac{\partial(\log X)}{\partial(\log I)} \right] \qquad (20)$$

If elasticities are assumed to be constants, then the demand curve becomes

$$X = K \cdot P_x{}^\eta \cdot P_y{}^{\eta XP_y} \cdot P_z{}^{\eta XP_z} \cdot I^{\eta XI} \tag{21}$$

NOTES TO CHAPTERS 2, 3, AND 4

THE THEORY OF THE CONSUMER

An Important Theorem. We recall from calculus that in order for the quadratic form

$$d^2u = \sum_{r=1}^{r=n} \sum_{s=1}^{s=n} u_{rs} dX_r dX_s$$

subject to the linear restriction

$$du = \sum_{r=1}^{r=n} u_r dX_r = 0$$

to be negative definite, the determinants

$$\begin{vmatrix} 0 & u_1 \\ u_1 & u_{11} \end{vmatrix} \quad \begin{vmatrix} 0 & u_1 & u_2 \\ u_1 & u_{11} & u_{12} \\ u_2 & u_{21} & u_{22} \end{vmatrix} \quad \cdots \quad \left. \begin{vmatrix} 0 & u_1 & u_2 & u_n \\ u_1 & u_{11} & u_{12} & u_{1n} \\ u_2 & u_{21} & u_{22} & u_{2n} \\ & \vdots & & \\ u_n & u_{n1} & u_{n2} & u_{nn} \end{vmatrix} \right\} \tag{22}$$

must be alternatively negative and positive. In what follows, the last determinant will be denoted by U, the cofactor of u_r by U_r, and the cofactor of u_{rs} by U_{rs}.

NECESSARY CONDITIONS FOR EQUILIBRIUM

Consider a consumer whose income per unit of time amounts to M dollars. He spends his entire income on commodities $X_1, X_2, \ldots, X_n$. By agreement X_r will denote both the rth commodity and the quantity demanded for that commodity and so on. The consumer is confronted with the prices P_1 for X_1, P_2 for X_2, and so on. He has no influence over these prices whatsoever.

Assume that the utility function of the consumer is

$$U = u(X_1, X_2, \ldots, X_n) \tag{23}$$

In equilibrium, Eq. 23 is maximized subject to the budget constraint

$$\sum_{r=1}^{r=n} P_r X_r = M$$

Let λ be the Lagrange multiplier; then we have to maximize

$$U + \lambda \cdot \left(M - \sum_{r=1}^{r=n} P_r X_r \right)$$

We assume that $u_r = \partial U / \partial X_r$, $r = 1, 2, \ldots, n$, exist. Differentiating it and equating to zero, plus the budget constraint, gives

$$\left. \begin{aligned} \sum_{r=1}^{r=n} P_r X_r &= M \\[2mm] -\lambda P_1 + u_1 &= 0 \\ -\lambda P_2 + u_2 &= 0 \\ &\vdots \\ -\lambda P_n + u_n &= 0 \end{aligned} \right\} \tag{24}$$

Note that u_r stands for the marginal utility of commodity X_r etc. It is easy to derive from Eq. 24 the set of equations

$$\frac{u_1}{P_1} = \frac{u_2}{P_2} = \cdots = \frac{u_n}{P_n} = \lambda \tag{25}$$

The marginal utility derived from spending the last dollar on commodity X_r is u_r / P_r and so on. Accordingly λ is the marginal utility of the last dollar spent or, as it is sometimes called, the marginal utility of money.

Note finally that Eq. 24 is a set of $n + 1$ equations. These equations determine the value of $n + 1$ unknowns; these are $X_1, X_2, \ldots, X_n$, and λ.

SUFFICIENT CONDITIONS FOR EQUILIBRIUM

Equation 24 does not tell us whether the consumer has really reached a point of maximum utility. In fact, the consumer may have minimized his utility, or he may have reached a saddle point. Making use of Eq. 24 the constraining $M - \sum_{r=1}^{r=n} P_r X_r = 0$ becomes

$$\lambda \cdot M - \sum_{r=1}^{r=n} u_r \cdot X_r = 0$$

Accordingly the linear side condition becomes

$$du = \sum_{r=1}^{r=n} u_r dX_r = 0$$

Equation 24 will indicate maximum utility only if

$$d^2u = \sum_{r=1}^{r=n} \sum_{s=1}^{s=n} u_{rs}\, dX_r\, dX_s$$

subject to the linear side condition

$$du = \sum_{r=1}^{r=n} u_r\, dX_r = 0$$

is negative definite. The conditions for it to be negative definite are that the determinants in Eq. 22 be alternatively negative and positive.

The reader should note that another way of approaching this problem would be to form the functions

$$Z = U + \lambda\left(M - \sum_{r=1}^{r=n} P_r X_r\right)$$

$$h = M - \sum_{r=1}^{r=n} P_r X_r$$

and form the determinants

$$\begin{vmatrix} Z_{11} & h_1 \\ h_1 & 0 \end{vmatrix} \quad \begin{vmatrix} Z_{11} & Z_{12} & h_1 \\ Z_{21} & Z_{22} & h_2 \\ h_1 & h_2 & 0 \end{vmatrix} \quad \cdots \quad \begin{vmatrix} Z_{11} & Z_{12}\ldots Z_{1n} & h_1 \\ Z_{21} & Z_{22}\ldots Z_{2n} & h_2 \\ \vdots & & \\ Z_{n1} & Z_{n2}\ldots Z_{nn} & h_n \\ h_1 & h_2\ \ldots h_n & 0 \end{vmatrix}$$

where

$$Z_{ij} = \frac{\partial Z^2}{\partial X_i\, \partial X_j}$$

and

$$h_i = \frac{\partial h}{\partial X_i}$$

The last determinant in the row is known as the bordered Hessian and the rest of the determinants are known as the bordered principal minors of the Hessian. The above determinants should be alternatively negative and positive for Z to be maximized, and negative for Z to be minimized.

A Change in Income. In what follows we shall keep all prices unchanged and differentiate Eq. 24 with respect to income M. This gives

$$P_1 \frac{\partial X_1}{\partial M} + P_2 \cdot \frac{\partial X_2}{\partial M} + \cdots + P_n \cdot \frac{\partial X_n}{\partial M} = 1$$

$$-P_1 \cdot \frac{\partial \lambda}{\partial M} + u_{11} \cdot \frac{\partial X_1}{\partial M} + u_{12} \cdot \frac{\partial X_2}{\partial M} + \cdots + u_{1n} \cdot \frac{\partial X_n}{\partial M} = 0 \qquad (26)$$

$$\vdots$$

$$-P_n \cdot \frac{\partial \lambda}{\partial M} + u_{n1} \cdot \frac{\partial X_1}{\partial M} + u_{n2} \cdot \frac{\partial X_2}{\partial M} + \cdots + u_{nn} \cdot \frac{\partial X_n}{\partial M} = 0$$

where

$$u_{rs} = \frac{\partial^2 u}{\partial X_r \cdot \partial X_s}$$

From Eq. 24 we know that $P_r = u_r/\lambda$. Thus, u_r/λ may be substituted for P_r, and Eq. 26 becomes

$$u_1 \cdot \frac{\partial X_1}{\partial M} + u_2 \cdot \frac{\partial X_2}{\partial M} + \cdots + u_n \cdot \frac{\partial X_n}{\partial M} = \lambda$$

$$u_1 \cdot \left(-\frac{1 \cdot \partial \lambda}{\lambda \cdot \partial M} \right) + u_{11} \cdot \frac{\partial X_1}{\partial M} + u_{12} \cdot \frac{\partial X_2}{\partial M} + \cdots + u_{1n} \cdot \frac{\partial X_n}{\partial M} = 0 \qquad (27)$$

$$\vdots$$

$$u_n \cdot \left(-\frac{1 \cdot \partial \lambda}{\lambda \cdot \partial M} \right) + u_{n1} \cdot \frac{\partial X_1}{\partial M} + u_{n2} \cdot \frac{\partial X_2}{\partial M} + \cdots + u_{nn} \cdot \frac{\partial X_n}{\partial M} = 0$$

Equation 27 is a set of $n + 1$ equations with $n + 1$ unknowns. The unknowns are $\partial X_r/\partial M$, $r = 1, 2, \ldots, n$, and $(-1/\lambda) \cdot (\partial \lambda/\partial M)$. Solving for $\partial X_r/\partial M$ by Cramer's rule gives

$$\frac{\partial X_r}{\partial M} = \frac{\begin{vmatrix} 0 & u_1 \cdots u_{r-1} & \lambda & u_{r+1} & \cdots u_n \\ u_1 & u_{11} \cdots u_{1(r-1)} & 0 & u_{1(r+1)} \cdots u_{1n} \\ \vdots \\ u_n & u_{n1} \cdots u_{n(r-1)} & 0 & u_{n(r+1)} \cdots u_{nn} \\ 0 & u_1 & \cdots & \cdots & \cdots u_n \\ u_1 & u_{11} & \cdots & \cdots & \cdots u_{1n} \\ \vdots \\ u_n & u_{n1} & \cdots & \cdots & \cdots u_{nn} \end{vmatrix}}{} = \frac{\lambda U_r}{U} \qquad (28)$$

where U_r is the cofactor of u_r. Since U_r may be either positive or negative, $\partial X_r/\partial M$ is either positive or negative.

Recall that income elasticity is obtained by multiplying $\partial X_r/\partial M$

by M/X_r which is positive. By definition, if $\partial X_r/\partial M$ is negative (and so income elasticity is also negative), X_r is an inferior commodity. If $\partial X_r/\partial M$ is positive (and so income elasticity is positive), X_r is a superior commodity.

A CHANGE IN PRICE

Let us keep income M and all prices but P_r unchanged. Differentiating Eq. 24 with respect to P_r gives

$$
\left.
\begin{aligned}
P_1\frac{\partial X_1}{\partial P_r}+P_2\frac{\partial X_2}{\partial P_r}+\cdots+P_s\frac{\partial X_s}{\partial P_r}+\cdots+P_n\frac{\partial X_n}{\partial P_r}&=-X_r\\[2mm]
-P_1\frac{\partial \lambda}{\partial P_r}+u_{11}\frac{\partial X_1}{\partial P_r}+u_{12}\frac{\partial X_2}{\partial P_r}+\cdots+u_{1s}\frac{\partial X_s}{\partial P_r}+\cdots+u_{1n}\frac{\partial X_n}{\partial P_r}&=0\\[2mm]
\vdots\qquad\qquad\qquad\qquad\qquad&\\[2mm]
-P_r\frac{\partial \lambda}{\partial P_r}+u_{r1}\frac{\partial X_1}{\partial P_r}+u_{r2}\frac{\partial X_2}{\partial P_r}+\cdots+u_{rs}\frac{\partial X_s}{\partial P_r}+\cdots+u_{rn}\frac{\partial X_n}{\partial P_r}&=\lambda\\[2mm]
\vdots\qquad\qquad\qquad\qquad\qquad&\\[2mm]
-P_n\frac{\partial \lambda}{\partial P_r}+u_{n1}\frac{\partial X_1}{\partial P_r}+u_{n2}\frac{\partial X_2}{\partial P_r}+\cdots+u_{ns}\frac{\partial X_s}{\partial P_r}+\cdots+u_{nn}\frac{\partial X_n}{\partial P_r}&=0
\end{aligned}
\right\} \quad (29)
$$

Substituting u_r/λ for $P_r, r = 1, 2, \ldots, n$, Eq. 29 gives

$$
\left.
\begin{aligned}
u_1\frac{\partial X_1}{\partial P_r}+u_2\frac{\partial X_2}{\partial P_r}+\cdots+u_s\frac{\partial X_s}{\partial P_r}+\cdots+u_n\frac{\partial X_n}{\partial P_r}&=-\lambda X_r\\[2mm]
u_1\left(-\frac{1}{\lambda}\frac{\partial \lambda}{\partial P_r}\right)+u_{11}\frac{\partial X_1}{\partial P_r}+u_{12}\frac{\partial X_2}{\partial P_r}+\cdots+u_{1s}\frac{\partial X_s}{\partial P_r}+\cdots+u_{1n}\frac{\partial X_n}{\partial P_r}&=0\\[2mm]
\vdots\qquad\qquad\qquad\qquad\qquad&\\[2mm]
u_r\left(-\frac{1}{\lambda}\frac{\partial \lambda}{\partial P_r}\right)+u_{r1}\frac{\partial X_1}{\partial P_r}+u_{r2}\frac{\partial X_2}{\partial P_r}+\cdots+u_{rs}\frac{\partial X_s}{\partial P_r}+\cdots+u_{rn}\frac{\partial X_n}{\partial P_r}&=\lambda\\[2mm]
\vdots\qquad\qquad\qquad\qquad\qquad&\\[2mm]
u_n\left(-\frac{1}{\lambda}\frac{\partial \lambda}{\partial P_r}\right)+u_{n1}\frac{\partial X_1}{\partial P_r}+u_{n2}\frac{\partial X_2}{\partial P_r}+\cdots+u_{ns}\frac{\partial X_s}{\partial P_r}+\cdots+u_{nn}\frac{\partial X_n}{\partial P_r}&=0
\end{aligned}
\right\} \quad (30)
$$

By Cramer's rule,

$$\frac{\partial X_s}{\partial P_r} = \frac{\begin{vmatrix} 0 & u_1 & u_2 & \cdots u_{s-1} & -X_r\lambda & u_{s+1} & \cdots u_n \\ u_1 & u_{11} & u_{12} & \cdots u_{1(s-1)} & 0 & u_{1(s+1)} & \cdots u_{1n} \\ \vdots & & & & & & \\ u_r & u_{r1} & u_{r2} & \cdots u_{r(s-1)} & \lambda & u_{r(s+1)} & \cdots u_{rn} \\ \vdots & & & & & & \\ u_n & u_{n1} & u_{n2} & \cdots u_{n(s-1)} & 0 & u_{n(s+1)} & \cdots u_{nn} \end{vmatrix}}{\begin{vmatrix} 0 & u_1 & \cdots & & & & \cdots u_n \\ u_1 & u_{11} & \cdots & & & & \cdots u_{1n} \\ \vdots & & & & & & \\ u_r & u_{n1} & \cdots & & & & \cdots u_{nn} \end{vmatrix}}$$

$$= \lambda \frac{U_{rs}}{U} - X_r \cdot \frac{\lambda U_s}{U} \tag{31}$$

From Eq. 28 it is clear that $\lambda U_s/U = \partial X_s/\partial M$. Thus, Eq. 31 may be written as

$$\frac{\partial X_s}{\partial P_r} = \lambda \cdot \frac{U_{rs}}{U} - X_r \frac{\partial X_s}{\partial M} \tag{32}$$

where the term $\lambda \cdot (U_{rs}/U)$ is the *substitution effect* and $-X_r (\partial X_s/\partial M)$ is the *income effect*. Equation 32, which is the fundamental theorem of the demand theory, is due to Slutsky.

Let us concentrate on the substitution effect. You will recall that if the change in price is dP_r then the change in apparent real income is $-X_r dP_r$. The change in demand for X_s is approximated by the change in apparent real income times the marginal propensity to consume X_s, which is $-X_r dP_r \frac{\partial X_s}{\partial M}$. Multiplying Eq. 32 by dP_r and subtracting this expression gives

$$\overline{dX_s} = \lambda \frac{U_{rs}}{U} dP_r - X_r dP_r \frac{\partial X_s}{\partial M} + X_r dP_r \frac{\partial X_s}{\partial M} = \lambda \frac{U_{rs}}{U} dP_r \tag{33}$$

where all prices, but P_r, are held constant. Dividing Eq. 33 by dP_r gives

$$\frac{\overline{\partial X_s}}{\partial P_r} = \lambda \frac{U_{rs}}{U} \tag{34}$$

where $\overline{\partial X_s}/\partial P_r$ is the change in the demand for X_s per one dollar change in the price of X_r due to the substitution effect only. Sometimes Eq. 34 is called the compensated change in demand.

In summary we may write

$$\frac{\partial X_s}{\partial P_r} = \frac{\overline{\partial X_s}}{\partial P_r} - X_r \frac{\partial X_s}{\partial M} \qquad (35)$$

Multiplying Eq. 35 through by P_r/X_s gives

$$\eta_{SP_r} = \overline{\eta}_{SP_r} - \frac{P_r X_r \cdot \partial X_s}{X_s \cdot \partial M}$$

$$= \overline{\eta}_{SP_r} - \frac{P_r \cdot X_r \cdot M \cdot \partial X_s}{M \cdot X_s \cdot \partial M}$$

$$= \overline{\eta}_{SP_r} - K_r \cdot \eta_{MS} \qquad (36)$$

where $K_r = P_r X_r/M$, and η_{MS} is income elasticity with respect to commodity X_s. Equation 36 was proved by a different method in the Appendix to Chapter 4. Consider Eq. 32. The income effect may be either positive or negative (see Eq. 28). In other words, when P_r changes, the income effect may be either a rightward or a leftward shift in the demand curve.

Let us focus on the substitution effect. Since the determinant U is symmetrical, $U_{rs} = U_{sr}$. Accordingly,

$$\lambda \frac{U_{rs}}{U} = \lambda \frac{U_{sr}}{U}$$

Making use of Eq. 34, we obtain

$$\frac{\overline{\partial X_s}}{\partial P_r} = \frac{\overline{\partial X_r}}{\partial P_s} \qquad (37)$$

We have made some use of Eq. 37 in Chapter 4. Finally, if $\partial \overline{X}_s/\partial P_r$ is positive, X_r and X_s are substitutes for each other. If $\partial \overline{X}_s/\partial P_r$ is negative, X_r and X_s are complements to each other.

Let us now consider the case $r = s$. If $r = s$, Eq. 32 becomes

$$\frac{\partial X_r}{\partial P_r} = \lambda \frac{U_{rr}}{U} - X_r \frac{\partial X_r}{\partial M} \qquad (38)$$

where $\lambda(U_{rr}/U)$ is the change in X_r per one dollar change in P_r due to the substitution effect only. The expression $\lambda(U_{rr}/U)$ may be denoted by $\partial \overline{X}_r/\partial P_r$ (see Eq. 34).

Equation 25, plus the assumption that prices and marginal utilities are positive, implies that λ must be positive. Since the determinants in Eq. 22 are alternatively positive and negative, U_{rr}/U is negative. (HINT: Arrange the commodities so that $r = n$.) Saying that $\partial \overline{X}/\partial P_r$ is negative is equivalent to saying that the *compensated* effect of lowering the price of one commodity is to consume more of it, and vice versa.

Note that when $r = s$, Eq. 36 becomes

$$\eta_{rP_r} = \bar{\eta}_{rP_r} - K_r \cdot \eta_{Mr} \tag{39}$$

Since $\partial \bar{X}_r / \partial P_r$ is negative and prices and quantities are positive, $\bar{\eta}_{rP_r}$ is negative. Use of Eqs. 36 and 39 was made in the Appendices to Chapter 3 and Chapter 4.

Consider the determinant U in Eq. 22. If the rth row is replaced by the first row, the value of the new determinant is zero. We may write it as

$$0 \cdot U_r + u_1 \cdot U_{r1} + u_2 \cdot U_{r2} + \cdots + u_n \cdot U_{rn} = 0$$

Substituting $\lambda \cdot P_s$ for u_s, $s = 1, 2, \ldots, n$, we obtain

$$0 \cdot U_r + P_1 \cdot \lambda \cdot U_{r1} + P_2 \cdot \lambda \cdot U_{r2} + \cdots + P_n \cdot \lambda \cdot U_{rn} = 0$$

Dividing through by U and making use of Eq. 34 gives

$$P_1 \frac{\overline{\partial X_1}}{\partial P_r} + P_2 \frac{\overline{\partial X_2}}{\partial P_r} + \cdots + P_r \frac{\overline{\partial X_r}}{\partial P_r} + \cdots + P_n \frac{\overline{\partial X_n}}{\partial P_r} = 0 \tag{40}$$

If there are only two commodities in the budget of the consumer, say, X_1 and X_2, then

$$P_1 \frac{\overline{\partial X_1}}{\partial P_1} + P_2 \frac{\overline{\partial X_2}}{\partial P_1} = 0$$

Since $\overline{\partial X_1} / \partial P_1$ is negative and P_1 and P_2 are positive, $\partial X_2 / \partial P_1$ must be positive and X_1 and X_2 are substitutes for each other. Accordingly, in order to assume complementarity the consumer must have at least three commodities in his budget.

Note, finally, that the theory of the consumer was derived under the assumption that utility Eq. 23 is a function of only the respective quantities consumed. Prices of the commodities do not appear in the utility function. In the case of prestige commodities, prices as well as quantities should appear in the utility function, and accordingly a new theory is developed.

ORDINAL UTILITY

The first and second order conditions for equilibrium have been derived under the assumption that there is a specific function U. Let us now consider the case of ordinal utility. Ordinal utility was assumed when we derived the demand curve by means of rotating the budget line in an indifference map. To illustrate the difference between the two approaches consider Fig. B.

Point G in Fig. B represents the combination of X_{1a} units of X_1

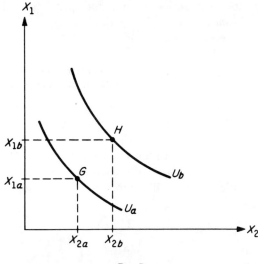

Fig B

and X_{2a} units of X_2. Let us denote it by (X_{1a}, X_{2a}). Point H represents a combination (X_{1b}, X_{2b}). If we assume that the utility function is known, then consumption of G yields u_a utils and the consumption of H yields u_b utils. The gain from moving from G to H is $u_b - u_a$ (where u_b is larger than u_a). It is clear, however, that the most the consumer can tell is that he prefers H to G, or in other words, he ranks H over G. If we assume that utility can be measured, then we are in the world of cardinal utility. If we restrict ourselves only to the possibility of ranking combinations of commodities, then we are in the world of ordinal utility.

The transformation from cardinal to ordinal utility is achieved by replacing u by any arbitrary function of itself, call it $f(u)$. The only restriction imposed on $f(u)$ is that it should rank combinations of commodities exactly as u does. That is if in Fig. B $u_b > u_a$, then $f(u_b)$ $> f(u_a)$, etc. (NOTE: Here u stands for utility and not for marginal utility!) Mathematically, this restriction is imposed by requiring that $f'(u) > 0$. (Why?)

Fortunately, the transformation from cardinal to ordinal utility does not invalidate the conclusions derived in the last sections. This will be proved in what follows. Differentiating $f(u)$ with respect to X_r gives

$$\frac{\partial}{\partial X_r} f(u) = f'(u) \cdot u_r \qquad (41)$$

Since $f(u)$ is arbitrary, $f'(u)$ is arbitrary too, and marginal utility cannot be determined. But the first order equilibrium conditions Eq. 25

are unchanged since the ratios are all multiplied by a common factor $f'(u)$ that cancels out.

Consider the second-order conditions

$$\frac{\partial^2}{\partial X_r \cdot \partial X_s} = f'(u) \cdot u_{rs} + f''(u) \cdot u_r u_s \tag{42}$$

Thus, the typical term in the determinants in Eq. 22 becomes $f'(u) \cdot u_{rs} + f''(u) \cdot u_r u_s$ instead of u_{rs}.

You will recall from algebra that adding a column multiplied by a scalar to another column does not change the value of the determinant. Thus, by performing the proper column operations, the second term on the right-hand side of Eq. 42 vanishes. For example, consider the following columns:

Column 1	Column s
0	$f'(u) \cdot u_s$
$f'(u) \cdot u_1$	$f'(u) \cdot u_{1s} + f''(u) \cdot u_1 u_s$
$f'(u) \cdot u_2$	$f'(u) \cdot u_{2s} + f''(u) \cdot u_2 u_s$
$\vdots$	$\vdots$
$f'(u) \cdot u_r$	$f'(u) \cdot u_{rs} + f''(u) \cdot u_r u_s$
$\vdots$	$\vdots$
$f'(u) \cdot u_n$	$f'(u) \cdot u_{ns} + f''(u) \cdot u_n u_s$

Multiplying column 1 by $(-f''(u)/f'(u)) \times u_s$ and adding it to column s causes the term $f''(u) u_r u_s$ in column s to vanish. Thus, instead of having the last determinant in Eq. 22, under the assumption of ordinal utility we have $[f'(u)]^{n+1}U$. By the same reason, the cofactor u_{rs} will become $[f'(u)]^n \cdot U_{rs}$. Since second order conditions are determined by the signs of the determinants rather than by their magnitudes, and since $f'(u)$ raised to any power is positive, the second order conditions are the same when the arbitrary function $f(u)$ replaces u.

NOTES TO CHAPTERS 5 AND 14

CONSTANT RETURNS TO SCALE

We recall from Chapter 5 that if the production function is governed by constant returns to scale, then increasing all factors of production λ fold will result in increasing production λ fold. A production function which is governed by constant returns to scale is known as homogeneous in the first degree. Let factors be denoted by A_1, A_2, . . . , A_n, and the production function be $Q = f(A_1, A_2, \ldots, A_n)$. In order for it to be homogeneous in the first degree, the following must hold:

$$f(\lambda A_1, \lambda A_2, \ldots, \lambda A_n) = \lambda \cdot f(A_1, A_2, \ldots, A_n) \qquad (43)$$

Let us denote A_2/A_1 by a_2, A_3/A_1 by a_3, and so on. Then, if $\lambda = 1/A_1$, Eq. 43 becomes

$$\frac{1}{A_1} Q = f\left(1, \frac{A_2}{A_1}, \ldots, \frac{A_n}{A_1}\right) = F(a_2, a_3, \ldots, a_n)$$

Multiplying through by A_1 gives

$$Q = A_1 \cdot F(a_2, a_3, \ldots, a_n)$$

Differentiating with respect to A_1 gives

$$MPP_{A_1} = \frac{\partial Q}{\partial A_1} = F(a_2, a_3, \ldots, a_n)$$

$$+ A_1 \cdot \left(F_{a_2} \frac{\partial a_2}{\partial A_1} + F_{a_3} \frac{\partial a_3}{\partial A_1} + \cdots + F_{a_n} \frac{\partial a_n}{\partial A_1} \right)$$

$$= F(a_2, a_3, \ldots, a_n) + A_1 \left(- F_{a_2} \frac{A_2}{A_1^2} - F_{a_3} \frac{A_3}{A_1^2} - \cdots - F_{a_n} \frac{A_n}{A_1^2} \right)$$

$$= F(a_2, a_3, \ldots, a_n) - F_{a_2} \cdot a_2 - F_{a_3} \cdot a_3 - \cdots - F_{a_n} \cdot a_n \qquad (44)$$

where F_{a2} is the derivative of F with respect to A_2/A_1, etc. Equation 44 proves that MPP_{A_1} is the function of the ratios $a_2(= A_2/A_1)$, $a_3(= A_3/A_1)$, and so on. Consider now any other factor, say A_2. Differentiating $Q = A_1 \cdot F(a_2, a_3, \ldots, a_n)$ gives

$$MPP_{A_2} = \frac{\partial Q}{\partial A_2} = A_1 \cdot F_{a2} \frac{\partial a_2}{\partial A_2} = A_1 \cdot F_{a_2} \frac{1}{A_1} = F_{a_2} \qquad (45)$$

Equation 45 can be applied to A_3, A_4, and so on. Thus we have proved the theorem telling that under constant returns to scale the marginal physical product is a function of the ratios such as $a_r = A_r/A_1$ for $r = 2$, 3, . . . , n. You will recall from Chapter 6 that this theorem is needed in order to show that variability of all factors and constant returns to scale give rise to a flat marginal cost curve.

EULER THEOREM

The Euler theorem was stated without proof in Chapter 5. We can now prove it. Substituting the right-hand term in Eq. 44 for MPP_{A1} the last term in Eq. 45 for MPP_{A2}, and so on gives

$$A_1 \cdot MPP_{A_1} + A_2 \cdot MPP_{A_2} + \cdots + A_n \cdot MPP_{A_n}$$

$$= A_1 \cdot F(a_2, a_3, \ldots, a_n) - A_2 F_{a_2} - A_3 F_{a_3} - \cdots - A_n F_{a_n}$$
$$+ A_2 F_{a_2} + A_3 F_{a_3} + \cdots + A_n F_{a_n}$$

$$= A_1 \cdot F(a_2, a_3; \ldots, a_n) = Q \tag{46}$$

THE COBB-DOUGLAS PRODUCTION FUNCTION

Consider the following Cobb-Douglas production function:

$$Q = KA^{\alpha} \cdot B^{\beta} \tag{47}$$

In the Appendix to Chapter 5 we showed that the Cobb-Douglas production function is governed by constant returns to scale, provided that $\alpha + \beta = 1$. Other properties were stated without proof. We shall now prove them.

The logarithm of Eq. 47 is

$$\log Q = \log K + \alpha \cdot \log A + \beta \cdot \log B$$

Taking the complete differential gives

$$\frac{dQ}{Q} = \alpha \frac{dA}{A} + \beta \frac{dB}{B} \tag{48}$$

Equation 48 shows that α is the elasticity of production with respect to factor A and so on. Next, let us keep B constant; then $dB = 0$. Dividing Eq. 48 by ∂A and multiplying it by Q gives

$$MPP_A = \frac{\partial Q}{\partial A} = \alpha \frac{Q}{A} \tag{49}$$

MPP_A can be expressed as

$$\frac{\partial Q}{\partial A} = K \alpha \cdot A^{\alpha-1} B^{\beta}$$

Differentiating it with respect to A gives

$$\frac{\partial^2 Q}{\partial A^2} = K \cdot \alpha \cdot (\alpha - 1) \cdot A^{\alpha-2} \cdot B^{\beta}$$

Since $\alpha + \beta = 1$ and $\alpha > 0, \beta > 0$, the term $\alpha - 1$ must be negative. Thus, $\partial^2 Q / \partial A^2$ is negative. This proves that the Cobb-Douglas production function is governed by diminishing marginal physical product. Differentiating $\partial Q / \partial A$ with respect to B gives

$$\frac{\partial^2 Q}{\partial A \partial B} = K \cdot \alpha \cdot \beta \cdot A^{\alpha-1} \cdot B^{\beta-1}$$

which is positive. This shows that the Cobb-Douglas production function assumes positive dependence between MPP_A and B and between MPP_B and A.

In the Appendix to Chapter 5, the elasticity of substitution σ between two factors was defined as

$$\sigma = \frac{[d(B/A)]/(B/A)}{[d(dB/dA)]/(dB/dA)} \qquad (50)$$

where output Q is constant, and so $dQ = 0$.

Then, from Eq. 48, $dB/dA = -(\alpha/\beta)\cdot(B/A)$ Substituting in Eq. 50 gives

$$\sigma = \frac{[(A \cdot dB - B \cdot dA)/A^2]/(B/A)}{[(-\alpha/\beta) \cdot (A \cdot dB - B \cdot dA)/A^2]/[(-\alpha/\beta) \cdot (B/A)]} = 1 \quad (51)$$

NOTES TO CHAPTER 7

TECHNOLOGICAL PROGRESS

In what follows, we shall present an approach to measuring technological change which is due to R. M. Sollow. Let Q stand for output, C for capital, L for labor, and t for time. Let us assume that the process of growth can be described by an aggregate production function

$$Q = A(t) \cdot f(C, L) \qquad (52)$$

where $A(t)$ takes care of the production function shift. For example, $A(t)$ may be e^{at}, etc. Equation 52 is governed by constant returns to scale. In other words, it is homogeneous of the first degree in C and L. Shifts in the production function are neutral. This is true because

$$\frac{\partial Q}{\partial C} = A(t) \frac{\partial f}{\partial C}$$

and

$$\frac{\partial Q}{\partial L} = A(t) \frac{\partial f}{\partial L}$$

Ceteris paribus, if $A(t)$ increases K fold, the respective marginal physical products will also increase K fold. You will recall from Chapter 7 that $A(t)$ is the shift in the production which measures the change in productivity. For example, if $A(t_0) = 1$ and $A(t_1) = 1.1$, it means that the output attainable from a given set of inputs at t_1 is 10 percent larger than it was at t_0. Differentiating Eq. 52 with respect to t gives

$$\frac{\partial Q}{\partial t} = A \cdot \frac{\partial}{\partial t} f(C, L) + f(C, L) \frac{\partial A}{\partial t}$$

$$= A \left(\frac{\partial f \cdot \partial C}{\partial C \cdot \partial t} + \frac{\partial f \cdot \partial L}{\partial L \cdot \partial t} \right) + \frac{Q}{A} \cdot \frac{\partial A}{\partial t}$$

$$= A \frac{\partial f \cdot \partial C}{\partial C \cdot \partial t} + A \frac{\partial f \cdot \partial L}{\partial L \cdot \partial t} + \frac{Q}{A} \cdot \frac{\partial A}{\partial t}$$

If we divide through by Q and substitute ∂Q for $A \times \partial f$, we obtain

$$\frac{1}{Q} \cdot \frac{\partial Q}{\partial t} = \frac{1}{Q} \cdot \frac{\partial Q \cdot \partial C}{\partial C \cdot \partial t} + \frac{1}{Q} \cdot \frac{\partial Q \cdot \partial L}{\partial L \cdot \partial t} + \frac{1}{A} \cdot \frac{\partial A}{\partial t}$$

If we denote $\partial Q/\partial t$ by Q^t, etc., we obtain

$$\frac{Q^t}{Q} = W_C \frac{C^t}{C} + W_L \frac{L^t}{L} + \frac{A^t}{A} \tag{53}$$

where $W_C = (C \cdot \partial Q)/(Q \cdot \partial C)$ and $W_L = (L \cdot \partial Q)/(Q \cdot \partial L)$. If we assume constant returns to scale and payment to factors of production according to their value of marginal product, then W_C is the share of capital and W_L the share of labor in total income. This is left as an exercise for the student.

Example: Assume that national income amounts to $100 billion, of which $75 billion are salaries and wages and $25 billion are returns to owners of capital. Assume that, during the last decade, output has been growing at an average rate of 7 percent, capital at 8 percent, and the labor force at 4 percent, all per annum. For simplicity, assume full employment in the economy. The value of A^t/A, which is the relative shift in the production function, can be estimated by use of Eq. 53.

Let us denote (A^t/A) 100 per cent by X. Then, $7\% = (\frac{1}{4}) \cdot 8\% + (\frac{3}{4})$ $\cdot 4\% + X$ and $X = 2\%$. In other words, on the average the production function has shifted 2 per cent per annum during the last decade.

NOTES TO CHAPTERS 5 AND 6

THE FIRM

Let the production function of a competitive firm be

$$Q = f(A_1, A_2, \ldots, A_n) \tag{54}$$

where Q is the quantity produced and A_1 stands for both the first factor and its quantity used, etc. The prices of the factors are $P_1, P_2, \ldots, P_n$. You will recall that the firm has no influence over these prices. Moreover, the firm has no influence over the product made by it. Let us denote the price of the product by P_Q. We shall now consider the problem of minimizing the cost of production, given that output is fixed at Q_0. Let total cost be denoted by C. We want to minimize $C = A_1P_1 + A_2P_2 +$

$\cdots + A_n P_n$ subject to the conditions that $f(A_1, A_2, \ldots, A_n) = Q_0$:

$$A_1 P_1 + A_2 P_2 + \ldots + A_n P_n + \lambda [Q_0 - f(A_1, A_2, \ldots, A_n)] = min. \quad (55)$$

where λ is the Lagrange multiplier.

Assume that first order derivatives exist. Let $\partial Q / \partial A_i$ be denoted by f_i $(i = 1, 2, \ldots, n)$. Note that f_i is positive under the realistic assumption that a firm will avoid the range of production in which marginal physical product is negative. The necessary conditions for Eq. 55 to be a minimum are that the partial derivatives be equal to zero; that is,

$$P_1 - \lambda f_1 = 0$$
$$P_2 - \lambda f_2 = 0$$
$$\vdots$$
$$P_n - \lambda f_n = 0$$

which may be written as

$$\frac{P_1}{f_1} = \frac{P_2}{f_2} = \cdots = \frac{P_n}{f_n} = \lambda \quad (56)$$

Note that Eq. 56 is a set of n equations. These n equations together with the side relation $Q_0 = f(A_1, A_2, \ldots, A_n)$ determine the respective amounts of the different factors used and λ. The complete differential of total cost is

$$dC = P_1 \cdot dA_1 + P_2 \cdot dA_2 + \cdots + P_n \cdot dA_n \quad (57)$$

The complete differential of output is

$$dQ = f_1 \cdot dA_1 + f_2 \cdot dA_2 + \cdots + f_n \cdot dA_n \quad (58)$$

Dividing Eq. 58 in Eq. 57 and taking advantage of Eq. 56 gives

$$\frac{dC}{dQ} = \frac{P_1 \cdot dA_1 + P_2 \cdot dA_2 + \cdots + P_n \cdot dA_n}{f_1 \cdot dA_1 + f_2 \cdot dA_2 + \cdots + f_n \cdot dA_n} = \lambda \quad (59)$$

Thus we proved that λ in Eq. 56 is the marginal cost. Since f_1 is the marginal physical product of the first factor and so on, Eq. 56 together with Eq. 58 prove the law of logic as stated in Chapter 6; that is,

$$\frac{P_1}{MPP_1} = \frac{P_2}{MPP_2} = \cdots = \frac{P_n}{MPP_n} = MC$$

We now turn to the second-order conditions. We assume that second-order derivatives exist and we denote $\partial^2 Q / \partial A_r \, \partial A_s$ by f_{rs}. In order for total cost C to be minimized, we must have $d^2 C > 0$ subject to the side relation $f_1 \cdot dA_1 + f_2 \cdot dA_2 + \cdots + f_n \cdot dA_n = 0$. The side relation determines A_1 as a function of the set $A_2, A_3, \ldots, A_n$. Accordingly, dA_1 is not a constant. Taking the complete differential of the side relation gives

$$d(f_1 \cdot dA_1 + f_2 \cdot dA_2 + \cdots + f_n \cdot dA_n)$$
$$= f_1 \cdot d^2A_1 + f_{11} \cdot dA_1^2 + 2f_{12} \cdot dA_1 \cdot dA_2 + \cdots + f_{nn} \cdot dA_n^2 = 0$$

and so,

$$d^2A_1 = -\frac{1}{f_1}\,(f_{11} \cdot dA_1^2 + 2f_{12} \cdot dA_1 \cdot dA_2 + \cdots + f_{nn} \cdot dA_n^2) \qquad (60)$$

Taking the complete differential of dC we have

$$d^2C = d(dC) = d(P_1 \cdot dA_1 + P_2 \cdot dA_2 + \cdots + P_n \cdot dA_n)$$
$$= d(P_1 \cdot dA_1) = P_1 \cdot d^2A_1 \qquad (61)$$

Substituting the right-hand side of Eq. 60 for d^2A_1 in Eq. 61 gives

$$d^2C = -\frac{P_1}{f_1}\,(f_{11} \cdot dA_1^2 + 2f_{12} \cdot dA_1 \cdot dA_2 + \cdots + f_{nn} \cdot dA_n^2) \qquad (62)$$

Making the realistic assumption that prices and marginal physical products of factors are positive implies that $-P_1/f_1$ is negative. Therefore, in order for d^2C in Eq. 62 to be positive definite, the quadratic form $f_{11} \cdot dA_1^2 + 2f_{12} \cdot dA_1 \cdot dA_2 + \cdots + f_{nn} \cdot dA_n^2$ must be negative definite. Recall also that the side relation is $f_1 \cdot dA_1 + f_2 \cdot dA_2 + \cdots + f_n \cdot dA_n = 0$. Thus, for a minimum cost the determinants

$$\left. \begin{vmatrix} 0 & f_1 \\ f_1 & f_{11} \end{vmatrix} \cdots \begin{vmatrix} 0 & f_1 & \ldots f_{n-1} \\ f_1 & f_{11} & \ldots f_{1(n-1)} \\ \vdots & & \\ f_{n-1} & f_{(n-1)1} & \ldots f_{(n-1)\ (n-1)} \end{vmatrix} \quad \begin{vmatrix} 0 & f_1 & \ldots f_n \\ f_1 & f_{11} & \ldots f_{1n} \\ \vdots & & \\ f_n & f_{n1} & \ldots f_{nn} \end{vmatrix} \right\} \quad (63)$$

must be alternatively negative and positive.

Another approach would be to form the functions

$$Z = \sum_{i=1}^{i=n} A_iP_i + \lambda\,[Q_0 - f(A_1, A_2, \ldots, A_n)]$$

$$h = Q_0 - f(A_1, A_2, \ldots, A_n)$$

and then form the proper Hessian and its principal minors. The determinants would contain second order partial derivatives of Z, each bordered by a column and a row made of the first order partial derivatives of h. The difficulty with this approach is that it yields determinants in which λ appears, and thus it takes a series of manipulations to bring it to the form of determinants 63.

Note also that instead of solving a problem of a constrained minimum, we can solve a problem of a constrained maximum and get the same results. The problem would be formulated as maximizing output given a fixed outlay.

Let us denote the last determinant in Eq. 63 by F, the cofactor of f_r by F_r, and the cofactor of f_{rs} by F_{rs}. Differentiating the production function $Q = f(A_1, A_2, \ldots, A_n)$ and Eq. 56 with respect to P_r gives

$$\left.\begin{aligned}
f_1 \frac{\partial A_1}{\partial P_r} + f_2 \frac{\partial A_2}{\partial P_r} + \cdots + f_s \frac{\partial A_s}{\partial P_r} + \cdots + f_n \frac{\partial A_n}{\partial P_r} &= 0 \\
f_1\left(\frac{1 \cdot \partial \lambda}{\lambda \cdot \partial P_r}\right) + f_{11}\frac{\partial A_1}{\partial P_r} + f_{12}\frac{\partial A_2}{\partial P_r} + \cdots + f_{1s}\frac{\partial A_s}{\partial P_r} + \cdots + f_{1n}\frac{\partial A_n}{\partial P_r} &= 0 \\
\vdots \qquad\qquad\qquad\qquad & \\
f_r\left(\frac{1 \cdot \partial \lambda}{\lambda \cdot \partial P_r}\right) + f_{r1}\frac{\partial A_1}{\partial P_r} + f_{r2}\frac{\partial A_2}{\partial P_r} + \cdots + f_{rs}\frac{\partial A_s}{\partial P_r} + \cdots + f_{rn}\frac{\partial A_n}{\partial P_r} &= \frac{1}{\lambda} \\
\vdots \qquad\qquad\qquad\qquad & \\
f_n\left(\frac{1 \cdot \partial \lambda}{\lambda \cdot \partial P_r}\right) + f_{n1}\frac{\partial A_1}{\partial P_r} + f_{n2}\frac{\partial A_2}{\partial P_r} + \cdots + f_{ns}\frac{\partial A_s}{\partial P_r} + \cdots + f_{nn}\frac{\partial A_n}{\partial P_r} &= 0
\end{aligned}\right\} \quad (64)$$

Solving for $\partial A_s/\partial P_r$ by Cramer's rule gives

$$\frac{\partial A_s}{\partial P_r} = \frac{1}{\lambda} \cdot \frac{F_{rs}}{F} \qquad (65)$$

Since there are no restrictions on the sign of $(1/\lambda) \cdot (F_{rs}/F)$, $\partial A_s/\partial P_r$ may be either positive or negative. If it is positive, then the factors A_r and A_s are called *substitutes*. If it is negative, these factors are called *complements*. If $r = s$, Eq. 65 becomes

$$\frac{\partial A_r}{\partial P_r} = \frac{1}{\lambda} \frac{F_{rr}}{F} \qquad (66)$$

Since the order of arranging the factors does not matter, we may require that $r = n$. Since the determinants in Eq. 63 are alternatively positive and negative (and since X is positive), F_{rr}/F must be negative.

In Chapter 5 we discussed the case of positive relationship between two factors of production. We claimed that positive relationship may be consistent with either factors that are substitutes for each other, or factors that are complements to each other. The proof is now available. Mathematically, positive relationship means that $f_{rs} > 0$. But this inequality may be consistent with either $F_{rs}/F < 0$ or $F_{rs}/F > 0$. It is left for the student to show (1) that $\partial A_r/\partial P_s = \partial A_s/\partial P_r$ and (2) that if only two factors are used in the process of production, they must be substitutes. (HINT: Show that $P_1(\partial A_1/\partial P_r) + P_2(\partial A_2/\partial P_r) + \cdots + P_n(\partial A_n/\partial P_r) = 0$.)

Our second problem is to determine the optimal production for a competitive firm. Recall that a competitive firm secures factors of production at given prices $P_1, P_2, \ldots, P_n$ and sells its product at a given price P_Q. The firm reaches its equilibrium when rent is maximized. Rent is obtained by substracting total cost from total revenue; that is,

$$\pi = P_Q \cdot Q - (P_1 A_1 + P_2 A_2 + \cdots + P_n A_n) \tag{67}$$

where π is rent. Note that here Q is variable and P_Q is constant. Differentiating Eq. 67 and equating to zero for maximum gives

$$P_Q \cdot f_1 - P_1 = P_Q \cdot f_2 - P_2 = \cdots = P_Q \cdot f_n - P_n = 0$$

Rearranging gives

$$\frac{P_1}{f_1} = \frac{P_2}{f_2} = \cdots = \frac{P_n}{f_n} = P_Q \tag{68}$$

Making use of Eqs. 59 and 68 gives

$$\frac{P_1}{f_1} = \frac{P_2}{f_2} = \cdots = \frac{P_n}{f_n} = MC = P_Q \tag{69}$$

The sufficient condition for maximum is that $d^2\pi$ is negative definite.

Let us take the complete differential of Eq. 67.

$$d\pi = P_Q dQ - P_1 dA_1 - P_2 dA_2 - \cdots - P_n dA_n \tag{70}$$

The factors $A_1, A_2, \ldots, A_n$ form a set of independent variables, thus

$$d(dA_1) = d(dA_2) = \cdots = d(dA_n) = 0$$

also

$$dP_Q = dP_1 = dP_2 = \cdots = dP_n = 0$$

Thus, the complete differential of Eq. 70 is

$$d(d\pi) = d^2\pi = P_Q d^2 Q \tag{71}$$

Since P_Q is positive, $d^2 Q$ must be negative definite in order for $d^2\pi$ to be negative definite. The quadratic form $f_{11} dA_1^2 + 2f_{12} dA_1 dA_2 + \cdots + f_{nn} dA_n$ is $d^2 Q$. Thus, $d^2 Q$ is positive definite if the determinants

$$f_{11}\cdots \begin{vmatrix} f_{11} & f_{12} & \cdots f_{1(n-1)} \\ f_{21} & f_{22} & \cdots f_{2(n-1)} \\ \vdots \\ f_{(n-1)1} & f_{(n-1)2} \cdots f_{(n-1)\ (n-1)} \end{vmatrix} \quad \begin{vmatrix} f_{11} & f_{12}\cdots f_{1n} \\ f_{21} & f_{22}\cdots f_{2n} \\ \vdots \\ f_{n1} & f_{n2}\cdots f_{nn} \end{vmatrix} \Bigg\} \quad (72)$$

are alternatively negative and positive.

An alternative approach would be to form the Hessian and its principal minors, where the Hessian contains the second order partial derivatives of π.

It is left for the reader to show that sufficient conditions for maximizing rent by a monopoly are satisfied when the following holds:

$$\frac{P_1}{f_1} = \frac{P_2}{f_2} = \cdots = \frac{P_n}{f_n} = MC = P_Q\left(1 + \frac{1}{\eta}\right) \qquad (73)$$

(HINT: When you differentiate Eq. 67, note that P_Q is a function of Q.)

Equations 65 and 66 summarize the effect of a change in the price of a factor on its quantity demanded and the demand for other factors of production under the assumption that output is fixed at Q_0. If we allow output to vary, we have a more difficult problem at hand. Let us assume that factor A_1 is used by practically all the firms in a certain industry. A decline in the price of factor A_1 will be followed by a rightward supply shift. Accordingly, more output will be produced at a lower price. Thus the price of the product which is made by the industry can no longer be assumed to be fixed. The mathematical analysis of this problem is postponed to a later point.

COST AND REVENUE FUNCTIONS

Given the production function, cost function, and the expansion function of the firm, one can express the total cost as a function of output. For example, consider the following Cobb-Douglas production function, its cost and expansion functions

$$Q = KA^\alpha \cdot B^\beta \qquad \alpha + \beta = 1$$

$$C = A \cdot P_a + B \cdot P_b$$

$$\frac{MPP_a}{P_a} = \frac{MPP_b}{P_b}$$

Making use of Eq. 49, the expansion function becomes $\alpha P_b B - \beta P_a A = 0$. We leave it for the reader to show that the production, cost, and expansion functions constitute three equations in four unknowns. Accordingly, in our example it converges to a linear cost function. That is,

$$C = hQ,$$

where

$$h = \frac{1}{K} \left(\frac{P_a}{\alpha} \right)^a \cdot \left(\frac{P_b}{\beta} \right)^\beta$$

In general, given the production, cost, and expansion functions, the cost function can be expressed as $C = C(Q)$. Also, since revenue is the product of price and output, and price is a function of output via the demand curve, revenue can be expressed as $R = R(Q)$. Thus $\pi = R(Q) - C(Q)$. The necessary condition for profit maximization is $R'(Q) - C'(Q) = 0$ which is the equality between marginal revenue and marginal cost. The sufficient condition is $\pi'' = R''(Q) - C''(Q) < 0$. Geometrically this means that for profit to be maximized, the marginal cost curve must cut the marginal revenue curve from below.

THE RELATIONSHIP BETWEEN AC AND MC

In Chapter 6, the functional relationship between AC and MC was stated as follows: when AC is declining, MC is smaller than AC, and vice versa. We shall now prove this theorem. When AC is falling, $d(AC)/dQ$ is negative; and when AC is rising, $d(AC)/dQ$ is positive. Total cost is the product of average cost and quantity; that is, $C = AC \times Q$. Differentiating C with respect to Q gives

$$MC = \frac{dC}{dQ} = AC + Q \frac{d(AC)}{dQ} \tag{74}$$

When AC is falling, $d(AC)/dQ$ is negative and marginal cost is smaller than average cost by $Q[d(AC)/dQ]$. When AC rises, $d(AC)/dQ$ is positive and marginal cost is higher than average cost by $Q[d(AC)/dQ]$. At the minimum point of the AC curve, $d(AC)/dQ = 0$. This implies that at the minimum point of the AC curve, $MC = AC$.

NOTES TO CHAPTER 8

Let K_i be the relative share of firm i in the total production of the industry, and let ϵ_i stand for its supply elasticity, where $i = 1, 2, \ldots, n$. Then it can be proved that

$$\epsilon = K_1 \cdot \epsilon_1 + K_2 \cdot \epsilon_2 + \cdots + K_n \cdot \epsilon_n \tag{75}$$

where ϵ is the supply elasticity of the industry. The proof is similar to Eq. 11.

NOTES TO CHAPTER 9

In Chapter 9, we discussed the effect of demand shifts and supply shifts on the price and the quantity. You will recall that we have analyzed only the direction of the change in prices and quantities, leaving out the order of magnitude of the change. In what follows, a method of estimating the order of magnitude of the change will be provided.

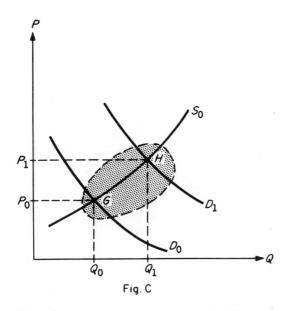

Fig. C

The demand curve may shift due to changes in income, due to changes in prices of other commodities, or due to changes in tastes. The supply curve may shift due to technological changes, or to the fact that factors of production are becoming either cheaper or dearer. For simplicity, assume that the demand curve shifts rightward due to a change in income per capita. Tastes of consumers and the number of consumers are unchanged. The supply curve does not shift at all. This is illustrated by Fig. C. If we knew the mathematical functions of S_0, D_0, and D_1, we would be able to determine the coordinates of point G and point H, respectively. In reality, we only have a rough idea of the order of magnitudes of elasticities, and we have to make some use of it. If we are ready to make the assumption that elasticities are fixed in the shaded area in Fig. C, then we can provide a crude estimate of the respective changes in the price and the quantity. It is left for the student to show that the smaller the shaded area in Fig. C is, the more realistic is the assumption of fixed elasticities.

At the point of intersection between supply and demand the following hold:

$$Q_D = K + \eta \cdot P + \alpha \cdot I \qquad (76)$$

$$Q_S = h + \epsilon \cdot P \qquad (77)$$

$$Q = Q_S = Q_D \tag{78}$$

where the subscripts D and S denote demand and supply, respectively; η is price elasticity of demand; α is income elasticity; ϵ is price elasticity of supply; and Q, I, and P are the logarithm of quantity, income per capita, and price, respectively. Since the variables are in logarithms, η, α, and ϵ are elasticities. Equation 76 is known as the demand structural equation, and Eq. 77 is known as the supply structural equation. The variables Q and P are endogenous: they are determined by Eqs. 76, 77, and 78. The variable I is predetermined: it is not influenced by the above system. Solving for P and Q gives the reduced forms

$$P = \frac{K - h}{\epsilon - \eta} + \frac{\alpha}{\epsilon - \eta} \cdot I \tag{79}$$

and

$$Q = \frac{\epsilon \cdot K - \eta \cdot h}{\epsilon - \eta} + \frac{\epsilon \cdot \alpha}{\epsilon - \eta} \cdot I \tag{80}$$

For example, the coefficient of I in Eq. 79 is the elasticity of the price with respect to income per capita, and the coefficient of I in Eq. 80 is the coefficient of the quantity with respect to income per capita.

Example: Assume that $\alpha = \frac{1}{2}$, $\epsilon = \frac{1}{4}$, and $\eta = -\frac{1}{2}$. Then

$$\frac{\alpha}{\epsilon - \eta} = \frac{\frac{1}{2}}{\frac{1}{4} + \frac{1}{2}} = 0.66$$

and

$$\frac{\epsilon \cdot \alpha}{\epsilon - \eta} = \frac{\frac{1}{4} \cdot \frac{1}{2}}{\frac{1}{4} + \frac{1}{2}} = 0.16$$

That is, elasticity of price with respect to income is 0.66 and elasticity of quantity with respect to income is 0.16. Accordingly, a 10 percent rise in income per capita will be followed by a 6.6 percent increase in price and 1.6 percent increase in the quantity marketed. Similarly, the effect of a demand shift due to a change in tastes on the price and the quantity may be estimated by changing K properly, and the effect of a supply shift on the price and quantity may be estimated by changing h properly.

Reducing a market system (Eqs. 76, 77, and 78) is more complex for inputs. This is true because the price of an input is equal to its marginal physical product multiplied by the price of output.[1]

[1] See Micha, Gisser, "Needed Adjustment in the Supply of Farm Labor," *Journal of Farm Economics*, Vol. XLIX, November, 1967.

NOTES TO CHAPTERS 5 AND 14

We are now ready to analyze the effect of the change in the price of a factor of production on the quantity demanded for that factor and on the demand for other factors of production. The analysis that follows is due to Allen. In what follows we shall analyze the case of two factors only. The case of n factors of production is too cumbersome to be presented here.[2]

In Chapter 5 the substitution elasticity σ was defined as

$$\sigma = \frac{dR/R}{dr/r} \tag{81}$$

where $R = B/A$ and $r = dB/dA$. Now consider the isoquant for $Q = Q_0$. The complete differential of the production function $f(A, B) = Q_0$ is $f_a \cdot dA + f_b \cdot dB = 0$, where $f_a = \partial f/\partial A$ and $f_b = \partial f/\partial B$. Factoring dB out gives

$$dB = -\frac{f_a}{f_b} \cdot dA = -r \cdot dA \tag{82}$$

Also,

$$dR = d\left(\frac{B}{A}\right) = \frac{A \cdot dB - B \cdot dA}{A^2}$$

$$= \frac{-A \cdot r \cdot dA - B \cdot dA}{A^2} = -\frac{Ar + B}{A^2} \cdot dA \tag{83}$$

Since r is a function of A and B, $dr = (\partial r/\partial A)dA + (\partial r/\partial B)dB$. Substituting $-r \cdot dA$ for dB gives

$$dr = -\left(r\frac{\partial r}{\partial B} - \frac{\partial r}{\partial A}\right) \cdot dA \tag{84}$$

Substituting the right-hand side of Eq. 83 for dR in Eq. 81 and substituting the right-hand side of Eq. 84 for dr in Eq. 81 gives

$$\sigma = \frac{r \cdot dR}{R \cdot dr} = \frac{r \cdot A \cdot dR}{B \cdot dr}$$

$$= \frac{r \cdot A(A \cdot r + B)}{BA^2\left(r\dfrac{\partial r}{\partial B} - \dfrac{\partial r}{\partial A}\right)} = \frac{r(A \cdot r + B)}{BA\left(r\dfrac{\partial r}{\partial B} - \dfrac{\partial r}{\partial A}\right)} \tag{85}$$

[2] See R. G. D. Allen, *Mathematical Analysis for Economists*, London: The Macmillan Company, 1956, Chapter 19.

Dividing Eq. 84 by dA gives

$$\frac{dr}{dA} = -\left(r\frac{\partial r}{\partial B} - \frac{\partial r}{\partial A}\right) \tag{86}$$

Substituting Eq. 86 in Eq. 85 gives

$$\sigma = \frac{-r(Ar + B)}{B \cdot A(dr/dA)} \tag{87}$$

Note that r is the additional amount of B that must be added per one unit of A diverted from production in order to maintain $Q = Q_0$. If r is constant, the two factors are said to be perfect substitutes. In such a case, $dr = 0$ and σ approaches infinity. If r increases when B is substituted for A, it means that it becomes increasingly difficult to substitute B for the scarcer A. In other words, r measures substitutability between A and B. Note that σ is positive. Consider Eq. 81. The ratio $R = B/A$ is positive. When B is substituted for A, the ratio R increases and so, dR is positive too. The ratio $r = dB/dA$ is negative. When B is substituted for A, the absolute value of r increases due to the law of diminishing returns (and/or dependence). Accordingly, algebraically dr is negative and dr/r is positive. This proves that σ is positive. Finally, when B replaces A in production, dA is negative. Thus dr/dA is positive. As indicated by Eq. 87, σ is a product of a certain positive coefficient and the inverse of dr/dA. That is, σ is inversely proportional to dr/dA. The interpretation of this is that the smaller the substitutability between A and B, the larger dr/dA and the smaller σ.

The Euler theorem, Eq. 46, for two factors is

$$A \cdot f_a + B \cdot f_b = Q$$

Differentiating it with respect to A gives

$$f_a + A \cdot f_{aa} + B \cdot f_{ba} = f_a$$

Factoring f_{aa} out we obtain

$$f_{aa} = -\frac{B}{A}f_{ba} \tag{88}$$

Similarly,

$$f_{bb} = -\frac{A}{B}f_{ba} \tag{89}$$

Making use of Eqs. 88, 89, 82, 85, and the Euler theorem we obtain

$$\sigma = \frac{r(Ar + B)}{A \cdot B\left(r\dfrac{\partial r}{\partial B} - \dfrac{\partial r}{\partial A}\right)} = \frac{r(Ar + B)}{A \cdot B\left[\dfrac{f_a}{f_b} \cdot \dfrac{\partial}{\partial B}\left(\dfrac{f_a}{f_b}\right) + \dfrac{\partial}{\partial A}\left(\dfrac{f_a}{f_b}\right)\right]}$$

$$= \frac{r(Ar + B)}{A \cdot B \left(\dfrac{f_a}{f_b} \cdot \dfrac{f_b f_{ab} - f_a f_{bb}}{f_b^2} + \dfrac{f_b f_{aa} - f_a f_{ba}}{f_b^2} \right)}$$

$$= \frac{r(Ar + B)}{(A \cdot B/f_b^3)(f_a f_b f_{ab} - f_a^2 f_{bb} + f_b^2 f_{aa} - f_a f_b f_{ab})}$$

$$= \frac{(-f_a/f_b)[A(-f_a/f_b) + B]}{(A \cdot B/f_b^3)(-f_a^2 f_{bb} + f_b^2 f_{aa})} = \frac{f_a f_b (A f_a - B f_b)}{A \cdot B (-f_a^2 f_{bb} + f_b^2 f_{aa})}$$

$$= \frac{f_a f_b (A f_a - B f_b)}{AB [f_a^2 (A/B) f_{ab} - f_b^2 (B/A) f_{ab}]} = \frac{f_a f_b (A f_a - B f_b)}{f_{ab} (A^2 f_a^2 - B^2 f_b^2)}$$

$$= \frac{f_a f_b (A f_a - B f_b)}{f_{ab} (A f_a + B f_b)(A f_a - B f_b)} = \frac{f_a f_b}{f_{ab} (A f_a + B f_b)} = \frac{f_a f_b}{Q \cdot f_{ab}} \quad (90)$$

Equation 90 may also be written as

$$\sigma = \frac{(\partial Q/\partial A) \cdot (\partial Q/\partial B)}{Q [\partial^2 Q/(\partial A \cdot \partial B)]} \quad (91)$$

Equations 88, 89, and 90 may be reduced to

$$f_{aa} = -\frac{B \cdot f_a \cdot f_b}{A \cdot Q \cdot \sigma} \quad (92)$$

$$f_{bb} = -\frac{A \cdot f_a \cdot f_b}{B \cdot Q \cdot \sigma} \quad (93)$$

$$f_{ab} = \frac{f_a f_b}{Q \cdot \sigma} \quad (94)$$

Equations 92, 93, and 94 will be used in the following section.

A CHANGE IN THE PRICE OF A FACTOR

Equations 65 and 66 summarize the effect of a change in the price of a factor of production on its quantity demanded and the demand for other factors of production, under the assumption that output is fixed at Q_0. Equations 65 and 66 were obtained by differentiating Eq. 56 and a production function, where $Q = Q_0$ with respect to the price of a factor. If the output is not fixed, then each firm will maximize its rent, and λ in Eq. 56 will equal the price of one unit of output which we shall denote by P. Moreover, since we assume a change in the price of a factor which is used by most of the firms in the industry, the industry will shift its supply curve, say rightward, and move down along the demand curve facing it. Accordingly, if the demand function is $Q = F(P)$, then $F(P)$ may be substituted for Q in the production function.

Since the case of n factors is quite cumbersome, we shall analyze only the case where there are two factors of production.[3] Accordingly, in a two-factor world, Eq. 56 becomes $P_a/f_a = P_b/f_b = P$, and the production function becomes $f(A, B) = F(P)$. This is summarized as

$$\left.\begin{aligned} f(A,B) &= F(P) \\ P_a &= P \cdot f_a \\ P_b &= P \cdot f_b \end{aligned}\right\} \tag{95}$$

Differentiating Eq. 95 with respect to P_a and making use of the equality

$$F'(P)\frac{\partial P}{\partial P_a} = \eta \frac{Q \cdot \partial P}{P \cdot \partial P_a}$$

gives

$$\left.\begin{aligned} f_a\frac{\partial A}{\partial P_a} + f_b\frac{\partial B}{\partial P_a} &= \eta\frac{Q \cdot \partial P}{P \cdot \partial P_a} \\ 1 &= f_a\frac{\partial P}{\partial P_a} + P\left(f_{aa}\frac{\partial A}{\partial P_a} + f_{ab}\frac{\partial B}{\partial P_a}\right) \\ 0 &= f_b\frac{\partial P}{\partial P_a} + P\left(f_{ab}\frac{\partial A}{\partial P_a} + f_{bb}\frac{\partial B}{\partial P_a}\right) \end{aligned}\right\} \tag{96}$$

Making use of Eqs. 92, 93, and 94; substituting P_a for $P \cdot f_a$ and P_b for $P \cdot f_b$; and multiplying the second equation in Eq. 96 by $(Q \cdot P \cdot \sigma)/P_a$ and the third equation by $(Q \cdot P \cdot \sigma)/P_b$; gives

$$\left.\begin{aligned} -\eta \cdot Q\frac{\partial P}{\partial P_a} + P_a\frac{\partial A}{\partial P_a} + P_b\frac{\partial B}{\partial P_a} &= 0 \\ \sigma \cdot Q\frac{\partial P}{\partial P_a} - \frac{B}{A}P_b\frac{\partial A}{\partial P_a} + P_b\frac{\partial B}{\partial P_a} &= \frac{Q \cdot P \cdot \sigma}{P_a} \\ \sigma \cdot Q\frac{\partial P}{\partial P_a} + P_a\frac{\partial A}{\partial P_a} - \frac{A}{B}P_a\frac{\partial B}{\partial P_a} &= 0 \end{aligned}\right\} \tag{97}$$

These three equations determine the value of $Q(\partial P/\partial P_a)$, $\partial A/\partial P_a$, and $\partial B/\partial P_a$. The Euler theorem for two factors is $Af_a + Bf_b = Q$. Multiplying it through by P gives

$$A \cdot P_a + B \cdot P_b = QP \tag{98}$$

under the assumption that factors are paid according to their value of the marginal physical product. Making use of Eq. 98 we obtain

[3] R. G. D. Allen, *Op. cit.*

$$\Delta = \begin{vmatrix} -\eta & P_a & P_b \\ \sigma & -\dfrac{B}{A}P_b & P_b \\ \sigma & P_a & -\dfrac{A}{B}P_a \end{vmatrix} = \dfrac{\sigma\,(P \cdot Q)^2}{A \cdot B} \tag{99}$$

By Cramer's rule,

$$\frac{\partial A}{\partial P_a} = \frac{\begin{vmatrix} -\eta & 0 & P_b \\ \sigma & \dfrac{Q \cdot P \cdot \sigma}{P_a} & P_b \\ \sigma & 0 & -\dfrac{A}{B}P_a \end{vmatrix}}{\Delta}$$

$$= \frac{A}{P_a}\,(-K_b \cdot \sigma + K_a \cdot \eta) \tag{100}$$

where

$$K_b = \frac{B \cdot P_b}{Q \cdot P}$$

and

$$K_a = \frac{A \cdot P_a}{Q \cdot P}$$

Or, in other words, K_b is the share of factor B in total cost and and K_a the share of factor A in total cost.

Under the assumption that η is negative, $\eta = -|\eta|$. Thus, if we multiply Eq. 100 through by P_a/A, we obtain

$$\frac{\partial A \cdot P_a}{\partial P_a \cdot A} = -(K_b \cdot \sigma + K_a \cdot |\eta|)$$

which may be written as

$$\frac{\% \text{ change in } A}{\% \text{ change in } P_a} = -(K_b \cdot \sigma + K_a \cdot |\eta|) \tag{101}$$

provided that the change in P_a is small.

Equation 101 may be interpreted as follows: Other things being the same, the larger the elasticity of substitution between factor A and factor B, the more elastic is the demand curve for A. Also, the more elastic the demand curve for the final product, the more elastic is the demand curve for factor A. Note that P_b is unchanged in Eq. 101. (In other words, we assume that the industry faces an horizontal supply curve of factor B. If the share of the industry in the total use of factor B is small, then this is a realistic assumption.) Let us estimate $\partial B/\partial P_a$. By Cramer's rule,

$$\frac{\partial B}{\partial P_a} = \frac{\begin{vmatrix} -\eta & P_a & 0 \\ \sigma & -\dfrac{B}{A}P_b & \dfrac{Q \cdot P \cdot \sigma}{P_a} \\ \sigma & P_a & 0 \end{vmatrix}}{\Delta}$$

$$= \frac{A \cdot B}{Q \cdot P} (\sigma + \eta) \tag{102}$$

Multiplying Eq. 102 through by P_a/B gives

$$\frac{\partial B \cdot P_a}{\partial P_a \cdot B} = \frac{A \cdot P_a}{Q \cdot P} (\sigma + \eta)$$

or

$$\frac{\% \text{ change in } B}{\% \text{ change in } P_a} = K_a (\sigma - |\eta|) \tag{103}$$

Equation 103 was used in the Appendix to Chapter 14 without proof.

NOTES TO CHAPTER 12

PRICE DISCRIMINATION

Let the two separate markets confronting a monopoly be denoted by 1 and 2. π, R, and C denote profit (rent) total revenue and total cost. The profit function is

$$\pi = R_1(Q_1) + R_2(Q_2) - C(Q) \tag{104}$$

where

$$Q = Q_1 + Q_2$$

The necessary conditions for profit maximization are

$$\frac{\partial \pi}{\partial Q_1} = R_1{}'(Q_1) - C'(Q) = 0$$

$$\frac{\partial \pi}{\partial Q_2} = R_2{}'(Q_2) - C'(Q) = 0$$

which can be written as

$$R_1'(Q_1) = R_2'(Q_2) = C'(Q) = 0 \qquad (105)$$

This result means that in equilibrium the marginal revenue in the first market must be equal to the marginal revenue in the second market and marginal cost.

Consider the following example:

$$C = 0.5Q^2$$

	Demand	*Revenue*
Market 1	$P_1 = 200 - Q_1$	$R_1 = 200Q_1 - Q_1^2$
Market 2	$P_2 = 100 - Q_2$	$R_2 = 100Q_2 - Q_2^2$

$$\pi = 200Q_1 - Q_1^2 + 100Q_2 - Q_2^2 - 0.5(Q_1 + Q_2)^2$$

Setting the partial derivatives equal to zero

$$\frac{\partial \pi}{\partial Q_1} = 200 - 3Q_1 - Q_2 = 0$$

$$\frac{\partial \pi}{\partial Q_2} = 100 - Q_1 - 3Q_2 = 0$$

The solution is

$$Q_1 = 62.5 \text{ and } Q_2 = 12.5$$

The reader can easily verify that

$$MR_1 = MR_2 = MC = \$75$$

and

$$\pi = \$6875$$

Sufficient conditions for profit maximization are satisfied as follows:

$$-3 < 0 \qquad \begin{vmatrix} -3 & -1 \\ -1 & -3 \end{vmatrix} \qquad = 8 > 0$$

MULTIPLE-PLANT MONOPOLY

Consider a monopolist operating two plants and selling in one market. His profit (rent) function is

$$\pi = R(Q) - C_1(Q_1) - C_2(Q_2) \qquad (106)$$

where

$$Q = Q_1 + Q_2$$

The necessary conditions for profit maximization are

$$\frac{\partial \pi}{\partial Q_1} = R'(Q) - C_1'(Q_1) = 0$$

$$\frac{\partial \pi}{\partial Q_2} = R'(Q) - C_2'(Q_2) = 0$$

That is

$$C_1'(Q_1) = C_2'(Q_2) = R'(Q) \qquad (107)$$

In equilibrium, the marginal cost of the first plant equals that of the second plant and marginal revenue.

Consider the following example:

$$\text{Demand: } P = 200 - Q$$
$$C_1 = 0.5Q_1{}^2$$
$$C_2 = Q_2{}^2$$

The profit function is

$$\pi = 200(Q_1 + Q_2) - (Q_1 + Q_2)^2 - 0.5Q_1{}^2 - Q_2{}^2$$

Setting the partial derivatives equal to zero

$$\frac{\partial \pi}{\partial Q_1} = 200 - 3Q_1 - 2Q_2 = 0$$

$$\frac{\partial \pi}{\partial Q_2} = 200 - 2Q_1 - 4Q_2 = 0$$

The solution is $Q_1 = 50$ and $Q_2 = 25$.

The student can verify that

$$MC_1 = MC_2 = MR = \$50$$

and

$$\pi = \$7500$$

Sufficient conditions for maximization are satisfied

$$-3 < 0 \qquad \begin{vmatrix} -3 & -2 \\ -2 & -4 \end{vmatrix} = 8 > 0$$

A monopolist may have to decide whether he should establish two plants or only one. If the plants incur fixed costs (which are avoidable by the nature of the problem), then the monopolist *may* be better off with a single plant.

TAXATION

The government imposes a specific tax of T dollars per unit of output made by a monopolist. The profit function of the monopolist after the tax is

$$\pi = R(Q) - C(Q) - T \cdot Q \tag{108}$$

The necessary condition for profit maximization is

$$\frac{d\pi}{dQ} = R'(Q) - C'(Q) - T = 0$$

Namely, in equilibrium,

$$R'(Q) = C'(Q) + T \tag{109}$$

In geometrical terms Eq. 109 means that the marginal cost curve after imposing the tax is T dollars higher than the original one. Taking the complete differential of 109 and rearranging we obtain

$$\frac{dQ}{dT} = \frac{1}{R''(Q) - C''(Q)} \tag{110}$$

The denominator of the right hand side of relation 110 is the sufficient condition for profit maximization. Accordingly, dQ/dT is negative: The higher the tax, the smaller is the level of output.

Example: The demand curve is $P = 200 - Q$ and the cost function is $C = Q^2$. The rent (profit) function after imposing the tax is

$$\pi = 200\,Q - Q^2 - Q^2 - TQ$$

The necessary condition for profit maximization is

$$\frac{d\pi}{dQ} = 200 - 4Q - T = 0$$

Since the second order derivative is negative, the sufficient condition for maximization is satisfied. The above relation implies that

$$Q = \frac{200 - T}{4}$$

The revenue collected by the government, G, is

$$G = TQ = \frac{T(200 - T)}{4} = \frac{200\,T - T^2}{4}$$

If the government desires to maximize revenue collection from the monopolist, it has to levy a tax T which would maximize G. Then,

$$\frac{dG}{dT} = \frac{200 - 2\,T}{4} = 0$$

The sufficient condition is met since the second order derivative is negative. Solving for the above relation yields $T = 100$, which implies a production of 25 units.

If the tax is imposed ad valorem, the result is similar to the above case. We leave it for the reader to show that an ad valorem tax (in which T is a certain proportion of the price) leads to the following necessary conditions:

$$(1 - T) \cdot R'(Q) = C'(Q) \tag{111}$$

By deriving the complete differential of Eq. 111 and making use of the sufficient condition for profit maximization, it can be shown that the higher the ad valorem tax the lower is the level of output.

The reader will also find it instructive to show that a fixed tax (lump-sum) does not affect the output level of the monopolist provided that the average cost curve does not shift entirely above the demand curve.

Note finally that the above theory of specific taxes applies to perfect competition. A firm in perfect competition may be considered a special case of monopoly where $R'(Q) = P$. Thus, under competition Eq. 109 becomes

$$P = C'(Q) + T \tag{112}$$

Equation 112 provides the supply curve of the individual firm under competition. Aggregating for all the firms in the industry yields the supply curve.

To make sure you understand this procedure solve Prob. 10-8.

If T is the rate of an ad valorem tax, then the equilibrium condition for the competitive firm is

$$(1 - T) \cdot P = C'(Q) \tag{113}$$

NOTES TO CHAPTER 13

A HOMOGENEOUS GOOD PRODUCED BY AN OLIGOPOLY

Unlike in competition or monopolistic competition, in oligopoly each producer must take into account the acts of other producers. In oligopoly, various models based on various modes of behavior are possible. In the case of a homogeneous product the following are the most important models:

(a) *Cournot:* The Cournot model (named after the French economist Augustin Cournot) assumes that each producer treats the quantities produced by other producers as parameters. Accordingly, differentiating his own profit function with respect to his own output, and setting the derivative equal to zero, each producer ends up with a *reaction function* in which the outputs of other producers are the independent variables, and his own output is the dependent variable.

(b) *Price leadership:* There are n oligopolists. $n - 1$ oligopolists agree to sell their output at whatever price set by the nth firm. Here, $n - 1$ firms are the *price-followers,* and the nth firm is the *price-leader.* It is clear that $n - 1$ followers behave like competitive firms. In order to maximize their profit they equate their marginal costs with the price established by the leader.

(c) *Stackelberg:* The Stackelberg model (named after the German economist Heinrich von Stackelberg) assumes that one producer is a "quantity" leader and the rest, $n - 1$, are followers. The leader does not have a reaction function. He assumes that $n - 1$ followers accept his leadership, and, accordingly, he "plugs" the reaction functions of his followers in his profit function and maximizes it.

The Stackelberg model makes some sense if applied to duopoly. If the oligopoly consists of more than two firms, then the Stackelberg model becomes vague. Although the relationships between the leader and each of the followers are clear, the relationships among the followers can follow various modes.

(d) *Collusion:* The oligopolists agree to form a management whose goal is profit maximization for the industry as a whole. Since the collusion yields the highest possible aggregate profit, each producer can earn at least as much as he did prior to the establishment of the collusion. Formally collusion is identical with the case of a multiple-plant monopoly.

In the following example we shall assume that the commodity is homogeneous, that is, the price is uniform. We shall impose the above modes of behavior upon the oligopolists and find an equilibrium for each model.

Example:

Demand: $P = 200 - Q$

Producer	Cost Function	
1	$C_1 = 0.5\, Q_1^2$	
2	$C_2 = Q_2^2$	(114)
3	$C_3 = 10 Q_3$	

$Q = Q_1 + Q_2 + Q_3$

(a) *Cournot:* The three profit functions are

$$\begin{aligned}
\pi_1 &= 200\, Q_1 - (Q_1 + Q_2 + Q_3)\, Q_1 - 0.5\, Q_1^2 \\
\pi_2 &= 200\, Q_2 - (Q_1 + Q_2 + Q_3)\, Q_2 - Q_2^2 \\
\pi_3 &= 200\, Q_3 - (Q_1 + Q_2 + Q_3)\, Q_3 - 10\, Q_3
\end{aligned} \qquad (115)$$

Differentiating the profit function of each oligopolist separately with respect to its own output gives the three reaction functions:

$$\left.\begin{array}{l} \partial\pi_1/\partial Q_1 = 200 - 3\,Q_1 - Q_2 - Q_3 = 0 \\ \partial\pi_2/\partial Q_2 = 200 - Q_1 - 4Q_2 - Q_3 = 0 \\ \partial\pi_3/\partial Q_3 = 190 - Q_1 - Q_2 - 2\,Q_3 = 0 \end{array}\right\} \qquad (116)$$

The second order partial derivatives are, respectively, -3, -4, and -2. Accordingly sufficient conditions for profit maximization of each producer are satisfied.

Solving Eq. 116 gives: $Q_1 = 37.06$, $Q_2 = 24.71$, and $Q_3 = 64.12$. $\Sigma Q = 125.89$. The price is \$74.11 ($= 200 - 125.89$). The profits are calculated by substituting the quantities in Eq. 115. They are shown in the summary table on page 393.

(b) *Price Leadership:* We assume that firms 1 and 2 decide to accept the price leadership of firm 3. The marginal cost curves of 1 and 2 (see Eq. 114) are $MC_1 = Q_1$ and $MC_2 = 2Q_2$. Since firms 1 and 2 accept the price set by the third firm as a parameter, they equate their marginal costs with the price, $MC_1 = MC_2 = P$. This can be written as $Q_1 = P$ and $Q_2 = 0.5P$. The net demand curve facing the price leader is

$$Q_3 = Q - (Q_1 + Q_2) = 200 - P - (P + 0.5P) = 200 - 2.5P$$

Accordingly, his profit function is

$$\pi_3 = \left(\frac{200 - Q_3}{2.5}\right) \cdot Q_3 - 10 \cdot Q_3 \qquad (117)$$

Differentiating Eq. 117 and setting the derivative equal to zero gives

$$d\pi_3/dQ_3 = (200 - 2\,Q_3)\,/\,2.5 - 10 = 0 \qquad (118)$$

The second order derivative is negative.

The solution of Eq. 118 is $Q_3 = 87.5$. Accordingly $MR_3 = MC_3 = \$10$. $Q_1 = 45$, $Q_2 = 22.5$, and $MC_1 = MC_2 = P = \$45$.

(c) *Stackelberg Solution:* Supposing firm 3 is the leader in the Stackelberg sense. Firms 1 and 2 accept the leadership of 3, but among themselves they adopt the Cournot mode of behavior. The profit function of firm 3 is

$$\pi_3 = [200 - (Q_1 + Q_2 + Q_3)]\,Q_3 - 10\,Q_3 \qquad (119)$$

The reaction functions of 1 and 2 are taken from Eq. 116:

$$\left.\begin{array}{l} \text{reaction function of 1: } 200 - 3\,Q_1 - Q_2 - Q_3 = 0 \\ \text{reaction function of 2: } 200 - Q_1 - 4\,Q_2 - Q_3 = 0 \end{array}\right\} \qquad (120)$$

Solving Eq. 120 for Q_1 and Q_2 we get

$$\left.\begin{array}{l} Q_1 = 54.54 - 0.27\,Q_3 \\ Q_2 = 36.36 - 0.18\,Q_3 \end{array}\right\} \qquad (121)$$

Substituting the right hand sides of Eq. 121 in Eq. 119 we obtain

$$\pi_3 = 99.10 - 0.55\,Q_3^2 \qquad (122)$$

Differentiating Eq. 122, and setting the derivative equal to zero,

$$d\pi_3/dQ_3 = 99.10 - 1.10\,Q_3 = 0 \qquad (123)$$

Thus the profit of 3 is maximized when $Q_3 = 90.09$. The second order derivative is negative. Making use of 121 the values of Q_1 and Q_2 are calculated to be 30.22 and 20.14.

(d) *Collusion:* The rent (profit) function of the entire industry is

$$\pi = 200\,(Q_1 + Q_2 + Q_3) - (Q_1 + Q_2 + Q_3)^2 - 0.5Q_1^2 - Q_2^2 - 10\,Q_3 \qquad (124)$$

The necessary condition for equilbrium is

$$\left.\begin{array}{l} \partial\pi/\partial Q_1 = 200 - 3\,Q_1 - 2\,Q_2 - 2\,Q_3 = 0 \\ \partial\pi/\partial Q_2 = 200 - 2\,Q_1 - 4\,Q_2 - 2\,Q_3 = 0 \\ \partial\pi/\partial Q_3 = 190 - 2\,Q_1 - 2\,Q_2 - 2\,Q_3 = 0 \end{array}\right\} \qquad (125)$$

The solution to Eq. 125 is $Q_1 = 10$, $Q_2 = 5$, and $Q_3 = 80$.

The reader can verify that $MC_1 = MC_2 = MC_3 = MR = \$10$. The price is $\$105$ $[= 200 - (10 + 5 + 80)]$. Sufficient conditions for profit maximization are satisfied:

$$-3 < 0 \quad \begin{vmatrix} -3 & -2 \\ -2 & -4 \end{vmatrix} = 8 > 0 \quad \begin{vmatrix} -3 & -2 & -2 \\ -2 & -4 & -2 \\ -2 & -2 & -2 \end{vmatrix} = -4 < 0$$

SUMMARY OF PROFITS

Firm	Mode of Behavior			
	Cournot	Price Leadership	Stackelberg	Collusion
1	2,059.80	1,012.50	1,342.98	
2	1,220.68	506.25	793.72	
3	4,110.73	3,062.50	4,463.96	
Total	7,391.21	4,581.25	6,600.66	9,100

SUMMARY OF QUANTITIES AND PRICES

	Mode of Behavior			
	Cournot	Price Leadership	Stackelberg	Collusion
Price	74.11	45	59.55	105
Quantity	125.89	155	140.45	95

The summaries indicate that collusion is the most desirable mode of behavior from the viewpoint of producers, but the least desirable from the viewpoint of consumers. Short of regulation, price leadership is the least desirable mode of behavior from the viewpoint of producers, but the most desirable to consumers.

If the oligopolists form a collusion, a situation may arise in which it pays them to shut down one or more plants. For example, suppose the demand curve is $P = 200 - Q$, but instead of Eq. 114 the cost functions are

$$C_1 = 0.50Q_1{}^2 + 100$$
$$C_2 = Q_2{}^2 + 25$$
$$C_3 = 10Q_3 + 75$$

(126)

and the fixed costs are avoidable.

It is left for the reader to show that the following is an exhaustive list of all the possible combinations of firms and the maximum profit per each combination:

(1) 6566.67	(1, 2) 7375	(1, 2, 3) 8900
(2) 4975.00	(1, 3) 8900	
(3) 8950.00	(3, 2) 8950	

Accordingly, production should either be left for 3 alone, or to 3 and 2 alone.

A HETEROGENEOUS GOOD PRODUCED BY AN OLIGOPOLY

In case of a differentiated product each oligopolist is confronted by a separate demand curve. The position of the demand curve confronting each producer is affected by the quantities sold by other firms. The modes of behavior most likely to arise when the commodity is differentiated are the familiar Cournot and Collusion plus a new model known as *market-shares*. In the market-shares model all firms, but one, maintain a fixed share of total output regardless of the price they secure in the market. The rational behind this model could be that the firm looks for a simple rule of thumb as a guidance under uncertainty.

Example:

Firm	Demand Function	Cost Function	
1	$P_1 = 100 - 2Q_1 - Q_2 - Q_3$	$C_1 = 0.5\,Q_1^2$	
2	$P_2 = 100 - Q_1 - 2Q_2 - Q_3$	$C_2 = Q_2^2$	(127)
3	$P_3 = 100 - Q_1 - Q_2 - 2Q_3$	$C_3 = 10\,Q_3$	

(a) *Cournot:* The three profit functions are

$$\pi_1 = (100 - 2\,Q_1 - Q_2 - Q_3)\,Q_1 - 0.5\,Q_1^2$$
$$\pi_2 = (100 - Q_1 - 2\,Q_2 - Q_3)\,Q_2 - Q_2^2$$
$$\pi_3 = (100 - Q_1 - Q_2 - 2\,Q_3)\,Q_3 - 10\,Q_3$$

(128)

Differentiating the profit function of each oligopolist separately with respect to its own output gives three reaction functions:

$$\partial\pi_1/\partial Q_1 = 100 - 5\,Q_1 - Q_2 - Q_3 = 0$$
$$\partial\pi_2/\partial Q_2 = 100 - Q_1 - 6\,Q_2 - Q_3 = 0$$
$$\partial\pi_3/\partial Q_3 = 90 - Q_1 - Q_2 - 4\,Q_3 = 0$$

(129)

The solution of Eq. 129 is $Q_1 = 14.49$, $Q_2 = 11.59$, and $Q_3 = 15.98$. The

profits are shown in the summary table on page 396. The second order derivatives, respectively, are -5, -6, and -4. Accordingly, profits are maximized.

(b) *Market Shares:* Assume that firms 2 and 3 decide to maintain a fixed
share of the aggregate quantity marketed. The share is defined as the proportion
of physical flow of output of one producer to the aggregate physical flow of output. The shares are

$$Q_2 = \frac{1}{3} Q$$

$$Q_3 = \frac{1}{5} Q$$

(130)

Equation 130 together with $Q = Q_1 + Q_2 + Q_3$ can be solved, yielding

$$Q_2 = \frac{5}{7} Q_1$$

$$Q_3 = \frac{3}{7} Q_1$$

(131)

Substituting Eq. 131 in the demand function confronting firm 1, gives a demand
curve

$$P_1 = 100 - \frac{22}{7} Q_1$$

(132)

Substituting Eq. 132 in the profit function of 1 gives

$$\pi_1 = (100 - \frac{22}{7} Q_1) Q_1 - 0.5 Q_1^2$$

(133)

Differentiating and setting the derivative equal to zero

$$d\pi_1 / dQ_1 = 100 - \frac{51}{7} Q_1 = 0$$

The second order derivative is negative.

The solution is $Q_1 = 13.72$, $Q_2 = 9.80$, and $Q_3 = 5.88$.

(c) *Collusion:* The profit function is

$$\begin{aligned}
\pi = {} & (100 - 2 Q_1 - Q_2 - Q_3) Q_1 - 0.5 Q_1{}^2 \\
& + (100 - Q_1 - 2 Q_2 - Q_3) Q_2 - Q_2{}^2 \\
& + (100 - Q_1 - Q_2 - 2 Q_2) Q_3 - 10 Q_3
\end{aligned}$$

(134)

The necessary conditions for maximum are

$$\left. \begin{aligned}
\partial\pi / \partial Q_1 &= 100 - 5 Q_1 - 2 Q_2 - 2 Q_3 = 0 \\
\partial\pi / \partial Q_2 &= 100 - 2 Q_1 - 6 Q_2 - 2 Q_3 = 0 \\
\partial\pi / \partial Q_3 &= 90 - 2 Q_1 - 2 Q_2 - 4 Q_3 = 0
\end{aligned} \right\}$$

(135)

The solution of Eq. 135 is $Q_1 = 11.58$, $Q_2 = 8.68$, and $Q_3 = 12.37$.
The sufficient conditions for maximum are satisfied:

$$-5 < 0 \quad \begin{vmatrix} -5 & -2 \\ -2 & -6 \end{vmatrix} = 26 > 0 \quad \begin{vmatrix} -5 & -2 & -2 \\ -2 & -6 & -2 \\ -2 & -4 & -4 \end{vmatrix} = -76 < 0$$

SUMMARY OF PROFITS (DOLLARS)

Firm	Mode of Behavior		
	Cournot	Market Shares	Collusion
1	524.61	686.27	579.00
2	402.87	499.80	434.09
3	510.72	321.75	556.65
Total	1438.20	1507.82	1569.74

SUMMARY OF QUANTITIES AND PRICES

Firm	Mode of Behavior					
	Cournot		Market Shares		Collusion	
	Q	P	Q	P	Q	P
1	14.49	43.45	13.72	56.88	11.58	55.79
2	11.59	46.35	9.80	60.80	8.68	58.69
3	15.98	41.96	5.88	64.72	12.37	55.00
Total Quantity, Average Price	42.06	43.21	29.40	59.41	32.63	55.95

MONOPOLISTIC COMPETITION

In monopolistic competition there are many firms, none of whom dominates the market, many consumers, ease of entry and exit, and a heterogeneous commodity. Since there are many producers and none of the producers dominates the market, the impact of the act of producer i upon producer j is negligible. Accordingly, each producer, when maximizing his profit, makes the assumption that his change of output does not affect the situations of other producers. Thus other producers are not expected to react. This leads the individual producer to accept the quantities marketed of other producers as parameters. In other words, monopolistic competition is an extension of Cournot mode of behavior under a differentiated good and a small number of producers to a situation of many producers making a differentiated good, where each shares a small fraction of the total market. Thus, under monopolistic competition, instead of having a set of three reaction functions in three unknowns (see Eq. 129), one can conceive of a set of 100 reaction functions in 100 unknowns. Since the impact of the act of one producer on another is negligible, if $Q_j = F(Q_1, Q_2, \ldots, Q_{j-1}, Q_{j+1}, \ldots, Q_{100})$ is a typical (explicit) reaction function of the jth producer, then $\partial Q_j/\partial Q_i$ $(i = 1, 2, \ldots, j - 1,$ $j + 1, \ldots, 100)$ is negative and relatively very small.

MONOPOLY AND MONOPSONY

Let the production function of a monopoly be $Q = f(A, B)$ where A is a factor bought in a monopsonistic market. That is, $P_a = F(A)$ and B is a factor bought in a competitive market. The assumption of monopoly also implies that $P = \phi(Q)$. The profit (rent) function is

$$\pi = P \cdot f(A, B) - P_a A - P_b B \qquad (136)$$

The necessary conditions for profit maximization are

$$\left. \begin{aligned} \partial\pi/\partial A &= P\frac{\partial Q}{\partial A} + Q\frac{dP}{dQ}\frac{\partial Q}{\partial A} - P_a - A\frac{dP_a}{dA} = 0 \\[2mm] \partial\pi/\partial B &= P\frac{\partial Q}{\partial B} + Q\frac{dP}{dQ}\frac{\partial Q}{\partial B} - P_b = 0 \end{aligned} \right\} \qquad (137)$$

Rearranging Eq. 137 we obtain

$$\left. \begin{aligned} \left(P + Q\frac{dP}{dQ}\right)\frac{\partial Q}{\partial A} &= P_a + A\frac{dP_a}{dA} \\[2mm] \left(P + Q\frac{dP}{dQ}\right)\frac{\partial Q}{\partial B} &= P_b \end{aligned} \right\} \qquad (138)$$

Factoring out prices and recognizing that

$$\eta = \frac{P \cdot dQ}{Q \cdot dp} \qquad \text{and} \qquad \epsilon = \frac{P_a \cdot dA}{A \cdot dP_a}$$

we obtain

$$\left. \begin{aligned} P\left(1 + \frac{1}{\eta}\right) \cdot MPP_a &= P_a\left(1 + \frac{1}{\epsilon}\right) \\[2mm] P\left(1 + \frac{1}{\eta}\right) \cdot MPP_a &= P_b \end{aligned} \right\} \qquad (139)$$

Since $P\left(1 + \dfrac{1}{\eta}\right)$ is marginal revenue and $P_a\left(1 + \dfrac{1}{\epsilon}\right)$ is marginal factor cost, Eq. 139 can be written

$$\left. \begin{aligned} MRP_a &= MFC_a \\ MRP_b &= P_b \end{aligned} \right\} \qquad (140)$$

Second order conditions and the case when output is sold competitively $(\eta = -\infty)$ are left for the reader.

NOTES TO CHAPTER 16

THE PROBLEM OF TREES, TIME, AND INTEREST

Consider this problem: Trees are presently planted. When should the timber be cut? Let t stand for time, Y for future values, X for the initial investment, and r for the interest rate.

If the compounding period is one year, then the value of X dollars t years hence is

$$Y = X (1 + r)^t$$

If the compounding period changes from a year to a month, then we have

$$Y = X (1 + r/12)^{12t}$$

In general, if the compounding period is $1/n$ of a year, then

$$Y = X (1 + r/n)^{n \cdot t} = X [(1 + r/n)^{n/r}]^{rt}$$

When $n \to \infty$ we have

$$Y = Xe^{rt} \tag{141}$$

which is known as the formula of continuous compounding.
The continuous discount rate is e^{-rt} because the discounted present value of Y dollars t years hence is

$$X = Y \cdot e^{-rt} \tag{142}$$

Let Y, the future value of the timber, be a function of X, the initial investment, and t, time.

$$Y = f(X, t) \tag{143}$$

The present value, V, of the timber is

$$V = f(X, t) \cdot e^{-rt} \tag{144}$$

Let us adopt the following notations:

$$\frac{\partial f}{\partial t} = f_1 \qquad \frac{\partial^2 f}{\partial t^2} = f_{11}$$

The profit, π, is

$$\pi = V - X \tag{145}$$

Differentiating Eq. 145 and equating to zero gives

$$\frac{\partial \pi}{\partial t} = f_1 e^{-rt} - fre^{-rt} = e^{-rt} (f_1 - rf) = 0 \tag{146}$$

Thus, the necessary condition for profit maximization is

$$f_1/f = r \tag{147}$$

In other words, f_1/f which is the relative change of the future value of timber over time, must be equal to the interest rate (expressed as a decimal). If we multiply Eq. 147 through by 100 percent, the interpretation is as follows: The firm should permit the trees to grow so long as the percentage rate of growth of the value of the trees is less than the interest rate (expressed as a percentage). The firm should cut the timber once the rate of growth is equal to the interest rate.

For second order conditions we redifferentiate profit

$$\frac{\partial^2 \pi}{\partial t^2} = f_{11}\, e^{-rt} - rf_1\, e^{-rt} + r^2 f e^{-rt} - rf_1\, e^{-rt} = e^{-rt}\, (f_{11} - rf_1) < 0 \tag{148}$$

Next, consider the necessary condition for maximization, $f_1 - rf = 0$, as expressed in relation Eq. 146. Taking the complete differential gives

$$f_{11} \cdot dt - rf_1 \cdot dt - f \cdot dr = 0 \tag{149}$$

Accordingly,

$$\frac{dt}{dr} = \frac{f}{f_{11} - rf_1} < 0 \tag{150}$$

$\dfrac{dt}{dr}$ must be negative because f is positive and $f_{11} - rf_1$ is negative by Eq. 148. The higher the interest rate, the shorter is the time period which is necessary for maximizing profit.

NOTES TO CHAPTER 17

EQUILIBRIUM OF CONSUMPTION

Let the utility function of the ith consumer be

$$U = u\,(X_1, X_2, \ldots, X_m) \tag{151}$$

Let his budget constraint be

$$\sum_{j=1}^{m} P_j\,(X_j - X_j^0) = 0 \tag{152}$$

The use of the subscript i is avoided in order to simplify the notations. Maximizing Eq. 151 subject to Eq. 152, namely, differentiating

$$Z = u\,(X_1, X_2, \ldots, X_m) + \lambda \left(\sum_{j=1}^{m} P_j\,(X_j - X_j^0) \right) \tag{153}$$

and setting the partial derivatives equal to zero gives

$$\frac{\partial Z}{\partial X_j} = MU_j + \lambda \cdot P_j = 0 \ (j = 1, 2, \ldots, m) \tag{154}$$

$$\frac{\partial Z}{\partial \lambda} = \sum_{j=1}^{m} P_j (X_j - X_j^0) = 0$$

where MU_j is $\dfrac{\partial U}{\partial X_j}$.

Solving for λ we get

$$\left. \begin{array}{c} \dfrac{MU_1}{P_1} = \dfrac{MU_2}{P_2} = \ldots = \dfrac{MU_m}{P_m} \\[2ex] \sum_{j=1}^{m} P_j (X_j - X_j^0) = 0 \end{array} \right\} \tag{155}$$

Some of the commodities are primary factors such as labor, land, and so on.

We leave it for the reader to derive the sufficient conditions for utility maximization. (Recall from calculus that you have to form the proper Hessian determinants containing the second order partial derivatives of Z, each bordered by a row and column of the first order derivatives of the constraint.) The bordered Hessians must alternate in sign.

EQUILIBRIUM OF PRODUCTION

Let the transformation function of the gth firm be

$$F (X_1, X_2, \ldots, X_m) = 0 \tag{156}$$

Let the profit function of the gth firm be

$$\pi = \sum_{j=1}^{m} P_j X_j \tag{157}$$

The use of the subscript g is avoided in order to simplify the notations. The firm has to maximize Eq. 157 subject to Eq. 156. We form the new function

$$W = \sum_{j=1}^{m} P_j X_j + \lambda \cdot F (X_1, X_2, \ldots, X_m) \tag{158}$$

Differentiating with respect to X_j $(j = 1, 2, \ldots, m)$ and λ, the Lagrange multiplier, and setting the partial derivatives equal to zero gives

$$
\left.
\begin{aligned}
\frac{\partial W}{\partial X_j} &= P_j + \lambda \cdot F_j \qquad (j = 1, 2, \ldots, m) \\[2mm]
\frac{\partial W}{\partial \lambda} &= F\ (X_1, X_2, \ldots, X_m)
\end{aligned}
\right\} \qquad (159)
$$

where F_j is the partial derivative $\dfrac{\partial F}{\partial X_j}$.

Any one of the first m equations in Eq. 159 can be used for finding a solution for λ. We arbitrarily choose the first equation for that purpose. Accordingly we get

$$
\frac{P_j}{P_1} = \frac{F_j}{F_1} \qquad (j = 2 \ldots m)
$$

Finally, recall from implicit differentiation that

$$
\frac{F_j}{F_1} = -\frac{dX_1}{dX_j} \qquad (j = 2 \ldots m)
$$

where all variables but X_j and X_1 are kept constant. Thus we obtain

$$
-\frac{dX_1}{dX_j} = \frac{P_j}{P_1} \qquad (j = 2 \ldots m) \qquad (160)
$$

These are $m - 1$ equations and, together with the transformation function, they constitute a set of m equations. This set determines the quantities demanded for inputs and the quantity supplied of outputs by the gth firm.

Sufficient conditions for profit maximization are formulated by obtaining the relevant Hessians. We leave it for the reader to construct the Hessians (containing second order partial derivatives $W_{jk} = \lambda F_{jk}$, $k, j = 1, 2, \ldots, m$, and bordered by the first order derivatives of the constraint, namely, F_j, $j = 1, 2, \ldots, m$). The Hessians should alternate in sign.

INTER-MARKET STABILITY

Consider an economy in which m commodities are made and traded. The Walrasian stability condition for a perfect market is based on the assumption that consumers would offer higher prices if at a given price the quantity demanded exceeds the quantity supplied. Producers would lower the prices they charge if at any given price the quantity supplied exceeds the quantity demanded. Accordingly, the Walrasian stability condition states that excess of quantity demanded over quantity supplied must be negatively related to the market price. Let excess demand be denoted by E, then for the jth commodity excess demand is

$$E_j = D_j\,(P_2, P_3, \ldots, P_m) - S_j\,(P_2, P_3, \ldots, P_m)$$

or simply

$$E_j = \psi_j\,(P_2, P_3, \ldots, P_m) \qquad j = 2, 3, \ldots, m \tag{161}$$

where P_1 is the numeraire.

The Walrasian stability condition states

$$\frac{dE_j}{dP_j} < 0 \tag{162}$$

The interpretation of the above inequality is left for the reader.

Taking the complete differential of Eq. 161 we obtain

$$\left.\begin{aligned}
dE_2 &= a_{22}\,dP_2 + a_{23}\,dP_3 + \ldots + a_{2m}\,dP_m \\
dE_3 &= a_{32}\,dP_2 + a_{33}\,dP_3 + \ldots + a_{3m}\,dP_m \\
&\ \vdots \\
dE_m &= a_{m2}\,dP_2 + a_{m3}\,dP_3 + \ldots + a_{mm}\,dP_m
\end{aligned}\right\} \tag{163}$$

where

$$a_{jt} = \partial E_j/\partial P_t \qquad j\ , \quad t = 2, 3, \ldots, m$$

Since we deal with small deviations from the equilibrium, a_{jt} are assumed to be constants.

Supposing the second market is upset. Since all markets are interrelated to each other, all markets are affected by a deviation from equilibrium in the second market. Prices in all markets are flexible. In order for stability to exist, we require that prices in markets $3, 4, \ldots, m$ adjust just until excess demand for each of these markets is zero. Formally,

$$dE_3 = dE_4 = \ldots = dE_m = 0$$

We also require that $dE_2/dP_2 < 0$ which ensures the restoration of equilibrium to the market where equilibrium was initially upset. Thus we have

$$\left.\begin{aligned}
dE_2 &= a_{22}\,dP_2 + a_{23}\,dP_3 + \ldots + a_{2m}\,dP_m \\
0 &= a_{32}\,dP_2 + a_{33}\,dP_3 + \ldots + a_{3m}\,dP_m \\
&\ \vdots \\
0 &= a_{m2}\,dP_2 + a_{m3}\,dP_3 + \ldots + a_{mm}\,dP_m
\end{aligned}\right\} \tag{164}$$

Solving by Cramer's rule gives

$$dP_2 = \frac{\begin{vmatrix} dE_2 & a_{23} & \dots & a_{2m} \\ 0 & a_{33} & \dots & a_{3m} \\ & \vdots & & \\ 0 & a_{m3} & \dots & a_{mm} \end{vmatrix}}{\begin{vmatrix} a_{22} & a_{23} & \dots & a_{2m} \\ a_{32} & a_{33} & \dots & a_{3m} \\ & \vdots & & \\ a_{m2} & a_{m3} & \dots & a_{mm} \end{vmatrix}}$$

Thus,

$$\frac{dE_2}{dP_2} = \frac{\begin{vmatrix} a_{22} & a_{23} & \dots & a_{2m} \\ a_{32} & a_{33} & \dots & a_{3m} \\ & \vdots & & \\ a_{m2} & a_{m3} & \dots & a_{mm} \end{vmatrix}}{\begin{vmatrix} a_{33} & \dots & a_{3m} \\ \vdots & & \\ a_{m3} & \dots & a_{mm} \end{vmatrix}} < 0 \tag{165}$$

Next, supposing prices $4, 5, \dots, m$ are rigid. Thus, after the second market is upset, it affects the third market and gets a feedback from the third market. But markets $4, 5, \dots, m$ do not react back on the second market. Thus, we ignore the equations of markets $4, 5, \dots, m$. Since

$$dP_4 = dP_5 = \dots = dP_m = 0$$

we now have

$$dE_2 = a_{22}\, dP_2 + a_{23}\, dP_3$$
$$0 = a_{32}\, dP_2 + a_{33}\, dP_3$$

Solving for dP_2 and rearranging gives

$$\frac{dE_2}{dP_2} = \frac{\begin{vmatrix} a_{22} & a_{23} \\ a_{32} & a_{33} \end{vmatrix}}{a_{33}} < 0 \tag{166}$$

Notice that a_{22} may be positive and dE_2/dP_2 may be negative as stated in Eq. 166.

NOTES TO CHAPTER 18

Let us assume that there are m sectors in the economy. Let X_j

stand for the total output of sector j. Let the flow of output from sector i to sector j be denoted by X_{ij}. Thus, $i = 1, 2, \ldots, m$ and $j = 1, 2, \ldots, m$. Let the flow of final demand from sector i to consumers be denoted by Y_i.

In equilibrium each sector satisfies the final demand for its product as well as demand of other sectors, as follows:

$$X_i = X_{i1} + X_{i2} + \ldots + X_{im} + Y_i \qquad i = 1, 2, \ldots, m \qquad (167)$$

Assuming fixed proportions in production we can write

$$\frac{X_{ij}}{X_j} = a_{ij} \qquad (168)$$

where a_{ij} is an input-output coefficient, telling how much of commodity i must be used (along with other inputs) in the production of one unit of commodity j.

Making use of Eq. 168 we can write Eq. 167 as

$$X_i - a_{i1} X_1 - a_{i2} X_2 - \ldots - a_{im} X_m = Y_i \qquad i = 1, 2, \ldots, m \qquad (169)$$

This can be written as

$$\begin{bmatrix} (1 - a_{11}) - a_{12} \ldots - a_{1m} \\ - a_{21} (1 - a_{22}) \ldots - a_{2m} \\ \vdots \\ - a_{m1} - a_{m2} \quad (1 - a_{mm}) \end{bmatrix} \begin{bmatrix} X_1 \\ X_2 \\ \\ X_m \end{bmatrix} = \begin{bmatrix} Y_1 \\ Y_2 \\ \\ Y_m \end{bmatrix} \qquad (170)$$

or in short matrix notations

$$(I - A)\, \vec{X} = \vec{Y} \qquad (171)$$

where I is an $m \times m$ identity matrix and A is the $m \times m$ matrix of input-output coefficients. $(I - A)$ is known as the Leontief matrix. $\vec{X}$ is the vertical vector of outputs X_j, $j = 1, 2, \ldots, m$, and $\vec{Y}$ is the vertical vector of final demands.

If A can be calculated and $\vec{Y}$ forecasted, then the forecast of $\vec{X}$ is

$$\vec{X} = (I - A)^{-1} \vec{Y} \qquad (172)$$

provided that $(I - A)$ is nonsingular.

Let $\vec{B}$ be a horizontal vector of input-output coefficients, say labor or imports. Then the forecast of the demand for the primary factor is

$$\vec{B}\, \vec{X} = \vec{B}\, (I - A)^{-1}\, \vec{Y} \qquad (173)$$

Solving Eq. 170 by Cramer's rule we get

$$X_j = \frac{(I-A)_{ij}}{det(I-A)} Y_1 + \frac{(I-A)_{2j}}{det(I-A)} Y_2 + \ldots + \frac{(I-A)_{mj}}{det(I-A)} Y_m$$

$$j = 1, 2, \ldots, m \tag{174}$$

where $(I-A)_{ij}$ is a co-factor.

Taking the complete differential of Eq. 174 and requiring that $dY_1 = dY_2 = \ldots dY_{i-1} = dY_{i+1} = \ldots = dY_m = 0$ gives a measure of the marginal effect of a change in the final consumption of commodity i on sector j as follows:

$$dX_j = \frac{(I-A)_{ij}}{det(I-A)} dY_i \tag{175}$$

GENERAL NOTES

DYNAMIC MODELS

One can generate as many dynamic economic models as the imagination allows. There is a one-one relationship between the profusion of market-behavior assumptions created by our imagination and dynamic models.

Let us illustrate a typical dynamic model by assuming the following:

$$\text{Demand function } D_t = \alpha P_t + \beta \tag{176}$$

$$\text{Supply function } S_t = \gamma P_{t-1} + \delta \tag{177}$$

$$\text{Market equilibrium } S_t = D_t \tag{178}$$

The solution of the general linear difference equation of the form $Y_t = K \cdot Y_{t-1} + H$ is

$$Y_t = CK^t + \frac{H}{1-K} \tag{179}$$

The demand function is normal in the sense that the quantity demanded in time period t is a function of the price prevailing in the same time period. But the supply function is lagged one time period. The quantity supplied in time period t is a function of the price which producers secured in time period $t - 1$. Substituting the right side of Eq. 176 and the right side of Eq. 177 in Eq. 178 we get

$$P_t = \frac{\gamma}{\alpha} P_{t-1} + \frac{\delta - \beta}{\alpha} \tag{180}$$

making use of Eq. 179 and setting $t = 0$ in order to solve for C we obtain

$$P_t = (P_0 - P_e) \left(\frac{\gamma}{\alpha} \right)^t + P_e \qquad (181)$$

where P_e is the static equilibrium price and P_0 is a certain non-equilibrium price which represents a deviation of $P_0 - P_e$ from equilibrium. The reader can easily show that $P_e = (\delta - \beta)/(\alpha - \gamma)$. If, after the deviation from equilibrium occurs, there are economic forces that automatically propel the market back into equilibrium, the market is said to be stable. If the initial divergence leads to further divergences, the market is said to be unstable. In our example stability conditions are

$$\left| \frac{\gamma}{\alpha} \right| \quad \begin{array}{l} < 0, \text{stable} \\ > 0, \text{unstable} \end{array} \qquad (182)$$

Namely, the absolute value of the slope of supply must be smaller than the absolute value of the slope of demand, where the slope is dQ/dP. If γ/α is negative, the price oscillates over time. If γ/α is positive, the price converges or diverges without oscillations.

The reader interested in this area is referred to R. G. D. Allen, *Mathematical Economics*.

REPAYING DEBT

A debt amounting to D_0 dollars has to be repaid in a period of n years. The rate of interest is r and the annual payment is K. If the periodic payment is made at the end of the year, then the outstanding debt after paying t annual payments is

$$D_t = D_{t-1} + rD_{t-1} - K \qquad (183)$$

Equation 183 can be written as a difference equation of the first order

$$D_t = (1 + r) D_{t-1} - K \qquad (184)$$

The solution of Eq. 184 is

$$D_t = (D_0 - \frac{K}{r}) (1 + r)^t + \frac{K}{r} \qquad (185)$$

It is required that after n years the debt be entirely repaid, that is, when $t = n$, $D_n = 0$. Notice that D_0 is the original debt. Accordingly, we have

$$0 = (D_0 - \frac{K}{r}) (1 + r)^n + \frac{K}{r} \qquad (186)$$

The solution is

$$K = \frac{r (1 + r)^n}{(1 + r)^n - 1} D_0 \qquad (187)$$

The reader can verify that the expression in Eq. 187 multiplied by D_0 is the capital recovery factor $r/[(1 + r)^n - 1] + r$.

SUGGESTED READINGS

ALLEN, R. G. D. *Mathematical Analysis for Economists*. London: The Macmillan Company, 1956.

———. *Mathematical Economics*. London. The Macmillan Company, 1960.

SAMUALSON, P. *Foundations of Economic Analysis*. Boston, Mass.: Harvard University Press, 1947.

Index

LIBRARY